PENGUIN
CUSTOM EDITIONS

THE WESTERN WORLD

Professor Sean Doyle
Western Humanities I
101
Moraine Valley Community College
Humanities

D0365979

Pearson
Custom
Publishing

Director of Database Publishing: Michael Payne
Sponsoring Editor: Natalie Danner
Development Editor: Katherine R. Gretz
Editorial Assistant: Samantha A. Goodman
Operations Manager: Eric M. Kenney
Marketing Manager: Nathan Wilbur
Production Editors: Mary Kaiser and Vikram Savkar
Cover Design: Renee Sartell

PENGUIN CLASSICS

PEARSON CUSTOM PUBLISHING
75 Arlington Street, Suite 300, Boston, MA 02116
A Pearson Education Company

Acknowledgments

As anyone could well imagine, creating *Penguin Custom Editions: The Western World* was an enormous undertaking. Not only did the project involve compiling a collection of more than a thousand selections—all of which had to be identified, excerpted, introduced, categorized, copy-edited, composed, proofread, and cleared for copyright, among other things—but as a new kind of publication, it raised a new and unpredictable set of challenges that demanded the creative skills of a dedicated team. The editors owe a sincere debt of gratitude to the scholars and professionals who worked with us to hone the original concept, to shape the materials as they emerged, and to transform idea into reality.

From the start, *Penguin Custom Editions* depended on the support of key people at Penguin Putnam, Inc. and at Penguin Books. In particular, Daniel T. Lundy's enthusiasm for the project buoyed us along, and John Schline's patience and perseverance remain much appreciated. Thanks also to Mary Sunden, Margaret Bluman, Andrew Rosenheim, and Florence Eichin.

The project benefited greatly from the advice of the many teachers who reviewed the original proposal and who, in the process, identified potential pitfalls and helped us to see how to avoid them: David A. Brewer, *The Ohio State University;* Denise Z. Davidson, *Georgia State University;* Barbara B. Diefendorf, *Boston University;* Daniel Gordon, *University of Massachusetts at Amherst;* Paul Halliday, *Union College;* Susan Hult, *Houston Community College, Central;* Ethan Knapp, *The Ohio State University;* Elizabeth A. Lehfeldt, *Cleveland State University;* Katharine J. Lualdi, *University of Southern Maine;* Christopher Martin, *Boston University;* Phillip C. Naylor, *Marquette University;* Catherine F. Patterson, *University of Houston;* John Paul Riquelme, *Boston University;* Barbara H. Rosenwein, *Loyola University of Chicago;* Charles J. Rzepka, *Boston University;* John Savage, *New York University;* and Daniel R. Schwarz, *Cornell University.*

As the manuscript neared completion, we had the good fortune to garner feedback from colleagues who helped us see what was working, what needed improvement, and how best to go about it. Many thanks to Feroz

Ahmad, *University of Massachusetts, Boston;* Joseph Aieta, *Babson College;* Kathleen Shine Cain, *Merrimack College;* Paul Doherty, *Boston College;* Paul Faler, *University of Massachusetts, Boston;* Julia Genster, *Tufts University;* Patricia A. Halpin, *Assumption College;* Robert Keohan, *Merrimack College;* Mary Kramer, *University of Massachusetts, Lowell;* Matthew Lenoe, *Assumption College;* Jennifer Morrison, *Regis College;* Janice Neuleib, *Illinois State University;* Shaun O'Connell, *University of Massachusetts, Boston;* Mark O'Connor, *Boston College;* Stuart Peterfreund, *Northeastern University;* Stephen Ruffus, *Salt Lake Community College;* Maurice Scharton, *Illinois State University;* Steven Scherwatzky, *Merrimack College;* Mary Shaner, *University of Massachusetts, Boston;* Louise Z. Smith, *University of Massachusetts, Boston;* Judith A. Stanford, *Rivier College;* Elizabeth Kowaleski Wallace, *Boston College;* James D. Wallace, *Boston College;* David Wick, *Gordon College;* and Alex Wilkes, *Northeastern University.*

Penguin Custom Editions simply would not have been possible without the talented people at Pearson Custom Publishing. Ellen Kuhl suggested the project to us and became its impresario extraordinaire throughout each step of the publishing process. Her ideas, hard work, and humor were key assets in bringing this work to fruition. Katherine Gretz invented the rules and held us to them; her creativity, her almost unbelievable organizational abilities, and her willingness to laugh at an endless stream of puns made it possible for us to finish what we started. Lydia Stuart Horton skillfully copy edited more than 15,000 pages of manuscript with a keen eye for detail and consistency. Among countless other things, Amy Hurd and Stephanie Tobin monitored the whereabouts of thousands upon thousands of files and pieces of paper without losing a single one; Mary Kaiser and Vikram Savkar wrestled all of that paper into finely crafted pages with the invaluable assistance of Melanie Aswell, her proofreading team, and Jim O'Malley at Stratford Publishing. Nathan Wilbur enthusiastically spread the news and Renee Sartell made it beautiful. Finally, a nod of grateful appreciation goes to Deborah Shaw, Francesca Marcantonio, Michael Payne, Pat Porter, Jay Schmidt, Eric Kenney, Lisa Cutler, Pat Boles, Don Kilburn, and to the many who contributed without our awareness. It has been a pleasure and we're looking forward to doing it again.

Mark Kishlansky
David Blackbourn
Virginia Brown
James Hankins

☞ CONTENTS ☜

Medieval Europe: Literature

Medieval Europe: Theatre

Renaissance Europe: History

Renaissance Europe: Religion

Renaissance Europe: Philosophy

Preface

This text, along with its companion Visual Arts CD and Music CD, truly constitutes a labor of love. When the full-time humanities faculty at Moraine Valley Community College opted to create a compilation of core content for its Western Humanities I: Foundations course (HUM 101), little did we realize what an intense period of self-examination and civil debate lie ahead of us. The selection of content that students "must know" after having completed a course, as opposed to content that students "should know," is a difficult task indeed, especially in the humanities where divergence of opinion is an exalted virtue rather than a despised vice. If the most fundamental questions of our existence, those that address the broadest and deepest aspects of our identity and those for which definitive answers are elusive at best, are truly at the heart of the humanities, then how can a finite set of works be chosen that represents the enduring quest of humans to, in the words of Seneca, ". . . cultivate our humanity." In truth, what we have created here is an educated guess and it will ultimately be up to you, the student, to decide if our choices have been wise. Despite the best efforts of your humanities teachers to package the content as neatly as possible and to provide as much context as humanly possible, in the end it is you, the student, who must confront these works directly.

Many colleagues here at Moraine contributed to the development of our core content for HUM 101 including Tammi Carlson, Linda Gruber, Gina Micelli-Hoffman, Justin Synnestvedt, Richard Wolf, and Robert Zbeeb. Each of these individuals is a teacher-scholar in the purest sense of the word and their endeavor to continually expose new generations of students to the splendor of the humanities is admirable. Of course, this package of core content would also not be possible without the efforts of the extremely skilled and highly competent staff at Pearson Custom Publishing and Prentice Hall including Natalie Danner, Evan Girard, Richard Rowe, and Debbie Schwartz.

—Sean William Doyle

Homo sum: humani nil a me alienum puto ("I am a human being, so nothing
human is strange to me")

— *Terence*

Some Words of Welcome. . . .

In order to more fully appreciate, interpret, and evaluate works of the
humanities, the acquisition of a critical vocabulary of fundamental concepts is highly desirable. The appropriation and use of these concepts
allow us to refine our powers of perception (a critical phase in any
encounter with a work of the humanities), communicate intelligibly
about the works, read and comprehend scholarly works in the field, and,
finally, to probe deeper and wider in our efforts to interpret and evaluate
works. However, the assimilation of such a lexicon should be neither an
esoteric nor pedantic exercise. For the attempt by the novice student to
comprehend the meanings of terms is a first step in immersing oneself in
the wonder of the humanities. Actively engaging a work of the humanities is not merely an intellectual exercise, but, indeed, an emotional and
spiritual experience as well. It would be a gross miscalculation to charac-
terize a work of the humanities as one would a cadaver upon which we
perform an autopsy to understand its anatomy and, hence, by such
mechanical operation, yield its meaning. A work of the humanities is as
organic as you and I and only yields its bounty to those who vigorously
seek it out. Like a great conversation between friends, a work of the
humanities requires two deeply impassioned participants. These concepts outlined here are useful across the whole spectrum of arts and disciplines that fall under the umbrella of the term "humanities."

A Brief History of the Origin
of the Humanities

Before we begin our exploration of the fundamental concepts in the
humanities, we should take a moment to acknowledge the origin, or ety-
mology, of the term "humanities." In Western (European or European-
derived) culture, the roots of what we call the humanities can be traced
all the way back to the ancient Greeks and their concept called Παιδεια
(Paideia). *Paideia* refers to the Classical Greek system of education and

training which included subjects as varied as gymnastics, grammar, rhetoric, poetry, music, mathematics, geography, natural history, astronomy and the physical sciences, history of society and ethics, and philosophy. The term *Paideia* commonly translates into English as "education." This curriculum was not intended for vocational training, but, instead, to develop a well-rounded individual (*Paideia* is the source from which we derive our contemporary sense of general education). It was the external manifestation of the ancient Greek educational ideal of developing a fit body conjoined with a sound mind, the spirit of which was later coined in the motto of the Benedictine monastic order: *mens sana in corpore sano* ("a sound mind in a sound body").

The next stop on our evolutionary tour of the origin of the humanities is ancient Rome. Scholarly consensus appears to support the arguable claim that the well-known Roman senator and eloquent orator Cicero (106–43 BCE) translated the ancient Greek word *Paideia* into the Latin term *Humanitas* (here the connection to our English word "humanities" is more obvious). *Humanitas* has come to refer to the ancient Roman educational program that focused on a liberal education founded upon the classics, which included subjects such as geometry, literature, poetry, natural science, ethics, and politics. *Humanitas* also typically translates into English as "kindness, culture, or refinement," and, hence, refers to the ability of these subjects to cultivate and refine our temperament. Although the Roman educational system also emphasized practical pursuits such as horsemanship and weaponry, the sense of "liberal" used here implies suitability for free people (as opposed to slaves), while the "classics" refers to the texts believed to be, in the judgment of scholars, the best that was ever thought and written.

In the Middle Ages, a curriculum emerged in the universities known as the seven liberal arts. The English term "liberal arts" stems from the Latin *artes liberales,* which means "arts appropriate for free men" (the Latin word libri meaning "free"). Early proponents of the liberal arts included Boethius (ca. 475–525 CE), Magnus Aurelius Cassiodorus (fifth century CE), and Martianus Capella (sixth century CE), but it was Alcuin of York, the head of Charlemagne's Palatine School in Aachen in the 8th century CE, who culled the medieval seven liberal arts from the subjects subsumed under the ancient Greek and Roman curricula of *Paideia* and *Humanitas,* respectively. The medieval seven liberal arts were comprised of two parts: the trivium and the quadrivium. The trivium, covered first in the curriculum, was composed of grammar, rhetoric, and logic (known as dialectic during that time). The student would then continue on the quadrivium, which consisted of arithmetic, astronomy, geometry, and music. Upon completion of the study of these subjects (which often required three to five years of study), the student would be subjected to an oral examination, which, if successfully passed, would lead to the awarding of a bachelor of arts (B.A.) degree. Students could then engage in specialized study in the professional fields of law, medicine, or theology, which would lead to the awarding of a master of arts (M.A.) degree. The doctorate involved independent research (often four years or more) beyond the master's degree and the defense of an original thesis before a board of scholars.

During the Renaissance, the curriculum evolved into what became known as the *Studia Humanitatis*, which roughly translates into English as "humanistic studies" or "study of humanity." Several figures were involved with its development including Petrarch (1304–1374), Coluccio Salutati (1331–1406), Guariono Veronese (1374–1406), and Vittorino da Feltre (1373–1446). The Florentine historian Leonardo Bruni (1374–1444) was instrumental in defining the *Studia Humanitatis* as the study, in Greek and Latin, of grammar, rhetoric, history, poetry, and ethics. With a more secular orientation compared with the predominance of theology in the medieval period, these subjects were intended to "make one human."

Unfortunately, today the humanities are often strictly thought of as an academic category of subjects including the fields of history, languages, literature, the fine arts, philosophy, and religion, as distinguished from the social sciences and natural or physical sciences. Indeed, it is just such an academic distinction that the Congress of the United States had in mind in creating the National Endowment for the Humanities with the National Foundation on the Arts and the Humanities Act of 1965: "The term 'humanities' includes, but is not limited to, the study of the following: language, both modern and classical; linguistics; literature; history; jurisprudence; philosophy; archaeology; comparative religion; ethics; the history, criticism and theory of the arts; those aspects of social sciences which have humanistic content and employ humanistic methods; and the study and application of the humanities to the human environment with particular attention to reflecting our diverse heritage, traditions, and history and to the relevance of the humanities to the current conditions of national life."

While there is nothing inherently immoral in defining the humanities by way of a listing of subjects that are currently judged to fall within its purview (notice how the list can historically be quite variable), I fear that, in doing so, we lose a sense of the immediacy and vitality of the concept. A rote listing of subjects resembles more of an obituary rather than a birth announcement. There is a risk that the humanities can come to be viewed by the public as a dead, rather than a living, concept, in the same spirit as Friedrich Nietzsche's claim "that which we find words for is something already dead in our hearts; there is always a kind of contempt in the act of speaking." We forget that each day, creative and thoughtful individuals around the globe diligently labor to create works of the humanities. Therefore, rather than simply consign ourselves to the academic definitions, I offer the following working definition of the term "humanities": the artistic and intellectual expression of and reflection on human existence. I qualify it as a "working" definition because, similar to the fate of the subjects that are claimed to encompass it, the definition of the term is something which is constantly evolving. Ask several humanities practitioners, scholars, or teachers how they define the term "humanities," and you will be amazed at the diversity of their responses.

The Branches of the Humanities

The humanities is often said to encompass two distinct realms: the arts and the disciplines. The term "art" is derived from the ancient Greek word Τέχνη *(techni)* which translates into English as "art, craft, or trade" and the Latin word *ars* which translates into English as "skill, method, technique, conduct, or character." The arts include literature (drama, non-fiction prose, poetry, prose fiction, etc.), the performing arts (dance, music, theater, etc.), and the visual arts (architecture, painting, sculpture, etc.). In discussing the arts, we must carefully differentiate between three distinct areas: the composition/performance/practice of the arts, the history and theory of the arts, and the criticism of the arts. Study in the humanities typically focuses on the history, theory, and criticism of the arts. The disciplines ("fields of study or inquiry") include history, philosophy, and religion.

A Brief Primer on Fundamental Concepts in the Humanities

- **Form/Composition** - the arrangement, design, organization, pattern, or structure of a work; the shape of its content.
- **Content/Subject Matter** - what the work is about.

- **Context** – the conditions under which a work is created including geographical and historical place of origin; purpose or function; biography of the creator of the work; public and critical reactions; political, economic, and social events of the time period; cultural values of the society; dominant styles/theories/influences/movements of the time period, etc.
- **Medium** - the physical materials that make up a work.
- **Technique** - a process or method used to produce a work.
- **Convention** - the customary practices, accepted underlying principles, or recurrent content/subject matter of an art or discipline.
- **Style** - the individual characteristics of a work that identify it with a particular artist or thinker, nationality, historical period, or school of artists or thinkers; typically used in reference to the arts rather then the disciplines of the humanities.
- **Genre** - a category of artistic composition (e.g. art, music, or literature) characterized by a particular style, form, technique or content/subject matter.
- **Historical Period** – an interval of time that has a certain unity because it is characterized by the prevalence of a unique culture, ideology, or technology or because it is bounded by defining historical events.
- **Movement** – the activities of large groups of people united to achieve a common goal; typically used in reference to the disciplines rather than the arts of the humanities.
- **Response**
  ○ **Cognitive** - intellectual; related to facts and objectivity
  ○ **Affective** - emotional; related to feelings or emotions and subjectivity.
- **Criticism** - the act of consciously defining, classifying, explaining, analyzing, interpreting and/or evaluating individual works of the humanities, as well as the formulation of general principles for the examination of such works.

A Three-Stage Model for Critiquing a Work of the Humanities

When we encounter a work of the humanities, we typically engage in three sequential stages:

o Stage 1: Perception - using any of the five senses to perceive and describe a work's form, content, and context as clearly, precisely, and comprehensively as possible.

o Stage 2: Interpretation – the act of and procedures for finding the meaning or significance of a work and the coherent communication of that meaning or significance to others, backed up by argument and evidence.

o Stage 3: Evaluation – making an informed value judgment concerning the merits and demerits of a work, either individually or in comparison with other works, in accordance with defined criteria.

As you interact with the works of the humanities, keep in mind these questions that will help you to create and express informed value judgments:

o What is the work's form?

o What is the work's content?

o What is the work's context?

o What does the work mean?

o Why is the work significant?

Parting Thoughts. . . .

Now that you have the rudiments, you are well prepared for your sojourn through the beguiling realm of the humanities. Like the prisoners in Plato's "Allegory of the Cave," you are ultimately responsible for your own intellectual liberation from ignorance. No matter how strong their back, no teacher is going to lift you up and carry you out. They can point the way and offer sage guidance, but they cannot do the heavy lifting for you. My sincere hope is that at least some of the passion your instructor feels for the subject is contagious and that the humanities will become, if it is not already, an integral part of your existence on this earth. The humanities are truly a fount of intellect and creativity from which you can eternally replenish your head, heart, and soul.

—Sean William Doyle

HERODOTUS

Thermopylae: Last Stand of the Spartans

Herodotus (c. 490–420 B.C.E.) was born in the Greek city of Halicarnassus in Asia Minor. He is called "the father of history" because he was the first in the western tradition to write a coherent account and explanation of past events. He lived in Athens for a time, then in 444 B.C.E. joined the new Athenian colony of Thurii in southern Italy, where he apparently spent the rest of his life. Herodotus traveled a great deal in Greece, Asia Minor, Egypt, Babylonia, and the Black Sea region. His personal observations and interviews add to the vividness of The Histories, *which describe and explain the wars between Greece and the Persian Empire in the context of all that was known of the world in his time. He wrote them in the 430s B.C.E.*

This selection presents what, for Herodotus, was the moment of greatest glory for the Greeks, when a force of 300 Spartans died fighting in a narrow pass to defend their country against the vast Persian army.

The Greeks at Thermopylae had their first warning of the death that was coming with the dawn from the seer Megistias, who read their doom in the victims of sacrifice; deserters, too, came in during the night with news of the Persian flank movement, and lastly, just as day was breaking, the look-out men came running from the hills. In council of war their opinions were divided, some urging that they must not abandon their post, others the opposite. The result was that the army split: some dispersed, contingents returning to their various cities, while others made ready to stand by Leonidas. It is said that Leonidas himself dismissed them, to spare their lives, but thought it unbecoming for the Spartans under his command to desert the post which they had originally come to guard.[1] I myself am inclined to think that he dismissed them when he realized that they had no heart for the fight and were unwilling to take their share of the danger; at the same time honour forbade that he himself should go. And indeed by remaining at his post he left great glory behind him, and Sparta did not lose her prosperity, as might otherwise have happened; for right at the outset of the war the Spartans had been told by the Delphic oracle that either their city must be laid waste by the foreigner or a Spartan king be killed. . . .

I believe it was the thought of this oracle, combined with his wish to lay up for the Spartans a treasure of fame in which no other city should share, that made Leonidas dismiss those troops; I do not think that they deserted, or went off without orders, because of a difference of opinion. Moreover, I am strongly supported in this view by the case of the seer Megistias, who was with the army—an Acarnanian, said to be of the clan of Melampus—who foretold the coming doom from his inspection of the sacrificial victims. He quite plainly received orders from Leonidas to quit Thermopylae, to save him from sharing the army's fate. He refused to go, but he sent his only son, who was serving with the forces.

Thus it was that the confederate troops, by Leonidas' orders, abandoned their posts and left the pass, all except the Thespians and the Thebans who remained with the Spartans. The Thebans were detained by Leonidas as hostages very much against their will; but the Thespians of their own accord refused to desert Leonidas and his men, and stayed, and died with them. They were under the command of Demophilus the son of Diadromes.[2]

In the morning Xerxes poured a libation to the rising sun, and then waited until the time when the market-place is filled before he began to move forward. This was according to Ephialtes' instructions, for the way down from the ridge is much shorter and more direct than the long and circuitous ascent. As the Persian army advanced to the assault, the Greeks under Leonidas, knowing that they were going to their deaths, went out into the wider part of the pass much further than they had done before; in the previous days' fighting they had been holding the wall and making sorties from behind it into the narrow neck, but now they fought outside the narrows. Many of the barbarians fell; behind them the company commanders plied their whips indiscriminately, driving the men on. Many fell into the sea and were drowned, and still more were trampled to death by one another. No one could count the number of the dead. The Greeks, who knew that the enemy were on their way round by the mountain track and that death was inevitable, put forth all their strength and fought with fury and desperation. By this time most of their spears were broken, and they were killing Persians with their swords.

In the course of that fight Leonidas fell, having fought most gallantly, and many distinguished Spartans with him—their names I have learned, as those of men who deserve to be remembered; indeed, I have learned the names of all the three hundred. Amongst the Persian dead, too, were many men of high distinction, including two brothers of Xerxes, Habrocomes and Hyperanthes, sons of Darius by Artanes' daughter Phratagune. Artanes, the son of Hystaspes and grandson of Arsames, was Darius' brother; as Phratagune was his only child, his giving her to Darius was equivalent to giving him his entire estate.

There was a bitter struggle over the body of Leonidas; four times the Greeks drove the enemy off, and at last by their valour rescued it.[3] So it went on, until the troops with Ephialtes were close at hand; and then, when the Greeks knew that they had come, the character of the fighting changed. They withdrew again into the narrow neck of the pass, behind the wall, and took up a position in a single compact body—all except the Thebans—on the little hill at the entrance to the pass, where the stone lion in memory of Leonidas stands today. Here they resisted to the last, with their swords, if they had them, and, if not, with their hands and teeth, until the Persians, coming on from the front over the ruins of the wall and closing in from behind, finally overwhelmed them with missile weapons.

Of all the Spartans and Thespians who fought so valiantly the most signal proof of courage was given by the Spartan Dieneces. It is said that before the battle he was told by a native of Trachis that, when the Persians shot their arrows, there were so many of them that they hid the sun. Dieneces, however, quite unmoved by the thought of the strength of the Persian army, merely remarked: 'This is pleasant news that the stranger from Trachis brings us: if the Persians hide the sun, we shall have our battle in the shade.' He is said to have left on record other sayings, too, of a similar kind, by which he will be remembered. After Dieneces the greatest distinction was won by two Spartan brothers, Alpheus and Maron, the sons of Orsiphantus; and of the Thespians the man to gain the highest glory was a certain Dithyrambus, the son of Harmatides.

The dead were buried where they fell, and with them the men who had been killed before those dismissed by Leonidas left the pass. Over them is this inscription, in honour of the whole force:

Four thousand here from Pelops' land
Against three million once did stand.[4]

The Spartans have a special epitaph; it runs:

Go tell the Spartans, you who read:
We took their orders, and here lie dead.

For the seer Megistias there is the following:

Here lies Megistias, who died
When the Mede passed Spercheius' tide.
A prophet; yet he scorned to save
Himself, but shared the Spartans' grave.

EXPLANATORY NOTES

1. On the Spartan prohibition against leaving their post see Demartus' words at ch. 104 [of the source material].
2. Plutarch, ... in one of the few places where he scores a hit against Herodotus, finds fault here for the treatment of the Thebans. Retaining people of doubtful loyalty in such a situation would have weakened Leonidas' position. Herodotus here has fallen for the anti-Theban propaganda that was rife in Athens before and during the Peloponnesian War. Diodorus (XI. 4. 7) says that the Thebans with Leonidas were members 'of the party', i.e. the one that was opposed to Persia. ...
3. The struggle for the body of Leonidas has epic associations: see the struggle for the body of Patroclus at *Il.* XVII. 274–5.
4. Herodotus's troops from the Peloponnese number 3100 in his army list (ch. 202).

THUCYDIDES

Pericles' Funeral Oration

———————

Thucydides' incomplete History of the Peloponnesian War *(431–404 B.C.E.), the greatest work of history surviving from the ancient world, depicts a mighty struggle between a federation of democratic city-states led by Athens and a federation of oligarchies headed by Sparta. Little is known of the author's life. He was an Athenian of the upper classes, born sometime between 460 and 455 B.C.E., who served as a general of the Athenian forces in 424 B.C.E., and was a devoted follower of the great Athenian politician Pericles. Thucydides tells his readers that he began to write his history soon after the beginning of the Peloponnesian war, so that it has much of the character of an eyewitness account, but internal evidence shows that he must have continued to revise his work down to the end of his life, around 400 B.C.E.*

After an introductory book, the work divides into four sections: an account of the Ten Years War (431–421 B.C.E., Books 2 to 5.24), the inter-war period (421–415 B.C.E., Book 5.25–116), the Sicilian Expedition (415–413 B.C.E., Books 6 and 7), and the so-called Decelian War (413–411 B.C.E., Book 8). These twenty years, in Thucydides' telling, describe an arc of political and moral decline for Athens, ending with her disastrous defeat in Sicily and the temporary triumph of oligarchic forces inside Athens herself. Such a story would seem to offer numerous opportunities for moralistic comment and patriotic bluster, but Thucydides resisted these temptations. His passion was constrained by a determination to be as truthful as possible, with a view to contributing to the scientific study of man. He was less interested in assigning blame than in understanding the workings of power and human nature. Such an understanding, he believed, was the true purpose of history, and its achievement in Thucydides' great book was the basis of his claim that his work would be "a possession for all time." The most famous passage in Thucydides' history is the funeral oration in Book 2 that he put in the mouth of Pericles, who describes movingly the ideals of Athenian democracy.

———————

"Pericles' Funeral Oration," from Book 2 of *Thucydides: History of the Peloponnesian War,* translated by Rex Warner, translation copyright © 1954 by Rex Warner, 143–151. Reprinted by permission of Penguin Books Ltd.

PERICLES' FUNERAL ORATION

In the same winter the Athenians, following their annual custom, gave a public funeral for those who had been the first to die in the war. These funerals are held in the following way: two days before the ceremony the bones of the fallen are brought and put in a tent which has been erected, and people make whatever offerings they wish to their own dead. Then there is a funeral procession in which coffins of cypress wood are carried on wagons. There is one coffin for each tribe, which contains the bones of members of that tribe. One empty bier is decorated and carried in the procession: this is for the missing, whose bodies could not be recovered. Everyone who wishes to, both citizens and foreigners, can join in the procession, and the women who are related to the dead are there to make their laments at the tomb. The bones are laid in the public burial-place, which is in the most beautiful quarter outside the city walls. Here the Athenians always bury those who have fallen in war. The only exception is those who died at Marathon, who, because their achievement was considered absolutely outstanding, were buried on the battlefield itself.

When the bones have been laid in the earth, a man chosen by the city for his intellectual gifts and for his general reputation makes an appropriate speech in praise of the dead, and after the speech all depart. This is the procedure at these burials, and all through the war, when the time came to do so, the Athenians followed this ancient custom. Now, at the burial of those who were the first to fall in the war Pericles, the son of Xanthippus, was chosen to make the speech. When the moment arrived, he came forward from the tomb and, standing on a high platform, so that he might be heard by as many people as possible in the crowd, he spoke as follows:

'Many of those who have spoken here in the past have praised the institution of this speech at the close of our ceremony. It seemed to them a mark of honour to our soldiers who have fallen in war that a speech should be made over them. I do not agree. These men have shown themselves valiant in action, and it would be enough, I think, for their glories to be proclaimed in action, as you have just seen it done at this funeral organized by the state. Our belief in the courage and manliness of so many should not be hazarded on the goodness or badness of one man's speech. Then it is not easy to speak with a proper sense of balance, when a man's listeners find it difficult to believe in the truth of what one is saying. The man who knows the facts and loves the dead may well think that an oration tells less than what he knows and what he would like to hear: others who do not know so much may feel envy for the dead, and think the orator over-praises them, when he speaks of exploits that are beyond their own capacities. Praise of other people is tolerable only up to a certain point, the point where one still believes that one could do oneself some of the things one is hearing about. Once you get beyond this point, you will find people becoming jealous and incredulous. However, the fact is that this institution was set up and approved by our forefathers, and it is my duty to follow the tradition and do my best to meet the wishes and the expectations of every one of you.

'I shall begin by speaking about our ancestors, since it is only right and proper on such an occasion to pay them the honour of recalling what they did. In this land of ours there have always been the same people living from generation to generation up till now, and they, by their courage and their virtues, have handed it on to us, a free country. They certainly deserve our praise. Even more so do our fathers deserve it. For to the inheritance they had received they added all the empire we have now, and it was not without blood and toil that they handed it down to us of the present generation. And then we ourselves, assembled here today, who are mostly in the prime of life, have, in most directions, added to the power of our empire and have organized our State in such a way that it is perfectly well able to look after itself both in peace and in war.

'I have no wish to make a long speech on subjects familiar to you all: so I shall say nothing about the warlike deeds by which we acquired our power or the battles in which we or our fathers gallantly resisted our enemies, Greek or foreign. What I want to do is, in the first place, to discuss the spirit in which we faced our trials and also our constitution and the way of life which has made us great. After that I shall speak in praise of the dead, believing that this kind of speech is not inappropriate to the present occasion, and that this whole assembly, of citizens and foreigners, may listen to it with advantage.

'Let me say that our system of government does not copy the institutions of our neighbours. It is more the case of our being a model to others, than of our imitating anyone else. Our constitution is called a democracy because power is in the hands not of a minority but of the whole people. When it is a question of settling private disputes, everyone is equal before the law; when it is a question of putting one person before another in positions of public responsibility, what counts is not membership of a particular class, but the actual ability which the man possesses. No one, so long as he has it in him to be of service to the state, is kept in political obscurity because of poverty. And, just as our political life is free and open, so is our day-to-day life in our relations with each other. We do not get into a state with our next-door neighbour if he enjoys himself in his own way, nor do we give him the kind of black looks which, though they do no real harm, still do hurt people's feelings. We are free and tolerant in our private lives; but in public affairs we keep to the law. This is because it commands our deep respect.

'We give our obedience to those whom we put in positions of authority, and we obey the laws themselves, especially those which are for the protection of the oppressed, and those unwritten laws which it is an acknowledged shame to break.

'And here is another point. When our work is over, we are in a position to enjoy all kinds of recreation for our spirits. There are various kinds of contests and sacrifices regularly throughout the year; in our own homes we find a beauty and a good taste which delight us every day and which drive away our cares. Then the greatness of our city brings it about that all the good things from all over the world flow in to us, so that to us it seems just as natural to enjoy foreign goods as our own local products.

'Then there is a great difference between us and our opponents, in our attitude towards military security. Here are some examples: Our city is open to the world, and we have no periodical deportations in order to prevent people observing or finding out secrets which might be of military advantage to the enemy. This is because we rely, not on secret weapons, but on our own real courage and loyalty. There is a difference, too, in our educational systems. The Spartans, from their earliest boyhood, are submitted to the most laborious training in courage; we pass our lives without all these restrictions, and yet are just as ready to face the same dangers as they are. Here is a proof of this: When the Spartans invade our land, they do not come by themselves, but bring all their allies with them; whereas we, when we launch an attack abroad, do the job by ourselves, and, though fighting on foreign soil, do not often fail to defeat opponents who are fighting for their own hearths and homes. As a matter of fact none of our enemies has ever yet been confronted with our total strength, because we have to divide our attention between our navy and the many missions on which our troops are sent on land. Yet, if our enemies engage a detachment of our forces and defeat it, they give themselves credit for having thrown back our entire army; or, if they lose, they claim that they were beaten by us in full strength. There are certain advantages, I think, in our way of meeting danger voluntarily, with an easy mind, instead of with a laborious training, with natural rather than with state-induced courage. We do not have to spend our time practising to meet sufferings which are still in the future; and when they are actually upon us we show ourselves just as brave as these others who are always in strict training. This is one point in which, I think, our city deserves to be admired. There are also others:

'Our love of what is beautiful does not lead to extravagance; our love of the things of the mind does not make us soft. We regard wealth as something to be properly used, rather than as something to boast about. As for poverty, no one need be ashamed to admit it: the real shame is in not taking practical measures to escape from it. Here each individual is interested not only in his own affairs but in the affairs of the state as well: even those who are mostly occupied with their own business are extremely well-informed on general politics—this is a peculiarity of ours: we do not say that a man who takes no interest in politics is a man who minds his own business; we say that he has no business here at all. We Athenians, in our own persons, take our decisions on policy or submit them to proper discussions: for we do not think that there is an incompatibility between words and deeds; the worst thing is to rush into action before the consequences have been properly debated. And this is another point where we differ from other people. We are capable at the same time of taking risks and of estimating them beforehand. Others are brave out of ignorance; and, when they stop to think, they begin to fear. But the man who can most truly be accounted brave is he who best knows the meaning of what is sweet in life and of what is terrible, and then goes out undeterred to meet what is to come.

'Again, in questions of general good feeling there is a great contrast between us and most other people. We make friends by doing good to others, not by receiving good from them. This makes our friendship all the more reliable, since we want to keep alive the gratitude of those who are in our debt by showing continued goodwill to them: whereas the feelings of one who owes us something lack the same enthusiasm, since he knows that, when he repays our kindness, it will be more like paying back a debt than giving something spontaneously. We are unique in this. When we do kindnesses to others, we do not do them out of any calculations of profit or loss: we do them without afterthought, relying on our free liberality. Taking everything together then, I declare that our city is an education to Greece, and I declare that in my opinion each single one of our citizens, in all the manifold aspects of life, is able to show himself the rightful lord and owner of his own person, and do this, moreover, with exceptional grace and exceptional versatility. And to show that this is no empty boasting for the present occasion, but real tangible fact, you have only to consider the power which our city possesses and which has been won by those very qualities which I have mentioned. Athens, alone of the states we know, comes to her testing time in a greatness that surpasses what was imagined of her. In her case, and in her case alone, no invading enemy is ashamed at being defeated, and no subject can complain of being governed by people unfit for their responsibilities. Mighty indeed are the marks and monuments of our empire which we have left. Future ages will wonder at us, as the present age wonders at us now. We do not need the praises of a Homer, or of anyone else whose words may delight us for the moment, but whose estimation of facts will fall short of what is really true. For our adventurous spirit has forced an entry into every sea and into every land; and everywhere we have left behind us everlasting memorials of good done to our friends or suffering inflicted on our enemies.

'This, then, is the kind of city for which these men, who could not bear the thought of losing her, nobly fought and nobly died. It is only natural that every one of us who survive them should be willing to undergo hardships in her service. And it was for this reason that I have spoken at such length about our city, because I wanted to make it clear that for us there is more at stake than there is for others who lack our advantages; also I wanted my words of praise for the dead to be set in the bright light of evidence. And now the most important of these words has been spoken. I have sung the praises of our city; but it was the courage and gallantry of these men, and of people like them, which made her splendid. Nor would you find it true in the case of many of the Greeks, as it is true of them, that no words can do more than justice to their deeds.

'To me it seems that the consummation which has overtaken these men shows us the meaning of manliness in its first revelation and in its final proof. Some of them, no doubt, had their faults; but what we ought to remember first is their gallant conduct against the enemy in defence of their native land. They have blotted out evil with good, and done more service to the commonwealth than they ever did harm in their private lives. No one of these men weakened because he wanted to go on enjoying his wealth: no one put off the awful day in the hope that he might live to escape his poverty and grow rich. More to be desired than such things, they chose to check the enemy's pride. This, to them, was a risk most glorious, and they accepted it, willing to strike down the enemy and relinquish everything else. As for success or failure, they left that in the doubtful hands of Hope, and when the reality of battle was before their faces, they put their trust in their own selves. In the fighting, they thought it more honourable to stand their ground and suffer death than to give in and save their lives. So they fled from the reproaches of men, abiding with life and limb the brunt of battle; and, in a small moment of time, the climax of their lives, a culmination of glory, not of fear, were swept away from us.

'So and such they were, these men worthy of their city. We who remain behind may hope to be spared their fate, but must resolve to keep the same daring spirit against the foe. It is not simply a question of estimating the advantages in theory. I could tell you a long story (and you know it as well as I do) about what is to be gained by beating the enemy back. What I would prefer is that you should fix your eyes every day on the greatness of Athens as she really is, and should fall in love with her. When you realize her greatness, then reflect that what made her great was men with a spirit of adventure, men who knew their duty, men who were ashamed to fall below a certain standard. If they ever failed in an enterprise, they made up their minds that at any rate the city should not find their courage lacking to her, and they gave to her the best contribution that they could. They gave her their lives, to her and to all of us, and for their own selves they won praises that never grow old, the most splendid of sepulchres—not the sepulchre in which their bodies are laid, but where their glory remains eternal in men's minds, always there on the right occasion to stir others to speech or to action. For famous men have the whole earth as their memorial: it is not only the inscriptions on their graves in their own country that mark them out; no, in foreign lands also, not in any visible form but in people's hearts, their memory abides and grows. It is for you to try to be like them. Make up your minds that happiness depends on being free, and freedom depends on being courageous. Let there be no relaxation in face of the perils of the war. The people who have most excuse for despising death are not the wretched and unfortunate, who have no hope of doing well for themselves, but those who run the risk of a complete reversal in their lives, and who would feel the difference most intensely, if things went wrong for them. Any intelligent man would find a humiliation caused by his own slackness more painful to bear than death, when death comes to him unperceived, in battle, and in the confidence of his patriotism.

'For these reasons I shall not commiserate with those parents of the dead, who are present here. Instead I shall try to comfort them. They are well aware that they have grown up in a world where there are many changes and chances. But this is good fortune—for men to end their lives with honour, as these have done, and for you honourably to lament them: their life was set to a measure where death and happiness went hand in hand. I know that it is difficult to convince you of this. When you see other people happy you will often be reminded of what used to make you happy too. One does not feel sad at not having some good thing which is outside one's experience: real grief is felt at the loss of something which one is used to. All the same, those of you who are of the right age must bear up and take comfort in the thought of having more children. In your own homes these new children will prevent you from brooding over those who are no more, and they will be a help to the city, too, both in filling the empty places, and in assuring her security. For it is impossible for a man to put forward fair and honest views about our affairs if he has not, like everyone else, children whose lives may be at stake. As for those of you who are now too old to have children, I would ask you to count as gain the greater part of your life, in which you have been happy, and remember that what remains is not long, and let your hearts be lifted up at the thought of the fair fame of the dead. One's sense of honour is the only thing that does not grow old, and the last pleasure, when one is worn out with age, is not, as the poet said, making money, but having the respect of one's fellow men.

'As for those of you here who are sons or brothers of the dead, I can see a hard struggle in front of you. Everyone always speaks well of the dead, and, even if you rise to the greatest heights of heroism, it will be a hard thing for you to get the reputation of having come near, let alone equalled, their standard. When one is alive, one is always liable to the jealousy of one's competitors, but when one is out of the way, the honour one receives is sincere and unchallenged.

'Perhaps I should say a word or two on the duties of women to those among you who are now widowed. I can say all I have to say in a short word of advice. Your great glory is not to be inferior to what God has made you, and the greatest glory of a woman is to be least talked about by men, whether they are praising you or criticizing you. I have now, as the law demanded, said what I had to say. For the time being our offerings to the dead have been made, and for the future their children will be supported at the public expense by the city, until they come of age. This is the crown and prize which she offers, both to the dead and to their children, for the ordeals which they have faced. Where the rewards of valour are the greatest, there you will find also the best and bravest spirits among the people. And now, when you have mourned for your dear ones, you must depart.'

LIVY

Romulus and Remus

Titus Livius (c. 59 B.C.E.–17 C.E.) was born in Padua in northern Italy, but spent much of his life in Rome, where he studied philosophy and oratory and attracted the attention of the emperor Augustus. He never held public office, but seems to have devoted most of his life to writing his enormous history of Rome, from its foundation down to 9 B.C.E. Of the original 142 books, 35 survive complete. He narrated history chronologically, and usually uncritically, but his work is notable for his vivid reconstruction of past events and people. In dealing with the earliest history, when Rome was ruled by kings (753–509 B.C.E.), Livy relied heavily on myth and oral tradition, using his material more as a source for moral examples and lessons— illustrations of ancient virtue—than as a true historical account.

The present selection recounts the mythical foundation of Rome by Romulus and Remus, who were miraculously suckled by a wolf.

Proca, the next king, had two sons, Numitor and Amulius, to the elder of whom, Numitor, he left the hereditary realm of the Silvian family; that, at least, was his intention, but respect for seniority was flouted, the father's will ignored and Amulius drove out his brother and seized the throne. One act of violence led to another; he proceeded to murder his brother's male children, and made his niece, Rhea Silvia, a Vestal, ostensibly to do her honour, but actually by condemning her to perpetual virginity to preclude the possibility of issue.

But (I must believe) it was already written in the book of fate that this great city of ours should arise, and the first steps be taken to the founding of the mightiest empire the world has known—next to God's. The Vestal Virgin was raped and gave birth to twin boys. Mars, she declared, was their father—perhaps she believed it, perhaps she was merely hoping by the pretence to palliate her guilt. Whatever the truth of the matter, neither gods nor men could save her or her babes from the savage hands of the king. The mother was bound and flung into prison; the boys, by the king's order, were condemned to be drowned in the river. Destiny, however, intervened; the Tiber had overflowed its banks; because of the flooded ground it was impossible to get to the actual river, and the men entrusted to do the deed thought that the flood-water, sluggish though it was, would serve their purpose. Accordingly they made shift to carry out the king's orders by leaving the infants on the edge of the first flood-water they came to, at the spot where now stands the Ruminal fig-tree—said to have once been known as the fig-tree of Romulus. In those days the country thereabouts was all wild and uncultivated, and the story goes that when the basket in which the infants had been exposed was left high and dry by the receding water, a she-wolf, coming down from the neighbouring hills to quench her thirst, heard the children crying and made her way to where they were. She offered them her teats to suck and treated them with such gentleness that Faustulus, the king's herdsman, found her licking them with her tongue. Faustulus took them to his hut and gave them to his wife Larentia to nurse. Some think that the origin of this fable was the fact that Larentia was a common whore and was called Wolf by the shepherds.

Such then, was the birth and upbringing of the twins. By the time they were grown boys, they employed themselves actively on the farm and with the flocks and began to go hunting in the woods; their strength grew with their resolution, until not content only with the chase they took to attacking robbers and sharing their stolen goods with their friends the shepherds. Other young fellows joined them, and they and the shepherds would fleet the time together, now in serious talk, now in jollity. . . .

Now Faustulus had suspected all along that the boys he was bringing up were of royal blood. He knew that two infants had been exposed by the king's orders, and the rescue of his own two fitted perfectly in point of time. Hitherto, however, he had been unwilling to declare what he knew, until either a suitable opportunity occurred or circumstances compelled him. Now the truth could no longer be concealed, so in his alarm he told Romulus the whole story; Numitor, too, when he had Remus in custody and was told that the brothers were twins, was set thinking about his grandsons; the young men's age and character, so different from the lowly born, confirmed his suspicions; and further inquiries led him to the same conclusion, until he was on the point of acknowledging Remus. The net was closing in, and Romulus acted. He was not strong enough for open hostilities, so he instructed a number of the herdsmen to meet at the king's house by different routes at a preordained time; this was done, and with the help of Remus, at the head of another body of men, the king was surprised and killed. Before the first blows were struck, Numitor gave it out that an enemy had broken into the town and attacked the palace; he then drew off all the men of military age to garrison the inner fortress, and, as soon as he saw Romulus and Remus, their purpose accomplished, coming to congratulate him, he summoned a meeting of the people and laid the facts before it: Amulius's crime against himself, the birth of his grandsons, and the circumstances attending it, how they were brought up and ultimately recognized, and, finally, the murder of the king for which he himself assumed responsibility. The two brothers marched through the crowd at the head of their men and saluted their grandfather as king, and by a shout of unanimous consent his royal title was confirmed.

Romulus and Remus, after the control of Alba had passed to Numitor in the way I have described, were suddenly seized by an urge to found a new settlement on the spot where they had been left to drown as infants and had been subsequently brought up. There was, in point of fact, already an excess of population at Alba, what with the Albans themselves, the Latins, and the addition of the herdsmen: enough, indeed, to justify the hope that Alba and Lavinium would one day be small places compared with the proposed new settlement. Unhappily the brothers' plans for the future were marred by the same source which had divided their grandfather and Amulius—jealousy and ambition. A disgraceful quarrel arose from a matter in itself trivial. As the brothers were twins and all question of seniority was thereby precluded, they determined to ask the tutelary gods of the countryside to declare by augury which of them should govern the new town once it was founded, and give his name to it. For this purpose Romulus took the Palatine hill and Remus the Aventine as their respective stations from which to observe the auspices. Remus, the story goes, was the first to receive a sign—six vultures; and no sooner was this made known to the people than double the number of birds appeared to Romulus. The followers of each promptly saluted their master as king, one side basing its claim upon priority, the other upon number. Angry words ensued, followed all too soon by blows, and in the course of the affray Remus was killed. There is another story, a commoner one, according to which Remus, by way of jeering at his brother, jumped over the half-built walls of the new settlement, whereupon Romulus killed him in a fit of rage, adding the threat, 'So perish whoever else shall overleap my battlements.'

This, then, was how Romulus obtained the sole power. The newly built city was called by its founder's name.

TACITUS

Nero and the Burning of Rome

---

*Cornelius Tacitus (c. 56–120 C.E.), whose mastery of language and powers
of analysis make him one of the greatest historians of Antiquity, had a distinguished civil career. He reached high office in his thirties, became consul
in 97 C.E., and governor of one of Rome's richest provinces, Asia (Western
Turkey), in 112 C.E. He was well educated in rhetoric and developed
tremendous skill as a public speaker, which he put to use as he turned to
writing history in the last decades of his life.*

Tacitus's major works, The Annals *and* The Histories, *covered the early
Empire from the death of Augustus in 14 C.E. to that of Domitian in 96 C.E.
He wrote in equal detail about politics, individuals, and military and foreign affairs, to provide a comprehensive history. Most of the* Annals, *but
only the first books of the* Histories, *have survived. They reflect Tacitus's
hatred of despotism in their damning portrayals of such emperors as
Tiberius and Nero, and their minions. His sarcastic, epigrammatic style
spares no one in the ruling classes, whom he considers an enemy of freedom
and decency. The present selection describes the great fire that destroyed
most of Rome in 64 C.E., together with its rebuilding along modern and
more sanitary lines by Nero, who placed the blame for the disaster on the
obscure but unpopular sect of the Christians.*

Disaster followed. Whether it was accidental or caused by a criminal act
on the part of the emperor is uncertain—both versions have supporters.
Now started the most terrible and destructive fire which Rome had ever
experienced. It began in the Circus, where it adjoins the Palatine and
Caelian hills. Breaking out in shops selling inflammable goods, and
fanned by the wind, the conflagration instantly grew and swept the
whole length of the Circus. There were no walled mansions or temples,
or any other obstructions, which could arrest it. First, the fire swept violently over the level spaces. Then it climbed the hills—but returned to
ravage the lower ground again. It outstripped every counter-measure.

"Nero and the Burning of Rome," from *The Annals of Imperial Rome,* by Tacitus, translated by Michael Grant, copyright © 1989 by Michael Grant Publications Ltd, 362–366.
Reprinted by permission of Penguin Books Ltd.

The ancient city's narrow winding streets and irregular blocks encouraged its progress.

Terrified, shrieking women, helpless old and young, people intent on their own safety, people unselfishly supporting invalids or waiting for them, fugitives and lingerers alike—all heightened the confusion. When people looked back, menacing flames sprang up before them or outflanked them. When they escaped to a neighbouring quarter, the fire followed—even districts believed remote proved to be involved. Finally, with no idea where or what to flee, they crowded on to the country roads, or lay in the fields. Some who had lost everything—even their food for the day—could have escaped, but preferred to die. So did others, who had failed to rescue their loved ones. Nobody dared fight the flames. Attempts to do so were prevented by menacing gangs. Torches, too, were openly thrown in, by men crying that they acted under orders. Perhaps they had received orders. Or they may just have wanted to plunder unhampered.

Nero was at Antium. He only returned to the city when the fire was approaching the mansion he had built to link the Gardens of Maecenas to the Palestine. The flames could not be prevented from overwhelming the whole of the Palatine, including his palace. Nevertheless, for the relief of the homeless, fugitive masses he threw open the Field of Mars, including Agrippa's public buildings, and even his own Gardens. Nero also constructed emergency accommodation for the destitute multitude. Food was brought from Ostia and neighbouring towns, and the price of corn was cut to less than ¼ sesterce a pound. Yet these measures, for all their popular character, earned no gratitude. For a rumour had spread that, while the city was burning, Nero had gone on his private stage and, comparing modern calamities with ancient, had sung of the destruction of Troy.

By the sixth day enormous demolitions had confronted the raging flames with bare ground and open sky, and the fire was finally stamped out at the foot of the Esquiline Hill. But before panic had subsided, or hope revived, flames broke out again in the more open regions of the city. Here there were fewer casualties; but the destruction of temples and pleasure arcades was even worse. This new conflagration caused additional ill-feeling because it started on Tigellinus' estate[1] in the Aemilian district. For people believed that Nero was ambitious to found a new city to be called after himself.

Of Rome's fourteen districts only four remained intact. Three were levelled to the ground. The other seven were reduced to a few scorched and mangled ruins. To count the mansions, blocks, and temples destroyed would be difficult. They included shrines of remote antiquity, such as Servius Tullius' temple of the Moon, the Great Altar and holy place dedicated by Evander to Hercules, the temple vowed by Romulus to Jupiter the Stayer, Numa's sacred residence, and Vesta's shrine containing Rome's household gods. Among the losses, too, were the precious spoils of countless victories, Greek artistic masterpieces, and authentic records of old Roman genius. All the splendour of the rebuilt city did not prevent the older generation from remembering these irreplaceable objects. It was noted that the fire had started on July 19th, the day on which the Senonian Gauls had captured and burnt the city. Others elaborately calculated that the two fires were separated by the same number of years, months, and days.[2]

But Nero profited by his country's ruin to build a new palace. Its wonders were not so much customary and commonplace luxuries like gold and jewels, but lawns and lakes and faked rusticity—woods here, open spaces and views there. With their cunning, impudent artificialities, Nero's architects and engineers, Severus and Celer, did not balk at effects which Nature herself had ruled out as impossible. . . .

In parts of Rome unfilled by Nero's palace, construction was not—as after the burning by the Gauls—without plan or demarcation. Streetfronts were of regulated alignment, streets were broad, and houses built round courtyards. Their height was restricted, and their frontages protected by colonnades. Nero undertook to erect these at his own expense, and also to clear debris from building-sites before transferring them to their owners. He announced bonuses, in proportion for rank and resources, for the completion of houses and blocks before a given date. Rubbish was to be dumped in the Ostian marshes by corn-ships returning down the Tiber.

A fixed proportion of every building had to be massive, untimbered stone from Gabii or Alba (these stones being fireproof). Furthermore, guards were to ensure a more abundant and extensive public watersupply, hitherto diminished by irregular private enterprise. Householders were obliged to keep fire-fighting apparatus in an accessible place; and semi-detached houses were forbidden—they must have their own walls. These measures were welcomed for their practicality, and they beautified the new city. Some, however, believed that the old town's configuration had been healthier, since its narrow streets and high houses had provided protection against the burning sun, whereas now the shadowless open spaces radiated a fiercer heat. . . .

But neither human resources, nor imperial munificence, nor appeasement of the gods, eliminated sinister suspicions that the fire had been instigated. To suppress this rumour, Nero fabricated scapegoats—and punished with every refinement the notoriously depraved Christians (as they were popularly called). Their originator, Christ, had been executed in Tiberius' reign by the governor of Judaea, Pontius Pilatus.[3] But in spite of this temporary setback the deadly superstition had broken out afresh, not only in Judaea (where the mischief had started) but even in Rome. All degraded and shameful practices collect and flourish in the capital.

First, Nero had self-acknowledged Christians arrested. Then, on their information, large numbers of others were condemned—not so much for incendiarism as for their anti-social tendencies.[4] Their deaths were made farcical. Dressed in wild animals' skins, they were torn to pieces by dogs, or crucified, or made into torches to be ignited after dark as substitutes for daylight. Nero provided his Gardens for the spectacle, and exhibited displays in the Circus, at which he mingled with the crowd— or stood in a chariot, dressed as a charioteer. Despite their guilt as Christians, and the ruthless punishment it deserved, the victims were pitied. For it was felt that they were being sacrificed to one man's brutality rather than to the national interest.[5]

EXPLANATORY NOTES

1. Its site is uncertain.
2. 418 years, 418 months, and 418 days had passed since the traditional date of the burning of Rome by the Gauls (390 B.C.).
3. This is the only mention in pagan Latin of Pontius Pilate's action.
4. But this phrase (*odio humani generis*) may instead mean 'because the human race detested them'.
5. Tacitus seems to hesitate (as often) between two versions. Were the Christians persecuted as incendiaries or as Christians? Our other sources know nothing of the former charge. Probably they were persecuted as an illegal association potentially guilty of violence or subversiveness (i.e. treason), but although the attack created a sinister precedent its main purpose at the time was merely to distract attention from rumours against Nero by finding a suitable scapegoat. Christian beliefs are unlikely to have been attacked as such. It has often been disputed whether Nero's government regarded the Christians as a sect of the Jews (whose Roman community had been penalized by Tiberius and Claudius, but may now have obtained protection through the influence of Poppaea). The martyrdoms of St Peter and St Paul are attributed to this or later persecutions of Nero. In the later Roman empire the Christian writer Tertullian attacked Tacitus for this passage (and for his slanders on the Jews in the *Histories*).

Religious Parties in Roman Judea

Flavius Josephus (c. 37–100 C.E.), originally called Joseph ben Mathias, was an aristocratic Jewish priest of the school of the Pharisees. Though a staunch defender of Jewish religion and culture, a visit to Rome in 64 C.E. convinced him that the Roman Empire was destined for success. He thereafter became notably pro-Roman and tried to control the excesses of the extreme Jewish nationalists. Because of his prominence, he was put in command of Galilee during the Jewish revolt (66–72 C.E.), but was captured in 67 C.E. He survived because he predicted that the general Vespasian would become emperor, as eventually happened. During the remainder of the war, he accompanied Titus, Vespasian's son, then returned with him to Rome, where he became a Roman citizen and enjoyed considerable influence. He devoted the rest of his life to writing a detailed and dramatic account of the Jewish revolt as well as a more general history of the Jews.

The present selection forms part of the background for the revolt by explaining the nature of the rival schools of thought in Judea on the eve of the Roman occupation of 6 C.E.

Among the Jews there are three schools of thought, whose adherents are called Pharisees, Sadducees, and Essenes respectively. The Essenes profess a severer discipline: they are Jews by birth and are peculiarly attached to each other. They eschew pleasure-seeking as a vice and regard temperance and mastery of the passions as virtue. Scorning wedlock, they select other men's children while still pliable and teachable, and fashion them after their own pattern—not that they wish to do away with marriage as a means of continuing the race, but they are afraid of the promiscuity of women and convinced that none of the sex remains faithful to one man. Contemptuous of wealth, they are communists to perfection, and none of them will be found to be better off than the rest: their rule is that novices admitted to the sect must surrender their property to the order, so that among them all neither humiliating poverty nor excessive wealth is ever seen, but each man's possessions go into the pool and as with brothers their entire property belongs to them all. Oil they regard as polluting, and if a man is unintentionally smeared with it he scrubs himself clean; for they think it desirable to keep the skin dry and always to wear white. Men to supervise the community's affairs are elected by show of hands, chosen for their tasks by universal suffrage.

They possess no one city but everywhere have large colonies.[1] When adherents arrive from elsewhere, all local resources are put at their disposal as if they were their own, and men they have never seen before entertain them like old friends. And so when they travel they carry no baggage at all, but only weapons to keep off bandits. In every town one of the order is appointed specially to look after strangers and issue clothing and provisions. In dress and personal appearance they are like children in the care of a stern tutor. Neither garments nor shoes are changed till they are dropping to pieces or worn out with age. Among themselves nothing is bought or sold: everyone gives what he has to anybody in need and receives from him in return something he himself can use; and even without giving anything in return they are free to share the possessions of anyone they choose.

They show devotion to the Deity in a way all their own. Before the sun rises they do not utter a word on secular affairs, but offer to Him some traditional prayers as if beseeching Him to appear.[2] After this their supervisors send every man to the craft he understands best, and they work assiduously till an hour before noon, when they again meet in one place and donning linen loincloths wash all over with cold water. After this purification they assemble in a building of their own which no one outside their community is allowed to enter; they then go into the refectory in a state of ritual cleanliness as if it was a holy temple and sit down in silence. Then the baker gives them their loaves in turn, and the cook sets before each man one plateful of one kind of food. The priest says grace before meat: to taste the food before this prayer is forbidden. After breakfast he offers a second prayer; for at beginning and end they give thanks to God as the Giver of life. Then removing their garments as sacred they go back to their work till evening. Returning once more they take supper in the same way, seating their guests beside them if any have arrived. Neither shouting nor disorder ever desecrates the house: in conversation each gives way to his neighbour in turn. To people outside the silence within seems like some dread mystery; it is the natural result of their unfailing sobriety and the restriction of their food and drink to a simple sufficiency.

In general they take no action without orders from the supervisors, but two things are left entirely to them—personal aid, and charity; they may of their own accord help any deserving person in need or supply the penniless with food. But gifts to their own kinsfolk require official sanction. Showing indignation only when justified, they keep their tempers under control; they champion good faith and serve the cause of peace. Every word they speak is more binding than an oath; swearing they reject as something worse than perjury, for they say a man is already condemned if he cannot be believed without God being named. They are wonderfully devoted to the work of ancient writers, choosing mostly books that can help soul and body; from them in their anxiety to cure disease they learn all about medicinal roots and the properties of stones.[3]

Persons desirous of joining the sect are not immediately admitted. For a whole year a candidate is excluded but is required to observe the same rule of life as the members, receiving from them a hatchet,[4] the loin-cloth mentioned above, and white garments. When he has given proof of his temperance during this period, he is associated more closely with the rule and permitted to share the purer waters of sanctification, though not yet admitted to the communal life. He has demonstrated his strength of purpose, but for two more years his character is tested, and if he is then seen to be worthy, he is accepted into the society. But before touching the communal food he must swear terrible oaths, first that he will revere the Godhead, and secondly that he will deal justly with men, will injure no one either of his own accord or at another's bidding, will always hate the wicked and co-operate with the good, and will keep faith at all times and with all men—especially with rulers, since all power is conferred by God. If he himself receives power, he will never abuse his authority and never by dress or additional ornament outshine those under him; he will always love truth and seek to convict liars, will keep his hands from stealing and his soul innocent of unholy gain, and will never hide anything from members of the sect or reveal any of their secrets to others, even if brought by violence to the point of death. He further swears to impart their teaching to no man otherwise than as he himself received it, to take no part in armed robbery, and to preserve the books of the sect and in the same way the names of the angels. Such are the oaths by which they make sure of their converts.

Men convicted of major offences are expelled from the order, and the outcast often comes to a most miserable end; for bound as he is by oaths and customs, he cannot share the diet of non-members, so is forced to eat grass till his starved body wastes away and he dies. Charity compels them to take many offenders back when at their last gasp, since they feel that men tortured to the point of death have paid a sufficient penalty for their offences. In trying cases they are most careful and quite impartial, and the verdict is given by a jury of not less than a hundred: when they reach a decision there is no appeal. What they reverence most after God is the Lawgiver,[5] and blasphemy against him is a capital offence. Obedience to older men and to the majority is a matter of principle: if ten sit down together one will not speak against the wish of the nine.

They are careful not to spit into the middle of other people or to the right, and they abstain from seventh-day work more rigidly than any other Jews; for not only do they prepare their meals the previous day so as to avoid lighting a fire on the Sabbath, but they do not venture to remove any utensil or to go and ease themselves. On other days they dig a hole a foot deep with their trenching-tool (for such is the hatchet they give to the novices) and draping their cloak round them so as not to affront the rays of the god, they squat over it; then they put the excavated soil back in the hole. On these occasions they choose the more secluded spots; and though emptying the bowels is quite natural, they are taught to wash after it, as if it defiled them.

They are divided into four grades, according to the stage they have reached in their preparation[6]; and so far are the juniors inferior to the seniors that if they touch them the persons touched must wash as though contaminated by an alien. They are long-lived, most of them passing the century, owing to the simplicity of their daily life, I suppose, and the regular routine. They despise danger and conquer pain by sheer will-power: death, if it comes with honour, they value more than life without end. Their spirit was tested to the utmost by the war with the Romans, who racked and twisted, burnt and broke them, subjecting them to every torture yet invented in order to make them blaspheme the Lawgiver or eat some forbidden food, but could not make them do either, or ever once fawn on their tormentors or shed a tear. Smiling in their agony and gently mocking those who tortured them, they resigned their souls in the joyous certainty that they would receive them back.[7]

It is indeed their unshakable conviction that bodies are corruptible and the material composing them impermanent, whereas souls remain immortal for ever. Coming forth from the most rarefied ether they are trapped in the prison-house of the body as if drawn down by one of nature's spells; but once freed from the bonds of the flesh, as if released after years of slavery, they rejoice and soar aloft. Teaching the same doctrine as the sons of Greece, they declare that for the good souls there waits a home beyond the ocean, a place troubled by neither rain nor snow nor heat, but refreshed by the zephyr that blows ever gentle from the ocean. Bad souls they consign to a darksome, stormy abyss, full of punishments that know no end. I think the Greeks had the same notion when they assigned to their brave men, whom they call heroes or demigods, the Islands of the Blest,[8] and to the souls of the wicked the place of the impious in Hades, where according to their stories certain people undergo punishment—Sisyphus and Tantalus, Ixion and Tityus,[9] and the like. They tell these tales firstly because they believe souls to be immortal, and secondly in the hope of encouraging virtue and discouraging vice, since the good become better in their lifetime through the hope of a reward after death, and the propensities of the bad are restrained by the fear that, even if they are not caught in this life, after their dissolution they will undergo eternal punishment. This then is the religious teaching of the Essenes about the soul, providing an inescapable inducement to those who have once tasted their wisdom.

Some of them claim to foretell the future, after a lifelong study of sacred literature, purifications of different kinds, and the aphorisms of prophets; rarely if ever do their predictions prove wrong.

There is a second order of Essenes, which agrees with the other in its way of life, customs, and rules, and differs only in its views on marriage. They think that the biggest thing in life—the continuance of the race—is forfeited by men who do not marry, and further, if everyone followed their example mankind would rapidly disappear. However, they put their brides on probation for three years, and do not marry them till the regularity of their periods proves them capable of child-bearing.[10] When conception has taken place intercourse ceases—proof that the object of the marriage was not pleasure but the begetting of children. When women bathe they wear a dress just as the men wear a loincloth. Such are the customs of the order.

Of the two schools named first, the Pharisees are held to be the most authoritative exponents of the Law and count as the leading sect.[11] They ascribe everything to Fate or to God: the decision whether or not to do right rests mainly with men, but in every action Fate takes some part. Every soul is imperishable, but only the souls of good men pass into other bodies,[12] the souls of bad men being subjected to eternal punishment. The Sadducees,[13] the second order, deny Fate altogether and hold that God is incapable of either committing sin or seeing it; they say that men are free to choose between good and evil, and each individual must decide which he will follow. The permanence of the soul, punishments in Hades, and rewards they deny utterly. Again, Pharisees are friendly to one another and seek to promote concord with the general public, but Sadducees, even towards each other, show a more disagreeable spirit, and in their relations with men like themselves they are as harsh as they might be to foreigners.

This is all I wish to say about the Jewish schools of thought.

EXPLANATORY NOTES

1. Almost certainly Qumran was one (Appendix E [of *The Jewish War*]).
2. Or 'offer prayers to it (the sun) as if beseeching it to rise', rather surprisingly implying sun-worship. But cf. their extraordinary respect for 'the rays of the god' (paragraph 7).
3. Probably for use as charms or amulets.
4. Its use is given in paragraph 7.
5. Moses.
6. The lowest three are presumably the novices passing through the three years of probation (above).
7. Josephus' account of the war of 66–70 contains no reference to Roman attacks on the Essenes, or indeed to the Essenes themselves except for the rather surprising appointment of one of them as a military commander (p. 180).
8. Hesiod, *Works and Days* 169 ff.; Pindar, *Olymp.* 2, 77 ff.
9. Notorious sinners who suffered picturesque punishments to fit their crimes.
10. The Greek here makes little sense. This suggestion of a possible meaning is based on the Latin translation of Josephus ascribed to the fourth-century writer Rufinus.
11. They stood for strict adherence to the law of Moses in every particular. The Pharisaic scholars and teachers, the rabbis, by discussion and interpretation of the basic law produced a vast quantity of traditional, oral law to supplement it and regulate every aspect of daily life.
12. cf. [later in *The Jewish War*], p. 219, where again acceptance of the doctrine of the transmigration of souls (i.e. the reincarnation of the dead for further lives on earth) held by the Greek philosophers Pythagoras and Plato is attributed to the Pharisees.
13. The Sadducees were the wealthy aristocracy from whom the high priests were drawn.

HESIOD

Theogony

Hail, daughters of Zeus! Give me sweet song,
To celebrate the holy race of gods
Who live forever, sons of starry Heaven
And Earth, and gloomy Night, and salty Sea.
Tell how the gods and earth arose at first,
And rivers and the boundless swollen sea
And shining stars, and the broad heaven above,
And how the gods divided up their wealth
And how they shared their honours, how they first
Captured Olympus with its many folds.
Tell me these things, Olympian Muses, tell
From the beginning, which first came to be?
Chaos was first of all, but next appeared
Broad-bosomed Earth, sure standing-place for all
The gods who live on snowy Olympus' peak,
And misty Tartarus, in a recess
Of broad-pathed earth, and Love, most beautiful
Of all the deathless gods. He makes men weak,
He overpowers the clever mind, and tames
The spirit in the breasts of men and gods.
From Chaos came black Night and Erebos.
And Night in turn gave birth to Day and Space
Whom she conceived in love to Erebos.
And Earth bore starry Heaven, first, to be
An equal to herself, to cover her
All over, and to be a resting-place,
Always secure, for all the blessed gods.
Then she brought forth long hills, the lovely homes
Of goddesses, the Nymphs who live among
The mountain clefts. Then, without pleasant love,
She bore the barren sea with its swollen waves,
Pontus. And then she lay with Heaven, and bore
Deep-whirling Oceanus and Koios; then
Kreius, Iapetos, Hyperion,
Theia, Rhea, Themis, Mnemosyne,
Lovely Tethys, and Phoebe, golden-crowned.
List, after these, most terrible of sons,
The crooked-scheming Kronos came to birth

Excerpt from *Theogony*, by Hesiod, reprinted from *Hesiod and Theogonis*, translated by
Dorothea Wender, (1973), by permission of Penguin Books, Ltd.

Who was his vigorous father's enemy.
Again, she bore the Cyclopes, whose hearts
Were insolent, Brontes and Steropes
And proud-souled Arges, those who found and gave
The thunder and the lightning-bolt to Zeus.
They were like other gods in all respects,
But that a single eye lay in the brow
Of each, and from this, they received the name,
Cyclopes, from the one round eye which lay
Set in the middle of each forehead. Strength
And energy and craft were in their works.
Then Ouranos and Gaia bore three sons
Mighty and violent, unspeakable
Kottos and Gyes and Briareus,
Insolent children, each with a hundred arms
On his shoulders, darting about, untouchable,
And each had fifty heads, standing upon
His shoulders, over the crowded mass of arms,
And terrible strength was in their mighty forms.

And these most awful sons of Earth and Heaven
Were hated by their father from the first.
As soon as each was born, Ouranos hid
The child in a secret hiding-place in Earth
And would not let it come to see the light,
And he enjoyed this wickedness. But she,
Vast Earth, being strained and stretched inside her, groaned.
And then she thought of a clever, evil plan.
Quickly she made grey adamant, and formed
A mighty sickle, and addressed her sons,
Urging them on, with sorrow in her heart,
'My sons, whose father is a reckless fool,
If you will do as I ask, we shall repay
Your father's wicked crime. For it was he
Who first began devising shameful acts.'

She spoke, but fear seized all of them, and none
Replied. Then crooked Kronos, growing bold,
Answered his well-loved mother with these words:
'Mother, I undertake to do the deed;
I do not care for my unspeakable
Father, for he first thought of shameful acts.'
He spoke, and giant Earth was glad at heart.
She set him in a hiding-place, and put
Into his hands the saw-toothed scimitar,

And told him all the plot she had devised.

Great Heaven came, and with him brought the night.
Longing for love, he lay around the Earth,
Spreading out fully. But the hidden boy
Stretched forth his left hand; in his right he took
The great long jagged sickle; eagerly
He harvested his father's genitals
And threw them off behind. They did not fall
From his hands in vain, for all the bloody drops
That leaped out were received by Earth; and when
The year's time was accomplished, she gave birth
To the Furies, and the Giants, strong and huge,
Who fought in shining armour, with long spears,
And the nymphs called Meliae on the broad earth.

The genitals, cut off with adamant
And thrown from land into the stormy sea,
Were carried for a long time on the waves.
White foam surrounded the immortal flesh,
And in it grew a girl. At first it touched
On holy Cythera, from there it came
To Cyprus, circled by the waves. And there
The goddess came forth, lovely, much revered,
And grass grew up beneath her delicate feet.
Her name is Aphrodite among men
And gods, because she grew up in the foam,
And Cytherea, for she reached that land,
And Cyprogenes from the stormy place
Where she was born, and Philommedes from
The genitals, by which she was conceived.
Eros is her companion; fair Desire
Followed her from the first, both at her birth
And when she joined the company of the gods.
From the beginning, both among gods and men,
She had this honour and received this power:
Fond murmuring of girls, and smiles, and tricks,
And sweet delight, and friendliness, and charm.

But the great father Ouranos reproached
His sons, and called them Titans, for, he said
They strained in insolence, and did a deed
For which they would be punished afterwards.

And Night bore frightful Doom and the black Ker,

And Death, and Sleep, and the whole tribe of Dreams.

Again, although she slept with none of the gods,
Dark Night gave birth to Blame and sad Distress,
And the Hesperides, who, out beyond
The famous stream of Oceanus, tend
The lovely golden apples, and their trees.
She bore the Destinies and ruthless Fates,
Goddesses who track down the sins of men
And gods, and never cease from awful rage
Until they give the sinner punishment.
Then deadly Night gave birth to Nemesis,
That pain to gods and men, and then she bore
Deceit and Love, sad Age, and strong-willed Strife.
And hateful Strife gave birth to wretched Work,
Forgetfulness, and Famine, tearful Pains,
Battles and Fights, Murders, Killings of men,
Quarrels and Lies and Stories and Disputes,
And Lawlessness and Ruin, both allied,
And Oath, who brings most grief to men on earth
When anyone swears falsely, knowing it.

And Pontus' firstborn child was Nereus,
The honest one, the truthful. The old man
Is called this name because he never errs,
And he is gentle and remembers Right,
And knows the arts of Mercy and the Law.

Then Pontus and Earth produced great Thaumas, proud
Phorkys, and Ceto with her lovely skin,
And Eurybie, with her heart of steel.

And Nereus and Doris, lovely-haired
Daughter of Oceanus, circling stream,
Begot and bore, in the unfruitful sea,
Their children, most beloved of goddesses:
Protho, Eukrante, Sao, Amphitrite,
Eudore, Thetis, Galene, Glauce, and
Cymothoe, Speio, and quick Thalia,
And lovely Pasithea, Erato and
Eunike with her rosy arms, and fair
Melite, Eulimene, Agave,
Doto, Proto, Pherousa, Dynamene,
Nesaia, Aktaia, Protomedeia, and
Doris, Panope, and the beautiful

Galatea, and the lovely Hippothoe,
Rosy-armed Hipponoe, Cymodoce,
Who, acting with trim-ankled Amphitrite
And Cymatolege, easily can still
Waves on the misty sea, and calm the blasts
Of raging winds; Cymo, Eione,
And garlanded Halimede, the one
Who loves to laugh, Glauconome, and next
Pontoporeia, and Leiagore,
Euagore, Laomedeia and
Poulunoe, and then Authonoe,
Lysianassa, and Euame, lovely-shaped,
Perfect to look at, graceful Psamathe,
Menippe, Neso, and Eupompe; next,
Themisto, Pronoe and Nemertes,
Whose mind is like her deathless father's. These
Are the fifty daughters of blameless Nereus;
And they, as well, are skilled in perfect works.

And Thaumas took Electra for his bride,
Deep-flowing Ocean's daughter, and she bore
Swift Iris and the Harpies; lovely-haired
Aello and Okypete, who fly
On their swift wings as fast as birds, or breath
Of wind; high through the air they hurl themselves.
And Ceto bore to Phorkys the fair-cheeked
Graiae, grey-haired from birth, whom gods and men
Who walk on earth call Grey Ones: Pemphredo
Well-gowned, and Enyo, with yellow robes,
And the Gorgons, they who lived beyond the stream
Of famous Ocean, on the edge near Night,
Where the clear-voiced Hesperides are found.
Their names were Sthenno and Euryale
And Medusa, she who suffered painfully.
Her sisters were immortal, always young,
But she was mortal, and the Dark-haired One
Lay down with her among the flowers of spring
In a soft meadow. And when Perseus
Cut off her head, great Chrysaor sprang out,
And Pegasus the horse, who is so called
Because his birth was near to Ocean's springs;
Chrysaor's name comes from the golden blade
He held when he was born. And Pegasus
Flew from the earth which nurtures sheep, and came
To join the immortal gods. And there he lives

In the house of Zeus, and brings the lightning-shaft
And thunder to wise Zeus. But Chrysaor
Lay with a child of Ocean, Callirhoe,
And fathered Geryon, who had three heads;
The power of Heracles killed Geryon
In sea-suffounded Erythea, near
The shuffling cattle. On that very day
The hero drove the broad-browed cattle home
To holy Tiryns, and crossed Ocean's ford,
And killed the herd Eurytion and the dog
Orthos, in the dark stalls, by Ocean's stream.

She bore another monster, terrible,
In a hollow cave, Echidna, fierce of heart,
Nothing like any mortal man, unlike
Any immortal god, for half of her
Is a fair-cheeked girl with glancing eyes, but half
Is a huge and frightening speckled snake; she eats
Raw flesh in a recess of the holy earth.
Down there she has a cave of hollow rock
Far from the deathless gods and mortal men;
There the gods gave a famous home to her,
And gloomy Echidna keeps her watch down there
Under the ground, among the Arimoi,
A nymph immortal and ageless all her days.

They say that Typho, terrible and proud
And lawless, loved this nymph with glancing eyes,
And she conceived and bore fierce progeny:
First, Orthos the dog of Geryon, and next,
Unspeakable Cerberus, who eats raw flesh,
The bronze-voiced hound of Hades, shameless, strong,
With fifty heads. And then again she bore
The Lernaean Hydra, skilled in wrong, the one
The goddess white-armed Hera raised, who was
Immensely angry with great Heracles.
With warlike Iolaus' help, and through
The plans of Athene, she who leads the host,
The son of Zeus, Amphitryonides,
Dispatched the Hydra with his ruthless sword.
She bore Chimaera, who breathed awful fire,
Three-headed, frightening, huge, swift-footed, strong,
One head a bright-eyed lion's, one a goat's,
The third a snake's, a mighty dragon-head.
Noble Bellerophon and Pegasus

Caught her. But she, subdued by Orthos, bore
The deadly Sphinx, a curse on the men of Thebes,
And the Nemean lion, a plague to men,
Brought up by Hera, the lady wife of Zeus,
Set down in the Nemean hills to live
Destroying the tribes of men; and he subdued
Nemean Tretus and Apesas. But he
Was conquered by the power of Heracles.
And Ceto, joined in love to Phorkys, bore
Her youngest child, a frightful snake which guards
The golden apples, in that secret place
Of the dark earth, at its great boundary-line.
And these are Phorkys' and Ceto's progeny.
Tethys bore whirling Rivers to her mate
Ocean: the Nile, Alpheios, and the deep
Eddying Eridanus, Strymon; then,
Meander, Ister's lovely-flowing stream,
And Phasis, Rhesus, and the silver pools
Of Achelous and Nessus, Rhodius,
Then Haliacmon, Heptaporus, and
Granicus, Aesepus, bright Simois,
Peneus, Hermus, gentle Caicus,
Sangarius the great, Parthenius,
Ladon, Euenus, and Aldescus; last,
She bore Scamander, shining holy stream.

And she bore daughters, holy progeny,
Who, with the Rivers and Apollo, lord,
Have charge of young men over all the earth,
For Zeus appointed them to do this work:
Peitho, Admete, and Ianthe; next,
Electra, Doris, Prymno, and divine
Ourania and Hippo, Clymene,
Rhodeia, Callirhoe, Zeuxo; and
Klutie, Iduia and Pasithoe,
Plexaure, Galaxaure and the loved
Dione, Melobosis, Thoe, fair
Polydore, Kerkeis with lovely shape,
And Pluto with her wide eyes, Perseis,
Ianeira, Akaste, Xanthe and the sweet
Petraie, Menestho, Europe, Metis; next,
Eurynome, Telesto, yellow-robed,
And Chryseis, Asie, lovable
Calypso and Eudore, Tyche, and
Amphiro, and Okuroe and Styx,

Who is the most important one of all.
These are the oldest daughters who were born
To Oceanus and Tethys, but there are
Many others beside them, Oceanids,
Three thousand nymphs with shapely ankles, who
Are scattered everywhere, over the earth
And on deep water, glorious goddesses.
There are as many roaring rivers, too,
Children of Ocean, lady Tethys' sons;
It is hard for mortal man to name their names,
But they are known to those who live nearby.

And Theia, mastered by Hyperion,
Bore Helios the great, bright Selene,
And Eos, who shines upon all men on earth
And on the deathless gods who hold broad heaven.

Eurybie, the shining goddess, joined
In love with Krios, bore to him the great
Astraios, Pallas and Perses, greatly wise.
And with the god Astraios, Eos lay
In love, a goddess herself, and bore the winds
With mighty hearts: the cleansing Zephyros,
And Notos, and swift-racing Boreas.
And Erigeneia brought forth, after these,
The star Eosphoros and all the stars
Which, shining, make a garland for the heavens.

Then Pallas slept with Ocean's daughter, Styx,
Who bore him shapely-ankled Victory
And Glory, in his house, and famous sons:
Power and Force. They have no house apart
From Zeus, nor any seat, nor any path
Except where God commands them, and they sit
Forever at the side of thundering Zeus.
Styx, Ocean's deathless daughter, planned it so,
The day the Lightener of Olympus called
To great Olympus all the deathless gods
And said, whichever of the gods should fight
With him against the Titans would not lose
His honours, but would keep the rights he had
Among the deathless gods up to that day;
And those, he said, who under Kronos had
No rank nor rights would be promoted now
To rank and honours both, as would be just.

And deathless Styx came to Olympus first
And brought her children, as her father advised.
Zeus gave her honour and unequalled gifts:
For she was made the great oath of the gods;
Her children always live at Zeus's side.
And as he promised, Zeus fulfilled his vows
To all; and he rules greatly, and is lord.

And Phoebe came to Koios' longed-for bed.
Loved by the god, the goddess conceived and bore
Leto the dark-robed, always mild and kind
To men and deathless gods; gentlest in all
Olympus; from the beginning, she was mild.
Then Phoebe bore renowned Asterie
Whom Perses led, a bride, to his great house.
Last she bore Hekate, who, above all,
Is honoured by the son of Kronos, Zeus.
He gave her glorious gifts: a share of earth
And of the barren sea. In starry heaven
She has her place, and the immortal gods
Respect her greatly. Even now, when men
Upon the earth, according to the rites,
Make handsome sacrifices, and entreat
The gods for favour, Hekate is called.
Great honours follow readily that man
Whose prayers the goddess graciously receives;
And she can give him wealth; that power is hers.
Of all the children Earth and Ocean bore,
Who once had privilege, she kept her due.
The son of Kronos never did her harm
Nor did he snatch away the rights she had
Under the Titan gods of old; she keeps
Her privilege in earth and sea and heaven
As it was portioned to her from the start.
Nor did she get a lesser share because
She had no brothers to defend her rights.
Her share is greater: Zeus is her advocate.
Help and success come to her favourites;
In court, she sits beside respected lords;
In the assembly of the people, he
Whom she has chosen, shines. And when men arm
For man-destroying war, the goddess helps
The men she wants to help, and eagerly
Brings victory and glorious fame to them.
A splendid ally in the games, when men

Compete, then, too, she brings success and help.
The man she favours wins by might and strength
And gains the lovely prize with ease and joy,
And brings his parents glory. She is good
To stand by horsemen, also good for those
Who work the rude grey sea, and those who pray
To Hekate and to the god who shakes
The earth with crashes, get great hauls from her,
The glorious goddess, if she wishes it,
But just as easily she takes away
All she has given, if she wants it so.
And she is helpful in the stables, too,
Along with Hermes, to increase the stock.
The herds of cattle and of goats, and flocks
Of woolly sheep grow numerous, from few,
If she is willing, or grow small from great.
Thus, among all the honoured, deathless gods
She is revered, although her mother bore
No sons. The son of Kronos also made
Her nurse and overseer of all the young
Who from that day were born and came to see
The light of Dawn who sees the world; and thus
She is a nurse; and these are her high tasks.
And Rhea, being forced by Kronos, bore
Most brilliant offspring to him: Hestia,
Demeter, golden-slippered Hera, strong
Hades, who has his home beneath the earth,
The god whose heart is pitiless, and him
Who crashes loudly and who shakes the earth,[29]
And thoughtful Zeus, father of gods and men,
Whose thunder makes the wide earth tremble. Then,
As each child issued from the holy womb
And lay upon its mother's knees, each one
Was seized by mightly Kronos, and gulped down.
He had in mind that no proud son of Heaven
Should hold the royal rank among the gods
Except himself. For he had learned from Earth
And starry Heaven, that his destiny
Was to be overcome, great though he was,
By one of his own sons, and through the plans
Of mighty Zeus. Therefore he never dropped
His guard, but lay in wait, and swallowed down
His children. Rhea suffered endless grief;
But when she was about to bring forth Zeus,
Father of gods and men, she begged the Earth

And starry Heaven, her parents, to devise
A plan to hide the birth of her dear son
And bring the Fury down on Kronos, for
His treatment of his father and his sons
Whom mighty, crooked Kronos swallowed down.
They heard their daughter and agreed, and told
Her all that fate would bring upon the king
Kronos, and to his mighty-hearted son.
They sent her to the fertile land of Crete,
To Lyctus, when she was about to bear
Her youngest child, great Zeus. And in broad Crete
Vast Earth received the child from her, to raise
And cherish. And she carried him, with speed,
Through the black night, and came to Lyctus first.
She took him in her arms and hid him, deep
Under the holy earth, in a vast cave,
On thickly-wooded Mount Aegeum. Then,
To the great lord, the son of Heaven, the past
King of the gods, she handed, solemnly,
All wrapped in swaddling-clothes, a giant stone.
He seized it in his hands and thrust it down
Into his belly, fool! He did not know
His son, no stone, was left behind, unhurt
And undefeated, who would conquer him
With violence and force, and drive him out
From all his honours, and would rule the gods.

The strength and glorious limbs of the young lord
Grew quickly and the years went by, and Earth
Entrapped great clever Kronos with shrewd words
Advising him to bring his offspring back.
(His son, by craft and power, conquered him.)
And first he vomited the stone, which he
Had swallowed last. At holy Pytho, Zeus
Set firm the stone in broad-pathed earth, beneath
Parnassus, in a cleft, to be a sign
In future days, for men to marvel at.

He freed his uncles from their dreadful bonds,
The sons of Heaven; his father, foolishly,
Had bound them. They remembered gratitude
And gave him thunder and the blazing bolt
And lightning, which, before, vast Earth had hid.
Trusting in them, he rules both men and gods.
And Klymene, the lovely-ankled nymph,

Daughter of Ocean, married Iapetos,
And went to bed with him, and bore a son,
Strong-hearted Atlas, then, notorious
Menoitios, and then, Prometheus
Brilliant and shifty, Epimetheus
The foolish one, who first brought harm to men
Who live on bread, for he took Woman in,
The manufactured maiden, gift of Zeus.
Far-seeing Zeus cast proud Menoitios
Down into Erebos; he struck him with
The smoking thunderbolt, because he was
Insanely bold and reckless in his pride.
And Atlas, forced by hard necessity,
Holds the broad heaven up, propped on his head
And tireless hands, at the last ends of Earth,
In front of the clear-voiced Hesperides;
For Zeus the Counsellor gave him this fate.
Clever Prometheus was bound by Zeus
In cruel chains, unbreakable, chained round
A pillar, and Zeus roused and set on him
An eagle with long wings, which came and ate
His deathless liver. But the liver grew
Each night, until it made up the amount
The long-winged bird had eaten in the day.
Lovely Alcmene's son, strong Heracles,
Killing the eagle, freed Prometheus
From his affliction and his misery,
And Zeus, Olympian, who rules on high,
Approved, so that the fame of Heracles
The Theban might be greater than before
Upon the fruitful earth; he showed respect,
And gave the honour to his famous son.
And angry though he was, he checked the rage
He felt against Prometheus, who dared
To match his wits against almighty Zeus.

The Six Days of Creation

_____

The Bible is the most authoritative text in the Judeo-Christian tradition, and is regarded as divinely inspired, even today, by the more conservative elements within Christianity and Judaism. It is divided into two large parts: the Jewish Scriptures, known to Christians as the Old Testament; and the New Testament, containing twenty-seven books recognized as authoritative by Christians but not by Jews. In addition to the thirty-nine books of the Old Testament recognized by Protestant Christianity and by normative Judaism are another fifteen books or parts of books that were handed down with the Jewish Scriptures in Greek (known as the Septuagint). Most of these are accepted as canonical by the Roman Catholic Church and are referred to in its tradition as the "deuterocanonical" books.

The Old Testament contains a great variety of writings including myths, legends, legal codes, chronicles, edifying stories, poetry, prophecy, and wisdom literature. The original texts were compiled at various times between the twelfth and the second centuries B.C.E. Almost all of them were written in classical Hebrew, except for a few short passages in Aramaic. The canon of the Hebrew scriptures (the so-called Massoretic text) was only established by Palestinian Jews toward the end of the first century C.E. and has remained substantially unchanged since that time. Greek Christians, however, made use of the Septuagint text, while Roman Catholic Christians in the Middle Ages used the Latin translation of St. Jerome (c. 342–420 C.E.) based on the Hebrew. Since the Reformation the customary practice in Protestant countries is to use vernacular translations based on the original Hebrew text.

In the first generations following the death of Christ (29/30 C.E.), Christians continued to use the Jewish Scriptures as sacred writings, interpreting them in the light of the teachings of Jesus and the apostle Paul. Gradually they assembled a body of their own writings, believed to be of apostolic origin. These were written in Greek during a seventy-five-year period between about 50 and 125 C.E. The first attested use of the expression "New

Testament," however, comes in the writings of Tertullian around 200 C.E., and the first serious attempts by the Church to define the canon of the New Testament date only from the late fourth century C.E. The New Testament includes four early accounts of the life and teachings of Christ (the Gospels); a historical account of the early missions of the Church (the Acts of the Apostles); letters of various apostles; and a book of prophecies (Revelation) attributed to the apostle John. The letters of the apostle Paul are particularly significant statements of early Christian theology, and all the apostolic epistles contain instructions concerning morality and Church discipline.

The passage excerpted here, one of the most famous in the Bible, comes from the beginning of Genesis, the first book of the Bible, and describes God's creation of the world.

---

1 In the beginning God created the heavens and the earth. ²The earth was a vast waste, darkness covered the deep, and the spirit of God hovered over the surface of the water. ³God said, 'Let there be light,' and there was light; ⁴and God saw the light was good, and he separated light from darkness. ⁵He called the light day, and the darkness night. So evening came, and morning came; it was the first day.

⁶God said, 'Let there be a vault between the waters, to separate water from water.' ⁷So God made the vault, and separated the water under the vault from the water above it, and so it was; ⁸and God called the vault the heavens. Evening came, and morning came, the second day.

⁹God said, 'Let the water under the heavens be gathered into one place, so that dry land may appear'; and so it was. ¹⁰God called the dry land earth, and the gathering of the water he called sea; and God saw that it was good. ¹¹Then God said, 'Let the earth produce growing things; let there be on the earth plants that bear seed, and trees bearing fruit each with its own kind of seed.' So it was; ¹²the earth produced growing things: plants bearing their own kind of seed and trees bearing fruit, each with its own kind of seed; and God saw that it was good. ¹³Evening came, and morning came, the third day.

¹⁴God said, 'Let there be lights in the vault of the heavens to separate day from night, and let them serve as signs both for festivals and for seasons and years. ¹⁵Let them also shine in the heavens to give light on earth.' So it was; ¹⁶God made two great lights, the greater to govern the day and the lesser to govern the night; he also made the stars. ¹⁷God put these lights in the vault of the heavens to give light on earth, ¹⁸to govern

day and night, and to separate light from darkness; and God saw that it was good. [19]Evening came, and morning came, the fourth day.

[20]God said, 'Let the water teem with living creatures, and let birds fly above the earth across the vault of the heavens.' [21]God then created the great sea-beasts and all living creatures that move and swarm in the water, according to their various kinds, and every kind of bird; and God saw that it was good. [22]He blessed them and said, 'Be fruitful and increase; fill the water of the sea, and let the birds increase on the land.' [23]Evening came, and morning came, the fifth day.

[24]God said, 'Let the earth bring forth living creatures, according to their various kinds: cattle, creeping things, and wild animals, all according to their various kinds.' So it was; [25]God made wild animals, cattle, and every creeping thing, all according to their various kinds; and he saw that it was good. [26]Then God said, 'Let us make human beings in our image, after our likeness, to have dominion over the fish in the sea, the birds of the air, the cattle, all wild animals on land, and everything that creeps on the earth.'

> [27]God created human beings in his own image;
> in the image of God he created them;
> male and female he created them.

[28]God blessed them and said to them, 'Be fruitful and increase, fill the earth and subdue it, have dominion over the fish in the sea, the birds of the air, and every living thing that moves on the earth.' [29]God also said, 'Throughout the earth I give you all plants that bear seed, and every tree that bears fruit with seed: they shall be yours for food. [30]All green plants I give for food to the wild animals, to all the birds of the air, and to everything that creeps on the earth, every living creature.' So it was; [31]and God saw all that he had made, and it was very good. Evening came, and morning came, the sixth day.

2 Thus the heavens and the earth and everything in them were completed. [2]On the sixth day God brought to an end all the work he had been doing; on the seventh day, having finished all his work, [3]God blessed the day and made it holy, because it was the day he finished all his work of creation.

EXPLANATORY NOTES

1:1–2 **In . . . earth was:** *or* When God began to create the heavens and the earth, [2]the earth was.

1:2 **the spirit . . . hovered:** *or* a great wind swept; *or* a wind from God swept.

2:2 **sixth:** *so some Vss.; Heb.* seventh.

The Ten Commandments

The Bible is the most authoritative text in the Judeo-Christian tradition, and is regarded as divinely inspired, even today, by the more conservative elements within Christianity and Judaism. It is divided into two large parts: the Jewish Scriptures, known to Christians as the Old Testament; and the New Testament, containing twenty-seven books recognized as authoritative by Christians but not by Jews. In addition to the thirty-nine books of the Old Testament recognized by Protestant Christianity and by normative Judaism are another fifteen books or parts of books that were handed down with the Jewish Scriptures in Greek (known as the Septuagint). Most of these are accepted as canonical by the Roman Catholic Church and are referred to in its tradition as the "deuterocanonical" books.

The Old Testament contains a great variety of writings including myths, legends, legal codes, chronicles, edifying stories, poetry, prophecy, and wisdom literature. The original texts were compiled at various times between the twelfth and the second centuries B.C.E. Almost all of them were written in classical Hebrew, except for a few short passages in Aramaic. The canon of the Hebrew scriptures (the so-called Massoretic text) was only established by Palestinian Jews toward the end of the first century C.E. and has remained substantially unchanged since that time. Greek Christians, however, made use of the Septuagint text, while Roman Catholic Christians in the Middle Ages used the Latin translation of St. Jerome (c. 342–420 C.E.) based on the Hebrew. Since the Reformation the customary practice in Protestant countries is to use vernacular translations based on the original Hebrew text.

In the first generations following the death of Christ (29/30 C.E.), Christians continued to use the Jewish Scriptures as sacred writings, interpreting them in the light of the teachings of Jesus and the apostle Paul. Gradually they assembled a body of their own writings, believed to be of apostolic origin. These were written in Greek during a seventy-five-year period between about 50 and 125 C.E. The first attested use of the expression "New

Testament," however, comes in the writings of Tertullian around 200 C.E., and the first serious attempts by the Church to define the canon of the New Testament date only from the late fourth century C.E. The New Testament includes four early accounts of the life and teachings of Christ (the Gospels); a historical account of the early missions of the Church (the Acts of the Apostles); letters of various apostles; and a book of prophecies (Revelation) attributed to the apostle John. The letters of the apostle Paul are particularly significant statements of early Christian theology, and all the apostolic epistles contain instructions concerning morality and Church discipline.

The passage below, from the book of Exodus, gives the text of the Ten Commandments, the basis of Judeo-Christian ethics, and describes how Moses brought the Commandments to the Israelites from Mount Sinai.

Israel at Mount Sinai

19 In the third month after Israel had left Egypt, they came to the wilderness of Sinai. ²They set out from Rephidim and, entering the wilderness of Sinai, they encamped there, pitching their tents in front of the mountain. ³Moses went up to God, and the LORD called to him from the mountain and said, 'This is what you are to say to the house of Jacob and tell the sons of Israel: ⁴You yourselves have seen what I did to Egypt, and how I have carried you on eagles' wings and brought you here to me. ⁵If only you will now listen to me and keep my covenant, then out of all peoples you will become my special possession; for the whole earth is mine. ⁶You will be to me a kingdom of priests, my holy nation. Those are the words you are to speak to the Israelites.'

⁷Moses went down, and summoning the elders of the people he set before them all these commands which the LORD had laid on him. ⁸As one the people answered, 'Whatever the LORD has said we shall do.' When Moses brought this answer back to the LORD, ⁹the LORD said to him, 'I am coming to you in a thick cloud, so that I may speak to you in the hearing of the people, and so their faith in you may never fail.'

When Moses reported to the LORD the pledge given by the people, ¹⁰the LORD said to him, 'Go to the people and hallow them today and tomorrow and have them wash their clothes. ¹¹They must be ready by the third day, because on that day the LORD will descend on Mount Sinai in the sight of all the people. ¹²You must set bounds for the people, saying, "Take care not to go up the mountain or even to touch its base." Anyone who touches the mountain shall be put to death. ¹³No hand may touch him; he is to be stoned to death or shot: neither man nor beast may live. But when the ram's horn sounds, they may go up the mountain.' ¹⁴Moses came down from the mountain to the people. He hallowed them and they washed their clothes. ¹⁵He said, 'Be ready by the third day; do not go near a woman.' ¹⁶At dawn on the third day there were peals of thunder and flashes of lightning, dense cloud on the mountain, and a loud trumpet-blast; all the people in the camp trembled.

¹⁷Moses brought the people out from the camp to meet God, and they took their stand at the foot of the mountain. ¹⁸Mount Sinai was enveloped in smoke because the Lord had come down on it in fire; the smoke rose like the smoke from a kiln; all the people trembled violently, ¹⁹and the sound of the trumpet grew ever louder. Whenever Moses spoke, God answered him in a peal of thunder. ²⁰The Lord came down on the top of Mount Sinai and summoned Moses up to the mountaintop. ²¹The Lord said to him, 'Go down; warn the people solemnly that they must not force their way through to the Lord to see him, or many of them will perish. ²²Even the priests, who may approach the Lord, must hallow themselves, for fear that the Lord may break out against them.' ²³Moses answered the Lord, 'The people cannot come up Mount Sinai, because you solemnly warned us to set bounds to the mountain and keep it holy.' ²⁴The Lord said, 'Go down; then come back, bringing Aaron with you, but let neither priests nor people force their way up to the Lord, for fear that he may break out against them.'²⁵ So Moses went down to the people and spoke to them.

20 God spoke all these words:
²I am the Lord your God who brought you out of Egypt, out of the land of slavery.

³You must have no other god besides me.

⁴You must not make a carved image for yourself, nor the likeness of anything in the heavens above, or on the earth below, or in the waters under the earth.

⁵You must not bow down to them in worship; for I, the Lord your God, am a jealous God, punishing the children for the sins of the parents to the third and fourth generation of those who reject me. ⁶But I keep faith with thousands, those who love me and keep my commandments.

⁷You must not make wrong use of the name of the Lord your God; the Lord will not leave unpunished anyone who misuses his name.

⁸Remember to keep the sabbath day holy. ⁹You have six days to labour and do all your work; ¹⁰but the seventh day is a sabbath of the Lord your God; that day you must not do any work, neither you, nor

your son or your daughter, your slave or your slave-girl, your cattle, or the alien residing among you; [11]for in six days the LORD made the heavens and the earth, the sea, and all that is in them, and on the seventh day he rested. Therefore the LORD blessed the sabbath day and declared it holy.

[12]Honour your father and your mother, so that you may enjoy long life in the land which the LORD your God is giving you.

[13]Do not commit murder.

[14]Do not commit adultery.

[15]Do not steal.

[16]Do not give false evidence against your neighbour.

[17]Do not covet your neighbour's household: you must not covet your neighbour's wife, his slave, his slave-girl, his ox, his donkey, or anything that belongs to him.

[18]When all the people saw how it thundered and the lightning flashed, when they heard the trumpet sound and saw the mountain in smoke, they were afraid and trembled. They stood at a distance [19]and said to Moses, 'Speak to us yourself and we will listen; but do not let God speak to us or we shall die.' [20]Moses answered, 'Do not be afraid. God has come only to test you, so that the fear of him may remain with you and preserve you from sinning.' [21]So the people kept their distance, while Moses approached the dark cloud where God was.

EXPLANATORY NOTES

19:1 **after . . . Egypt:** *prob. rdg; Heb. adds* on this day.

19:13 **shot:** *or* hurled to his death.

19:18 **the people:** *so some MSS; others* the mountain.

19:19 **in . . . thunder:** *or* by voice.

20:3 **god:** *or* gods.

20:6 **with thousands:** *or* for a thousand generations with.

THE BIBLE

The Sermon on the Mount

---

*The Bible is the most authoritative text in the Judeo-Christian tradition,
and is regarded as divinely inspired, even today, by the more conservative
elements within Christianity and Judaism. It is divided into two large
parts: the Jewish Scriptures, known to Christians as the Old Testament; and
the New Testament, containing twenty-seven books recognized as authoritative by Christians but not by Jews. In addition to the thirty-nine books
of the Old Testament recognized by Protestant Christianity and by normative Judaism are another fifteen books or parts of books that were
handed down with the Jewish Scriptures in Greek (known as the Septuagint). Most of these are accepted as canonical by the Roman Catholic
Church and are referred to in its tradition as the "deuterocanonical" books.*

*The Old Testament contains a great variety of writings including
myths, legends, legal codes, chronicles, edifying stories, poetry, prophecy,
and wisdom literature. The original texts were compiled at various times
between the twelfth and the second centuries B.C.E. Almost all of them
were written in classical Hebrew, except for a few short passages in Aramaic. The canon of the Hebrew scriptures (the so-called Massoretic text)
was only established by Palestinian Jews toward the end of the first century C.E. and has remained substantially unchanged since that time.
Greek Christians, however, made use of the Septuagint text, while
Roman Catholic Christians in the Middle Ages used the Latin translation
of St. Jerome (c. 342–420 C.E.) based on the Hebrew. Since the Reformation the customary practice in Protestant countries is to use vernacular
translations based on the original Hebrew text.*

*In the first generations following the death of Christ (29/30 C.E.), Chris-
tians continued to use the Jewish Scriptures as sacred writings, interpreting
them in the light of the teachings of Jesus and the apostle Paul. Gradually
they assembled a body of their own writings, believed to be of apostolic
origin. These were written in Greek during a seventy-five-year period
between about 50 and 125 C.E. The first attested use of the expression "New*

*Testament," however, comes in the writings of Tertullian around 200 C.E.,
and the first serious attempts by the Church to define the canon of the New
Testament date only from the late fourth century C.E. The New Testament
includes four early accounts of the life and teachings of Christ (the Gospels);
a historical account of the early missions of the Church (the Acts of the
Apostles); letters of various apostles; and a book of prophecies (Revelation)
attributed to the apostle John. The letters of the apostle Paul are particularly significant statements of early Christian theology, and all the apostolic
epistles contain instructions concerning morality and Church discipline.*

*The following passage, from the Gospel of Matthew, contains the most
famous and characteristic teachings of Jesus Christ.*

---

5 WHEN he saw the crowds he went up a mountain. There he sat down,
and when his disciples had gathered round him [2]he began to address
them. And this is the teaching he gave:

> [3]'Blessed are the poor in spirit;
>   the kingdom of Heaven is theirs.
> [4]Blessed are the sorrowful;
>   they shall find consolation.
> [5]Blessed are the gentle;
>   they shall have the earth for their possession.
> [6]Blessed are those who hunger and thirst to see right prevail;
>   they shall be satisfied.
> [7]Blessed are those who show mercy;
>   mercy shall be shown to them.
> [8]Blessed are those whose hearts are pure;
>   they shall see God.
> [9]Blessed are the peacemakers;
>   they shall be called God's children.
> [10]Blessed are those who are persecuted in the cause of right;
>   the kingdom of Heaven is theirs.

[11]'Blessed are you, when you suffer insults and persecution and calumnies
of every kind for my sake. [12]Exult and be glad, for you have a rich reward
in heaven; in the same way they persecuted the prophets before you.

[13]'You are salt to the world. And if salt becomes tasteless, how is its
saltness to be restored? It is good for nothing but to be thrown away and
trodden underfoot.

[14]"You are light for all the world. A town that stands on a hill cannot be hidden. [15]When a lamp is lit, it is not put under the meal-tub, but on the lampstand, where it gives light to everyone in the house. [16]Like the lamp, you must shed light among your fellows, so that, when they see the good you do, they may give praise to your Father in heaven.

[17]'Do NOT suppose that I have come to abolish the law and the prophets; I did not come to abolish, but to complete. [18]Truly I tell you: so long as heaven and earth endure, not a letter, not a dot, will disappear from the law until all that must happen has happened. [19]Anyone therefore who sets aside even the least of the law's demands, and teaches others to do the same, will have the lowest place in the kingdom of Heaven, whereas anyone who keeps the law, and teaches others to do so, will rank high in the kingdom of Heaven. [20]I tell you, unless you show yourselves far better than the scribes and Pharisees, you can never enter the kingdom of Heaven.

[21]'You have heard that our forefathers were told, "Do not commit murder; anyone who commits murder must be brought to justice." [22]But what I tell you is this: Anyone who nurses anger against his brother must be brought to justice. Whoever calls his brother "good for nothing" deserves the sentence of the court; whoever calls him "fool" deserves hell-fire. [23]So if you are presenting your gift at the altar and suddenly remember that your brother has a grievance against you, [24]leave your gift where it is before the altar. First go and make your peace with your brother; then come back and offer your gift. [25]If someone sues you, come to terms with him promptly while you are both on your way to court; otherwise he may hand you over to the judge, and the judge to the officer, and you will be thrown into jail. [26]Truly I tell you: once you are there you will not be let out until you have paid the last penny.

[27]'You have heard that they were told, "Do not commit adultery." [28]But what I tell you is this: If a man looks at a woman with a lustful eye, he has already committed adultery with her in his heart. [29]If your right eye causes your downfall, tear it out and fling it away; it is better for you to lose one part of your body than for the whole of it to be thrown into hell. [30]If your right hand causes your downfall, cut it off and fling it away; it is better for you to lose one part of your body than for the whole of it to go to hell.

[31]'They were told, "A man who divorces his wife must give her a certificate of dismissal." [32]But what I tell you is this: If a man divorces his wife for any cause other than unchastity he involves her in adultery; and whoever marries her commits adultery.

³³'Again, you have heard that our forefathers were told, "Do not break your oath," and "Oaths sworn to the Lord must be kept." ³⁴But what I tell you is this: You are not to swear at all—not by heaven, for it is God's throne, ³⁵nor by the earth, for it is his footstool, nor by Jerusalem, for it is the city of the great King, ³⁶nor by your own head, because you cannot turn one hair of it white or black. ³⁷Plain "Yes" or "No" is all you need to say; anything beyond that comes from the evil one.

³⁸'You have heard that they were told, "An eye for an eye, a tooth for a tooth." ³⁹But what I tell you is this: Do not resist those who wrong you. If anyone slaps you on the right cheek, turn and offer him the other also. ⁴⁰If anyone wants to sue you and takes your shirt, let him have your cloak as well. ⁴¹If someone in authority presses you into service for one mile, go with him two. ⁴²Give to anyone who asks; and do not turn your back on anyone who wants to borrow.

⁴³'You have heard that they were told, "Love your neighbour and hate your enemy." ⁴⁴But what I tell you is this: Love your enemies and pray for your persecutors; ⁴⁵only so can you be children of your heavenly Father, who causes the sun to rise on good and bad alike, and sends the rain on the innocent and the wicked. ⁴⁶If you love only those who love you, what reward can you expect? Even the tax-collectors do as much as that. ⁴⁷If you greet only your brothers, what is there extraordinary about that? Even the heathen do as much. ⁴⁸There must be no limit to your goodness, as your heavenly Father's goodness knows no bounds.

6 'BE careful not to parade your religion before others; if you do, no reward awaits you with your Father in heaven.

²'So, when you give alms, do not announce it with a flourish of trumpets, as the hypocrites do in synagogues and in the streets to win the praise of others. Truly I tell you: they have their reward already. ³But when you give alms, do not let your left hand know what your right is doing; ⁴your good deed must be secret, and your Father who sees what is done in secret will reward you.

⁵'Again, when you pray, do not be like the hypocrites; they love to say their prayers standing up in synagogues and at street corners for everyone to see them. Truly I tell you: they have their reward already. ⁶But when you pray, go into a room by yourself, shut the door, and pray to your Father who is in secret; and your Father who sees what is done in secret will reward you.

⁷'In your prayers do not go babbling on like the heathen, who imagine that the more they say the more likely they are to be heard. ⁸Do not

imitate them, for your Father knows what your needs are before you ask him.

⁹"This is how you should pray:

> Our Father in heaven,
> may your name be hallowed;
> ¹⁰your kingdom come,
> your will be done,
> on earth as in heaven.
> ¹¹Give us today our daily bread.
> ¹²Forgive us the wrong we have done,
> as we have forgiven those who have wronged us.
> ¹³And do not put us to the test,
> but save us from the evil one.

¹⁴"For if you forgive others the wrongs they have done, your heavenly Father will also forgive you; ¹⁵but if you do not forgive others, then your Father will not forgive the wrongs that you have done.

¹⁶"So too when you fast, do not look gloomy like the hypocrites: they make their faces unsightly so that everybody may see that they are fasting. Truly I tell you: they have their reward already. ¹⁷But when you fast, anoint your head and wash your face, ¹⁸so that no one sees that you are fasting, but only your Father who is in secret; and your Father who sees what is done in secret will give you your reward.

¹⁹"Do NOT store up for yourselves treasure on earth, where moth and rust destroy, and thieves break in and steal; ²⁰but store up treasure in heaven, where neither moth nor rust will destroy, nor thieves break in and steal. ²¹For where your treasure is, there will your heart be also.

²²"The lamp of the body is the eye. If your eyes are sound, you will have light for your whole body; ²³if your eyes are bad, your whole body will be in darkness. If then the only light you have is darkness, how great a darkness that will be.

²⁴"No one can serve two masters; for either he will hate the first and love the second, or he will be devoted to the first and despise the second. You cannot serve God and Money.

²⁵"This is why I tell you not to be anxious about food and drink to keep you alive and about clothes to cover your body. Surely life is more than food, the body more than clothes. ²⁶Look at the birds in the sky; they do not sow and reap and store in barns, yet your heavenly Father feeds them. Are you not worth more than the birds? ²⁷Can anxious thought add a single day to your life? ²⁸And why be anxious about

clothes? Consider how the lilies grow in the fields; they do not work, they do not spin; ²⁹yet I tell you, even Solomon in all his splendour was not attired like one of them. ³⁰If that is how God clothes the grass in the fields, which is there today and tomorrow is thrown on the stove, will he not all the more clothe you? How little faith you have! ³¹Do not ask anxiously, "What are we to eat? What are we to drink? What shall we wear?" ³²These are the things that occupy the minds of the heathen, but your heavenly Father knows that you need them all. ³³Set your mind on God's kingdom and his justice before everything else, and all the rest will come to you as well. ³⁴So do not be anxious about tomorrow; tomorrow will look after itself. Each day has troubles enough of its own.

7 'Do NOT judge, and you will not be judged. ²For as you judge others, so you will yourselves be judged, and whatever measure you deal out to others will be dealt to you. ³Why do you look at the speck of sawdust in your brother's eye, with never a thought for the plank in your own? ⁴How can you say to your brother, "Let me take the speck out of your eye," when all the time there is a plank in your own? ⁵You hypocrite! First take the plank out of your own eye, and then you will see clearly to take the speck out of your brother's.

⁶'Do not give dogs what is holy; do not throw your pearls to the pigs: they will only trample on them, and turn and tear you to pieces.

⁷'Ask, and you will receive; seek, and you will find; knock, and the door will be opened to you. ⁸For everyone who asks receives, those who seek find, and to those who knock, the door will be opened.

⁹'Would any of you offer his son a stone when he asks for bread, ¹⁰or a snake when he asks for a fish? ¹¹If you, bad as you are, know how to give good things to your children, how much more will your heavenly Father give good things to those who ask him!

¹²'Always treat others as you would like them to treat you: that is the law and the prophets.

¹³'Enter by the narrow gate. Wide is the gate and broad the road that leads to destruction, and many enter that way; ¹⁴narrow is the gate and constricted the road that leads to life, and those who find them are few.

¹⁵'Beware of false prophets, who come to you dressed up as sheep while underneath they are savage wolves. ¹⁶You will recognize them by their fruit. Can grapes be picked from briars, or figs from thistles? ¹⁷A good tree always yields sound fruit, and a poor tree bad fruit. ¹⁸A good tree cannot bear bad fruit, or a poor tree sound fruit. ¹⁹A tree that does not yield sound fruit is cut down and thrown on the fire. ²⁰That is why I say you will recognize them by their fruit.

21'Not everyone who says to me, "Lord, Lord" will enter the kingdom of Heaven, but only those who do the will of my heavenly Father. 22When the day comes, many will say to me, "Lord, Lord, did we not prophesy in your name, drive out demons in your name, and in your name perform many miracles?" 23Then I will tell them plainly, "I never knew you. Out of my sight; your deeds are evil!"

24"So whoever hears these words of mine and acts on them is like a man who had the sense to build his house on rock. 25The rain came down, the floods rose, the winds blew and beat upon that house, but it did not fall, because its foundations were on rock. 26And whoever hears these words of mine and does not act on them is like a man who was foolish enough to build his house on sand. 27The rain came down, the floods rose, the winds blew and battered against that house; and it fell with a great crash!

28When Jesus had finished this discourse the people were amazed at his teaching; 29unlike their scribes he taught with a note of authority.

EXPLANATORY NOTES

5:6 **to ... prevail:** *or* to do what is right.
5:18 **until ... happened:** *or* before all that it stands for is achieved.
6:11 **our ... bread:** *or* our bread for the morrow.
6:13 **from the evil one:** *or* from evil. *Some witnesses add* For yours is the kingdom and the power and the glory, for ever. Amen.
6:27 **add ... life:** *or* add one foot to your height.
6:28 **Consider ... spin:** *one witness reads* Consider the lilies: they neither card, nor spin, nor work.

The Revelation of John

The Bible is the most authoritative text in the Judeo-Christian tradition, and is regarded as divinely inspired, even today, by more conservative elements within Christianity and Judaism. It is divided into two large parts: the Jewish Scriptures, known to Christians as the Old Testament; and the New Testament, containing twenty-seven books recognized as authoritative by Christians but not by Jews. In addition to the thirty-nine books of the Old Testament recognized by Protestant Christianity and by normative Judaism are another fifteen books or parts of books that were handed down with the ancient Greek version of the Jewish Scriptures, known as the Septuagint. Most of these are accepted as canonical by the Roman Catholic Church and are referred to in its tradition as the "deuterocanonical" books.

The Old Testament contains a great variety of writings including myths, legends, legal codes, chronicles, edifying stories, poetry, prophecy, and wisdom literature. The original texts were compiled at various times between the twelfth and the second centuries B.C.E. Almost all of them were written in classical Hebrew, except for a few short passages in Aramaic. The canon of the Hebrew scriptures (the so-called Massoretic text) was only established by Palestinian Jews toward the end of the first century C.E. and has remained substantially unchanged since that time. Greek Christians, however, made use of the Septuagint text, while Roman Catholic Christians in the Middle Ages used the Latin translation of St. Jerome (c. 342–420 C.E.) based on the Hebrew. Since the Reformation the customary practice in Protestant countries is to use vernacular translations based on the original Hebrew text.

In the first generations following the death of Christ (29/30 C.E.), Christians continued to use the Jewish Scriptures as sacred writings, interpreting them in the light of the teachings of Jesus and the apostle Paul. Gradually they assembled a body of their own writings, believed to be of apostolic origin. These were written in Greek during a seventy-five-year period between about 50 and 125 C.E. The first attested use of the expression "New Testament," however, comes in the writings of Tertullian around 200 C.E., and the first serious attempts by the Church to define the canon of the New Testament date only from the late fourth century C.E. The New Testament includes four early accounts of the life and teachings of Christ (the Gospels); a historical account of the early missions of the Church (the Acts of the Apostles); letters of various apostles; and a book of prophecies (Revelation) attributed to the apostle John. The letters of the apostle Paul are particularly significant statements of early Christian theology, and all the apostolic epistles contain instructions concerning morality and Church discipline.

In this passage from the Apocalypse (or Book of Revelation), the last book in the Bible, an angel reveals to John (traditionally identified with the Apostle John) what will happen in the last days before the destruction of the world to Christians and unbelievers. The emotionally charged, symbolical language of this text inspired many later prophets, radicals, and doomsayers in the Western tradition.

Visions of heaven

4 AFTER this I had a vision: a door stood open in heaven, and the voice that I had first heard speaking to me like a trumpet said, 'Come up here, and I will show you what must take place hereafter.' ²At once the Spirit came upon me. There in heaven stood a throne. On it sat One ³whose appearance was like jasper or cornelian, and round it was a rainbow, bright as an emerald. ⁴In a circle about this throne were twenty-four other thrones, and on them were seated twenty-four elders, robed in white and wearing gold crowns. ⁵From the throne came flashes of lightning and peals of thunder. Burning before the throne were seven flaming torches, the seven spirits of God, ⁶and in front of it stretched what looked like a sea of glass or a sheet of ice.

In the centre, round the throne itself, were four living creatures, covered with eyes in front and behind. ⁷The first creature was like a lion, the second like an ox, the third had a human face, and the fourth was like an eagle in flight. ⁸Each of the four living creatures had six wings, and eyes all round and inside them. Day and night unceasingly they sing:

> 'Holy, holy, holy is God the sovereign Lord of all, who was, and is, and is to come!'

⁹Whenever the living creatures give glory and honour and thanks to the One who sits on the throne, who lives for ever and ever, ¹⁰the twenty-

four elders prostrate themselves before the One who sits on the throne and they worship him who lives for ever and ever. As they lay their crowns before the throne they cry:

> [11]'You are worthy, O Lord our God, to receive glory and honour and power, because you created all things; by your will they were created and have their being!'

5 I saw in the right hand of the One who sat on the throne a scroll with writing on both sides, and sealed with seven seals. [2]And I saw a mighty angel proclaiming in a loud voice, 'Who is worthy to break the seals and open the scroll?' [3] But there was no one in heaven or on earth or under the earth able to open the scroll to look inside it. [4]And because no one was found worthy to open the scroll and look inside, I wept bitterly. [5]One of the elders said to me: 'Do not weep; the Lion from the tribe of Judah, the shoot growing from David's stock, has won the right to open the scroll and its seven seals.'

[6]Then I saw a Lamb with the marks of sacrifice on him, standing with the four living creatures between the throne and the elders. He had seven horns and seven eyes, the eyes which are the seven spirits of God sent to every part of the world. [7]The Lamb came and received the scroll from the right hand of the One who sat on the throne. [8]As he did so, the four living creatures and the twenty-four elders prostrated themselves before the Lamb. Each of the elders had a harp; they held golden bowls full of incense, the prayers of God's people, [9]and they were singing a new song:

> 'You are worthy to receive the scroll and break its seals, for you were slain and by your blood you bought for God people of every tribe and language, nation and race. [10]You have made them a royal house of priests for our God, and they shall reign on earth.'

[11]As I looked I heard, all round the throne and the living creatures and the elders, the voices of many angels, thousands on thousands, myriads on myriads. [12]They proclaimed with loud voices:

> 'Worthy is the Lamb who was slain, to receive power and wealth, wisdom and might, honour and glory and praise!'

[13]Then I heard all created things, in heaven, on earth, under the earth, and in the sea, crying:

> 'Praise and honour, glory and might, to him who sits on the throne and to the Lamb for ever!'

[14]The four living creatures said, 'Amen,' and the elders prostrated themselves in worship.

The seven seals

6 I WATCHED as the Lamb broke the first of the seven seals, and I heard one of the four living creatures say in a voice like thunder, 'Come!' ²There before my eyes was a white horse, and its rider held a bow. He was given a crown, and he rode forth, conquering and to conquer.

³The Lamb broke the second seal, and I heard the second creature say, 'Come!' ⁴Out came another horse, which was red. Its rider was given power to take away peace from the earth that men might slaughter one another; and he was given a great sword.

⁵He broke the third seal, and I heard the third creature say, 'Come!' There, as I looked, was a black horse, and its rider was holding in his hand a pair of scales. ⁶I heard what sounded like a voice from among the four living creatures: it said, 'A day's wage for a quart of flour, a day's wage for three quarts of barley-meal! But do not damage the olive and the vine!'

⁷He broke the fourth seal, and I heard the fourth creature say, 'Come!' ⁸There, as I looked, was another horse, sickly pale; its rider's name was Death, and Hades followed close behind. To them was given power over a quarter of the earth, power to kill by sword and famine, by pestilence and wild beasts.

⁹He broke the fifth seal, and I saw beneath the altar the souls of those who had been slaughtered for God's word and for the testimony they bore. ¹⁰They gave a great cry: 'How long, sovereign Lord, holy and true, must it be before you will vindicate us and avenge our death on the inhabitants of the earth?' ¹¹They were each given a white robe, and told to rest a little longer, until the number should be complete of all their brothers in Christ's service who were to be put to death, as they themselves had been.

¹²I watched as the Lamb broke the sixth seal. There was a violent earthquake; the sun turned black as a funeral pall and the moon all red as blood; ¹³the stars in the sky fell to the earth, like figs blown off a tree in a gale; ¹⁴the sky vanished like a scroll being rolled up, and every mountain and island was dislodged from its place. ¹⁵The kings of the earth, the nobles and the commanders, the rich and the powerful, and all men, slave or free, hid themselves in caves and under mountain crags; ¹⁶and they called out to the mountains and the crags, 'Fall on us, hide us from the One who sits on the throne and from the wrath of the Lamb, ¹⁷for the great day of their wrath has come, and who can stand?'

7 After that I saw four angels stationed at the four corners of the earth, holding back its four winds so that no wind should blow on land or sea or on any tree: [2]I saw another angel rising from the east, bearing the seal of the living God. To the four angels who had been given the power to ravage land and sea, he cried out: [3]'Do no damage to land or sea or to the trees until we have set the seal of our God upon the foreheads of his servants.' [4]I heard how many had been marked with the seal—a hundred and forty-four thousand from all the tribes of Israel: [5]twelve thousand from the tribe of Judah, twelve thousand from the tribe of Reuben, twelve thousand from the tribe of Gad, [6]twelve thousand from the tribe of Asher, twelve thousand from the tribe of Naphtali, twelve thousand from the tribe of Manasseh, [7]twelve thousand from the tribe of Simeon, twelve thousand from the tribe of Levi, twelve thousand from the tribe of Issachar, [8]twelve thousand from the tribe of Zebulun, twelve thousand from the tribe of Joseph, and twelve thousand from the tribe of Benjamin.

[9]After that I looked and saw a vast throng, which no one could count, from all races and tribes, nations and languages, standing before the throne and the Lamb. They were robed in white and had palm branches in their hands, [10]and they shouted aloud:

'Victory to our God who sits on the throne, and to the Lamb!'

[11]All the angels who stood round the throne and round the elders and the four living creatures prostrated themselves before the throne and worshipped God, [12]crying:

'Amen! Praise and glory and wisdom, thanksgiving and honour, power and might, be to our God for ever! Amen.'

[13]One of the elders turned to me and asked, 'Who are these all robed in white, and where do they come from?' [14]I answered, 'My lord, it is you who know.' He said to me, 'They are those who have passed through the great ordeal; they have washed their robes and made them white in the blood of the Lamb. [15]That is why they stand before the throne of God and worship him day and night in his temple; and he who sits on the throne will protect them with his presence. [16]Never again shall they feel hunger or thirst; never again shall the sun beat on them or any scorching heat, [17]because the Lamb who is at the center of the throne will be their shepherd and will guide them to springs of the water of life; and God will wipe every tear from their eyes.'

8 Now when the Lamb broke the seventh seal, there was silence in heaven for about half an hour.

The seven trumpets

²I SAW the seven angels who stand in the presence of God: they were given seven trumpets.

³Another angel came and stood at the altar, holding a golden censer. He was given much incense to offer with the prayers of all God's people on the golden altar in front of the throne, ⁴and the smoke of the incense from the angel's hand went up before God with his people's prayers. ⁵The angel took the censer, filled it with fire from the altar, and threw it down on the earth; and there came peals of thunder, lightning-flashes, and an earthquake.

⁶THE seven angels who held the seven trumpets prepared to blow them.

⁷The first angel blew his trumpet. There came hail and fire mingled with blood, and this was hurled upon the earth; a third of the earth was burnt, a third of the trees, and all the green grass.

⁸The second angel blew his trumpet. What looked like a great mountain flaming with fire was hurled into the sea; a third of the sea was turned to blood, ⁹a third of the living creatures in it died, and a third of the ships on it were destroyed.

¹⁰The third angel blew his trumpet. A great star shot from the sky, flaming like a torch, and fell on a third of the rivers and springs; ¹¹the name of the star was Wormwood. A third of the water turned to wormwood, and great numbers of people died from drinking the water because it had been made bitter.

¹²The fourth angel blew his trumpet. A third part of the sun was struck, a third of the moon, and a third of the stars, so that a third part of them turned dark and a third of the light failed to appear by day or by night.

¹³As I looked, I heard an eagle calling with a loud cry as it flew in mid-heaven: 'Woe, woe, woe to the inhabitants of the earth at the sound of the other trumpets which the next three angels must now blow!'

9 The fifth angel blew his trumpet. I saw a star that had fallen from heaven to earth, and the star was given the key to the shaft of the abyss. ²He opened it, and smoke came up from it like smoke from a great furnace and darkened the sun and the air. ³Out of the smoke came locusts over the earth, and they were given the powers of scorpions. ⁴They were told not to do damage to the grass or to any plant or tree, but only to those people who had not received God's seal on their foreheads. ⁵They were given permission to torment them for five months

with torment like a scorpion's sting; but they were not to kill them. [6]During that time people will seek death, but will not find it; they will long to die, but death will elude them.

[7]In appearance the locusts were like horses equipped for battle. On their heads were what looked like gold crowns; their faces were like human faces [8]and their hair like women's hair; they had teeth like lions' teeth [9]and chests like iron breastplates; the sound of their wings was like the noise of many horses and chariots charging into battle; [10]they had tails like scorpions, with stings in them, and in their tails lay their power to injure people for five months. [11]They had for their king the angel of the abyss, whose name in Hebrew is Abaddon, and in Greek Apollyon, the Destroyer.

[12]The first woe has now passed; but there are still two more to come.

[13]The sixth angel blew his trumpet. I heard a voice coming from the horns of the golden altar that stood in the presence of God. [14]To the sixth angel, who held the trumpet, the voice said: 'Release the four angels held bound at the Great River, the Euphrates!' [15]So the four angels were let loose, to kill a third of mankind; they had been held in readiness for this very year, month, day, and hour. [16]And their squadrons of cavalry numbered twice ten thousand times ten thousand; this was the number I heard.

[17]This was how I saw the horses and their riders in my vision: they wore breastplates, fiery red, turquoise, and sulphur-yellow; the horses had heads like lions' heads, and from their mouths issued fire, smoke, and sulphur. [18]By these three plagues, the fire, the smoke, and the sulphur that came from their mouths, a third of mankind was killed. [19]The power of the horses lay in their mouths and in their tails; for their tails had heads like serpents, and with them they inflicted injuries.

[20]The rest of mankind who survived these plagues still did not renounce the gods their hands had made, or cease their worship of demons and of idols fashioned from gold, silver, bronze, stone, and wood, which cannot see or hear or walk; [21]nor did they repent of their murders, their sorcery, their fornication, or their robberies.

10 I saw another mighty angel coming down from heaven. He was wrapped in cloud, with a rainbow over his head; his face shone like the sun and his legs were like pillars of fire. [2]In his hand he held a little scroll which had been opened. He planted his right foot on the sea and his left on the land, [3]and gave a great shout like the roar of a lion; when he shouted, the seven thunders spoke. [4]I was about to write down what the seven thunders had said, but I heard a voice from heaven saying, 'Put

under seal what the seven thunders have said; do not write it down.' [5]Then the angel whom I saw standing on the sea and the land raised his right hand towards heaven [6]and swore by him who lives for ever, who created heaven and earth and the sea and everything in them: 'There shall be no more delay; [7]when the time comes for the seventh angel to sound his trumpet, the hidden purpose of God will have been fulfilled, as he promised to his servants the prophets.'

[8]The voice which I had heard from heaven began speaking to me again; it said, 'Go and take the scroll which is open in the hand of the angel who stands on the sea and the land.' [9]I went to the angel and asked him to give me the little scroll. He answered, 'Take it, and eat it. It will turn your stomach sour, but in your mouth it will taste as sweet as honey.' [10]I took the scroll from the angel's hand and ate it, and in my mouth it did taste as sweet as honey, but when I swallowed it my stomach turned sour.

[11]Then I was told, 'Once again you must utter prophecies over many nations, races, languages, and kings.'

11 I was given a long cane to use as a measuring rod, and was told: 'Go and measure the temple of God and the altar, and count the worshippers. [2]But leave the outer court of the temple out of your measurements; it has been given over to the Gentiles, and for forty-two months they will trample the Holy City underfoot. [3]I will give my two witnesses authority to prophesy, dressed in sackcloth, for those twelve hundred and sixty days.' [4]They are the two olive trees and the two lamps that stand in the presence of the Lord of the earth. [5]If anyone tries to injure them, fire issues from their mouths and consumes their enemies; so shall anyone die who tries to do them injury. [6]These two have the power to shut up the sky, so that no rain falls during the time of their prophesying; and they have power to turn water into blood and to afflict the earth with every kind of plague whenever they like. [7]But when they have completed their testimony, the beast that comes up from the abyss will wage war on them and will overcome and kill them. [8]Their bodies will lie in the street of the great city, whose name in prophetic language is Sodom, or Egypt, where also their Lord was crucified. [9]For three and a half days people from every nation and tribe, language, and race, gaze on their corpses and refuse them burial. [10]The earth's inhabitants gloat over them; they celebrate and exchange presents, for these two prophets were a torment to them. [11]But at the end of the three and a half days the breath of life from God came into their bodies, and they rose to their

feet, to the terror of those who saw them. [12]A loud voice from heaven was heard saying to them, 'Come up here!' and they ascended to heaven in a cloud, in full view of their enemies. [13]At that moment there was a violent earthquake, and a tenth of the city collapsed. Seven thousand people were killed in the earthquake; the rest, filled with fear, did homage to the God of heaven.

[14]The second woe has now passed; but the third is soon to come.

[15]Then the seventh angel blew his trumpet. Voices in heaven were heard crying aloud:

> 'Sovereignty over the world has passed to our Lord and his Christ, and he shall reign for ever!'

[16]The twenty-four elders, who sit on their thrones before God, prostrated themselves before him in adoration, [17]saying:

> 'O Lord God, sovereign over all, you are and you were; we give you thanks because you have assumed full power and entered upon your reign. [18]The nations rose in wrath, but your day of wrath has come. Now is the time for the dead to be judged; now is the time for rewards to be given to your servants the prophets, to your own people, and to all who honour your name, both small and great; now is the time to destroy those who destroy the earth.'

[19]God's sanctuary in heaven was opened, and within his sanctuary was seen the ark of his covenant. There came flashes of lightning and pearls of thunder, an earthquake, and a violent hailstorm.

Seven visions

12 AFTER that there appeared a great sign in heaven: a woman robed with the sun, beneath her feet the moon, and her head a crown of twelve stars. [2]She was about to bear a child, and in the anguish of her labour she cried out to be delivered. [3]Then a second sign appeared in heaven: a great, fiery red dragon with seven heads and ten horns. On his heads were seven diadems, [4]and with his tail he swept down a third of the stars in the sky and hurled them to the earth. The dragon stood in front of the woman who was about to give birth, so that when her child was born he might devour it. [5]But when she gave birth to a male child, who is destined to rule all nations with a rod of iron, the child was snatched up to God and to his throne. [6]The woman herself fled into the wilderness, where she was to be looked after for twelve hundred and sixty days in a place prepared for her by God.

[7]Then war broke out in heaven; Michael and his angels fought against

the dragon. The dragon with his angels fought back, [8]but he was too weak, and they lost their place in heaven. [9]The great dragon was thrown down, that ancient serpent who led the whole world astray, whose name is the Devil, or Satan; he was thrown down to the earth, and his angels with him.

[10]I heard a loud voice in heaven proclaim: 'This is the time of victory for our God, the time of his power and sovereignty, when his Christ comes to his rightful rule! For the accuser of our brothers, he who day and night accused them before our God, is overthrown. [11]By the sacrifice of the Lamb and by the witness they bore, they have conquered him; faced with death they did not cling to life. [12]Therefore rejoice, you heavens and you that dwell in them! But woe to you, earth and sea, for the Devil has come down to you in great fury, knowing that his time is short!'

[13]When the dragon saw that he had been thrown down to the earth, he went in pursuit of the woman who had given birth to the male child. [14]But she was given the wings of a mighty eagle, so that she could fly to her place in the wilderness where she was to be looked after for three and a half years, out of reach of the serpent. [15]From his mouth the serpent spewed a flood of water after the woman to sweep her away with its spate. [16]But the earth came to her rescue: it opened its mouth and drank up the river which the dragon spewed from his mouth. [17]Furious with the woman, the dragon went off to wage war on the rest of her offspring, those who keep God's commandments and maintain their witness to Jesus.

13

[1]He took his stand on the seashore.

Then I saw a beast rising out of the sea. It had ten horns and seven heads; on the horns were ten diadems, and on each head was a blasphemous name. [2]The beast I saw resembled a leopard, but its feet were like a bear's and its mouth like a lion's. The dragon conferred on it his own power, his throne, and great authority. [3]One of the heads seemed to have been given a death blow, yet its mortal wound was healed. The whole world went after the beast in wondering admiration, [4]and worshipped the dragon because he had conferred his authority on the beast; they worshipped the beast also. 'Who can fight against it?'

[5]The beast was allowed to mouth bombast and blasphemy, and was granted permission to continue for forty-two months. [6]It uttered blasphemies against God, reviling his name and his dwelling-place, that is, those who dwell in heaven. [7]It was also allowed to wage war on God's people and to defeat them, and it was granted authority over every tribe,

nation, language, and race. [8]All the inhabitants of the earth will worship it, all whose names have not been written in the book of life of the Lamb, slain since the foundation of the world.

[9]You have ears, so hear! [10]Whoever is to be made prisoner, to prison he shall go; whoever is to be slain by the sword, by the sword he must be slain. This calls for the endurance and faithfulness of God's people.

[11]Then I saw another beast; it came up out of the earth, and had two horns like a lamb's, but spoke like a dragon. [12]It wielded all the authority of the first beast in its presence, and made the earth and its inhabitants worship this first beast, whose mortal wound had been healed. [13]It worked great miracles, even making fire come down from heaven to earth, where people could see it. [14]By the miracles it was allowed to perform in the presence of the beast it deluded the inhabitants of the earth, and persuaded them to erect an image in honour of the beast which had been wounded by the sword and yet lived. [15]It was allowed to give breath to the image of the beast, so that it could even speak and cause all who would not worship the image to be put to death. [16]It caused everyone, small and great, rich and poor, free man and slave, to have a mark put on his right hand or his forehead, [17]and no one was allowed to buy or sell unless he bore this beast's mark, either name or number. [18](This calls for skill; let anyone who has intelligence work out the number of the beast, for the number represents a man's name, and the numerical value of its letters is six hundred and sixty-six.)

14 I LOOKED, and there on Mount Zion stood the Lamb, and with him were a hundred and forty-four thousand who had his name and the name of his Father written on their foreheads. [2]I heard a sound from heaven like a mighty torrent or a great peal of thunder; what I heard was like harpists playing on their harps. [3]They were singing a new song before the throne and the four living creatures and the elders, and no one could learn it except the hundred and forty-four thousand ransomed from the earth. [4]These men who have kept themselves chaste and have not defiled themselves with women; these follow the Lamb wherever he goes. They have been ransomed as the firstfruits of mankind for God and the Lamb. [5]No lie was found on their lips; they are without fault.

[6]Then I saw an angel flying in mid-heaven, with an eternal gospel to proclaim to those on earth, to every race, tribe, language, and nation. [7]He spoke in a loud voice: 'Fear God and pay him homage, for the hour of his judgement has come! Worship him who made heaven and earth, the sea and the springs of water!'

[8]A second angel followed, saying, 'Fallen, fallen in Babylon the great,

who has made all nations drink the wine of God's anger roused by her fornication!'

[9]A third angel followed, saying in a loud voice, 'Whoever worships the beast and its image and receives its mark on his forehead or hand, [10]he too shall drink the wine of God's anger, poured undiluted into the cup of his wrath. He shall be tormented in sulphurous flames in the sight of the holy angels and the Lamb. [11]The smoke of their torment will rise for ever; there will be no respite day or night for those who worship the beast and its image, or for anyone who receives the mark of its name.' [12]This calls for the endurance of God's people, all those who keep his commands and remain loyal to Jesus.

[13]I heard a voice from heaven say, 'Write this: "Happy are the dead who henceforth die in the faith of the Lord!" "Yes," says the Spirit, "let them rest from their labours, for the record of their deeds goes with them."'

[14]As I looked there appeared a white cloud, on which was seated a figure like a man; he had a gold crown on his head and a sharp sickle in his hand. [15]Another angel came out of the temple and called in a loud voice to him who sat on the cloud: 'Put in your sickle and reap, for harvest time has come and earth's crop is fully ripe.' [16]So the one who sat on the cloud swept over the earth with his sickle and the harvest was reaped.

[17]Another angel came out of the heavenly sanctuary, and he also had a sharp sickle. [18]Then from the altar came yet another, the angel who has authority over fire, and he called aloud to the one with the sharp sickle: 'Put in your sharp sickle, and gather in earth's grape harvest, for its clusters are ripe.' [19]So the angel swept over the earth with his sickle and gathered in its grapes, and threw them into the great winepress of God's wrath. [20]The winepress was trodden outside the city, and for a distance of two hundred miles blood flowed from the press to the height of horses' bridles.

The seven bowls

15 THEN I saw in heaven another great and astonishing sign: seven angels with seven plagues, the last plagues of all, for with them the wrath of God was completed.

[2]I saw what looked like a sea of glass shot through with fire. Standing beside it and holding the harps which God had given them were those who had been victorious against the beast, its image, and the number of its name.

[3]They were singing the song of Moses, the servant of God, and the song of the Lamb:

'Great and marvellous are your deeds,
O Lord God, sovereign over all;
just and true are your ways,
O King of the ages.
⁴Who shall not fear you, Lord,
and do homage to your name?
For you alone are holy.
All nations shall come and worship before you,
for your just decrees stand revealed.'

⁵After this, as I looked, the sanctuary of the heavenly Tent of Testimony was opened, ⁶and from it came the seven angels with the seven plagues. They were robed in fine linen, pure and shining, and had golden girdles round their breasts. ⁷One of the four living creatures gave to the seven angels seven golden bowls full of the wrath of God who lives for ever. ⁸The sanctuary was filled with smoke from the glory of God and from his power, so that no one could enter it until the seven plagues of the seven angels were completed.

16 I heard a loud voice from the sanctuary say to the seven angels, 'Go and pour out the seven bowls of God's wrath on the earth.'

²The first angel went and poured out his bowl on the earth; and foul malignant sores appeared on the men that wore the mark of the beast and worshipped its image.

³The second angel poured out his bowl on the sea; and the sea turned to blood like the blood from a dead body, and every living thing in it died.

⁴The third angel poured out his bowl on the rivers and springs, and they turned to blood.

⁵And I heard the angel of the waters say, 'You are just in these your judgements, you who are, and were, O Holy One; ⁶for they shed the blood of your people and your prophets, and blood you have given them to drink. They have what they deserve!' ⁷I heard a voice from the altar cry, 'Yes, Lord God, sovereign over all, true and just are your judgements!'

⁸The fourth angel poured out his bowl on the sun; and it was allowed to burn people with its flames. ⁹They were severely burned, and cursed the name of God who had the power to inflict such plagues, but they did not repent and do him homage.

¹⁰The fifth angel poured out his bowl on the throne of the beast; and its kingdom was plunged into darkness. Men gnawed their tongues in

agony, [11]and cursed the God of heaven for their pain and sores, but they would not repent of what they had done.

[12]The sixth angel poured out his bowl on the Great River, the Euphrates; and its water was dried up to prepare a way for the kings from the east.

[13]I saw three foul spirits like frogs coming from the mouths of the dragon, the beast, and the false prophet. [14]These are demonic spirits with power to work miracles, sent out to muster all the kings of the world for the battle on the great day of God the sovereign Lord. [15]('See, I am coming like a thief! Happy the man who stays awake, and keeps his clothes at hand so that he will not have to go naked and ashamed for all to see!') [16]These spirits assembled the kings at the place called in Hebrew Armageddon.

[17]The seventh angel poured out his bowl on the air; and out of the sanctuary came a loud voice from the throne, which said, 'It is over!' [18]There followed flashes of lightning and peals of thunder, and a violent earthquake, so violent that nothing like it had ever happened in human history.

The destruction of Babylon
[19]THE great city was split in three, and the cities of the nations collapsed in ruin. God did not forget Babylon the great, but made her drink the cup which was filled with the fierce wine of his wrath. [20]Every island vanished, and not a mountain was to be seen. [21]Huge hailstones, weighing as much as a hundredweight, crashed down from the sky on the people; and they cursed God because the plague of hail was so severe.

17 ONE of the seven angels who held the seven bowls came and spoke to me; 'Come,' he said, 'I will show you the verdict on the great whore, she who is enthroned over many waters. [2]The kings of the earth have committed fornication with her, and people the world over have made themselves drunk on the wine of her fornication.' [3]He carried me in spirit into the wilderness, and I saw a woman mounted on a scarlet beast which was covered with blasphemous names and had seven heads and ten horns. [4]The woman was clothed in purple and scarlet, and decked out with gold and precious stones and pearls. In her hand she held a gold cup full of obscenities and the foulness of her fornication. [5]Written on her forehead was a name with a secret meaning: 'Babylon the great, the mother of whores and of every obscenity on earth.' [6]I saw that the woman was drunk with the blood of God's people, and with the blood of those who had borne their testimony to Jesus.

At the sight of her I was greatly astonished. [7]But the angel said to me, 'Why are you astonished? I will tell you the secret of the woman and of the beast she rides, with the seven heads and the ten horns. [8]The beast you saw was once alive, and is alive no longer, but has yet to ascend out of the abyss before going to be destroyed. All the inhabitants of the earth whose names have not been written in the book of life since the foundation of the world will be astonished to see the beast, which once was alive, and is alive no longer, and has still to appear.

[9]'This calls for a mind with insight. The seven heads are seven hills on which the woman sits enthroned. [10]They also represent seven kings: five have already fallen, one is now reigning, and the other has yet to come. When he does come, he is to last for only a little while. [11]As for the beast that once was alive and is alive no longer, he is an eighth—and yet he is one of the seven, and he is going to destruction. [12]The ten horns you saw are ten kings who have not yet begun to reign, but who for a brief hour will share royal authority with the beast. [13]They have a single purpose and will confer their power and authority on the beast. [14]They will wage war on the Lamb, but the Lamb will conquer them, for he is Lord of lords and King of kings, and those who are with him are called and chosen and faithful.'

[15]He continued: 'The waters you saw, where the great whore sat enthroned, represent nations, populations, races, and languages. [16]As for the ten horns you saw, and the beast, they will come to hate the whore. They will strip her naked and leave her destitute; they will devour her flesh and burn her up. [17]For God has put it into their minds to carry out his purpose, by making common cause and conferring their sovereignty on the beast until God's words are fulfilled. [18]The woman you saw is the great city that holds sway over the kings of the earth.'

18 After this I saw another angel coming down from heaven; he possessed great authority and the earth shone with his splendour. [2]In a mighty voice he proclaimed, 'Fallen, fallen is Babylon the great! She has become a dwelling for demons, a haunt for every unclean spirit, for every unclean and loathsome bird. [3]All the nations have drunk the wine of God's anger roused by her fornication; the kings of the earth have committed fornication with her, and merchants the world over have grown rich on her wealth and luxury.'

[4]I heard another voice from heaven saying: 'Come out from her, my people, lest you have any part in her sins and you share in her plagues, [5]for her sins are piled high as heaven, and God has not forgotten her crimes. [6]Pay her back in her own coin, repay her twice over for her

deeds! Give her a potion twice as strong as the one she mixed! [7]Measure out torment and grief to match her pomp and luxury! "I am a queen on my throne!" she says to herself. "No widow's weeds for me, no mourning!" [8]That is why plagues shall strike her in a single day, pestilence, bereavement, and famine, and she shall perish in flames; for mighty is the Lord God who has pronounced her doom!'

[9]The kings of the earth who committed fornication with her and wallowed in her luxury will weep and wail over her, as they see the smoke of her burning. [10]In terror at her torment they will keep their distance and say, 'Alas, alas for you great city, mighty city of Babylon! In a moment your doom has come upon you!'

[11]The merchants of the world will weep and mourn for her, because no one buys their cargoes any more, [12]cargoes of gold and silver, precious stones and pearls, purple and scarlet cloth, silks and fine linens; all sorts of fragrant wood, and all kinds of objects made of ivory or of costly woods, bronze, iron, or marble; [13]cinnamon and spice, incense, perfumes, and frankincense; wine, oil, flour and wheat, cattle and sheep, horses, chariots, slaves, and human lives. [14]"The harvest you longed for', they will say, 'is gone from you; all the glitter and glamour are lost, never to be found again!' [15]The traders in all these goods, who grew rich on her, will keep their distance in terror at her torment; weeping and mourning [16]they will say: 'Alas, alas for the great city that was clothed in fine linen and purple and scarlet, decked out with gold and precious stones and pearls [17]So much wealth laid waste in a moment!'

All the sea-captains and voyagers, the sailors and those who made a living on the sea, stayed at a distance; [18]as they saw the smoke of her burning, they cried out, 'Was there ever a city like the great city?' [19]They threw dust on their heads and, weeping and mourning, they cried aloud: 'Alas, alas for the great city, where all who had ships at sea grew rich from her prosperity! In a single hour she has been laid waste!'

[20]But let heaven exult over her; exult, God's people, apostles and prophets, for he has imposed on her the sentence she passed on you!

[21]Then a mighty angel picked up a stone like a great millstone and hurled it into the sea, saying, 'Thus shall Babylon, the great city, be sent hurtling down, never to be seen again! [22]The sound of harpists and minstrels, flute-players and trumpeters, shall no more be heard in you; no more shall craftsmen of any trade be found in you, or the sound of the mill be heard in you; [23]no more shall the light of the lamp appear in you, no more the voices of the bridegroom and bride be heard in you! Your traders were once the merchant princes of the world, and with your sor-

cery you deceived all the nations.' ²⁴The blood of the prophets and of God's people was found in her, the blood of all who had been slain on earth.

19

After this I heard what sounded like a vast throng in heaven shouting:

> 'Hallelujah! Victory and glory and power belong to our God, ²for true and just are his judgements! He has condemned the great whore who corrupted the earth with her fornication; he has taken vengeance on her for the blood of his servants.'

³Once more they shouted:

> 'Hallelujah! The smoke from her burning will rise for ever!'

⁴The twenty-four elders and the four living creatures bowed down and worshipped God who sits on the throne; they cried: 'Amen! Hallelujah!'

⁵THERE came a voice from the throne saying: 'Praise our God, all you his servants, you that fear him, both small and great!' ⁶And I heard what sounded like a vast throng, like the sound of a mighty torrent or of great peals of thunder, and they cried:

> 'Hallelujah! The Lord our God, sovereign over all, has entered on his reign! ⁷Let us rejoice and shout for joy and pay homage to him, for the wedding day of the Lamb has come! His bride has made herself ready, ⁸and she has been given fine linen, shining and clean, to wear.'

(The fine linen signifies the righteous deeds of God's people.)

⁹The angel said to me, 'Write this: "Happy are those who are invited to the wedding banquet of the Lamb!"' He added, 'These are the very words of God.' ¹⁰I prostrated myself to worship him, but he said, 'You must not do that! I am a fellow-servant with you and your brothers who bear their witness to Jesus. It is God you must worship. For those who bear witness to Jesus have the spirit of prophecy.

More visions

¹¹I SAW heaven wide open, and a white horse appeared; its rider's name was Faithful and True, for he is just in judgement and just in war. ¹²His eyes flamed like fire, and on his head were many diadems. Written on him was a name known to none but himself; ¹³he was robed in a garment dyed in blood, and he was called the Word of God. ¹⁴The armies of

heaven followed him, riding on white horses and clothed in fine linen, white and clean. ¹⁵Out of his mouth came a sharp sword to smite the nations; for it is he who will rule them with a rod of iron, and tread the winepress of the fierce wrath of God the sovereign Lord. ¹⁶On his robe and on his thigh was written the title: 'King of kings and Lord of lords'.

¹⁷I saw an angel standing in the sun. He cried aloud to all the birds flying in mid-heaven: 'Come, gather together for God's great banquet, ¹⁸to eat the flesh of kings, commanders, and warriors, the flesh of horses and their riders, the flesh of all, the free and the slave, the small and the great!' ¹⁹I saw the beast and the kings of the earth with their armies mustered to do battle against the rider and his army. ²⁰The beast was taken prisoner, along with the false prophet who had worked miracles in its presence and deluded those who had received the mark of the beast and worshipped its image. The two of them were thrown alive into the lake of fire with its sulphurous flames. ²¹The rest were killed by the sword which came out of the rider's mouth, and the birds all gorged themselves on their flesh.

20 I saw an angel coming down from heaven with the key to the abyss and a great chain in his hand. ²He seized the dragon, that ancient serpent who is the Devil, or Satan, and chained him up for a thousand years; ³he threw him into the abyss, shutting and sealing it over him, so that he might not seduce the nations again till the thousand years were ended. After that he must be let loose for a little while.

⁴I saw thrones, and on them sat those to whom judgement was committed. I saw the souls of those who, for the sake of God's word and their witness to Jesus, had been beheaded, those who had not worshipped the beast and its image or received its mark on forehead or hand. They came to life again and reigned with Christ for a thousand years, ⁵though the rest of the dead did not come to life until the thousand years were ended. This is the first resurrection. ⁶Blessed and holy are those who share in this first resurrection! Over them the second death has no power; but they shall be priests of God and of Christ, and shall reign with him for the thousand years.

⁷When the thousand years are ended, Satan will be let loose from his prison, ⁸and he will come out to seduce the nations in the four quarters of the earth. He will muster them for war, the hosts of Gog and Magog, countless as the sands of the sea. ⁹They marched over the breadth of the land and laid siege to the camp of God's people and the city that he loves. But fire came down on them from heaven and consumed them. ¹⁰Their

seducer, the Devil, was flung into the lake of fire and sulphur, where the beast and the false prophet had been flung to be tormented day and night for ever.

[11]I saw a great, white throne, and the One who sits upon it. From his presence earth and heaven fled away, and there was no room for them any more. [12]I saw the dead, great and small, standing before the throne; and books were opened. Then another book, the book of life, was opened. The dead were judged by what they had done, as recorded in these books. [13]The sea gave up the dead that were in it, and Death and Hades gave up the dead in their keeping. Everyone was judged on the record of his deeds. [14]Then Death and Hades were flung into the lake of fire. This lake of fire is the second death; [15]into it were flung any whose names were not to be found in the book of life.

21

I saw a new heaven and a new earth, for the first heaven and the first earth had vanished, and there was no longer any sea. [2]I saw the Holy City, new Jerusalem, coming down out of heaven from God, made ready like a bride adorned for her husband. [3]I heard a loud voice proclaiming from the throne: 'Now God has his dwelling with mankind! He will dwell among them and they shall be his people, and God himself will be with them. [4]He will wipe every tear from their eyes. There shall be an end to death, and to mourning and crying and pain, for the old order has passed away!'

[5]The One who sat on the throne said, 'I am making all things new!' ('Write this down,' he said, 'for these words are trustworthy and true.') [6]Then he said to me, 'It is done! I am the Alpha and the Omega, the beginning and the end. To the thirsty I will give water from the spring of life as a gift. [7]This is the victors' heritage; and I will be their God and they will be my children. [8]But as for the cowardly, the faithless, and the obscene, the murderers, fornicators, sorcerers, idolaters, and liars of every kind, the lake that burns with sulphurous flames will be their portion, and that is the second death.

The new Jerusalem

[9]ONE of the seven angels who held the seven bowls full of the seven last plagues came and spoke to me. 'Come,' he said, 'and I will show you the bride, the wife of the Lamb.' [10]So in the spirit he carried me away to a great and lofty mountain, and showed me Jerusalem, the Holy City, coming down out of heaven from God. [11]It shone with the glory of God; it had the radiance of some priceless jewel, like a jasper, clear as crystal.

[12]It had a great and lofty wall with twelve gates, at which were stationed twelve angels; on the gates were inscribed the names of the twelve tribes of Israel. [13]There were three gates to the east, three to the north, three to the south, and three to the west. [14]The city wall had twelve foundation-stones, and on them were the names of the twelve apostles of the Lamb.

[15]The angel who spoke with me carried a gold measuring rod to measure the city, its gates, and its wall. [16]The city had four sides, and it was as wide as it was long. Measured by his rod, it was twelve thousand furlongs, its length and breadth and height being equal. [17]Its wall was one hundred and forty-four cubits high, by human measurements, which the angel used. [18]The wall was built of jasper, while the city itself was of pure gold, bright as clear glass. [19]The foundations of the city wall were adorned with precious stones of every kind, the first of the foundation-stones being jasper, the second lapis lazuli, the third chalcedony, the fourth emerald, [20]the fifth sardonyx, the sixth carnelian, the seventh chrysolite, the eighth beryl, the ninth topaz, the tenth chrysoprase, the eleventh turquoise, and the twelfth amethyst. [21]The twelve gates were twelve pearls, each gate fashioned from a single pearl. The great street of the city was of pure gold, like translucent glass.

[22]I saw no temple in the city, for its temple was the sovereign Lord God and the Lamb. [23]The city did not need the sun or the moon to shine on it, for the glory of God gave it light, and its lamp was the Lamb. [24]By its light shall the nations walk, and to it the kings of the earth shall bring their splendour. [25]The gates of the city shall never be shut by day, nor will there be any night there. [26]The splendour and wealth of the nations shall be brought into it, [27]but nothing unclean shall enter, nor anyone whose ways are foul or false; only those shall enter whose names are inscribed in the Lamb's book of life.

22 Then the angel showed me the river of the water of life, sparkling like crystal, flowing from the throne of God and of the Lamb [2]down the middle of the city's street. On either side of the river stood a tree of life, which yields twelve crops of fruit, one for each month of the year. The leaves of the trees are for the healing of the nations. [3]Every accursed thing shall disappear. The throne of God and of the Lamb will be there, and his servants shall worship him; [4]they shall see him face to face and bear his name on their foreheads. [5]There shall be no more night, nor will they need the light of lamp or sun, for the Lord God will give them light; and they shall reign for ever.

Conclusion

[6]He said to me, 'These words are trustworthy and true. The Lord God who inspires the prophets has sent his angel to show his servants what must soon take place. [7]And remember, I am coming soon!'

Happy is the man who takes to heart the words of prophecy contained in this book! [8]It was I, John, who heard and saw these things. When I had heard and seen them,. I prostrated myself to worship the angel who had shown them to me. [9]But he said, 'You must not do that! I am a fellow-servant with you and your brothers the prophets and with those who take to heart the words of this book. It is God you must worship.' [10]He told me, 'Do not seal up the words of the prophecy that are in this book, for the time of fulfillment is near. [11]Meanwhile, let the evildoers persist in doing evil and the filthy-minded continue in their filth, but let the good persevere in their goodness and the holy continue in holiness.'

[12]'I am coming soon, and bringing with me my recompense to repay everyone according to what he has done! [13]I am the Alpha and the Omega, the first and the last, the beginning and the end.'

[14]Happy are those who wash their robes clean! They shall be free to eat from the tree of life and may enter the city by the gates. [15]Outside are the perverts, the sorcerers and fornicators, the murderers and idolaters, and all who love and practise deceit.

[16]'I, Jesus, have sent my angel to you with this testimony for the churches, I am the offspring of David, the shoot growing from his stock, the bright star of dawn.'

[17]'Come!' say the Spirit and the bride.

'Come!' let each hearer reply.

Let the thirsty come; let whoever wishes accept the water of life as a gift.

[18]I, John, give this warning to everyone who is listening to the words of prophecy in this book: if anyone adds to them, God will add to him the plagues described in this book; [19]if anyone takes away from the words in this book of prophecy, God will take away from him his share in the tree of life and in the Holy City, which are described in this book.

[20]He who gives this testimony says: 'Yes, I am coming soon!'

Amen. Come, Lord Jesus!

[21]The grace of the Lord Jesus be with all.

EXPLANATORY NOTES

5:6 **standing . . . elders:** *or* standing in the middle of the throne, inside the circle of living creatures and the circle of elders.

6:9 **beneath:** *or* at the foot of.

12:11 **the witness they bore:** *or* the word of God to which they bore witness.

13:8 **written . . . world:** *or* written, since the foundation of the world, in the book of life of the slain Lamb.

13:10 **whoever . . . slain by the sword:** *or* whoever takes the sword to slay.

13:18 **the numerical . . . letters:** *lit.* his number.

14:13 **the dead . . . the Spirit:** *some witnesses read* the dead who die trusting in the Lord! Henceforth", says the Spirit.

17:10 **kings:** *or* emperors.

22:15 **perverts:** *lit.* dogs.

PLATO

Death Cannot Harm the Good Man

Plato of Athens (c. 429–347 B.C.E.) stands with Aristotle as one of the two most important philosophers of Antiquity and as a major shaper of the Western intellectual history as a whole. Descended from a wealthy and aristocratic family, his intellectual outlook was decisively formed by his teacher, Socrates. Socrates' judicial murder at the hands of political opponents helped turn Plato into a critic of democracy and a supporter of aristocracy, in his special sense of the term, that is, rule by the wise and virtuous (or "philosopher-kings"). From Socrates Plato learned a mode of inquiry that consisted of subjecting received opinions to systematic cross-examination ("dialectic"), as well as certain moral doctrines such as the view that the source of wrongdoing is ignorance, or that the gods' approval or disapproval does not render actions right or wrong. Plato attempted to put his political ideas into practice by serving as counselor to Dionysius II, tyrant of Syracuse, but the young ruler's sporadic enthusiasm for philosophy did not survive political reality, and the two men became estranged. Plato was more successful as the founder of a philosophical school, the Academy, established in a grove dedicated to the hero Academus outside Athens during the early fourth century B.C.E. The school continued for several centuries and was instrumental in preserving Plato's teachings and writings.

Plato's surviving writings are cast in dialogue form to force the reader to make up his or her own mind about the positions and arguments presented. Plato never appears, though students of the dialogues often assume, perhaps correctly, that his point of view is represented by Socrates. Modern scholarship largely agrees in dividing the dialogues into three broad groupings: early, middle, and late. Attempts to coordinate these groupings with known events in Plato's life or with the development of his thought, however, are more controversial.

The Apology, a work of Plato's early period, is an idealized reconstruction of the speech given by Socrates in his own defense in the trial before the Athenian people that led eventually to his execution. In the present passage, the noble peroration of his speech, Socrates maintains that death can be only a blessing for the man who has lived well.

As for you who voted for my acquittal, I should very much like to say a few words to reconcile you to this result, while the officials are busy and I am not yet on my way to the place where I must die. I ask you, gentlemen, to spare me these few moments; there is no reason why we should not exchange a few words while the law permits. I look upon you as my friends, and I want to show you the meaning of what has now happened to me.

Gentlemen of the jury—for you deserve to be so called—I have had a remarkable experience. In the past the prophetic voice to which I have become accustomed has always been my constant companion, opposing me even in quite trivial things if I was going to take the wrong course. Now something has happened to me, as you can see, which might be thought and is commonly considered to be a supreme calamity; yet neither when I left home this morning, nor when I was taking my place here in the court, nor at any point in any part of my speech, did the divine sign oppose me. In other discussions it has often checked me in the middle of a sentence; but this time it has never opposed me in any part of this business in anything that I have said or done. What do I suppose to be the explanation? I will tell you. I suspect that this thing that has happened to me is a blessing, and we are quite mistaken in supposing death to be an evil. I have good grounds for thinking this, because my accustomed sign could not have failed to oppose me if what I was doing had not been sure to bring some good result.

We should reflect that there is much reason to hope for a good result on other grounds as well. Death is one of two things. Either it is annihilation, and the dead have no consciousness of anything; or, as we are told, it is really a change: a migration of the soul from this place to another. Now if there is no consciousness but only a dreamless sleep, death must be a marvellous gain. I suppose that if anyone were told to pick out the night on which he slept so soundly as not even to dream, and then to compare it with all the other nights and days of his life, and then were told to say, after due consideration, how many better and happier days and nights than this he had spent in the course of his life—well, I think that the Great King himself, to say nothing of any private person, would find these days and nights easy to count in comparison with the rest. If death is like this, then, I call it gain; because the whole of time, if you look at it in this way, can be regarded as no more than one single night. If on the other hand death is a removal from here to some other place, and if what we are told is true, that all the dead are there, what greater blessing could there be than this, gentlemen of the jury? If on arrival in the other world, beyond the reach of these so-called jurors here, one will find there the true jurors who are said to preside in those courts, Minos and Rhadamanthys and Aeacus and Triptolemus and all those other demi-gods who were upright in their earthly life, would that be an unrewarding place to settle? Put it in this way: how much would one of you give to meet Orpheus and Musaeus, Hesiod and Homer? I am willing to die ten times over if this account is true. For me at least it would be a wonderful personal experience to join them there, to meet Palamedes and Ajax the son of Telamon and any other heroes of the old days who met their death through an unjust trial, and to compare my fortunes with theirs—it would be rather amusing, I think—and above all I should like to spend my time there, as here, in examining and searching people's minds, to find out who is really wise among them, and who only thinks that he is. What would one not give, gentlemen, to be able to scrutinize the leader of that great host against Troy, or Odysseus, or Sisyphus, or the thousands of other men and women whom one could mention, their company and conversation— like the chance to examine them—would be unimaginable happiness? At any rate I presume that they do not put one to death there for such conduct; because apart from the other happiness in which their world surpasses ours, they are now immortal for the rest of time, if what we are told is true.

You too, gentlemen of the jury, must look forward to death with confidence, and fix your minds on this one belief, which is certain: that nothing can harm a good man either in life or after death, and his ortunes are not a matter of indifference to the gods. This present experience of mine does not result from mere earthly causes; I am quite clear that the time had come when it was better for me to die and be released from my distractions. That is why my sign never turned me back. For my own part I bear no grudge at all against those who condemned me and accused me, although it was not with this kind intention that they did so, but because they thought that they were hurting me; and that is culpable of them. However, I ask them to grant me one favour. When my sons grow up, gentlemen, if you think that they are putting money or any-thing else before goodness, take your revenge by plaguing them as I plagued you; and if they fancy themselves for no reason, you must scold them just as I scolded you, for neglecting the important things and thinking that they are good for something when they are good for nothing. If you do this, I shall have had justice at your hands—I *and* my children.

Well, now it is time to be off, I to die and you to live; but which of us has the happier prospect is unknown to anyone but God.

PLATO

The Simile of the Cave

Plato of Athens (c. 429–347 B.C.E.) stands with Aristotle as one of the two most important philosophers of Antiquity and as a major shaper of the Western intellectual history as a whole. Descended from a wealthy and aristocratic family, his intellectual outlook was decisively formed by his teacher, Socrates. Socrates' judicial murder at the instance of political opponents helped turn Plato into a critic of democracy and a supporter of aristocracy, in his special sense of the term, that is, rule by the wise and virtuous (or "philosopher-kings"). From Socrates Plato learned a mode of inquiry that consisted of subjecting received opinions to systematic cross-examination ("dialectic"), as well as certain moral doctrines such as the view that the source of wrongdoing is ignorance, or that the gods' approval or disapproval does not render actions right or wrong. Plato attempted to put his political ideas into practice by serving as counselor to Dionysius II, tyrant of Syracuse, but the young ruler's sporadic enthusiasm for philosophy did not survive political reality, and the two men were finally estranged. Plato was more successful as the founder of a philosophical school, the Academy, which he established in a grove dedicated to the hero Academus outside Athens during the early fourth century B.C.E. The school continued for several centuries and was instrumental in preserving Plato's teachings and writings. Plato's surviving writings are cast in dialogue form, to force the reader to make up his or her own mind about the positions and arguments presented. Plato himself never appears, though students of the dialogues often assume, perhaps correctly, that his point of view is represented by Socrates. Modern scholarship largely agrees in dividing the dialogues into three broad groupings: early, middle, and late. Attempts to coordinate these groupings with known events in Plato's life or with the development of his thought, however, are more controversial.

The Republic, Plato's most famous dialogue, is considered a work of Plato's mature, or middle period, where his ethical and political beliefs have struck root in more fundamental metaphysical and epistemological convictions. The major question animating the dialogue is the nature of justice. Plato's Socrates defends the view that justice consists in a harmony of soul stemming from a vision of transcendental Good, which in turn provides a standard for rational control of the passions and appetites, lead-ing to happiness. In this famous passage from Book VII, Plato illustrated his metaphysics and epistemology using the famous simile of the Cave, which shows the obstacles philosophers face in their search for truth, and emphasizes the obligation philosophers are under to use their knowledge for the good of the state.

This is a more graphic presentation of the truths presented in the analogy of the Line; in particular, it tells us more about the two states of mind called in the Line analogy Belief and Illusion. We are shown the ascent of the mind from illusion to pure philosophy, and the difficulties which accompany its progress. And the philosopher, when he has achieved the supreme vision, is required to return to the cave and serve his fellows, his very unwillingness to do so being his chief qualification.

As Cornford pointed out, the best way to understand the simile is to replace 'the clumsier apparatus' of the cave by the cinema, though today television is an even better comparison. It is the moral and intellectual condition of the average man from which Plato starts; and though clearly the ordinary man knows the difference between substance and shadow in the physical world, the simile suggests that his moral and intellectual opinions often bear as little relation to the truth as the average film or tel-evision programme does to real life.

'I want you to go on to picture the enlightenment or ignorance of our human condition somewhat as follows. Imagine an underground cham-ber like a cave, with a long entrance open to the daylight and as wide as the cave. In this chamber are men who have been prisoners there since they were children, their legs and necks being so fastened that they can only look straight ahead of them and cannot turn their heads. Some way off, behind and higher up, a fire is burning, and between the fire and the prisoners and above them runs a road, in front of which a curtain-wall has been built, like the screen at puppet shows between the operators and their audience, above which they show their puppets.'

'I see.'

'Imagine further that there are men carrying all sorts of gear along behind the curtain-wall, projecting above it and including figures of men and animals made of wood and stone and all sorts of other materials, and that some of these men, as you would expect, are talking and some not.'

'An odd picture and an odd sort of prisoner.'

'They are drawn from life,'[1] I replied. 'For, tell me, do you think our prisoners could see anything of themselves or their fellows except the shadows thrown by the fire on the wall of the cave opposite them?'

'How could they see anything else if they were prevented from moving their heads all their lives?'

'And would they see anything more of the objects carried along the road?'

'Of course not.'

'Then if they were able to talk to each other, would they not assume that the shadows they saw were the real things?'

'Inevitably.'

'And if the wall of their prison opposite them reflected sound, don't you think that they would suppose, whenever one of the passers-by on the road spoke, that the voice belonged to the shadow passing before them?'

'They would be bound to think so.'

'And so in every way they would believe that the shadows of the objects we mentioned were the whole truth.'[2]

'Yes, inevitably.'

'Then think what would naturally happen to them if they were released from their bonds and cured of their delusions. Suppose one of them were let loose, and suddenly compelled to stand up and turn his head and look and walk towards the fire; all these actions would be painful and he would be too dazzled to see properly the objects of which he used to see the shadows. What do you think he would say if he was told that what he used to see was so much empty nonsense and that he was now nearer reality and seeing more correctly, because he was turned towards objects that were more real, and if on top of that he were compelled to say what each of the passing objects was when it was pointed out to him? Don't you think he would be at a loss, and think that what he used to see was far truer[3] than the objects now being pointed out to him?'

'Yes, far truer.'

'And if he were made to look directly at the light of the fire, it would hurt his eyes and he would turn back and retreat to the things which he could see properly, which he would think really clearer than the things being shown him.'

'Yes.'

'And if,' I went on, 'he were forcibly dragged up the steep and rugged ascent and not let go till he had been dragged out into the sunlight, the process would be a painful one, to which he would much object, and when he emerged into the light his eyes would be so dazzled by the glare of it that he wouldn't be able to see a single one of the things he was now told were real.'[4]

'Certainly not at first,' he agreed.

'Because, of course, he would need to grow accustomed to the light before he could see things in the upper world outside the cave. First he would find it easiest to look at shadows, next at the reflections of men and other objects in water, and later on at the objects themselves. After that he would find it easier to observe the heavenly bodies and the sky itself at night, and to look at the light of the moon and stars rather than at the sun and its light by day.'

'Of course.'

'The thing he would be able to do last would be to look directly at the sun itself, and gaze at it without using reflections in water or any other medium, but as it is in itself.'

'That must come last.'

'Later on he would come to the conclusion that it is the sun that produces the changing seasons and years and controls everything in the visible world, and is in a sense responsible for everything that he and his fellow-prisoners used to see.'

'That is the conclusion which he would obviously reach.'

'And when he thought of his first home and what passed for wisdom there, and of his fellow-prisoners, don't you think he would congratulate himself on his good fortune and be sorry for them?'

'Very much so.'

'There was probably a certain amount of honour and glory to be won among the prisoners, and prizes for keensightedness for those best able to remember the order of sequence among the passing shadows and so be best able to divine their future appearances. Will our released prisoner hanker after these prizes or envy this power or honour? Won't he be more likely to feel, as Homer says, that he would far rather be "a serf in the house of some landless man",[5] or indeed anything else in the world, than hold the opinions and live the life that they do?'

'Yes,' he replied, 'he would prefer anything to a life like theirs.'

'Then what do you think would happen,' I asked, 'if he went back to sit in his old seat in the cave? Wouldn't his eyes be blinded by the darkness, because he had come in suddenly out of the sunlight?'

'Certainly.'

'And if he had to discriminate between the shadows, in competition with the other prisoners, while he was still blinded and before his eyes got used to the darkness—a process that would take some time—wouldn't he be likely to make a fool of himself? And they would say that his visit to the upper world had ruined his sight, and that the ascent was not worth even attempting. And if anyone tried to release them and lead them up, they would kill him if they could lay hands on him.'

'They certainly would.'

'Now, my dear Glaucon,' I went on, 'this simile must be connected throughout with what preceded it.[6] The realm revealed by sight corresponds to the prison, and the light of the fire in the prison to the power of the sun. And you won't go wrong if you connect the ascent into the upper world and the sight of the objects there with the upward progress of the mind into the intelligible region. That at any rate is my interpretation, which is what you are anxious to hear; the truth of the matter is, after all, known only to god. But in my opinion, for what it is worth, the final thing to be perceived in the intelligible region, and perceived only with difficulty, is the form of the good; once seen, it is inferred to be responsible for whatever is right and valuable in anything, producing in the visible region light and the source of light, and being in the intelligible region itself controlling source of truth and intelligence. And anyone who is going to act rationally either in public or private life must have sight of it.'

'I agree,' he said, 'so far as I am able to understand you.'

'Then you will perhaps also agree with me that it won't be surprising if those who get so far are unwilling to involve themselves in human affairs, and if their minds long to remain in the realm above. That's what we should expect if our simile holds good again.'

'Yes, that's to be expected.'

'Nor will you think it strange that anyone who descends from contemplation of the divine to human life and its ills should blunder and make a fool of himself, if, while still blinded and unaccustomed to the surrounding darkness, he's forcibly put on trial in the law-courts or elsewhere about the shadows of justice or the figures[7] of which they are shadows, and made to dispute about the notions of them held by men who have never seen justice itself.'

'There's nothing strange in that.'

'But anyone with any sense,' I said, 'will remember that the eyes may be unsighted in two ways, by a transition either from light to darkness or from darkness to light, and will recognize that the same thing applies to the mind. So when he sees a mind confused and unable to see clearly he will not laugh without thinking, but will ask himself whether it has come from a clearer world and is confused by the unaccustomed darkness, or whether it is dazzled by the stronger light of the clearer world to which it has escaped from its previous ignorance. The first condition of life is a reason for congratulation, the second for sympathy, though if one wants to laugh at it one can do so with less absurdity than at the mind that has descended from the daylight of the upper world.'

'You put it very reasonably.'

'If this is true,' I continued, 'we must reject the conception of education professed by those who say that they can put into the mind knowledge that was not there before—rather as if they could put sight into blind eyes.'

'It is a claim that is certainly made,' he said.

'But our argument indicates that the capacity for knowledge is innate in each man's mind, and that the organ by which he learns is like an eye which cannot be turned from darkness to light unless the whole body is turned; in the same way the mind as a whole must be turned away from the world of change until its eye can bear to look straight at reality, and at the brightest of all realities which is what we call the good. Isn't that so?'

'Yes.'

'Then this turning around of the mind itself might be made a subject of professional skill,[8] which would effect the conversion as easily and effectively as possible. It would not be concerned to implant sight, but to ensure that someone who had it already was not either turned in the wrong direction or looking the wrong way.'

'That may well be so.'

'The rest, therefore, of what are commonly called excellences[9] of the mind perhaps resemble those of the body, in that they are not in fact innate, but are implanted by subsequent training and practice; but knowledge, it seems, must surely have a diviner quality, something which never loses its power, but whose effects are useful and salutary or again useless and harmful according to the direction in which it is turned. Have you never noticed how shrewd is the glance of the type of men commonly called bad but clever? They have small minds, but their sight is sharp and piercing enough in matters that concern them; it's not that their sight is weak, but that they are forced to serve evil, so that the keener their sight the more effective that evil is.'

'That's true.'

'But suppose,' I said, 'that such natures were cut loose, when they were still children, from all the dead weights natural to this world of change and fastened on them by sensual indulgences like gluttony, which twist their minds' vision to lower things, and suppose that when so freed they were turned towards the truth, then this same part of these same individuals would have as keen a vision of truth as it has of the objects on which it is at present turned.'

'Very likely.'

'And is it not also likely, and indeed a necessary consequence of what we have said, that society will never be properly governed either by the uneducated, who have no knowledge of the truth, or by those who are allowed to spend all their lives in purely intellectual pursuits? The uneducated have no single aim in life to which all their actions, public and private, are to be directed; the intellectuals will take no practical action of their own accord, fancying themselves to be out of this world in some kind of earthly paradise.'

'True.'

'Then our job as lawgivers is to compel the best minds to attain what we have called the highest form of knowledge, and to ascend to the vision of the good as we have described, and when they have achieved this and see well enough, prevent them behaving as they are now allowed to.'

'What do you mean by that?'

'Remaining in the upper world, and refusing to return again to the prisoners in the cave below and share their labours and rewards, whether trivial or serious.'

'But surely,' he protested, 'that will not be fair. We shall be compelling them to live a poorer life than they might live.'

'The object of our legislation,' I reminded him again, 'is not the special welfare of any particular class in our society, but of the society as a whole;[10] and it uses persuasion or compulsion to unite all citizens and make them share together the benefits which each individually can confer on the community; and its purpose in fostering this attitude is not to leave everyone to please himself, but to make each man a link in the unity of the whole.'

'You are right; I had forgotten,' he said.

'You see, then, Glaucon,' I went on, 'we shan't be unfair to our philosophers, but shall be quite fair in what we say when we compel them to have some care and responsibility for others. We shall tell them that philosophers born in other states can reasonably refuse to take part in the hard work of politics; for society produces them quite involuntarily and unintentionally, and it is only just that anything that grows up on its own should feel it has nothing to repay for an upbringing which it owes to no one. "But," we shall say, "we have bred you both for your own sake and that of the whole community to act as leaders and king-bees in a hive; you are better and more fully educated than the rest and better qualified to combine the practice of philosophy and politics. You must therefore each descend in turn and live with your fellows in the cave and get used to seeing in the dark; once you get used to it you will see a thousand times better than they do and will distinguish the various shadows, and know what they are shadows of, because you have seen the truth about things admirable and just and good. And so our state and yours will be really awake, and not merely dreaming like most societies today, with their shadow battles and their struggles for political power, which they treat as some great prize. The truth is quite different: the state whose prospective rulers come to their duties with least enthusiasm is bound to have the best and most tranquil government, and the state whose rulers are eager to rule the worst."[11]

'I quite agree.'

'Then will our pupils, when they hear what we say, dissent and refuse to take their share of the hard work of government, even though spending the greater part of their time together in the pure air above?'

'They cannot refuse, for we are making a just demand of just men. But of course, unlike present rulers, they will approach the business of government as an unavoidable necessity.'

'Yes, of course,' I agreed. 'The truth is that if you want a well-governed state to be possible, you must find for your future rulers some way of life they like better than government; for only then will you have government by the truly rich, those, that is, whose riches consist not of gold, but of the true happiness of a good and rational life. If you get, in public affairs, men whose life is impoverished and destitute of personal satisfactions, but who hope to snatch some compensation for their own inadequacy from a political career, there can never be good government. They start fighting for power, and the consequent internal and domestic conflicts ruin both them and society.'

'True indeed.'

'Is there any life except that of true philosophy which looks down on positions of political power?'

'None whatever.'

'But what we need is that the only men to get power should be men who do not love it, otherwise we shall have rivals' quarrels.'

'That is certain.'

'Who else, then, will you compel to undertake the responsibilities of Guardians of our state, if it is not to be those who know most about the principles of good government and who have other rewards and a better life than the politician's?'

'There is no one else.'

EXPLANATORY NOTES

1. Lit: 'like us'. How 'like' has been a matter of controversy. Plato can hardly have meant that the ordinary man cannot distinguish between shadows and

real things. But he does seem to be saying, with a touch of caricature (we must not take him too solemnly), that the ordinary man is often very uncritical in his beliefs, which are little more than a 'careless acceptance of appearances' (Crombie).

2. Lit: 'regard nothing else as true but the shadows'. The Greek word *alēthēs* (true) carries an implication of genuineness, and some translators render it here as 'real'.

3. Or 'more real'.

4. Or 'true', 'genuine'.

5. *Odyssey*, xi, 489.

6. I.e. the similes of the Sun and the Line. The detailed relations between the three similes have been much disputed, as has the meaning of the word here translated 'connected'. Some interpret it to mean a detailed correspondence ('every feature . . . is meant to fit'—Cornford), others to mean, more loosely, 'attached' or 'linked to'. That Plato intended some degree of 'connection' between the three similes cannot be in doubt in view of the sentences which follow. But we should remember that they are similes, not scientific descriptions, and it would be a mistake to try to find too much detailed precision. Plato has just spoken of the prisoners getting their hands' on their returned fellow and killing him. How could they do that if fettered as described at the opening of the simile? But Socrates was executed, so of course they must.

This translation assumes the following main correspondences:

Tied prisoner in the cave	Illusion
Freed prisoner in the cave	Belief
Looking at shadows and reflections in the world outside the cave and the ascent thereto	Reason
Looking at real things in the world outside the cave	Intelligence
Looking at the sun	Vision of the form of the good.

7. Cf. 514*b–c*.

8. *Technē*.

9. *Aretē*.

10. Cf. 420*b* and 466*a*.

11. Socrates takes up here a point made to Thrasymachus at 347*b*.

ARISTOTLE

The Golden Mean

Aristotle (384–322 B.C.E.) ranks among the greatest philosophers of classical Antiquity, and is arguably the most influential thinker in the western tradition. Although large parts of his philosophical system were no longer accepted after the seventeenth century, many of his writings (especially on ethics, politics, and psychology) continue to arouse interest today. Born at Stageira in Macedonia (and thus often called the Stagirite), at the age of seventeen Aristotle went to study in Athens, where he became a student of Plato and a member of the Platonic Academy until his master's death in 347 B.C.E. After an unsuccessful bid to lead the Academy, Aristotle spent several years teaching and doing research in Asia Minor, then became tutor to Alexander the Great, the son of King Philip of Macedonia. After Alexander's accession to the throne, Aristotle returned to Athens, where he stayed from around 334 B.C.E. until shortly before his death. There he established his own school and research center, the Lyceum, in competition with the Platonic Academy. This is symbolic of the divergences between Aristotle's and Plato's thought on a number of key philosophical issues.

Among the more significant differences between Plato and Aristotle are the Stagirite's rejection of the theory of ideas and his attempt to construct a systematic philosophy embracing not only moral philosophy, but also logic, natural philosophy, and metaphysics. Furthermore, the style of the works is significantly different. Many of Aristotle's works have been lost, so it is not possible to speak of his total production authoritatively; most of the surviving works are either lecture notes or systematic treatises not designed for a broad public, and in some cases the history of these texts' transmission has done them a real disservice. The result is a rather dry, "scientific" style dictated by the systematic scope of the works and their procedure by proof and argumentation, although this is often enlivened by Aristotle's polemical stance toward other thinkers. The lecture notes often suffer from extreme conciseness and editorial interventions; these can make for slow reading and have given rise to a rich commentary literature. However, most readers agree that the works more than repay the effort involved in studying them.

"The Golden Mean," in *Nicomachean Ethics*, by Aristotle, translated by J. A. K. Thomson, revised edition, copyright © 1976 by Hugh Trennedick, 98–110.

The Nicomachean Ethics, *written probably during his second sojourn in Athens (Nicomachus, Aristotle's son, seems to be the dedicatee), is one of Aristotle's best known works. A collection of the Stagirite's lectures on ethics in ten books, it discusses the end of man (happiness) and its connection with virtue (whether moral or intellectual), as well as related topics such as pleasure and friendship. Aristotle's driving assumption is that man—like other natural entities—is a creature designed by Nature to seek his proper and final end, and that this end is the same for all mankind. In the present selection from Book II, Aristotle offered a definition of moral virtue and emphasized its function as a mean between extremes, a famous theory later referred to as the "golden mean." Aristotle then illustrated his doctrine by discussing a number of virtues and the extremes against which they should be seen. In his conclusion, Aristotle offered some advice for practical conduct in which he showed that one's judgment plays an important part in the exercise of virtue, so that it is impossible to be virtuous simply by mechanically applying general rules to one's conduct.*

In order to define virtue we must decide to what class or genus it belongs. It is not a feeling or a faculty, but a disposition

v.   We must now consider what virtue is. Since there are three kinds of modification that are found in the soul, viz. feelings, faculties and dispositions, virtue must be one of these three. By feelings I mean desire, anger, fear, daring, envy, joy, friendliness, hatred, longing, jealousy, pity, and in general all conditions that are attended by pleasure or pain. By faculties I mean those susceptibilities in virtue of which we are said to be capable of the feelings in question, e.g. capable of anger or sorrow or pity. By dispositions I mean conditions in virtue of which we are well or ill disposed in respect of the feelings concerned. We have, for instance, a bad disposition towards anger if our tendency is too strong or too weak, and a good one if our tendency is moderate. Similarly with the other feelings.

Now neither the virtues nor the vices are feelings, because we are not called good or bad on the ground of our feelings, but we are so called on the ground of our virtues and vices; nor are we either praised or blamed for our feelings (a man is not praised for being frightened or angry, nor is he blamed just for being angry; it is for being angry in a particular way); but we *are* praised and blamed for our virtues and vices. Again, when we are angry or frightened it is not by our choice;[1] but our virtues are

95

expressions of our choice, or at any rate imply choice. Besides, we are said to be moved in respect of our feelings, but in respect of our virtues and vices we are said to be not moved but disposed in a particular way. By the same line of reasoning they are not faculties either. We are not called good or bad, nor are we praised or blamed, merely because we are *capable* of feeling. Again, what faculties we have, we have by nature; but it is not nature that makes us good or bad (we mentioned this point above). So if the virtues are neither feelings nor faculties, it remains that they are dispositions.

We have now stated what virtue is generically.

But what is its differentia? Any excellence enables its possessor to function; therefore this is true of human excellence, i.e. virtue

vi.   But we must not only make the simple statement that it is a disposition; we must also say what *kind* of disposition. Let us assert, then, that any kind of excellence renders that of which it is the excellence *good,* and makes it perform its function *well.* For example, the excellence of the eye makes both the eye and its function good (because it is through the excellence of the eye that we see well). Similarly the excellence of a horse makes him both a fine horse and good at running and carrying his rider and facing the enemy. If this rule holds good for all cases, then *human* excellence will be the disposition that makes one a good man and causes him to perform his function well. We have already explained how this will be; but it will also become clear in another way if we consider what is the specific nature of virtue.

This is confirmed by the doctrine of the Mean

In anything continuous and divisible it is possible to take a part which is greater or less than, or equal to, the remainder; and that in relation either to the thing divided or to us. The equal part is a sort of mean between excess and deficiency; and I call mean in relation to the *thing* whatever is equidistant from the extremes, which is one and the same for everybody; but I call mean in relation to *us* that which is neither excessive nor deficient, and this is *not* one and the same for all. For example, if ten is 'many' and two 'few' of some quantity, six is the mean if one takes it in relation to the thing, because it exceeds the one number and is exceeded by the other by the same amount; and this is the mean by arithmetical reckoning. But the mean in relation to *us* is not to be obtained in this way. Supposing that ten pounds of food is a large and two pounds a small allowance for an athlete, it does not follow that the trainer will prescribe six pounds; for even this is perhaps too much or too little for the person who is to receive it—too little for Milo[2] but too much for one who is only beginning to train. Similarly in the case of running and wrestling. In this way, then, every knowledgeable person avoids excess and deficiency, but looks for the mean and chooses it—not the mean of the thing, but the mean relative to us.

If, then, every science[3] performs its function well only when it observes the mean and refers its products to it (which is why it is customary to say of well-executed works that nothing can be added to them or taken away, the implication being that excess and deficiency alike destroy perfection, while the mean preserves it)—if good craftsmen, as we hold, work with the mean in view; and if virtue, like nature, is more exact and more efficient than any art, it follows that virtue aims to hit the mean. By virtue I mean moral virtue since it is this that is concerned with feelings and actions, and these involve excess, deficiency and a mean. It is possible, for example, to feel fear, confidence, desire, anger, pity, and pleasure and pain generally, too much or too little; and both of these are wrong. But to have these feelings at the right times on the right grounds towards the right people for the right motive and in the right way is to feel them to an intermediate, that is to the best, degree; and this is the mark of virtue. Similarly there are excess and deficiency and a mean in the case of actions. But it is in the field of actions and feelings that virtue operates; and in them excess and deficiency are failings, whereas the mean is praised and recognized as a success: and these are both marks of virtue. Virtue, then, is a mean condition, inasmuch as it aims at hitting the mean.

Again, failure is possible in many ways (for evil, as the Pythagoreans represented it, is a form of the Unlimited, and good of the Limited), but success is only one. That is why the one is easy and the other difficult; it is easy to miss the target and difficult to hit it. Here, then, is another reason why excess and deficiency fall under evil, and the mean state under good;

For men are bad in countless ways, but good in only one.[4]

A provisional definition of virtue

So virtue is a purposive disposition, lying in a mean that is relative to us and determined by a rational principle, and by that which a prudent man would use to determine it.[5] It is a mean between two kinds of vice, one of excess and the other of deficiency; and also for this reason, that whereas these vices fall short of or exceed the right measure in both feelings and actions, virtue discovers the mean and chooses it. Thus from the point of view of its essence and the definition of its real nature, virtue is a mean; but in respect of what is right and best, it is an extreme.

. . .

The doctrine of the mean applied to particular virtues

vii.   But a generalization of this kind is not enough; we must apply it to particular cases. When we are discussing actions, although general statements have a wider application, particular statements are closer to the truth. This is because actions are concerned with particular facts, and theories must be brought into harmony with these. Let us, then, take these instances from the diagram.[6]

In the field of Fear and Confidence[7] the mean is Courage; and of those who go to extremes the man who exceeds in fearlessness has no name to describe him (there are many nameless cases), the one who exceeds in confidence is called Rash, and the one who shows an excess of fear and a deficiency of confidence is called Cowardly. In the field of Pleasures and Pains—not in all, especially not in all pains—the mean is Temperance,[8] the excess Licentiousness; cases of defective response to pleasures scarcely occur, and therefore people of this sort too have no name to describe them, but let us class them as Insensible. In the field of Giving and Receiving Money the mean is Liberality, the excess and deficiency are Prodigality and Illiberality; but these show excess and deficiency in contrary ways to one another: the prodigal man goes too far in spending and not far enough in getting, while the illiberal man goes too far in getting money and not far enough in spending it. This present account is in outline and summary, which is all that we need at this stage; we shall give a more accurate analysis later.

TABLE OF VIRTUES AND VICES

SPHERE OF ACTION OR FEELING	EXCESS	MEAN	DEFICIENCY
Fear and Confidence	Rashness *thrasutēs*	Courage *andreia*	Cowardice *deilia*
Pleasure and Pain	Licentiousness *akolasia*	Temperance *sōphrosunē*	Insensibility *anaisthēsia*
Getting and Spending (minor)	Prodigality *asōtia*	Liberality *eleutheriotēs*	Illiberality *aneleutheria*

TABLE OF VIRTUES AND VICES (*continued*)

SPHERE OF ACTION OR FEELING	EXCESS	MEAN	DEFICIENCY
Getting and Spending (major)	Vulgarity *apeirokalia, banausia*	Magnificence *megaloprepeia*	Pettiness *mikroprepeia*
Honour and Dishonour (major)	Vanity *chaunotēs*	Magnanimity *megalopsúchia*	Pusillanimity *mikropsúchia*
Honour and Dishonour (minor)	Ambition *philotīmia*	Proper ambition	Unambitiousness *aphilotīmia*
Anger	Irascibility *orgilotēs*	Patience *prāotēs*	Lack of spirit *aorgēsia*
Self-expression	Boastfulness *alazoneia*	Truthfulness *alētheia*	Understatement *eirōneia*
Conversation	Buffoonery *bōmolochia*	Wittiness *eutrapelia*	Boorishness *agroikia*
Social Conduct	Obsequiousness *areskeia* Flatter *kolakeia*	Friendliness *philia*(?)	Cantankerousness *duskolia* (*duseris*)
Shame	Shyness *kataplēxis*	Modesty *aidōs*	Shamelessness *anaischuntia*
Indignation	Envy *phthonos*	Righteous indignation *nemesis*	Malicious enjoyment *epichairekakia*

But there are other dispositions too that are concerned with money. There is a mean called Magnificence (because the magnificent is not the same as the liberal man: the one deals in large and the other in small outlays); the excess is Tastelessness and Vulgarity, the deficiency Pettiness. These are different from the extremes between which liberality lies; how they differ will be discussed later. In the field of Public Honour and Dishonour the mean is Magnanimity, the excess is called a sort of Vanity, and the deficiency Pusillanimity. And just a liberality differs, as we said,[9] from magnificence in being concerned with small outlays, so there is a state related to Magnanimity in the same way, being concerned with small honours, while magnanimity is concerned with great ones; because it is possible to aspire to <small> honours in the right way, or to a greater or less degree than is right. The man who goes too far in his aspirations is called Ambitious, the one who falls short, Unambitious; the one who is a mean between them has no name. This true also of the corresponding dispositions, except that the ambitious man's is called Ambitiousness. This is why the extremes lay claim to the intermediate territory. We ourselves sometimes call the intermediate man ambitious and sometimes unambitious; that is, we sometimes commend the ambitious and sometimes the unambitious. Why it is that we do this will be explained in our later remarks. Meanwhile let us continue our discussion of the remaining virtues and vices, following the method already laid down.

In the field of Anger, too, there is excess, deficiency and the mean. They do not really possess names, but we may call the intermediate man Patient and the mean Patience; and of the extremes the one who exceeds can be Irascible and his vice Irascibility, while the one who is deficient can be Spiritless and the deficiency Lack of Spirit.

There are also three other means which, though different, somewhat resemble each other. They are all concerned with what we do and say in social intercourse, but they differ in this respect, that one is concerned with truthfulness in such intercourse, the other two with pleasantness— one with pleasantness in entertainment, the other with pleasantness in every department of life. We must therefore say something about these too, in order that we may better discern that in all things the mean is to be commended, while the extremes are neither commendable nor right, but reprehensible. Most of these too have no names; but, as in the other cases, we must try to coin names for them in the interest of clarity and to make it easy to follow the argument.

Well, then, as regards Truth the intermediate man may be called Truthful and the mean Truthfulness; pretension that goes too far may be Boastfulness and the man who is disposed to it a Boaster, while that which is deficient[10] may be called Irony and its exponent Ironical. As for Pleasantness in Social Entertainment, the intermediate man is Witty, and the disposition Wit; the excess is Buffoonery and the indulger in it a Buffoon; the man who is deficient is a kind of Boor and his disposition Boorishness. In the rest of the sphere of the Pleasant—life in general—the person who is pleasant in the right way is Friendly and the mean is Friendliness; the person who goes too far, if he has no motive, is Obsequious; if his motive is self-interest, he is a Flatterer. The man who is deficient and is unpleasant in all circumstances is Cantankerous and Ill-tempered.

There are mean states also in the sphere of feelings and emotions. Modesty is not a virtue, but the modest man too is praised. Here too one person is called intermediate and another excessive—like the Shy man who is overawed at anything. The man who feels too little shame or none at all is Shameless, and the intermediate man is Modest. Righteous Indignation is a mean between Envy and Spite, and they are all concerned with feelings of pain or pleasure at the experiences of our neighbours. The man who feels righteous indignation is distressed at instances of undeserved good fortune, but the envious man goes further and is distressed at *any* good fortune, while the spiteful man is so far from feeling distress[11] that he actually rejoices.

However, we shall have occasion to continue this discussion elsewhere.[12] After that we shall treat of Justice, distinguishing its two kinds—because the word is used in more senses than one—and explain in what way each of them is a mean. [We shall also treat similarly of the rational virtues.]

. . .

Summing up of the foregoing discussion, together with three practical rules for good conduct

ix. We have now said enough to show that moral virtue is a mean, and in what sense it is so: that it is a mean between two vices, one of excess and the other of deficiency, and that it is such because it aims at hitting the mean point in feelings and actions. For this reason it is a difficult business to be good; because in any given case it is difficult to find the midpoint[13]—for instance, not everyone can find the centre of a circle; only the man who knows how. So too it is easy to get angry—anyone can do that—or to give and spend money; but to feel or act towards the right person to the right extent at the right time for the right reason in the right way—that is not easy, and it is not everyone that can do it. Hence to do these things well is a rare, laudable and fine achievement.

For this reason anyone who is aiming at the mean should (1) keep away from that extreme which is more contrary to the mean, just as Calypso advises:

Far from this surf and surge keep thou thy ship.

For one of the extremes is always more erroneous than the other; and since it is extremely difficult to hit the mean, we must take the next best course, as they say, and choose the lesser of the evils; and this will be most readily done in the way that we are suggesting. (2) We must notice the errors into which we ourselves are liable to fall (because we all have differ-ent natural tendencies—we shall find out what ours are from the pleasure and pain that they give us), and we must drag ourselves in the contrary direction; for we shall arrive at the mean by pressing well away from our failing—just like somebody straightening a warped piece of wood. (3) In every situation one must guard especially against pleasure and pleasant things, because we are not impartial judges of pleasure. So we should adopt the same attitude towards it as the Trojan elders did towards Helen, and constantly repeat their pronouncement;[14] because if in this way we relieve ourselves of the attraction, we shall be less likely to go wrong.

To sum up: by following these rules we shall have the best chance of hitting the mean. But this is presumably difficult, especially in particular cases; because it is not easy to determine what is the right way to be angry, and with whom, and on what grounds, and for how long. Indeed we sometimes praise those who show deficiency, and call them patient, and sometimes those who display temper, calling them manly. However, the man who deviates only a little from the right degree, either in excess or in deficiency, is not censured—only the one who goes too far, because he is noticeable. Yet it is not easy to define by rule for how long, and how much, a man may go wrong before he incurs blame; no easier than it is to define any other object of perception. Such questions of degree occur in particular cases, and the decision lies with our perception.[15]

This much, then, is clear: in all our conduct it is the mean that is to be commended. But one should incline sometimes towards excess and sometimes towards deficiency, because in this way we shall most easily hit upon the mean, that is, the right course.

EXPLANATORY NOTES

1. *proairesis*
2. A prodigiously strong wrestler from Croton in S. Italy.
3. He means *practical* science, as is evident from the context.
4. The source of the quotation is unknown.
5. It is purposive as being a deliberately cultivated and exercised state of the appetitive faculty; and the mean is determined not merely by a general prin-ciple but by the application of it to particular circumstances by a man of good character and intelligence; cf. ch. ix. below.
6. Or 'table'; see table, where the Greek names of the several virtues and vices are shown.
7. These should be regarded (for the understanding of A.'s general theory) as forming a single continuum with extremes Rashness and Cowardice; the reference to Fearlessness may be ignored.

8. Generally 'self-control' is a better rendering.
9. Just above.
10. By understating the truth; in fact 'understatement' is often a better equivalent than 'irony'.
11. At their *bad* fortune, because the Greek work means literally 'rejoicing at misfortune'.
12. In Book V.
13. Or 'mean'.
14. As a sort of charm or spell. The elders paid tribute to her beauty, but said that she ought to be sent back to Greece, for fear of the consequences for Troy if she remained (*Iliad* iii. 156–60).
15. e.g. a person of good character *feels* that he is getting too angry; he does not, in a particular case, refer to a general principle of ethics.

LUCRETIUS

Epicurus, Victor over Superstition

Titus Lucretius Carus (c. 94–55 or 51 B.C.E.), in addition to being one of the greatest of Roman poets, is also an important source for the study of ancient Epicureanism. Little is known about his life. His didactic poem On the Nature of the Universe, *written in hexameters, is a philosophical poem explaining the basic doctrines of the Greek sage Epicurus. It is dedicated to a certain Memmius, identifiable as a Roman politician who had been exiled to Athens after a corruption scandal. The story that the poem was composed during brief intervals of sanity while Lucretius was being driven mad by a love potion administered secretly by his wife is probably an invention.*

Lucretius's great poem is divided into six books, each of which has a prologue and a concluding section, so that every book constitutes a unity in itself. Book 1 lays out the basic scientific premises of Epicureanism and atomism. Book 2 explains atomist physics, the relationship between primary and secondary qualities, and defends the proposition that the universe contains an infinite number of worlds. Book 3 describes the nature of the soul and argues that it is mortal, and therefore death is not to be feared. Book 4 discusses various psychological phenomena and concludes with an attack on love, which Lucretius, following Epicurus, saw as a dangerous delusion causing nothing but misery. Book 5 argues for the mortality of the world and against the idea of providence, concluding with a famous account of the origins of civilization. Book 6 deals with natural phenomena such as earthquakes and thunder, the ignorance of which tends to lead to fear of the gods, and ends with an account of the plague at Athens.

After a long period of neglect in the Middle Ages, Lucretius's work was revived in the Renaissance, and its ideas about natural philosophy and superstition had a powerful impact on the development of modern science, especially thinkers such as Giordano Bruno, Galileo, Pierre Gassendi, and David Hume, and on modern philosophical materialisms. The present passage contains Lucretius's famous praise of Epicurus, whose philosophy saves the world from superstition and the fear of death.

"Epicurus, Victor over Superstition," from Book 1 in *Lucretius: On the Nature of the Universe,* translated by R. E. Latham, revised with an introduction by John Godwin, translation copyright © 1951 by R. E. Latham, revisions, introduction, and notes copyright © 1994 by John Godwin, 11–14, 200. Reprinted by permission of Penguin Books Ltd.

When human life lay grovelling in all men's sight, crushed to the earth under the dead weight of superstition whose grim features loured menacingly upon mortals from the four quarters of the sky, a man of Greece[1] was first to raise mortal eyes in defiance, first to stand erect and brave the challenge. Fables of the gods did not crush him, nor the lightning flash and the growling menace of the sky.[2] Rather, they quickened the keen courage of his heart, so that he, first of all men, longed to smash the constraining locks of nature's doors. The vital vigour of his mind prevailed. He ventured far out beyond the flaming ramparts of the world and voyaged in mind throughout infinity. Returning victorious, he proclaimed to us what can be and what cannot: how the power of each thing is limited, and its boundary-stone sticks buried deep. Therefore superstition in its turn lies crushed beneath his feet, and we by his triumph are lifted level with the skies.

One thing that worries me is the fear that you may fancy yourself embarking on an impious course of philosophy, setting your feet on the path of sin. Far from it. More often it is this very superstition that is the mother of sinful and impious deeds. Remember how at Aulis[3] the altar of the virgin goddess was foully stained with the blood of Iphigeneia by the leaders of the Greeks, the patterns of chivalry. The headband was bound about her virgin tresses and hung down evenly over both her cheeks. Suddenly she caught sight of her father standing sadly in front of the altar, the attendants beside him hiding the knife and her people bursting into tears when they saw her. Struck dumb with terror, she sank on her knees to the ground. Poor girl, at such a moment it did not help her that she had been first to give the name of father to a king. Raised by the hands of men, she was led trembling to the altar. Not for her the sacrament of marriage and the loud chant of Hymen. It was her fate in the very hour of marriage to fall a sinless victim to a sinful rite, slaughtered to her greater grief by a father's hand, so that a fleet might sail under happy auspices. Such are the heights of wickedness to which men have been driven by superstition.

You yourself, if you surrender your judgement at any time to the blood-curdling declamations of the prophets, will want to desert our ranks. Only think what phantoms they can conjure up to overturn the tenor of your life and wreck your happiness with fear. And not without cause. For, if men saw that a term was set to their troubles, they would find strength in some way to withstand the hocus-pocus and intimidations of the prophets. As it is, they have no power of resistance, because they are haunted by the fear of eternal punishment after death. They know nothing of the nature of the spirit. Is it born, or is it implanted in us at birth? Does it perish with us, dissolved by death, or does it visit the murky depths and dreary sloughs of the Underworld? Or is it transplanted by divine power into other creatures, as described in the poems of our own Ennius,[4] who first gathered on the delectable slopes of Helicon[5] an evergreen garland destined to win renown among the nations of Italy? Ennius indeed in his immortal verses proclaims that there is also a Hell, which is peopled not by our actual spirits or bodies but only by shadowy images, ghastly pale. It is from this realm that he pictures the ghost of Homer,[6] of unfading memory, as appearing to him, shedding salt tears and revealing the nature of the universe.

I must therefore give an account of celestial phenomena, explaining the movements of sun and moon and also the forces that determine events on earth. Next, and no less important, we must look with keen insight into the make-up of spirit and mind: we must consider those alarming phantasms that strike upon our minds when they are awake but disordered by sickness, or when they are buried in slumber, so that we seem to see and hear before us men whose dead bones lie in the embraces of earth.

I am well aware that it is not easy to elucidate in Latin verse the obscure discoveries of the Greeks. The poverty of our language[7] and the novelty of the theme often compel me to coin new words for the purpose. But your merit and the joy I hope to derive from our delightful friendship[8] encourage me to face any task however hard. This it is that leads me to stay awake through the quiet of the night, studying how by choice of words and the poet's art I can display before your mind a clear light by which you can gaze into the heart of hidden things.

This dread and darkness of the mind cannot be dispelled by the sunbeams, the shining shafts of day, but only by an understanding of the outward form and inner workings of nature. In tackling this theme, our starting-point will be this principle: *Nothing is ever created by divine power out of nothing.* The reason why all mortals are so gripped by fear is that they see all sorts of things happening on the earth and in the sky with no discernible cause, and these they attribute to the will of a god. Accordingly, when we have seen that nothing can be created out of nothing, we shall then have a clearer picture of the path ahead, the problem of how things are created and occasioned without the aid of gods.

EXPLANATORY NOTES

1. Epicurus.
2. L. attacks the theory that the gods cause thunder and lightning in 6.379–422.

3. At Aulis (in Boeotia) Iphigeneia was sacrificed by her father, the Greek general Agamemnon, to placate Artemis (the virgin goddess) and cause the wind to blow the fleet to Troy—to fight the Trojan War.
4. Early Roman Poet (239–169 B.C.), believer in reincarnation, who at the beginning of his *Annales* claimed that his soul had 'been' Homer and Pythagoras in previous existences.
5. Mountain in Boeotia where the Muses were said to live.
6. Early Greek epic poet said to have composed the *Iliad* and the *Odyssey*.
7. Latin lacked the technical philosophical and scientific vocabulary of Greek.
8. Friendship was especially praised by Epicurus as both an ethical ideal and as one of the highest pleasures available to man.

SENECA

Should a Philosopher Withdraw from the World?

One of the most influential writers of Antiquity, Lucius Annaeus Seneca (4 B.C.E.–65 C.E.) was born in Cordoba (Spain), spent part of his youth in Egypt, then settled in Rome where he studied law and pursued a political career. He obtained the office of quaestor and was a successful speaker in the Senate, but his rise was a cause for jealousy and he was twice (in 37 and 41 C.E., by successive emperors) condemned to death. His punishment was in each case commuted to exile, and he spent eight years on the island of Corsica, dedicating himself to literature and philosophy. In 49 C.E. he was recalled to Rome and made praetor. He was also entrusted with tutoring a twelve-year-old child who was later to become Emperor Nero. Upon Nero's accession to the throne in 54 C.E., Seneca became, together with an army officer named Burrus, the power behind the throne. For a period of eight years, the two men managed to direct imperial policy and redirect the emperor's baser instincts. This period was remembered by historians as one of the best in imperial government. But Nero became increasingly independent of his tutors, and Seneca's enemies whispered to the emperor that the philosopher had become corrupt, and his popularity a danger to the throne. In 62 C.E., Seneca thought it wise to retire from public life; but the discovery of a plot against the emperor, in which Seneca was implicated, spelled the philosopher's end, and he was forced to commit suicide.

Though an adherent of Stoicism (an austere philosophy that emphasized the pursuit of virtue, a modest lifestyle, and immunity to pain, grief, fear of death, and superstition), Seneca sought to humanize its more forbidding aspects and make the Stoic ideal seem attractive and attainable to a larger circle. He stressed the universal brotherhood of man and expressed, for the time, remarkable views on the natural equality of man. Furthermore, his writings have a religious flavor that proved appealing to Christians as well as to pagans. Although Seneca penned works in a variety of genres, including political speeches, dialogues, poems, letters, and treatises, his surviving oeuvre consists mainly of tragedies in verse and philosophical writings in prose. The latter took the form of letters, essays, and treatises, and includes titles such as The Happy Life, The Shortness of Life, Providence, Anger, *and* Clemency. *These works are known not only for their philosophical insight, but for their style, which combines brevity, conversational ease, and wit in a way that contrasts sharply with the fulsome style of Seneca's predecessor Cicero.*

Seneca's 124 Letters, *directed to Lucilius Junior, a civil servant from Pompeii who had some interest in literature and philosophy, are mostly essays on moral topics, as is indicated by the Latin title* Epistulae morales. *It is not clear whether these letters were actually sent, or whether Seneca simply decided to use the letter form as a convenient vehicle for his ethical considerations. However, it is certain that the letters, whose style is highly polished, were meant for publication, and that Seneca worked on them especially during the last three years of his life. Full of pithy sentences as well as references to life in contemporary Rome, they offer a supple vehicle to communicate Seneca's chief philosophical concerns. The present selection, taken from letters VII–VIII, is an inquiry into how the philosopher should relate to those around him. In the first letter, Seneca described some gladiatorial combats and the crowd's thirst for the blood of the combatants. He recommended that, to avoid being influenced by such base instincts, a philosopher should as much as possible retire within himself, without however avoiding more intimate relationships. In the second letter, Seneca advanced the view that philosophical writing was more useful than the active political life.*

LETTER VII

You ask me to say what you should consider it particularly important to avoid. My answer is this: a mass crowd. It is something to which you cannot entrust yourself yet without risk. I at any rate am ready to confess my own frailty in this respect. I never come back home with quite the same moral character I went out with; something or other becomes unsettled where I had achieved internal peace, some one or other of the things I had put to flight reappears on the scene. We who are recovering from a prolonged spiritual sickness are in the same condition as invalids who have been affected to such an extent by prolonged indisposition that they cannot once be taken out of doors without ill effects. Associating with people in large numbers is actually harmful: there is not one of them that will not make some vice or other attractive to us, or leave us carrying the imprint of it or bedaubed all unawares with it. And inevitably enough, the larger the size of the crowd we mingle with, the greater the danger. But nothing is as ruinous to the character as sitting away one's time at a show—for it is then, through the medium of entertainment, that vices creep into one with more than usual ease. What do you take me to mean? That I go home more selfish, more self-seeking and more self-indulgent? Yes, and what is more, a person crueller and less humane through having been in contact with human beings. I happened to go to one of these shows at the time of the lunch-hour interlude, expecting there to be some light and witty entertainment then, some respite for the purpose of affording people's eyes a rest from human blood. Far from it. All the earlier contests were charity in comparison. The nonsense is dispensed with now: what we have now is murder pure and simple. The combatants have nothing to protect them; their whole bodies are exposed to the blows; every thrust they launch gets home. A great many spectators prefer this to the ordinary matches and even to the special, popular demand ones. And quite naturally. There are no helmets and no shields repelling the weapons. What is the point of armour? Or of skill? All that sort of thing just makes the death slower in coming. In the morning men are thrown to the lions and the bears: but it is the spectators they are thrown to in the lunch hour. The spectators insist that each on killing his man shall be thrown against another to be killed in his turn; and the eventual victor is reserved by them for some other form of butchery; the only exit for the contestants is death. Fire and steel keep the slaughter going. And all this happens while the arena is virtually empty.

'But he was a highway robber, he killed a man.' And what of it? Granted that as a murderer he deserved this punishment, what have you done, you wretched fellow, to deserve to watch it? 'Kill him! Flog him! Burn him! Why does he run at the other man's weapon in such a cowardly way? Why isn't he less half-hearted about killing? Why isn't he a bit more enthusiastic about dying? Whip him forward to get his wounds! Make them each offer the other a bare breast and trade blow for blow on them.' And when there is an interval in the show: 'Let's have some throats cut in the meantime, so that there's something happening!' Come now, I say, surely you people realize—if you realize nothing else—that bad examples have a way of recoiling on those who set them? Give thanks to the immortal gods that the men to whom you are giving a lesson in cruelty are not in a position to profit from it.

When a mind is impressionable and has none too firm a hold on what is right, it must be rescued from the crowd: it is so easy for it to go over to the majority. A Socrates, a Cato or a Laelius might have been shaken in his principles by a multitude of people different from himself: such is the measure of the inability of any of us, even as we perfect our personality's adjustment, to withstand the onset of vices when they come with such a mighty following. A single example of extravagance or greed does a lot of harm—an intimate who leads a pampered life gradually makes one soft and flabby; a wealthy neighbour provokes cravings in one; a companion with a malicious nature tends to rub off some of his rust even on someone of an innocent and open-hearted nature—what then do you imagine the effect on a person's character is when the assault comes from the world at large? You must inevitably either hate or imitate the world. But the right thing is to shun both courses: you should neither become like the bad because they are many, nor be an enemy of the many because they are unlike you. Retire into yourself as much as you can. Associate with people who are likely to improve you. Welcome those whom you are capable of improving. The process is a mutual one: men learn as they teach. And there is no reason why any pride in advertising your talents abroad should lure you forward into the public eye, inducing you to give readings of your works or deliver lectures. I should be glad to see you doing that if what you had to offer them was suitable for the crowd I have been talking about: but the fact is, not one of them is really capable of understanding you. You might perhaps come across one here and there, but even they would need to be trained and developed by you to a point where they could grasp your teaching. 'For whose benefit, then, did I learn it all?' If it was for your own benefit that you learnt it you have no call to fear that your trouble may have been wasted.

Just to make sure that I have not been learning solely for my own benefit today, let me share with you three fine quotations I have come across, each concerned with something like the same idea—one of them is by way of payment of the usual debt so far as this letter is concerned, and the other two you are to regard as an advance on account. 'To me,' says Democritus, 'a single man is a crowd, and a crowd is a single man.' Equally good is the answer given by the person, whoever it was (his identity is uncertain), who when asked what was the object of all the trouble he took over a piece of craftsmanship when it would never reach more than a few people, replied: 'A few is enough for me; so is one; and so is none.' The third is a nice expression used by Epicurus in a letter to one of his colleagues. 'I am writing this,' he says, 'not for the eyes of the many, but for yours alone: for each of us is audience enough for the other.' Lay these up in your heart, my dear Lucilius, that you may scorn the pleasure that comes from the majority's approval. The many speak highly of you, but have you really any grounds for satisfaction with yourself if you are the kind of person the many understand? Your merits should not be outward facing.

LETTER VIII

'ARE you, of all people', you write, 'really telling me to avoid the crowd, to retire from the world and find contentment in a good conscience? Where are those Stoic rules of yours that call on a man to die in harness?' Come now, do I really give you the impression that I advocate a life of inactivity? I have only buried myself away behind closed doors in order to be able to be of use to more people. With me no day is ever whiled away at ease. I claim a good part of my nights for study; I have no time for sleep: I just succumb to it, keeping my eyes at their work when they are heavy-lidded and exhausted from lack of rest. I have withdrawn from affairs as well as from society, and from my own affairs in particular: I am acting on behalf of later generations. I am writing down a few things that may be of use to them; I am committing to writing some helpful recommendations, which might be compared to the formulae of successful medications, the effectiveness of which I have experienced in the case of my own sores, which may not have been completely cured but have at least ceased to spread. I am pointing out to others the right path, which I have recognized only late in life, when I am worn out with my wanderings. 'Avoid,' I cry, 'whatever is approved of by the mob, and things that are the gift of chance. Whenever circumstance brings some welcome thing your way, stop in suspicion and alarm: wild animals and fish alike are taken in by this or that inviting prospect. Do you look on them as presents given you by fortune? They are snares. Anyone among you who wishes to lead a secure life will do his very best to steer well wide of these baited bounties, which comprise yet another instance of the errors we miserable creatures fall into: we think these things are ours when in fact it is we who are caught. That track leads to precipices; life on that giddy level ends in a fall. Once, moreover, prosperity begins to carry us off course, we are no more capable even of bringing the ship to a standstill than of going down with the consolation that she has been held on her course, or of going down once and for all; fortune does not just capsize the boat: she hurls it headlong on the rocks and dashes it to pieces. Cling, therefore, to this sound and wholesome plan of life: indulge the body just so far as suffices for good health. It needs to be treated somewhat strictly to prevent it from being disobedient to the spirit. Your food should appease your hunger, your drink quench your thirst, your

112

clothing keep out the cold, your house be a protection against inclement weather. It makes no difference whether it is built of turf or of variegated marble imported from another country: what you have to understand is that thatch makes a person just as good a roof as gold does. Spurn everything that is added on by way of decoration and display by unnecessary labour. Reflect that nothing merits admiration except the spirit, the impressiveness of which prevents it from being impressed by anything.'

If these are the things I'm saying to myself, if these are the things I'm saying to future generations, don't you think I'm doing more good than when I go into court to enter into a recognizance on someone's behalf, or stamp my seal on a will, or lend my assistance by word or action in the Senate to some candidate for office? Those who appear inactive are, believe me, engaged in far more important activity; they're dealing with matters divine and human at the same moment.

But the time has come to make an end, and in accordance with the practice I've started to make some disbursement on this letter's behalf. For this I shall not draw on my own resources. I'm still turning over the pages of Epicurus, and the following saying, one I read today, comes from him: 'To win true freedom you must be a slave to philosophy.' A person who surrenders and subjects himself to her doesn't have his application deferred from day to day; he's emancipated on the spot, the very service of philosophy being freedom.

Quite possibly you'll be demanding to know why I'm quoting so many fine sayings from Epicurus rather than ones belonging to our own school. But why should you think of them as belonging to Epicurus and not as common property? Think how many poets say things that philosophers have said—or ought to have said! Not to mention the tragedians or our native Roman drama (which has a serious element in it as well and stands halfway between comedy and tragedy), think of the quantity of brilliant lines to be found lying about in farces alone! Think of the number of Publilius' verses that really ought to be spoken by actors wearing the tragic buskins instead of barefooted pantomime actors! I'll quote one verse of his which belongs to philosophy, and the same facet of philosophy that I was occupied with just now, a verse in which he proclaims that gifts which chance brings our way are not to be regarded as possessions:

> If you pray a thing may
> And it does come your way,
> 'Tis a long way from being your own.

I recall your expressing the same idea a good deal more happily and suc-
cinctly:

What fortune has made yours is not your own.

And I can't pass over that even happier expression of yours:

The boon that could be given can be withdrawn.

(This being from your own stock, I'm not debiting it to your account!)

HOMER

Odysseus Fools the Cyclops

Homer's two epic poems, The Iliad *and* The Odyssey, *are the first works of European literature and the greatest of their kind, but nothing is known about their author. Homer probably lived in the eighth century* B.C.E., *in the eastern Greek world; Smyrna in Asia Minor and the island of Chios, among many others, claimed him. According to tradition, he was blind. In any case, the poems are the product of a long oral tradition that preserved the memory of events in the Bronze Age, four hundred years before the poems were composed. They incorporate many ancient elements and stories, but each is the coherent work of one author who carefully produced a unified epic that also reflects the life of his own time. Whether* The Iliad *and* The Odyssey *are both by the same poet has been argued for more than two thousand years, and the issue is unlikely ever to be resolved. If both are by Homer,* The Iliad *is probably a work of his youth and* The Odyssey *of his old age. But differences of style, treatment, and characterization are striking. There is also a possibility that the poems were altered before they assumed their final form in the sixth century* B.C.E.

Here, Odysseus describes how he tricked and blinded the savage one-eyed Cyclops, who has eaten his men.

'Evening came, and with it the Cyclops, shepherding his plump flocks, every one of which he herded into the broad cave, leaving none out in the walled yard, either because he suspected something or because a god had ordered him to. He lifted the great doorstone, set it in its place, and then sat down to milk his ewes and bleating goats, which he did methodically, giving each mother its young one in due course. When he had efficiently completed all these tasks, he once more snatched two of us and prepared his supper. Then with an olive-wood bowl of my dark wine in my hands, I went up to him and said: "Here, Cyclops, have some wine to wash down that meal of human flesh, and find out for yourself what kind of vintage was stored away in our ship's hold. I brought it for you as an offering in the hope that you would take pity on me and help me on my homeward way. But your savagery is more than we can bear. Hard-hearted man, how can you expect ever to have a visitor again from the world of men? You have not behaved rightly."

'The Cyclops took the wine and drank it up. And the delicious drink gave him such exquisite pleasure that he asked me for another bowlful. "Give me more, please, and tell me your name, here and now—I would like to make you a gift that will please you. We Cyclopes have wine of our own made from the grapes that our rich soil and rains from Zeus produce. But this vintage of yours is a drop of the real nectar and ambrosia."

'So said the Cyclops, and I handed him another bowlful of the sparkling wine. Three times I filled it for him; and three times the fool drained the bowl to the dregs. At last, when the wine had fuddled his wits, I addressed him with soothing words.

'"Cyclops," I said, "you ask me my name. I'll tell it to you; and in return give me the gift you promised me. My name is Nobody. That is what I am called by my mother and father and by all my friends."

'The Cyclops answered me from his cruel heart. "Of all his company I will eat Nobody last, and the rest before him. That shall be your gift."

'He had hardly spoken before he toppled over and fell face upwards on the floor, where he lay with his great neck twisted to one side, and all-compelling sleep overpowered him. In his drunken stupor he vomited, and a stream of wine mixed with morsels of men's flesh poured from his throat. I went at once and thrust our pole deep under the ashes of the fire to make it hot, and meanwhile gave a word of encouragement to all my men, to make sure that no one would hang back through fear. When the fierce glow from the olive stake warned me that it was about to catch alight in the flames, green as it was, I withdrew it from the fire and my men gathered round. A god now inspired them with tremendous courage. Seizing the olive pole, they drove its sharpened end into the Cyclops' eye, while I used my weight from above to twist it home, like a man boring a ship's timber with a drill which his mates below him twirl with a strap they hold at either end, so that it spins continuously. In much the same way we handled our pole with its red-hot point and twisted it in his eye till the blood boiled up round the burning wood. The scorching heat singed his lids and brow all round, while his eyeball blazed and the very roots crackled in the flame. The Cyclops' eye hissed round the olive stake in the same way that an axe or adze hisses when a smith plunges it into cold water to quench and strengthen the iron. He gave a dreadful shriek, which echoed round the rocky walls, and we backed away from him in terror, while he pulled the stake from his eye, streaming with blood. Then he hurled it away from him with frenzied hands and raised a great shout to the other Cyclopes who lived in neighbouring caves along the windy heights. Hearing his screams they came up from every quarter, and gathering outside the cave asked him what the matter was.

'"What on earth is wrong with you, Polyphemus? Why must you disturb the peaceful night and spoil our sleep with all this shouting? Is a robber driving off your sheep, or is somebody trying by treachery or violence to kill you?"

'Out of the cave came mighty Polyphemus' voice in reply: "O my friends, it's Nobody's treachery, not violence, that is doing me to death."

'"Well then," came the immediate reply, 'if you are alone and nobody is assaulting you, you must be sick and sickness comes from almighty Zeus and cannot be helped. All you can do is to pray to your father, the Lord Poseidon."

'And off they went, while I laughed to myself at the way in which my cunning *notion*[1] of a false name had taken them in. The Cyclops, still moaning in agonies of pain, groped about with his hands and pushed the rock away from the mouth of the cave. Then he sat himself down in the doorway and stretched out both arms in the hope of catching us in the act of slipping out among the sheep. What a fool he must have thought me! Meanwhile I was cudgelling my brains for the best possible course, trying to hit on some way of saving my friends as well as myself. I thought up plan after plan, scheme after scheme. It was a matter of life or death: we were in mortal peril.

'This was the scheme that eventually seemed best. The rams of the flock were of good stock, thick-fleeced, fine, big animals in their coats of black wool. These I quietly lashed together with the plaited willow twigs which the inhuman monster used for his bed. I took them in threes. The middle one was to carry one of my followers, with its fellows on either side to protect him. Each of my men thus had three rams to bear him. But for myself I chose a full-grown ram who was the pick of the whole flock. Seizing him by the back, I curled myself up under his shaggy belly and lay there upside down, with a firm grip on his wonderful fleece and with patience in my heart. In this way, with sighs and groans, we waited for the blessed Dawn.

'As soon as she arrived, fresh and rosy-fingered, the he-goats and the rams began to scramble out and make for the pastures, but the females, unmilked as they were and with udders full to bursting, stood bleating by the pens. Their master, though tortured and in terrible agony, passed his hands along the backs of all the animals as they stopped in front of him; but the idiot never noticed that my men were tied under the chests of his own woolly rams. The last of the flock to come up to the doorway was the big ram, burdened by his own fleece and by me with my thoughts racing. As he felt him with his hands the great Polyphemus broke into speech:

'"Sweet ram," he said, "why are you the last of the flock to pass out of the cave like this? You have never before lagged behind the others, but always step so proudly out and are the first of them to crop the lush shoots of the grass, first to make your way to the flowing stream, and first to want to return to the fold when evening falls. Yet today you are the last of all. You must be grieved for your master's eye, blinded by a wicked man and his accursed friends, when he had robbed me of my wits with wine. Nobody was his name; and I swear that he has not yet saved his skin! Ah, if only you could feel as I do and find a voice to tell me where he's hiding from my fury! I'd hammer him and splash his brains all over the floor of the cave, and my heart would find some relief from the suffering which that nothing, that Nobody, has caused me!"

'So he let the ram pass through the entrance and when we had put a little distance between ourselves and the courtyard of the cave, I first let go my ram and then untied my men. Then, quickly, though with many a backward look, we drove our long-striding sheep and goats—a rich, fat flock—right down to the ship. My dear companions were overjoyed when they caught sight of us survivors, but broke into loud lamentations for the others. With nods and frowns I indicated silently that they should stop their weeping and hurry to bundle the fleecy sheep and goats on board and put to sea. So they went on board at once, took their places at the oars, and all together struck the white water with the blades.'

EXPLANATORY NOTE

1. The Greek for 'no one' is *me tis,* but run together as *metis* it means 'wily scheme, resourcefulness'. Odysseus laughs to himself because *metis* (no one/resourcefulness) has foiled the Cyclops. '*Notion*' is an attempt to get the pun.

HOMER

Death of a Hero

Homer's two epic poems, The Iliad *and* The Odyssey, *are the first works of European literature and the greatest of their kind, but nothing is known about their author. Homer probably lived in the eighth century* B.C.E., *in the eastern Greek world; Smyrna in Asia Minor and the island of Chios, among many others, claimed him. According to tradition, he was blind. In any case, the poems are the product of a long oral tradition that preserved the memory of events in the Bronze Age, four hundred years before the poems were composed. They incorporate many ancient elements and stories, but each is the coherent work of one author who carefully produced a unified epic that also reflects the life of his own time. Whether* The Iliad *and* The Odyssey *are both by the same poet has been argued for more than two thousand years, and the issue is unlikely ever to be resolved. If both are by Homer,* The Iliad *is probably a work of his youth and* The Odyssey *of his old age. But differences of style, treatment, and characterization are striking. There is also a possibility that the poems were altered before they assumed their final form in the sixth century* B.C.E.

Homer describes the final battle between the two greatest heroes of the Trojan War, Achilles and Hector. Achilles kills Hector and proposes further dishonor by mistreating his body.

. . . When the two men had advanced to close range, great Hektor of the glinting helmet was first to speak: 'Son of Peleus, I shall not run from you any more, as I did when you chased me three times round the great city of Priam, and I did not dare to stop and take your attack. But now my heart prompts me to stand and face you—I shall kill or be killed. But first let us swear here before our gods—they will be the best witnesses to keep watch on our agreement. I swear that I will inflict no outrage on you, if Zeus grants me the endurance and I take away your life: but after I have stripped you of your famous armour, Achilleus, I will give your body back to the Achaians—and you do the same.'

Then swift-footed Achilleus scowled at him and said: 'Hektor, do not talk to me of agreements, you madman. There are no treaties of trust between lions and men: wolves and lambs share no unity of heart, but are fixed in hatred of each other for all time—so there can be no friendship for you and me, there will be no oaths between us, before one or the other falls and gives his glut of blood to Ares, the fighter with the bull's-hide shield. Call to mind now all your fighting skills: now is the time above all to show yourself a spearman and a brave warrior. But I tell you there is no escape for you any longer, but soon Pallas Athene will beat you down under my spear. And now you will make me lump payment for the pain of my companions' deaths, all those you killed when your spear was raging.'

So he spoke, and steadying his long-shadowed spear he let it fly. But glorious Hektor had looked ahead and avoided it. He watched it come and crouched down, and the bronze spear flew over him and fixed in the earth: and unseen by Hektor, shepherd of the people, Pallas Athene pulled up the spear and gave it back to Achilleus. Hektor then spoke to the excellent son of Peleus: 'You missed! So, godlike Achilleus, it seems you knew nothing from Zeus about my death—and yet you said you did. No, you turn out a mere ranter—all your talk is bluff, to frighten me and make me lose my courage for the fight. Well, I shall not run and let you fix your spear in my back, but you must drive it through my chest as I charge straight for you, if that is what god has granted you. But now you try to avoid this bronze spear of mine—how I hope you take it entire in your flesh! Then the war would go lighter for the Trojans, with you dead, their greatest danger.'

So he spoke, and steadying his long-shadowed spear he let it fly, and did not miss, hitting in the centre of the son of Peleus' shield: but the spear rebounded far from the shield. Hektor was angered that his swift spear had flown wasted from his hand, and stood there in dismay, as he had no second ash spear. He called in a great shout to Deïphobos of the white shield, and asked him for a long spear. But Deïphobos was not there near him. Then Hektor realised in his heart, and cried out: 'Oh, for sure now the gods have called me to my death! I thought the hero Deïphobos was with me: but he is inside the wall, and Athene has tricked me. So now vile death is close on me, not far now any longer, and there is no escape. This must long have been the true pleasure of Zeus and Zeus' son the far-shooter, and yet before now they readily defended me: but now this time my fate has caught me. Even so, let me not die ingloriously, without a fight, without some great deed done that future men will hear of.'

So speaking he drew the sharp sword that hung long and heavy at his side, gathered himself, and swooped like a high-flying eagle which darts down to the plain through the dark clouds to snatch up a baby lamb or a cowering hare. So Hektor swooped to attack, flourishing his sharp sword. And Achilleus charged against him, his heart filled with savage fury. In front of his chest he held the covering of his lovely decorated shield, and the bright four-bossed helmet nodded on his head, with the beautiful golden hairs that Hephaistos had set thick along the crest shimmering round it. Like the Evening Star on its path among the stars in the darkness of the night, the loveliest star set in the sky, such was the light gleaming from the point of the sharp spear Achilleus held quivering in his right hand, as he purposed death for godlike Hektor, looking over his fine body to find the most vulnerable place. All the rest of his body was covered by his bronze armour, the fine armour he had stripped from mighty Patroklos when he killed him. But flesh showed where the collarbones hold the join of neck and shoulders, at the gullet, where a man's life is most quickly destroyed. Godlike Achilleus drove in there with his spear as Hektor charged him, and the point went right through his soft neck: but the ash spear with its weight of bronze did not cut the windpipe, so that Hektor could still speak and answer Achilleus. He crashed in the dust, and godlike Achilleus triumphed over him: 'Hektor, doubtless as you killed Patroklos you thought you would be safe, and you had no fear of me, as I was far away. You fool—behind him there was I left to avenge him, a far greater man than he, waiting there by the hollow ships, and I have collapsed your strength. Now the dogs and birds will maul you hideously, while the Achaians will give Patroklos full burial.'

Then with the strength low in him Hektor of the glinting helmet answered: 'I beseech you by your life and knees and by your parents, do not let the dogs of the Achaian camp eat me by the ships, but take the ransom of bronze and gold in plenty that my father and honoured mother will offer you, and give my body back to my home, so that the Trojans and the wives of the Trojans can give me in death my due rite of burning.'

Then swift-footed Achilleus scowled at him and said: 'Make me no appeals, you dog, by knees or parents. I wish I could eat you myself, that the fury in my heart would drive me to cut you in pieces and eat your flesh raw, for all that you have done to me. So no man is going to keep the dogs away from your head, not even if they bring here and weigh out ten times or twenty times your ransom, not even if Dardanian Priam offers to pay your own weight in gold. Not even so will your honoured mother lay you on the bier and mourn for you, her own child, but the dogs and birds will share you for their feast and leave nothing.'

Then, dying, Hektor of the glinting helmet said to him: 'Yes, I can tell it—I know you well, and I had no chance of swaying you: your heart is like iron in your breast. But take care now, or I may bring the gods' anger on you, on that day when for all your bravery Paris and Phoibos Apollo will destroy you at the Skaian gates.'

As he spoke the end of death enfolded him: and his spirit flitted from his body and went on the way to Hades, weeping for its fate, and the youth and manhood it must leave. Then godlike Achilleus spoke to him, dead though he was: 'Die! I shall take my death at whatever time Zeus and the other immortal gods wish to bring it on me.'

So he spoke, and pulled his bronze spear out of the body and laid it on one side, then stripped the blood-stained armour from Hektor's shoulders. And the other sons of the Achaians came running round, and stared with admiration at the size and wonderful looks of Hektor—and none who came up to the body left without stabbing it. And a man would glance at his neighbour and say: 'Look, Hektor is much milder to handle now than when he fired our ships with burning flame.'

This is what they said as they came up and stabbed him. When swift-footed Achilleus had stripped the body, he stood up and spoke winged words to the Achaians: 'Friends, leaders and lords of the Argives, now that the gods have granted us the mastering of this man, who has done so much harm, more than all the rest of them together, come then, let us test them with an armed attack around the city, to see if we can now find out what is in the Trojans' minds—whether they will abandon their citadel now that this man has fallen, or are determined to stay there even though Hektor is no longer with them. But yet how can my heart debate like this, when a dead man is lying by the ships unwept and unburied—Patroklos. I shall not forget him, as long as I am in the company of the living and there is lift in my knees—and if the dead forget their dead in the house of Hades, yet even there I shall remember my dear companion. So come now, young Achaians, let us return to the hollow ships singing a song of victory, and carrying this body with us. We have won great glory—we have killed glorious Hektor, whom the Trojans venerated like a god in their city.'

VIRGIL

Book I—The Aeneid

a man on the run, strugglin' [handwritten annotation]

I sing of arms and of a man: his fate
had made him fugitive; he was the first
to journey from the coasts of Troy as far
as Italy and the Lavinian shores.
Across the lands and waters he was battered   5
beneath the violence of High Ones, for
the savage Juno's unforgetting anger;

Able & Hera's sister [handwritten annotation]

and many sufferings were his in war—
until he brought a city into being
and carried in his gods to Latium: 10
from this have come the Latin race, the lords
of Alba, and the ramparts of high Rome.

Tell me the reason, Muse: what was the wound
to her divinity, so hurting her
that she, the queen of gods, compelled a man   15
remarkable for goodness to endure
so many crises, meet so many trials?
Can such resentment hold the minds of gods?

There was an ancient city they called Carthage—
a colony of refugees from Tyre—   20
a city facing Italy, but far
away from Tiber's mouth: extremely rich
and, when it came to waging war, most fierce.
This land was Juno's favorite—it is said—
more dear than her own Samos; here she kept   25
her chariot and armor, even then
the goddess had this hope and tender plan:
for Carthage to become the capital
of nations, if the Fates would just consent.
But she had heard that, from the blood of Troy,   30
a race had come that some day would destroy
the citadels of Tyre; from it, a people
would spring, wide-ruling kings, men proud in battle
and destined to annihilate her Libya.
The Fates had so decreed. And Saturn's daughter—   35

Excerpt from the *Aeneid*, by Virgil, reprinted from *The Aneid of Virgil*, translated by Allen Mandelbaum, (1981), reprinted by permission of Bantom Books

in fear of this, remembering the old war
that she had long since carried on at Troy
for her beloved Argos (and, indeed,
the causes of her bitterness, her sharp
and savage hurt, had not yet left her spirit;   40
for deep within her mind lie stored the judgment
of Paris and the wrong done to her scorned
beauty, the breed she hated, and the honors
that had been given ravished Ganymede)—
was angered even more; for this, she kept   45
far off from Latium the Trojan remnant
left by the Greeks and pitiless Achilles.
For long years they were cast across all waters,
fate-driven, wandering from sea to sea.
It was so hard to found the race of Rome.   50

With Sicily scarce out of sight, the Trojans
had gladly spread their canvas on the sea,
turning the salt foam with their brazen prows,
when Juno, holding fast within her heart
the everlasting insult, asked herself: 55
"Am I defeated, simply to stop trying,
unable to turn back the Trojan king
from Italy? No doubt, the Fates won't have it.
But Pallas—was she powerful enough
to set the Argive fleet on fire, to drown   60
the crewmen in the deep, for an outrage done
by only one infuriated man,
Ajax, Oileus' son? And she herself
could fling Jove's racing lightning from the clouds
and smash their galleys, sweep the sea with tempests.   65
Then Ajax' breath was flame from his pierced chest;
she caught him up within a whirlwind; she
impaled him on a pointed rock. But I,
the queen of gods, who stride along as both
the sister and the wife of Jove, have warred   70
so many years against a single nation.
For after this, will anyone adore
the majesty of Juno or, before
her altars, pay her honor, pray to her?"

Then—burning, pondering—the goddess reaches,   75
Aeolia, the motherland of storms,
a womb that always teems with raving south winds.
In his enormous cave King Aeolus

restrains the wrestling winds, loud hurricanes;
he tames and sways them with his chains and prison.   80
They rage in indignation at their cages;
the mountain answers with a mighty roar.
Lord Aeolus sits in his high citadel;
he holds his scepter, and he soothes their souls
and calms their madness. Were it not for this,   85
then surely they would carry off the sea
and lands and steepest heaven, sweeping them
across the emptiness. But fearing that,
the all-able Father hid the winds within
dark caverns, heaping over them high mountains,   90
and he assigned to them a king who should,
by Jove's sure edict, understand just when
to jail and when, commanded, to set free.
Then Juno, suppliant, appealed to him:

"You, Aeolus—to whom the king of men   95
and father of the gods has given this:
to pacify the waves or, with the wind,
to incite them—over the Tyrrhenian
now sails my enemy, a race that carries
the beaten household gods of Ilium   100
to Italy. Hammer your winds to fury
and rain their swamped ships, or scatter them
and fling their crews piecemeal across the seas.
I have twice-seven nymphs with splendid bodies;
the loveliest of them is Deiopea,   105
and I shall join her to you in sure marriage
and name her as your own, that she may spend
all of her years with you, to make you father
of fair sons. For such service, such return."

And Aeolus replied: "O Queen, your task   110
is to discover what you wish; and mine,
to act at your command. For you have won
this modest kingdom for me, and my scepter,
and Jove's goodwill. You gave me leave to lean
beside the banquets of the gods, and you   115
have made me lord of tempests and of clouds."

. . .

And here to right and left he can see others:
some feasting on the lawns; and some chanting   870

glad choral paeans in a fragrant laurel
grove. Starting here, Eridanus in flood
flows through a forest to the world above.
Here was the company of those who suffered
wounds, fighting for their homeland; and of those 875
who, while they lived their lives, served as pure priests;
and then the pious poets, those whose songs
were worthy of Apollo; those who had
made life more civilized with newfound arts;
and those whose merits won the memory 880
of men: all these were crowned with snow-white garlands.
And as they streamed around her there, the Sibyl
addressed them, and Musaeus before all—
he stood, his shoulders towering above
a thronging crowd whose eyes looked up to him. 885
"O happy souls and you the best of poets,
tell us what land, what place it is that holds
Anchises. It is for his sake we have come
across the mighty streams of Erebus."

The hero answered briefly: "None of us 890
has one fixed home: we live in shady groves
and settle on soft riverbanks and meadows
where fresh streams flow. But if the will within
your heart is bent on this, then climb the hill
and I shall show to you an easy path." 895
He spoke, and led the way, and from the ridge
he pointed out bright fields. Then they descend.

But in the deep of a green valley, father
Anchises, lost in thought, was studying
the souls of all his sons to come—though now 900
imprisoned, destined for the upper light.
And as it happened, he was telling over
the multitude of all his dear descendants,
his heroes' fates and fortunes, works and ways.
And when he saw Aeneas cross the meadow, 905
he stretched out both hands eagerly, the tears
ran down his cheeks, these words fell from his lips:

"And have you come at last, and has the pious
love that your father waited for defeated
the difficulty of the journey? Son, 910
can I look at your face, hear and return
familiar accents? So indeed I thought,

126

imagining this time to come, counting
the moments, and my longing did not cheat me.
What lands and what wide waters have you journeyed   915
to make this meeting possible? My son,
what dangers battered you? I feared the kingdom
of Libya might do so much harm to you."

Then he: "My father, it was your sad image,
so often come, that urged me to these thresholds.   920
My ships are moored on the Tyrrhenian.
O father, let me hold your right hand fast,
do not withdraw from my embrace." His face
was wet with weeping as he spoke. Three times
he tried to throw his arms around Anchises'   925
neck; and three times the Shade escaped from that
vain clasp—like light winds, or most like swift dreams.

Meanwhile, Aeneas in a secret valley
can see a sheltered grove and sounding forests
and thickets and the stream of Lethe flowing   930
past tranquil dwellings. Countless tribes and peoples
were hovering there: as in the meadows, when
the summer is serene, the bees will settle
upon the many-colored flowers and crowd
the dazzling lilies—all the plain is murmuring.   935
The sudden sight has startled him. Aeneas,
not knowing, asks for reasons, wondering
about the rivers flowing in the distance,
the heroes swarming toward the riverbanks.
Anchises answers him: "These are the spirits   940
to whom fate owes a second body, and
they drink the waters of the river Lethe,
the care-less drafts of lone forgetfulness.
How much, indeed, I longed to tell you of them,
to show them to you face to face, to number   945
all of my seed and race, that you rejoice
the more with me at finding Italy."

"But, Father, can it be that any souls
would ever leave their dwelling here to go
beneath the sky of earth, and once again   950
take on their sluggish bodies? Are they madmen?
Why this wild longing for the light of earth?"
"Son, you will have the answer; I shall not

keep you in doubt," Anchises starts and then
reveals to him each single thing in order.   955

"First, know, a soul within sustains the heaven
and earth, the plains of water, and the gleaming
globe of the moon, the Titan sun, the stars;
and mind, that pours through every member, mingles
with that great body. Born of these: the race   960
of men and cattle, flying things, and all
the monsters that the sea has bred beneath
its glassy surface. Fiery energy
is in these seeds, their source is heavenly;
but they are dulled by harmful bodies, blunted   965
by their own earthly limbs, their mortal members.
Because of these, they fear and long, and sorrow
and joy, they do not see the light of heaven;
they are dungeoned in their darkness and blind prison.
And when the final day of life deserts them,   970
then, even then, not every ill, not all
the plagues of body quit them utterly;
and this must be, for taints so long congealed
cling fast and deep in extraordinary
ways. Therefore they are schooled by punishment   975
and pay with torments for their old misdeeds:
some there are purified by air, suspended
and stretched before the empty winds; for some
the stain of guilt is washed away beneath
a mighty whirlpool or consumed by fire.   980
First each of us must suffer his own Shade;
then we are sent through wide Elysium—
a few of us will gain the Fields of Gladness—
until the finished cycle of the ages,
with lapse of days, annuls the ancient stain   985
and leaves the power of ether pure in us,
the fire of spirit simple and unsoiled.
But all the rest, when they have passed time's circle
for a millennium, are summoned by
the god to Lethe in a great assembly   990
that, free of memory, they may return
beneath the curve of the upper world, that they
may once again begin to wish for bodies."

Anchises ended, drew the Sibyl and
his son into the crowd, the murmuring throng,   995
then gained a vantage from which he could scan

all of the long array hat moved toward them,
to learn their faces as they came along:

"Listen to me: my tongue will now reveal
the fame that is to come from Dardan sons   1000
and what Italian children wait for you—
bright souls that are about to take your name;
in them I shall unfold your fates. The youth
you see there, leaning on his headless spear,
by lot is nearest to the light, and he   1005
will be the first to reach the upper air
and mingle with Italian blood; an Alban,
his name is Silvius, your last-born son.
For late in your old age Lavinia,
your wife, will bear him for you in the forest;   1010
and he will be a king and father kings;
through him our race will rule in Alba Longa.
Next Procas stands, pride of the Trojan race;
then Capys, Numitor, and he who will
restore your name as Silvius Aeneas,   1015
remarkable for piety and arms
if he can ever gain his Alban kingdom.
What young men you see here, what powers they
display, and how they bear the civic oak
that shades their brows! For you they will construct   1020
Nomentum, Gabii, Fidena's city,
and with the ramparts of Collatia,
Pometia and Castrum Inui,
and Bola, Cora, they will crown the hills.
These will be names that now are nameless lands.   1025

"More: Romulus, a son of Man. He will
join Numitor, his grandfather, on earth
when Ilia, his mother, gives him birth
out of the bloodline of Assaracus.
You see the double plumes upon his crest: 1030
his parent Mars already marks him out
with his own emblem for the upper world.
My son, it is beneath his auspices
that famous Rome will make her boundaries
as broad as earth itself, will make her spirit   1035
the equal of Olympus, and enclose
her seven hills within a single wall,
rejoicing in her race of men: just as
the Berecynthian mother, tower-crowned,
when, through the Phrygian cities, she rides on   1040

her chariot, glad her sons are gods, embraces
a hundred sons of sons, and every one
a heaven-dweller with his home on high.

"Now turn your two eyes here, to look upon
your Romans, your own people. Here is Caesar   1045
and all the line of Iülus that will come
beneath the mighty curve of heaven. This,
this is the man you heard so often promised—
Augustus Caesar, son of a god, who will
renew a golden age in Latium,   1050
in fields where Saturn once was king, and stretch
his rule beyond the Garamantes and
the Indians—a land beyond the paths
of year and sun, beyond the constellations,
where on his shoulders heaven-holding Atlas   1055
revolves the axis set with blazing stars.
And even now, at his approach, the kingdom
of Caspia and land of Lake Maeotis
shudder before the oracles of gods;
the seven mouths of Nile, in terror, tremble.   1060
For even Hercules himself had never
crossed so much of the earth, not even when
he shot the brazen-footed stag and brought
peace to the groves of Erymanthus and
made Lerna's monster quake before his arrows;   1065
nor he who guides his chariot with reins
of vine leaves, victor Bacchus, as he drives
his tigers down from Nysa's steepest summits.
And do we, then, still hesitate to extend
our force in acts of courage? Can it be   1070
that fear forbids our settling in Ausonia?

"But who is he who stands apart, one crowned
with olive boughs and bearing offerings?
I recognize his hair and his white beard:
when called from humble Cures, a poor land,   1075
to mighty rulership, he will become
first king of Rome to found the city's laws.
And after Numa: Tullus, who will shatter
his country's idleness and wake to arms
the indolent and ranks unused to triumph.   1080
Beside him is the ever-boastful Ancus,
one even now too glad when people hail him.
And would you see the Tarquin kings? And, too,

the haughty spirit of avenging Brutus,
the fasces he regained? He will be first   1085
to win the power of a consul, to use
the cruel axes; though a father, for
the sake of splendid freedom he will yet
condemn his very sons who stirred new wars.
Unhappy man! However later ages   1090
may tell his acts, his love of country will
prevail, as will his passion for renown.

"Then see, far off, the Decii and Drusi;
Torquatus of the ruthless ax; Camillus
as he brings back the standards. But those spirits   1095
you see there—gleaming in their equal armor
and now, while night restrains them, still at peace—
if they but reach the light of life, how great
a war they will incite against each other,
what armies and what slaughter! There is Caesar,   1100
descending from the summits of the Alps,
the fortress of Monoecus, and Pompey,
his son-in-law, arrayed against him with
the legions of the East. My sons, do not
let such great wars be native to your minds,   1105
or turn your force against your homeland's vitals:
and Caesar, be the first to show forbearance;
may you, who come from heaven's seed, born of
my blood, cast down the weapon from your hand!

"And there is Mummius, who—famous for   1110
his slaying of Achaeans, conqueror
of Corinth—will yet drive his chariot
triumphantly to the high Capitol.
There stands Aemilius Paulus, the destroyer
of Agamemnon's own Mycenae and   1115
of Argos and the sons of Aeacus,
the seed of powerful-in-arms Achilles:
he will yet avenge the Trojan elders and
Minerva's outraged altars. Who could leave
to silence you, great Cato, or you, Cossus?   1120
Who can ignore the Gracchi or the Scipios,
twin thunderbolts of war, the lash of Libya;
Fabricius, so strong and with so little;
or you, Serranus, as you sow your furrow?
And Fabii, where does your prodding lead me—   1125
now weary—with your many deeds and numbers!

You are that Maximus, the only man
who, by delaying, gave us back our fortunes.
For other peoples will, I do not doubt,
still cast their bronze to breathe with softer features,   1130
or draw out of the marble living lines,
plead causes better, trace the ways of heaven
with wands and tell the rising constellations;
but yours will be the rulership of nations,
remember, Roman, these will be your arts: 1135
to teach the ways of peace to those you conquer,
to spare defeated peoples, tame the proud."

So, while Aeneas and the Sibyl marveled,
father Anchises spoke to them, then added:
"And see Marcellus there, as he advances   1140
in glory, with his splendid spoils, a victor
who towers over all! A horseman, he
will set the house of Rome in order when
it is confounded by great mutiny;
he will lay low the Carthaginians   1145
and rebel Gaul; then for a third time father
Quirinus will receive his captured arms."

At this, Aeneas had to speak; he saw
beside that Shade another—one still young,
of handsome form and gleaming arms, and yet   1150
his face had no gladness, his eyes looked down:
"Who, Father, moves beside this man? A son
or one of the great race of his sons' sons?
For how his comrades clamor as they crowd!
What presence—his! And yet, around his head   1155
black night is hovering with its sad shade!"

With rising tears Anchises answered him:
"My son, do not search out the giant sorrow
your people are to know. The Fates will only
show him to earth; but they will not allow   1160
a longer stay for him. The line of Rome,
o High Ones, would have seemed too powerful
for you, if his gifts, too, had been its own.
What cries of mourning will the Field of Mars
send out across that overwhelming city,   1165
what funerals, o Tiber, will you see
when you glide past the new-made tomb! No youth
born of the seed of Ilium will so

132

excite his Latin ancestors to hope;
the land of Romulus will never boast   1170
with so much pride of any of its sons.
I weep for righteousness, for ancient trust,
for his unconquerable hand: no one
could hope to war with him and go untouched,
whether he faced the enemy on foot   1175
or dug his foaming horse's flank with spurs.
O boy whom we lament, if only you
could break the bonds of fate and be Marcellus.
With full hands, give me lilies; let me scatter
these purple flowers, with these gifts, at least,   1180
be generous to my descendant's spirit,
complete this service, although it be useless."

And so they wander over all that region,
across the wide and misted plains, surveying
everything. And when father Anchises   1185
has shown his son each scene and fired his soul
with love of coming glory, then he tells
Aeneas of the wars he must still wage,
of the Laurentians, of Latinus' city,
and how he is to flee or face each trial.   1190

There are two gates of Sleep: the one is said
to be of horn, through it an easy exit
is given to true Shades; the other is made
of polished ivory, perfect, glittering,
but through that way the Spirits send false dreams   1195
into the world above. And here Anchises,
when he is done with words, accompanies
the Sibyl and his son together; and
he sends them through the gate of ivory.
Aeneas hurries to his ships, rejoins   1200
his comrades, then he coasts along the shore
straight to Caieta's harbor. From the prow
the anchor is cast. The sterns stand on the beach.

SAPPHO

Love and Politics

Sappho (ca. 612–555 B.C.E.) is best known for her exquisite lyric poetry. Her poetry was famed in the ancient world in her own time, and for centuries after she was regarded as the equal of Homer, even as the Tenth Muse. In 1850, Philip Smith wrote in the Dictionary of Greek and Roman Biography and Mythology: *"It is almost superfluous to refer to the numerous passages in which the ancient writers have expressed their unbounded admiration of the poetry of Sappho. . . . It may safely be affirmed that the loss of Sappho's poems is the greatest over which we have to mourn in the whole range of Greek literature." She continues to have a unique place among ancient poets, and in a collection focusing on contemporary Greek women poets, she is praised for "her rhythmic lyricism, her faith in the poetic idea, and the free expression of her emotions," which allowed Sappho to break "through the patriarchal structure of society and the moral authority of the male." Her influence has been felt for over two millenia, and remains powerful today. Little is known with certainty about the life of Sappho, whose birth and death dates have been set variously by scholars at about 612 (or 630) to 555 (or 570) B.C.E. Contradictions abound concerning her biography: It is held that Sappho was born on the island of Lesbos in the city of Mytilene, or perhaps in Eresus; she married a man named Kerkylas, or that this name is a crude pun and that she never married; she had a daughter named Cleis, or that Cleis was not really her daughter; she was a prostitute, or she was not; she committed suicide by throwing herself off a cliff for love of Phaon, a ferryman, or that she did no such thing; she taught a school for girls on Lesbos, or she did not; the women named in her poems, such as Atthis and Anaktoria, were her students, or that they were simply her friends, or that they were her lovers, or that they were not; and her flight from Lesbos to Sicily was a political banishment, or it was not. Sappho's poetry was collected in nine volumes in Hellenistic Alexandria, around the second century B.C.E. They appear to have been preserved in the West through at least the early middle ages, despite public condemnations and orders that they be destroyed—for example, by St. Gregory, Bishop of Constantinople, about the year 380 C.E., and by Pope Gregory VII in 1073 C.E.. The persistence of quotations from her poems in later works suggests that not all copies were destroyed, but today only one complete poem and numerous fragments are known to have survived, in part from papyri found in Egypt, many in shreds used for wrapping the dead in tombs.*

There are numerous editions of the surviving fragments, in Greek or in translation, often along with compilations of testimonia *or biographical references and commentaries on Sappho. The following selections include verses on war and politics as well as her more familiar love poetry.*

SELECTED FRAGMENTS AND VERSE RENDITIONS

1.A. FROM A SECOND-CENTURY PAPYRUS

Some say a host of cavalry, others of infantry, and others of ships, is the most beautiful thing on the black earth, but I say it is whatsoever a person loves. It is perfectly easy to make this understood by everyone: for she who far surpassed mankind in beauty, Helen, left her most noble husband and went sailing off to Troy with no thought at all for her child or dear parents, but (love) led hey astray ... lightly ... (and she?) has reminded me now of Anactoria who is not here; I would rather see her lovely walk and the bright sparkle of her face than the Lydians' chariots and armed infantry ... impossible to happen ... mankind ... but to pray to share ... unexpectedly.

1.B. [VERSE TRANSLATION BY GUY DAVENPORT]

A company of horsemen or of infantry
Or a fleet of ships, some say,
Is the black earth's finest sight,
But to me it is what you love.

This can be understood in its round truth   5
By all, clearly, for she who in her beauty
Surpassed all mankind, Elena, left her husband,
The best of men,

And sailed to Troia, mindless of her daughter,
And of her parents whom she loved.   10
But[   ]
[   ]led her astray.

[   ]
[   ]lightness in her heart[ ]
That I remember Anaktoria now   15
So far away.

I would rather see the fetching way she walks
And the smiling brightness of her eyes
Than the chariots and charioteers of Lydia
In full armor charging.   20

[   ]cannot become
[   ]man[   ]approach with sacrifice
    and pray
[   ]
[   ].   25

1.C. [VERSE TRANSLATION
BY WILLIS BARNSTONE]

To Anaktoria

Some say cavalry and others claim
infantry or a fleet of long oars
is the supreme sight on the black earth.
        I say it is   5

the one you love. And easily proved.
Did not Helen, who was queen of mortal
beauty, choose as first among mankind
        the very scourge

of Trojan honor? Haunted by Love   10
she forgot kinsmen, her own dear child,
and wandered off to a remote country.
        Weak and fitful

woman bending before any man!
So Anaktoria, although you are   15
far, do not forget your loving friends.
        And I for one

would rather listen to your soft step
and see your radiant face—than watch
all the dazzling chariots and armored   20
        hoplites of Lydia.

2. FROM HEPHAESTION, SECOND CENTURY

I have a beautiful child who looks like golden flowers, my darling Cleis, for whom I would not (take) all Lydia or lovely . . .

3. FROM DIONYSIUS OF HALICARNASSUS, FIRST CENTURY B.C.E.

Ornate-throned immortal Aphrodite, wile-weaving daughter of Zeus, I entreat you: do not overpower my heart, mistress, with ache and anguish, but come here, if ever in the past you heard my voice from afar and acquiesced and came, leaving your father's golden house, with chariot yoked: beautiful swift sparrows whirring fast-beating wings brought you above the dark earth down from heaven through the mid-air, and soon they arrived; and you, blessed one, with a smile on your Immortal face asked what was the matter with me this time and why I was calling this time and what in my maddened heart I most wished to happen for myself: "Whom am I to persuade this time to lead you back to her love? Who wrongs you, Sappho? If she runs away, soon she shall pursue; if she does not accept gifts, why, she shall give them instead; and if she does not love, soon she shall love even against her will." Come to me now again and deliver me from oppressive anxieties; fulfil all that my heart longs to fulfil, and you yourself be my fellow-fighter.

4. FROM HEPHAESTION

I loved you, Atthis, once long ago.

5. FROM "LONGINUS," FIRST CENTURY

He seems as fortunate as the gods to me, the man who sits opposite you and listens nearby to your sweet voice and lovely laughter. Truly that sets my heart trembling in my breast. For when I look at you for a moment, then it is no longer possible for me to speak; my tongue has snapped, at once a subtle fire has stolen beneath my flesh, I see nothing with my eyes, my ears hum, sweat pours from me, a trembling seizes me all over, I am greener than grass, and it seems to me that I am little short of dying. But all can be endured, since . . . even a poor man . . .

6. FROM HEPHAESTION

Once again limb-loosening Love makes me tremble, the bitter-sweet, irresistible creature.

7. FROM HEPHAESTION

(But?), Atthis, the thought of me has grown hateful to you, and you fly off to Andromeda.

8. FROM HEPHAESTION

The moon has set and the Pleiades; it is midnight, and time goes by, and I lie alone.

9. SIXTH CENTURY PARCHMENT

. . . and honestly I wish I were dead. She was leaving me with many tears and said this: "Oh what bad luck has been ours, Sappho; truly I leave you against my will." I replied to her thus:

"Go and fare well and remember me, for you know how we cared for you. If not, why then I want to remind you . . . and the good times we had. You put on many wreaths of violets and roses and (crocuses?) together by my side, and round your tender neck you put many woven garlands made from flowers and . . . with much flowery perfume, fit for a queen, you anointed yourself stirring . . . and on soft beds . . . you would satisfy your longing (for?) tender . . .

10. FROM THE SAME PARCHMENT

. . . Sardis . . . often turning her thoughts in this direction . . . (she honoured) you as being like a goddess for all to see and took most delight in your song. Now she stands out among Lydian women like the rosyfingered moon after sunset, surpassing all the stars, and its light spreads alike over the salt sea and flowery fields; the dew is shed in beauty, and roses bloom and tender chervil and flowery melilot. Often as she goes to and from she remembers gentle Atthis and doubtless her tender heart is consumed because of your fate . . . to go there . . . this . . . mind . . . much . . . sings . . .

11. PAPYRUS FRAGMENT WRITTEN IN
SECOND OR THIRD CENTURY

. . . (golden-haired Phoebus), whom the daughter of Coeus bore, having lain with Cronus' son, (god of high clouds), whose name is great; but Artemis swore the (gods') great oath; "By your head, I shall always be a virgin (unwed), (hunting) on the peaks of the (lonely) mountains; come, grant this for my sake." So she spoke, and the father of the blessed gods nodded his consent; and gods (and men) call her (the virgin, shooter of deer), huntress, a great title. Love, (loosener of limbs), never approaches her . . .

12. FROM ARISTOTLE, RHETORIC, *fourth century* B.C.E.

[Alcaeus said:] "I wish to say something to you, but shame prevents me."
   [Sappho replied:] ". . . but if you had a desire for what is honourable or good, and your tongue were not stirring up something evil to say, shame would not cover your eyes, but you would state your claim."

13. FROM GALEN, SECOND CENTURY

for he that is beautiful is beautiful as far as appearances go, while he that is good will consequently also be beautiful.

14. FROM THE SCHOLIAST, FIFTH CENTURY?

Wealth without virtue is no harmless neighbour. [The blending of both brings the height] of happiness.

15. FROM STOBAEUS, EARLY FIFTH CENTURY

[Sappho to an uneducated woman]: But when you die you will lie there, and afterwards there will never be any recollection of you or any longing for you since you have no share in the roses of Pieria; unseen in the house of Hades also, flown from our midst, you will go to and fro among the shadowy corpses.

16. FROM SYRIANUS, SECOND CENTURY

As the sweet-apple reddens on the bough-top, on the top of the topmost bough; the apple-gatherers have forgotten it—no they have not forgotten it entirely, but they could not reach it.

17. DIO CHRYSOSTOM, FIRST CENTURY

Someone, I say, will remember us in the future . . .

SELECTED VERSES FROM SAPPHO: A NEW TRANSLATION

3

Standing by my bed
In gold sandals
Dawn that very
moment awoke me

4

I asked myself   5
What, Sappho, can
you give one who
has everything,
like Aphrodite?

5

And I said   10
I shall burn the
fat thigh-bones of
a white she-goat
on her altar

6

I confess   15
I love that
which caresses
me. I believe

Love has his
share in the
Sun's brilliance
and virtue   20

7

At noontime
When the earth is
bright with flaming   25
heat falling straight down

the cricket sets
up a high-pitched
singing in his wings

8

I took my lyre and said: 30
Come now, my heavenly
tortoise shell: become
a speaking instrument

9

Although they are
Only breath, words   35
which I command
are immortal

10

That afternoon
Girls ripe to marry
FIRST
VOICE   wove the flower-   40
heads into necklaces

SECOND
VOICE   ### 11

We heard them chanting:
Young Adonis is
dying! O Cytherea
What shall we do now?   45

Batter your breasts
with your fists, girls—
tatter your dresses!

12

It's no use
Mother dear, I   50
can't finish my
weaving
        You may
blame Aphrodite

soft as she is   55

she has almost
killed me with
love for that boy

16

You are the herdsman of evening
Hesperus, you herd   60
homeward whatever
Dawn's light dispersed

You herd sheep—herd
goats—herd children
home to their mothers   65

17

Sleep, darling
I have a small
daughter called
Cleis, who is

like a golden   70
flower
        I wouldn't
take all Croesus'
kingdom with love
thrown in, for her   75

18

Although clumsy
Mnasidica has a more
shapely figure than
our gentle Gyrinno

19

Tomorrow you had better   80
Use your soft hands,
Dica, to tear off
dill shoots, to cap
your lovely curls

She who wears flowers   85
attracts the happy
Graces: they turn
back from a bare head

22

In the spring twilight
The full moon is shining: 90
Girls take their places
as though around an altar

23

And their feet move
Rhythmically, as tender
feet of Cretan girls   95
danced once around an

FIRST
VOICE

altar of love, crushing
a circle in the soft
smooth flowering grass

27

It is time now   100
For you who are so
pretty and charming

SECOND
VOICE

to share in games
that the pink-ankled
Graces play, and   105

143

gold Aphrodite

O never!

I shall be a
virgin always

28

For her sake 110
We ask you
to come now

O Graces O
rosy-armed
perfection: 115

God's daughters

33

They're locked in, oh!
The doorkeeper's
feet are twelve
yards long! ten shoe- 120

FIRST
VOICE

makers used five
oxhides to cobble
sandals for them!

34

SECOND
VOICE

Lament for a maidenhead
Like a quince-apple 125
ripening on a top
branch in a tree top

not once noticed by
harvesters or if
not unnoticed, not reached 130

Like a hyacinth in
the mountains, trampled
by shepherds until
only a purple stain
remains on the ground 135

37

You know the place: then
Leave Crete and come to us
waiting where the grove is
pleasantest, by precincts

sacred to you; incense   140
smokes on the altar, cold
streams murmur through the

apple branches, a young
rose thicket shades the ground
and quivering leaves pour   145

down deep sleep; in meadows
where horses have grown sleek
among spring flowers, dill

scents the air. Queen! Cyprian!
Fill our gold cups with love   150
stirred into clear nectar

39

He is more than a hero
He is a god in my eyes—
the man who is allowed
to sit beside you—he   155

who listens intimately
to the sweet murmur of
your voice, the enticing

laughter that makes my own
heart beat fast. If I meet   160
you suddenly, I can't

speak—my tongue is broken;
a thin flame runs under
my skin; seeing nothing,

hearing only my own ears   165
drumming, I drip with sweat;
trembling shakes my body

and I turn paler than
dry grass. At such times
death isn't far from me   170

40

Yes, Atthis, you may be sure
                    Even in Sardis
Anactoria will think often of us

of the life we shared here, when you seemed
the Goddess incarnate   175
to her and your singing pleased her best

Now among Lydian women she in her
turn, stands first as the red-
fingered moon rising at sunset takes

precedence over stars around her;   180
her light spreads equally
on the salt sea and fields thick with bloom

Delicious dew pours down to freshen
roses, delicate thyme
and blossoming sweet clover; she wanders   185

aimlessly, thinking of gentle
Atthis, her heart hanging
heavy with longing in her little breast

She shouts aloud, Come! we know it;
thousand-eared night repeats that cry   190
across the sea shining between us

43

It was you, Atthis, who said
"Sappho, if you will not get
up and let us look at you
I shall never love you again!   195

"Get up, unleash your suppleness,
lift off your Chian nightdress
and, like a lily leaning into

"a spring, bathe in the water.
Cleis is bringing your best   200
purple frock and the yellow

"tunic down from the clothes chest;
you will have a cloak thrown over
you and flowers crowning your hair . . .

"Praxinoa, my child, will you please   205
roast nuts for our breakfast? One
of the gods is being good to us:

"today we are going at last
into Mitylene, our favorite
city, with Sappho, loveliest   210

"of its women; she will walk
among us like a mother with
all her daughters around her

"when she comes home from exile . . ."

But you forget everything   215

49

She was dressed well:
Her feet were hidden
under embroidered sandal straps—fine
handwork from Asia

50

But you, monkey face   220
Atthis, I loved you
long ago while you
still seemed to me a
small ungracious child

51

I was proud of you, too   225
In skill I think
you need never
bow to any girl

not one who may
see the sunlight   230
in time to come

52

After all this
Atthis, you hate
even the thought

of me. You dart   235
off to Andromeda

61

Pain penetrates
Me drop
by drop

75

Well!   240
Andromeda has
got herself a
fair exchange

76

Sappho, when some fool
Explodes rage   245
in your breast
hold back that
yapping tongue!

77

Strange to say
Those whom I treated   250
well are those who do
me the most injury now

78

I taught the talented
And furthermore, I did
well in instructing   255
Hero, who was a girl
track star from Gyara

81

Greetings to Gorgo
I salute, madam,

the descendant of   260
many great kings

a great many times

82

Rich as you are
Death will finish
you: afterwards no   265
one will remember

or want you: you
had no share in
the Pierian roses

You will flitter   270
invisible among
the indistinct dead
in Hell's palace
darting fitfully

83

Don't ask me what to wear   275
I have no embroidered
headband from Sardis to
give you, Cleis, such as
I wore
        and my mother   280
always said that in her
day a purple ribbon
looped in the hair was thought
to be high style indeed

but we were dark: 285
            a girl
whose hair is yellower than
torchlight should wear no
headdress but fresh flowers

89

Then the god of war   290
Ares, boasted to us
that he could haul off
Hephaistos, master of
the Forges, by sheer force

90

As for the exiles   295
I think they had
never found you,
Peace, more diffi-
cult to endure!

91

In memory   300
Of Pelagon, a fisherman,
his father Meniscus placed

here a fishbasket and oar:
tokens of an unlucky life

92

Do you remember   305
How a golden
broom grows on
the sea beaches

93

Be kind to me
Gongyla; I ask only   310
that you wear the cream
white dress when you come

Desire darts about your
loveliness, drawn down in
circling flight at sight of it   315

and I am glad, although
once I too quarrelled
with Aphrodite
        to whom
I pray that you will   320
come soon

94

You remind me
Of a very gentle
little girl I once
watched picking flowers   325

95

When they were tired
Night rained her
thick dark sleep
upon their eyes

96

The gods bless you   330
May you sleep then
on some tender
girl friend's breast

97

I have often asked you
not to come now   335

Hermes, Lord, you
who lead the ghosts
home:
        But this time
I am not happy; I   340
want to die, to see
the moist lotus open
along Acheron

98

It is the Muses
Who have caused me   345
to be honored: they
taught me their craft

99

Must I remind you, Cleis,
That sounds of grief
are unbecoming in   350
a poet's household?

and that they are not
suitable in ours?

100

I have no complaint
Prosperity that   355
the golden Muses
gave me was no
delusion: dead, I
won't be forgotten

HORACE

Love of Money

Quintus Horatius Flaccus (65–8 B.C.E.), known in English as Horace, was ancient Rome's greatest lyric poet, a writer of great originality and versatility. He supposedly came from a poor family, but was educated in Rome and Athens and rose to be commander of a legion under Caesar's assassin Brutus. He returned to Italy to find his family lands confiscated by the victorious party of Octavian, so he determined to make a living by writing. He got a job with the government, met Virgil, and attracted the patronage of the wealthy Maecenas, the emperor's closest adviser. He was given a farm in the country south of Rome and devoted himself to poetry. He began with the Epodes, *humorous verses in the Greek tradition, then turned to a Roman genre with the* Satires. *These generally good-natured and somewhat philosophical poems on such themes as greed, ambition, gluttony, and sex were published in 30 B.C.E. His next achievement, the* Odes *of 23 B.C.E., gave him unquestioned recognition as Rome's greatest lyric poet; he was never surpassed. The* Epistles, *written during the next decade, are discourses full of good advice cast in the form of letters. A final volume of* Odes *appeared in 17 B.C.E.*

Horace's works were enormously popular and influential, especially in the seventeenth and eighteenth centuries. Many of his phrases became part of the English poetic vocabulary. In this Satire, *Horace uses many examples to explain the vanity of piling up money.*

However, joking aside, let's take the matter seriously.
That fellow turning the heavy soil with his rough plough,
the crooked barman, the soldier, and the sailors who dash so bravely
across the seven seas maintain that their only object   30
in enduring hardship is to make their pile, so when they are old
they can then retire with an easy mind. In the same way
the tiny ant with immense industry (for he is their model)

hauls whatever he can with his mouth and adds it to the heap
he is building, thus making conscious and careful provision for the
[future.
Then, as the year wheels round into dismal Aquarius, the ant
never sets foot out of doors but, very sensibly, lives
on what he has amassed. But you—neither scorching heat nor the cold
of winter can divert you from your money-grubbing; fire, tempest,
[sword—
nothing can stop you; no one else must be richer than you.   40
Why have a huge mass of silver and gold if it makes you
so nervous that you dig a hole in the ground and furtively bury it?
    'If you once broke in on it you'd soon be down to your last penny.'
If you don't break in on it what's so fine about having a heap?
Suppose your floor has threshed a hundred thousand bushels,
that doesn't mean your stomach will hold any more than mine.
If you belonged to a slave-gang and happened to be carrying the
[bread-bag
on your aching shoulders, you wouldn't get any more than the chap
who had carried nothing. Tell me, if a man lives within nature's
limits, what matter whether he has a hundred or a thousand acres   50
of ploughed land?
                'But it's nice to draw from a big pile!'
But if you let us draw the same amount from our *little* pile,
why should your granaries be superior to our bins?
It's as if you needed only a jug or a glass of water
and said 'I'd sooner draw it from a big river than from this
piddling stream, although the amount would be just the same.'
That's how people who like more than their fair share
get swept away, bank and all, by the raging Aufidus,
while the man who wants only what he needs doesn't drink water
clouded with mud, nor does he lose his life in the torrent.   60

But many people are enticed by a desire which continually cheats
[them.
'Nothing is enough,' they say, 'for you're only worth what you
[have.'
What can you do with a man like that? You may as well tell him
to be miserable, since misery is what he enjoys. He's like the rich
Athenian miser who treated the people's remarks with contempt.
'The people hiss me,' he would say, 'but I applaud myself
when I reach home and set eyes on all the cash in my box!'

Tantalus thirstily strains at the waters eluding his lips—
what are you laughing at? Change the name and you are the subject
of the story. You scrape your money-bags together and fall asleep   70

on top of them with your mouth agape. They must remain unused
like sacred objects, giving no more pleasure than if painted on canvas.
Do you realize what money is for, what enjoyment it gives?
You can buy bread and vegetables, half a litre of wine,
and the other things which human life can't do without.
Or maybe you prefer to lie awake half dead with fright,
to spend your days and nights in dread of burglars or fire
or your own slaves, who may fleece you and then disappear? For
                                [myself,
I think I can always do without blessings like those!

But if, you say, you happen to have caught a feverish chill,   80
or some other bit of bad luck has nailed you to your bed, you have
                                [someone
to sit beside you, prepare poultices, and get the doctor
to come and put you on your feet and restore you to your nearest
                              [and dearest.
Don't you believe it. Your wife and son don't want you to recover.
Friends and neighbours, young and old, they all hate you.
Since you put money before all else small wonder that no one
offers you any affection. What do you do to earn it?
Or take your relatives, given you by nature with no effort
on your part—I suppose if you tried to hold and keep their love
you'd find it a futile waste of time, like training a donkey   90
to answer the rein and making him run in the Park races.

So let's put a limit to the scramble for money. As your wealth increases
your fear of poverty should diminish, and having got what you
                              [wanted
you ought to begin to bring that struggle to an end. Or else
you may finish up like Ummidius. The story won't take long:
this Ummidius was so rich that instead of counting
his money he weighed it, and so stingy that his clothes were never
better than a servant's, and yet to his dying day he was sure
he'd succumb to starvation. In fact he was split down the middle
                              [with an axe
swung by a freedwoman, one of Clytemnestra's indomitable breed.   100

CICERO

The Dream of Scipio

----

*Marcus Tullius Cicero (106–43 B.C.E.), the greatest of Rome's public speak-
ers as well as a leading philosopher and writer, also had an active political
career. Although he was born in a provincial town and was not an aristocrat, he became a successful advocate and started to establish a reputation
in his twenties. After studying philosophy in Greece, he returned to Rome
and entered public life, serving in a series of high offices at the youngest
statutory age. His attacks on a corrupt governor of Sicily in 70 brought him
considerable fame. During his term as consul (chief magistrate) in 63, he
suppressed an attempted revolution, gaining both popularity and a hostility
that led to his exile from Rome for four years. Thereafter, though he
remained a public figure, he was increasingly sidelined as generals like
Pompey and Caesar seized power. He used these years to publish a great
variety of works, including fifty-eight of his speeches, numerous treatises on
philosophy and rhetoric, and hundreds of letters. He returned to the political stage in 44 when he launched a series of attacks on Marc Antony—the
famous* Philippics. *This act of political courage in defense of the old republican values of Rome led to his execution in the following year.*

In the present selection, from the sixth book of Cicero's fragmentary On
the Republic, *the structure of the universe was revealed to a dreaming Scipio Africanus, along with such famous Platonic/Pythagorean doctrines as
the music of the spheres, the transmigration of souls, and the immortality of
great men. Scipio learned that even the glory of the Roman Empire is a
small thing from the perspective of the cosmos and eternity.*

As you know, I was military tribune in the Fourth Legion in Africa
under the command of the consul Manius Manilius. When I arrived
there I was particularly eager to meet King Masinissa, who for good reason was a close friend of my family.[1] When I came into his presence the
old man embraced me and wept. Then, after a moment, he lifted his eyes
to heaven and uttered these words.

'Most glorious Sun and other heavenly beings, I offer you my thanks![2] For before I depart from this life, I am now seeing with my own eyes, within this kingdom of mine and beneath my roof, Publius Cornelius Scipio. The very sound of his name revives my strength. For never a moment has the recollection of his glorious, invincible forbear faded from my memory.'[3]

Then I began asking him questions about his kingdom, and he in turn interrogated me about Rome; and so we spent the whole day in conversation. Afterwards, he entertained me in regal splendour, and we continued our discussion far into the night, as the aged king wanted nothing better than to talk of Africanus. He had not forgotten a single deed the great man had ever done, or a single word he had ever uttered.

When we finally parted and retired to bed, my journey and the lateness of the hour had made me tired, and I fell into a deeper sleep than usual. As I slept I had a dream, prompted no doubt by what we had been talking about. For it frequently happens that the subjects of our meditations and discussions reappear in our dreams. This happened for example to the poet Ennius; he writes of his dream about Homer, who was naturally the constant subject of his thoughts and conversations when he was awake.[4] And so I dreamt that Africanus was with me; his appearance recalled his portrait busts rather than his actual living self.[5]

I recognized him—and trembled with fear. But he spoke to me; and this is what he said.

'Calm yourself, Scipio. Do not be afraid. But remember carefully the things I am about to tell you. Do you see that city there? It was I who made its people submit to Rome. But now they are starting up the old conflicts once again; they refuse to remain at peace!' And from where he stood amid the bright illumination of radiant stars, he pointed down at Carthage, and began speaking once more. 'This,' he declared, 'is the city you have come to attack. At present you are not much more than an ordinary soldier. But within the space of two years you will have been elected consul, and then you will overthrow the place utterly. Thereafter the surname, which you now bear as an inheritance from myself, will be yours by your own right. Later on, after you have destroyed Carthage and celebrated a Triumph, after you have held the office of censor and undertaken missions to Egypt, Syria, Asia and Greece, you will be elected to the consulship for the second time, while you are absent, and you will win a very great war and raze Numantia to the ground. But at the time when you yourself are proceeding in Triumph to the Capitol, you will find the government in a state of confusion: for which the machinations of my grandson will be responsible.[6]

'After that, Africanus, it will be your duty to devote to your people the full splendid benefit of all your integrity, talent and wisdom. But at that juncture I see two divergent paths of destiny opening up before you. For when your life has completed seven times eight circuitous revolutions of the sun, and when these two numbers, each of which for a different reason is regarded as possessing some quality of perfection,[7] have in their natural course brought you to your supreme moment of destiny, that is the time when the entire Roman State will turn to you and all that you stand for: the Senate, every right-minded citizen, our subject allies, the entire Latin people. The fate of the whole country, at that juncture, will depend on you and you alone. In other words, it will be your duty to assume the role of dictator, and restore order to our commonwealth— provided only that death does not overtake you at the criminal hands of your own kinsman!'[8]

At this, Laelius cried out aloud, and a deep groan was heard from all.[9] But the younger Scipio smiled serenely, and went on: 'Hush! Do not, I beg you, awaken me from my sleep. Listen a little longer, and take heed of what my ancestor went on to say next.'

For then he continued speaking. 'But consider this, Africanus,' he said, 'and the thought will make your determination to defend your homeland even greater than it is already. Every man who has preserved or helped his country, or has made its greatness even greater, is reserved a special place in heaven, where he may enjoy an eternal life of happiness. For all things that are done on earth nothing is more acceptable to the Supreme God, who rules the whole universe, than those gatherings and assemblages of men who are bound together by law, the communities which are known as states. Indeed, it is from here in heaven that the rulers and preservers of those states once came; and it is to here that they eventually return.[10]

By now I was thoroughly alarmed. It was not the idea of death that frightened me so much, but the thought of treachery inside my own family. Nevertheless, I managed to ask Africanus a question. Was he, was my father Paullus, were the other men we think of as having died, really dead? Or were they still alive?[11]

'To be sure they are still living,' he replied, 'seeing that they have escaped from the prison-house of their bodies—that is to say from "life", as you call it, which is, in fact, death.[12] Look: do you not see your father Paullus coming towards you?'

Indeed I now saw him approaching; and I burst into a flood of tears. But my father put his arms round me and kissed me, and told me not to weep. So when I had suppressed my tears and felt able to speak, I cried out, 'Since this, most revered and best of fathers, is true life, as I hear Africanus declare, why must I stay any longer upon earth? Why should I not come and join you, with the utmost possible speed?'

'That must not be,' replied Paullus. 'For unless God whose sacred domain is all that you see around you here[13] has freed you from your confinement in the body, you cannot be admitted to this place. For men were brought into existence in order that they should inhabit the globe known as the earth, which you see here at the centre of this holy space. They have been endowed with souls made out of the everlasting fires called stars and constellations, consisting of globular, spherical bodies which are animated by the divine mind and move with marvellous speed, each in its own orbit and cycle. Therefore it is destined that you, Publius, and all other righteous men, shall suffer your souls to stay in the custody of the body. You must not abandon human life except at the command of him who gave it to you. For otherwise you would have failed in the duty which you, like the rest of humanity, have to fulfil.[14]

'Instead, then, Scipio, do upon earth as your grandfather has done. Do as I have done, who begot you. Cherish justice and devotion. These qualities in abundance are owed to parents and kinsmen; and most of all they are owed to one's country.

'That is the life which leads to heaven, and to the company of those who, having completed their lives in the world, are now released from their bodies and dwell in that region you see over there, which the Greeks have taught you people on earth to call the Milky Way.' And he pointed to a circle of light, blazing brilliantly among all the other fires.

As I gazed out from where I stood, first in one direction and then another, the whole prospect looked marvellously beautiful. There were stars we never see from the earth, and they were larger than we could possibly have imagined. The smallest was the luminary which is farthest away from heaven and nearest to the earth, and shines with reflected light.[15] These starry spheres were much larger than the earth. Indeed the earth now seemed to me so small that I began to think less of this empire of ours, which only amounts to a pinpoint on its surface.

While I looked more and more intently down at the earth Africanus checked me. 'How long,' he asked, 'do you propose to keep your eyes fastened down there upon that world of yours? Look up, instead, and look round at the sacred region into which you have now entered.

'The universe is held together by nine concentric spheres. The outer-most sphere is heaven itself, and it includes and embraces all the rest. For it is the Supreme God in person, enclosing and comprehending every-thing that exists, that is to say all the stars which are fixed in the sky yet rotate upon their eternal courses. Within this outermost sphere are eight others. Seven of them contain the planets—a single one in each sphere, all moving in the contrary direction to the great movement of heaven itself. The next sphere to the outermost is occupied by the orb which people on earth name after Saturn. Below Saturn shines the brilliant light of Jupiter, which is benign and healthful to mankind. Then comes the star we call Mars, red and terrible to men upon earth.

'Next, almost midway between heaven and earth, blazes the Sun. He is the prince, lord and ruler of all the other worlds, the mind and guiding principle of the entire universe, so gigantic in size that everything, every-where, is pervaded and drenched by his light. In attendance upon the Sun are Venus and Mercury, each in its own orbit; and the lowest sphere of all contains the Moon, which takes its light, as it revolves, from the rays of the sun. Above the Moon there is nothing which is not eternal, but beneath that level everything is moral and transient (except only for the souls in human beings, which are a gift to mankind from the gods). For there below the Moon is the earth, the ninth and lowest of the spheres, lying at the centre of the universe. The earth remains fixed and without motion; all things are drawn to it, because the natural force of gravity pulls them down.'[16]

I surveyed the scene in a stupor. But finally I recovered enough to ask: 'What is this sound, so strong and so sweet, which fills my ears?'

'That,' he replied, 'is the music of the spheres.[17] They create it by their own motion as they rush upon their way. The intervals between them, although differing in length, are all measured according to a fixed scheme of proportions; and this arrangement produces a melodious blend of high and low notes, from which emerges a varied harmony. For it cannot be that these vast movements should take place in silence, and nature has ordained that the spheres utter music, those at the summit giving forth high sounds, whereas the sounds of those beneath are low and deep. That is to say, the spheres containing the uppermost stars, comprising those regions of the sky where the movements are speediest, give out a high and piercing sound, whereas the Moon, which lies beneath all the others, sends forth the lowest note.

'The ninth of the spheres, the earth, fixed at the centre of the universe, is motionless and silent. But the other I eight spheres produce seven dif-ferent sounds on the scale—not eight, since two of these orbs move at identical speeds, but seven, a number which is the key to almost all things that exist. Clever men, by imitating these musical effects with their stringed instruments and voices, have given themselves the possibility of eventually returning to this place; and the same chance exists for others too, who during their earthly lives have devoted their outstanding talents to heavenly activities.

'The ears of mankind are filled with this music all the time. But they have become completely deaf to its melody; no other human faculty has become so atrophied as this. The same thing happens where the Nile rushes down from high mountains to the place known as Catadupa.[18] For the sound there is so loud that the people who live nearby have entirely lost their sense of hearing. And that, too, is why the mighty music of the spheres, created by the immeasurably fast rotations of the I whole universe, cannot be apprehended by the human ears—any more than you can look at the light of the Sun, which is so intense it blots out your power of vision altogether.'

The scene filled me with awe and delight. And yet all the time I still could not help riveting my eyes upon our own world there below. Africanus noticed this, and spoke again. 'I see,' he said, 'that your gaze is still fastened, even now, upon the places where mortals dwell upon the earth. But can you not understand that the earth is totally insignificant? Contemplate these heavenly regions instead! Scorn what is mortal!

'For the lips of mankind can give you no fame or glory worth the seeking. Note how few and minute are the inhabited portions of the earth, and look upon the vast deserts that divide each one of these patches from the next. See, the inhabitants of the world are so cut off from one another that their different centres cannot even communicate with each other. The place where you yourself dwell, for example, is far removed from certain of the other populated areas, both in latitude and longitude; and some people live in regions that are at the very opposite end of the world from yours. Surely you cannot expect *them* to honour your name.

'Furthermore, you will observe that the surface of the earth is girdled and encompassed by a number of different zones; and that the two which are most widely separated from one another, and lie beneath opposite poles of the heavens, are rigid with icy cold, while the central, broadest zone is burnt up with the heat of the sun. Two others, situated between the hot zones and the cold, are habitable. The zone which lies towards the south has no connexion with yours at all; it represents your antipodes. As to its northern counterpart, where you yourselves live, you will realize, if you look, what a diminutive section of this region can really be regarded as your property. For the territory you occupy is nothing more than a small island, narrow from north to south, somewhat less narrow from east to west, and surrounded by the sea which is known, on earth as the Atlantic, or the Great Sea, or the Ocean.[19] In spite of the grand name this stretch of water bears, you can tell from here how tiny it really is.

'And I must disabuse you of any idea that your own fame, or the fame of any one of us, could ever be great enough to extend beyond these known and settled lands. It could never scale the Caucasus mountains (you see them down there);[20] it could never swim the river Ganges. Not one of the inhabitants of all those eastern tracts, or the remote west either, or the far off north and south, will ever so much as hear the sound of your name! And once you leave all these hosts of people out of account, you will have to conclude that the area over which your glory is so eager to extend itself is really of the most trifling dimensions.

'And now about the people who *do* know and speak about us. The point is, how long will this go on? Assume, if you like, that future generations, having inherited our praises from their fathers, will indeed retain the desire to hand them down to their children as well. Even so the deluges and conflagrations which inevitably descend upon the earth at fixed intervals will make it impossible for any glory we may gain in this way to be eternal—or even to last for any length of time.[21] But in any case why do you regard it as so important to be talked about by people who have not yet been born? After all, you were never spoken of by all the multitudes who lived before you—and they were every bit as numerous, and were better men.

'It is also necessary to remind ourselves that even the people who may in fact hear our names mentioned will not retain the recollection even for as much as the space of one year. I am not referring to the year as it is commonly understood, which is measured according to the revolution of the sun, that is to say according the movements of one single star. But when *all* the stars return to the places where they started from, so that after an immense interval has elapsed the entire heavens finally resume their original configuration, then that great period of rotation can truly be called a year—but how many generations of human life it comprises, I should not venture to say.[22]

'Long ago, when the spirit of Romulus ascended into these sacred expanses, it seemed to those living at the time that a shadow suddenly passed over the sun, and its light was blotted out. When, once again, the sun shall go into eclipse in the very same position and at the very same hour, that will signify that all the constellations and stars have returned to their original positions: and then you will know that the Year has been completed. But you must understand that, up to now, not one twentieth part of its course has been run.[23]

'As for yourself, do not abandon hope of coming back here one day. For this is the place which offers great and eminent men their authentic reward—and, after all, such fame as you are able to win among mere human beings can evidently be disregarded, seeing that it is scarcely capable of enduring even for a small part of one single year. Look upwards, then! Contemplate this place which is a habitation for all eternity! Then you will not need any longer to be at the mercy of what the multitude says about you: then you will not have to put your trust in whatever human rewards your achievements may earn.

'Instead let Virtue herself, by her own unaided allurements, summon you to a glory that is genuine and real. Feel no concern about what other people may say about you. They will say it in any case. Besides, whatever words they may choose to utter will not pass beyond the narrow limits you now see below you. No utterance of man about his fellowmen has ever been lasting. When a person dies his words die with him. Posterity forgets them; and they pass into annihilation.

He stopped speaking, and I cried out my assent. 'Even when I was only a boy, Africanus,' I declared, 'I was already exerting myself to the utmost to follow in your footsteps, and in those of my father. I longed to be not unworthy of your fame! And if there is really a path leading right to the entrance of heaven for those who have served their country well, the knowledge of this great goal before me will inspire me to redouble my endeavours.'

'Strive on,' he replied. 'And rest assured that it is only your body that is mortal; your true self is nothing of the kind. For the man you outwardly appear to be is not yourself at all. Your real self is not that corporeal, palpable shape, but the spirit inside. *Understand that you are god.*[24] You have a god's capacity of aliveness and sensation and memory and foresight; a god's power to rule and govern and direct the body that is your servant, in the same way as God himself, who reigns over us, directs the entire universe. And this rule exercised by eternal God is mirrored in the dominance of your frail body by your immortal soul.

'That which is always in motion is eternal;[25] yet that which communicates motion to something else, but is itself moved by another force, must necessarily cease to live when the transmission of this motion to it has ceased. Consequently the only thing that never ceases to move is something which has the power of starting up motion all *on its own*—it can go on moving because its power to achieve motion depends on itself and itself alone. This, therefore, it must be concluded, is the source and first principle of motion for all things that move.

'Being the first principle, it never had a beginning: since the first principle is what everything else has originated from, it cannot possibly have originated from anything itself. For if it owed its origin to something else, it could not be described as the first principle.

'And since it never had a beginning it will never have an end. For if the first principle were destroyed it could never be reborn from any other source and would no longer be able to create things on its own account—which is obviously what the first principle has to do.

'The beginning of all movement, then, comes from that which has set itself in motion: which can neither be born nor die. For if that were not so, one would have to envisage the entire heavens and all things that have ever been created crashing down and coming to an end—for that is what would happen if the force generating their motion were taken away from them.

'Since, therefore, it is plain that the self-moving principle is eternal, the same must evidently apply to the human soul. For unlike lifeless objects which can only be set in motion from outside, the soul, by its very essence and nature, is a living thing such as can only derive its life and motion from within itself. And since, uniquely, it possesses this characteristic of self-impulsion, surely it has no beginning, and lives for ever.

'Use this eternal force, therefore, for the most splendid deeds it is in you to achieve! And the very best deeds are those which serve your country. A soul devoted to such pursuits will find it easiest of all to soar upwards to this place, which is its proper habitation and home.[26] And its flight will be all the more rapid if already during the period of its confinement within the body it has ranged freely abroad, and, by contemplating what lies outside itself, has contrived to detach itself from the body to the greatest possible degree.

'When, on the other hand, a man has failed to do this, and has abandoned himself instead to bodily indulgence and become its slave, letting the passions which serve pleasure impel him to flout the laws both of gods and of men, his soul, after departing from his body, hovers about close to the earth. Nor does it return to this place until many ages of torment have been undergone.'[27]

Then Africanus vanished; and I awoke from my sleep.

EXPLANATORY NOTES

1. Manius Manilius, consul in 149 B.C., was in command of the Roman force which besieged Carthage at the beginning of the Third Punic War. King Masinissa of Numidia (eastern Algeria) had helped the elder Scipio Africanus to win his decisive victory in the Second Punic War (at Zama in 203). In 150 Masinissa goaded the Carthaginians to attack him, thus provoking the Romans to intervene on his side and start the Third Punic War. He died in 149.

2. The peoples of north Africa paid special attention to the worship of the Sun which played so great a art in current Mediterranean religion (p. 338) [of original text].

3. For the Scipio family see Genealogical Table (II), p. 361 [of original text].

4. A reference to a passage in the *Annals* of Ennius (239–169 B.C.); elsewhere Cicero quotes his actual words. It was said that Ennius believed himself to be a reincarnation of Homer.

5. In fact, however, the younger Scipio did not know his older relation, since he was born in about the year of the elder Scipio's death (184).

6. The younger Scipio was consul in 147 B.C., destroyed Carthage in 146, held the censorship in 142, headed a delegation in the eastern Mediterranean in c. 140–138, was consul for the second time in 134, and destroyed Numantia in Spain in 133. The grandson to whom the elder Scipio refers is the tribune Tiberius Gracchus, who was killed in the same year (p. 199 [of original text]). Scipio's Triumph was in 132.

7. The idea of 'perfect' numbers went back to Pythagoras (p. 22 [of original text]). There are various contradictory explanations why seven and eight were perfect.

8. After the death of Tiberius Gracchus the younger Scipio had stepped in to check Tiberius's 'democratic' followers, who were trying to implement their dead leader's land law. The Italian allies resented the law and appealed to Scipio in 129. When Scipio died later in the year, there were rumours of foul play (p. 182 [of original text]), and the names of Tiberius's mother Cornelia, his sister Sempronia and his brother Gaius were among those mentioned.

9. For Gaius Laelius, who was one of the spokesmen in *On the State* see *On Friendship*.

10. An echo of Plato. For the insistence of the Stoics on the unity of the divine and human mind, see p. 26 [of original text].

11. Lucius Aemilius Paullus Macedonicus, consul in 182 and again in 168 B.C., when he was victor over King Perseus of Macedonia at Pydna.

12. The Pythagoreans believed that the soul was a fallen divinity confined within the body as a tomb and condemned to a cycle of reincarnation (p. 22 [of original text]).

13. The word *templum* originally meant a region of the sky marked off for purposes of divination, and then it came to signify a sacred space generally.

14. Plato had compared men who commit suicide to soldiers who desert their posts. But for a different view see p. 115 [of original text].

15. The Moon. Anaxagoras of Clazomenae had discovered that its light was reflected.

16. This was the system gradually elaborated by the Pythagoreans, and described by Plato. The seven internal spheres containing the planets were believed to rotate from west to east through the signs of the zodiac, whereas the outermost sphere of fixed stars rotated from, east to west. The reference to Jupiter is based on astrological teaching. In the fourth century B.C. Heraclides of Pontus had classified both Venus and Mercury as satellites of the Sun. The Sun and Moon are counted as planets. Cicero takes the order of the planets from Archimedes and the Chaldaean astrologers, whereas Plato placed the Sun between the Moon and Mercury.

17. The doctrine of the harmony of the spheres (p. 338 [of original text]) may have originated early in the fifth century B.C.. Pythagoras had discovered that the intervals of the musical scale could be expressed as numerical ratios; and later Pythagoreans concluded that the arrangement of the heavens was based on the principles of musical harmony. Venus and Mercury were believed to have the same speed.

18. Catadupa ('thundering falls') is the First Cataract of the Nile at Syene (Assuan). The reference to the mountains is confusing. Pliny the elder and Seneca the younger (first century A.D.) confirmed the deafness of the inhabitants. The Pythagoreans, however, ascribed human inability to catch the music of the spheres to habit.

19. The great stream believed to flow round the earth.

20. The Hindu Kush (Paropamisus, see p. 94 [of original text]).

21. The Stoics (though not Panaetius) believed in this cycle of periodical destruction by flood and then fire (occurring at winter solstice and summer solstice respectively) or by alternate flood and fire. They, attributed the doctrine of conflagration, wrongly, to Heraclitus of Ephesus (c. 500 B.C.), basing it on his belief that the basic world principle is Fire.

22. This is the Great Year, an idea which goes back as far as Hesiod. It was variously estimated as 30,000, 15,000 and 10,800 years, or as 300,000 generations.

23. The traditional date of Romulus's death and departure to heaven, where he became the god Quirinus, was 716 B.C. or 567 years before the date at which Scipio was supposed to be speaking.

24. An echo of Plato, his disciple Xenocrates of Chalcedon (head of the Academy 339–314 B.C.), and the Stoics.

25. The passage that follows is a translation from Plato's *Phaedrus,* 254 C–E.

26. According to Plato political virtue was the highest form of virtue; but philosophical speculation, on which the highest good depended, could only be attained by keeping the soul free from the disturbing influence of the body.

27. Plato estimates this purgatory of the soul at different durations varying between three thousand and ten thousand years.

SOPHOCLES

The Horrible Truth

---

*Sophocles (496–406 B.C.E.), one of the greatest and the most prolific of the
ancient Greek tragedians, a skilled poet and dramatic innovator, also played
a major role in public life. Even in his youth, he led the song of victory in
the celebrations at Athens for the successes in the Persian wars. In 468 B.C.E.,
he won his first victory in the competition for tragic drama, defeating the
great master Aeschylus. He went on to write 123 plays of which only seven
have survived. As a leading citizen from a rich family in a democratic state,
he actively performed his civic duties and rose to the highest positions. He
was treasurer of the Delian League (the states dominated by Athens) in 443
B.C.E. He was twice elected general, the highest post in the state and one that
was given only to people of wide popularity and proven military ability. He
was also priest of the healing god Asclepius and active in discussing and writing about literature. Sophocles introduced the use of a third actor into the
tragic drama, (previously there had been only two on the stage at once),
which made it possible for him to create more complex situations and portray his characters in greater depth. His greatest tragedies, which deal with
the myth of Oedipus (and inspired Freud's idea of the Oedipus complex), are
models of the classical theme of a character going beyond the normal bounds
of human behavior, moved by pride and arrogance (hubris); despite warn-
ings, he persists in his blind pig-headedness (Ate); and so suffers the bitter
punishment of the gods (nemesis). Sophocles' ability to portray the com-
plexities of his characters, and his use of rapid exchange, rhetoric, or sublime
lyric poetry have rarely been excelled. His works have had tremendous
influence on drama, from his time to today.*

*The present selection portrays the horrible culmination of Oedipus's
story, when he finds out that he really did murder his father and marry
his mother.*

"The Horrible Truth," excerpted from *King Oedipus*, reprinted from *The Theban
Plays*, by Sophocles, translated by E.F. Watling. Copyright © 1974 by E.F. Watling.
Reprinted by permission of Penguin Books, Ltd.

OEDIPUS:

My wife, you know the man whom we have sent for. Is that the man
he means?

JOCASTA: (*white with terror*):

What does it matter
What man he means? It makes no difference now . . .
Forget what he has told you . . . It makes no difference.

OEDIPUS:

Nonsense: I must pursue this trail to the end,
Till I have unravelled the mystery of my birth.

JOCASTA:

No! In God's name—if you want to live, this quest
Must not go on. Have I not suffered enough?

OEDIPUS:

There is nothing to fear. Though I be proved slave-born
To the third generation, *your* honour is not impugned.

JOCASTA:

Yet do not do it. I implore you, do not do it.

OEDIPUS:

I must. I cannot leave the truth unknown.

JOCASTA:

I know I am right. I am warning you for your good.

OEDIPUS:

My 'good' has been my bugbear long enough.

JOCASTA:

Doomed man! O never live to learn the truth!

OEDIPUS:

Go, someone; fetch the shepherd. Leave the lady
To enjoy her pride of birth.

JOCASTA:

O lost and damned!
This is my last and only word to you
For ever!

Exit.

CHORUS:

Why has the Queen, sir, left us in such deep passion?
I fear some vile catastrophe will out
From what she dare not tell.

OEDIPUS:

Let all come out,
However vile! However base it be,
I must unlock the secret of my birth.
The woman, with more than woman's pride, is shamed
By my low origin. I am the child of Fortune,
The giver of good, and I shall not be shamed.
She is my mother; my sisters are the Seasons;
My rising and my falling march with theirs.
Born thus, I ask to be no other man
Than that I am, and *will know who I am.*

CHORUS:

If my prophetic eye fails not, tomorrow's moon
Makes known to all the earth
The secret of our master's birth.
Cithaeron's name shall fill
Our song; his father, mother, nurse was she,
And for this boon
To our great King, praised shall Cithaeron be.
Phoebus our Lord, be this according to thy will.

Was this the offspring born of some primeval sprite
By the love-glance beguiled
Of mountain-haunting Pan? Or child
Of Loxias, very son
To our bright God who walks the high grass-lands ?
Did he delight
Cyllene's lord? Did Dionysus' hands
Receive him from a nymph he loved on Helicon?

OEDIPUS:

Elders, I think I see our shepherd approaching.
I guess it is he, though I never set eyes on him.
He and our Corinehian friend are of like age.
And those are my men that bring him. It must be he.
But you could tell more surely, if you know him.

CHORUS:
> Yes, it is he. I know him. Laius' shepherd—
> As good a man as any in his service.

Enter an elderly SHEPHERD, *escorted by attendants.*

OEDIPUS:
> Now good Corinthian, your evidence first —
> Is this the man you spoke of?

MESSENGER:
> This is the man.

OEDIPUS:
> Come now, old shepherd—please to look at me,
> And answer my questions Were you in Laius' service?

SHEPHERD:
> Indeed I was, sir; born and bred, not bought.

OEDIPUS:
> What trade or occupation did you follow?

SHEPHERD:
> The most part of my life a shepherd, sir.

OEDIPUS:
> What part of the country did you mostly work?

SHEPHERD:
> 'Twould be . . . Cithaeron—or somewhere thereabouts.

OEDIPUS:
> Do you remember having seen this man before?

SHEPHERD:
> What man is that, sir? Where would I have seen him?

OEDIPUS:
> This man. Did you ever meet him anywhere?

SHEPHERD:
> I cannot say I did, sir—not to remember.

MESSENGER:
> I am not surprised. I'll jog his memory.
> He won't forget the days when he and I
> Were neighbours on Cithaeron—he with two flocks
> And I with one; three seasons we were there
> From spring to autumn; and I would drive my flock

Back Corinth way for winter, and he to Thebes
To Laius' folds. Was that the way it was?

SHEPHERD:

Ay, that's how it was. 'Tis many years ago.

MESSENGER:

Well then, maybe you remember a baby boy
You gave me, and asked me to rear it as my own?

SHEPHERD (*with frightened eyes*):

What do you mean? What are you asking me to say?

MESSENGER:

Why, my old friend, here stands your baby boy!

SHEPHERD:

Damn you, man, hold your tongue!

OEDIPUS:

Come, come, old fellow;
He speaks more honestly than you, I think.

SHEPHERD:

Why, how have I offended, honourable master?

OEDIPUS:

Not answering straightly his question about that child.

SHEPHERD:

He doesn't know what he is saying. He is making a mistake.

OEDIPUS:

If you won't speak willingly, we must make you speak.

SHEPHERD:

Don't hurt an old man, sir, for the love of God!

OEDIPUS:

Pinion his arms, there!

SHEPHERD:

O sir, why, what is this?
What more do you ask to know?

OEDIPUS:

This child he speaks of
Was it you that gave it to him?

SHEPHERD:

Yes, it was.
I wish I might have died that very day.

OEDIPUS:

As you shall now, unless you tell the truth.

SHEPHERD:

Twill be my death to tell it.

OEDIPUS:

Evasion still!

SHEPHERD:

Have I not said I gave it him? What more?

OEDIPUS:

Where did it come from? Your home or another's?

SHEPHERD:

Not mine. Another man's.

OEDIPUS:

What man? What house?

SHEPHERD:

By all the gods, master, ask me no morel

OEDIPUS:

Answer! If I must speak again, you die!

SHEPHERD:

It was a...child of Laius...house.

OEDIPUS:

A slave?
Or of his own begetting?

SHEPHERD:

Must I tell?

OEDIPUS:

You must. And I must hear.

SHEPHERD:

IT WAS HIS CHILD,
They said. Your lady could tell the truth of it.

OEDIPUS:

She gave it you?

SHEPHERD:

Yes, master.

OEDIPUS:

To what purpose?

SHEPHERD:
  To be destroyed.
OEDIPUS:
  The child she bore!
SHEPHERD:
  Yes, master.
  They said 'twas on account of some wicked spell.
OEDIPUS:
  What spell?
SHEPHERD:
  Saying the child should kill its father.
OEDIPUS:
  In God's name, what made you give it to this man?
SHEPHERD:
  I hadn't the heart to destroy it, master. I thought
  'He will take it away to another country, his home'.
  He took it and saved its life—to come to this!
  If you are the man, O then your life is lost!
OEDIPUS:
  Alas! All out! All known, no more concealment!
  O Light! May I never look on you again,
  Revealed as I am, sinful in my begetting,
  Sinful in marriage, sinful in shedding of blood!

Exit.

The MESSENGER *and* SHEPHERD *depart.*

CHORUS:
All the generations of mortal man add up to nothing!
Show me the man whose happiness was anything more than illusion
Followed by disillusion.
Here is the instance, here is Oedipus, here is the reason
Why I will call no mortal creature happy.

With what supreme sureness of aim he winged his quarry;
Grasped every prize, by Zeus! once he had drowned the She-devil,
The Claw-foot Lady.
He was our bastion against disaster, our honoured King;
All Thebes was proud of the majesty of his name.

And now, where is a more heart-rending story of affliction?
Where a more awful swerve into the arms of torment?
O Oedipus, that proud head!
When the same bosom enfolded the son and the father,
Could not the engendering clay have shouted aloud its indignation?

Time sees all; and now he has found you, when you least expected it;
Has found you and judged that marriage-mockery, bride-groom-son!
This is your elegy:
I wish I had never seen you, offspring of Laius,
Yesterday my morning of light, now my night of endless darkness!

. . .

EXPLANATORY NOTES

1. *What does it matter?* At what point in the scene does Jocasta guess the whole truth? 'Cithaeron', 'ankles', 'shepherd', have driven daggers into her heart, and she is now at the extremity of her endurance.
2. *Chorus:* suspecting nothing but good in the discovery, or seeking to put the most hopeful construction on it, they anticipate a romantic and supernatural explanation. Oedipus and the Corinthian presumably remain on the stage during these lines Cyllene's lord: Hermes.

ARISTOPHANES

The Women Go on Strike

Aristophanes (c. 457–385 B.C.E.), the greatest of the ancient comic drama-
tists, was an Athenian from a respectable family. Details of his life are
unknown, but he clearly moved in the highest political and intellectual cir-
cles. He was a friend of Plato and is portrayed sympathetically in that
philosopher's Symposium, *where he discourses on the nature of love. Aris-*
tophanes is best known however for his plays, of which eleven out of more
than forty have survived. They were produced between 425 and 388 B.C.E.,
a time of great transitions in Athens. When Aristophanes was born, Athens
was at its height, the richest and most powerful city in Greece. He lived to
see it involved in a disastrous war with Sparta (431–404 B.C.E.), the Pelo-
ponnesian War, that brought eventual defeat and a series of revolutions.
War, peace, and politics therefore are constant themes of these comedies.

Aristophanes was a conservative, who looked back to the glorious days
before the war, but never uncritically. Since he lived in a democracy that
allowed free speech, he outspokenly attacked its political leaders, mocks
corruption, and frequently expressed the universal longing for peace. At
the same time, he was an incisive literary and social critic, who lam-
pooned the writers and philosophers of the day, especially any he con-
sidered to be corrupting established moral values. His weapons, which
struck rich and poor alike, were satire and a humor that ranges from the
subtle to the scatological. He was one of the leading literary figures of his
time and has never lost his popularity.

In this scene, from one of his three plays that feature women, Aris-
tophanes portrays the women refusing sex to their husbands as a way of
bringing an end to the war.

MYRRHINE: Yes, dear, tell us what this important business is.

LYSISTRATA: I will tell you. But before I do, I want to ask you just one
little question.

MYRRHINE: By all means.

LYSISTRATA: The fathers of your children—don't you miss them when they're away at the war? I know not one of you has a husband at home.

CALONICE: I know, my dear. My husband has been away for five months, five months, my dear, in Thrace I think, keeping an eye on our general there.[1]

MYRRHINE: And mine has been in Pylos[2] for the last seven months.

LAMPITO: And as for my mon, if he ever turns up at home, it's anely to pit a new strap on his shield and fly off again.

LYSISTRATA: That's what it's like. There isn't anyone even to have an affair with—not a sausage! Talking of which, now the Milesians have rebelled, we can't even get our six-inch Ladies' Comforters which we used to keep as leather rations for when all else failed. Well then, if I found a way to do it, would you be prepared to join with me in stopping the war?

MYRRHINE: By the Holy Twain,[3] I would! Even if I had to take off my cloak this very day and—drink!

CALONICE: And so would I—even if I had to cut myself in two, like a flatfish, and give half of myself for the cause.

LAMPITO: And I too, if I had tae climb tae the top o' Taygetus,[4] so I cuid see the licht o' peace whenas I got there.

LYSISTRATA: Then I will tell you my plan: there is no need to keep it back. Ladies, if we want to force our husbands to make peace, we must give up—[*She hesitates.*]

CALONICE: What must we give up? Go on.

LYSISTRATA: Then you'll do it?

CALONICE: If need be, we'll lay down our lives for it.

LYSISTRATA: Very well then. We must give up—sex.

[*Strong murmurs of disapproval, shaking of heads, etc.
Several of the company begin to walk off.*]

Why are you turning away from me? Where are you going? What's all this pursing of lips and shaking of heads mean? You're all going pale—I can see tears! Will you do it or won't you? Answer!

MYRRHINE: I won't do it. Better to let the war go on.

CALONICE: I won't do it either. Let the war go on.

LYSISTRATA: Weren't you the flatfish who was ready to cut herself in half a moment ago?

CALONICE: I still am! I'll do that, or walk through the fire, or anything—but give up sex, never! Lysistrata, darling, there's just nothing like it.

LYSISTRATA [*to* MYRRHINE]: How about you?

MYRRHINE: I'd rather walk through the fire too!

LYSISTRATA: I didn't know we women were so beyond redemption. The tragic poets are right about us after all: all we're interested in is having our fun and then getting rid of the baby. My Spartan friend, will you join me? Even if it's just the two of us, we might yet succeed.

LAMPITO: Well—it's a sair thing, the dear knows, for a woman tae sleep alone wi'oot a prick—but we maun do it, for the sake of peace.

LYSISTRATA [*enthusiastically embracing her*]: Lampito, darling, you're the only real woman among the lot of them.

CALONICE: But look, suppose we did give up—what you said—which may heaven forbid—but if we did, how would that help to end the war?

LYSISTRATA: How? Well, just imagine: we're at home, beautifully made up, wearing our sheerest lawn negligées and nothing underneath, and with our—our triangles carefully plucked; and the men are all like ramrods and can't wait to leap into bed, and then we absolutely refuse—that'll make them make peace soon enough, you'll see.

LAMPITO: Din ye mind how Menelaus threw away his sword when he saw but a glimpse of Helen's breasties?[5]

CALONICE: But look, what if they divorce us?

LYSISTRATA: Well, that wouldn't help them much, would it? Like Pherecrates[6] says, it would be no more use than skinning the same dog twice.

CALONICE [*misunderstanding her*]: You know what you can do with those imitation dogskin things. Anyway, what if they take hold of us and drag us into the bedroom by force?

LYSISTRATA: Cling to the door.

CALONICE: And if they hit us and force us to let go?

LYSISTRATA: Why, in that case you've got to be as damned unresponsive as possible. There's no pleasure in it if they have to use force and give pain. They'll give up trying soon enough. And no man is ever happy if he can't please his woman.

CALONICE: Well—if you really think it's a good idea—we agree.

LAMPITO: And we'll do the same thing and see if we can persuade oor men tae mak peace and mean it. But I dinna see how ye're ever going to get the Athenian riff-raff tae see sense.

LYSISTRATA: We will, you'll see.

LAMPITO: Not sae lang as their warships have sails and they have that bottomless fund o' money in Athena's temple.

LYSISTRATA: Oh, don't think we haven't seen to that! We're going to occupy the Acropolis. While we take care of the sexual side of things, so to speak, all the older women have been instructed to seize the Acropolis under pretence of going to make sacrifices.

LAMPITO: A guid notion; it soonds as if it will wark.

LYSISTRATA: Well then, Lampito, why don't we confirm the whole thing now by taking an oath?

LAMPITO: Tell us the aith and we'll sweir.

LYSISTRATA: Well spoken. Officeress!

[*Enter a* SCYTHIAN POLICEWOMAN, *with bow and arrows and a shield. She stares open-eyed about her.*]

Stop gawping like an idiot! Put your shield face down in front of you—so. Now someone give me the limbs of the sacrificial victim.

[*The severed limbs of a ram are handed to her.*]

CALONICE [*interrupting*]: Lysistrata, what sort of oath is this you're giving us?

LYSISTRATA: Why, the one that Aeschylus talks about somewhere, 'filling a shield with blood of fleecy sheep'.[7]

CALONICE: But Lysistrata, this oath is about peace! We can't possibly take it over a shield.

LYSISTRATA: What do you suggest, then?

CALONICE: Well, if we could slaughter a full-grown cock . . .

LYSISTRATA: You've got a one-track mind.

CALONICE: Well, how *are* you going to take the oath, then?

MYRRHINE: I've got an idea, if you like. Put a large black cup on the ground, and pour some Thasian vine's blood[8] into it, and then we can swear over the cup that we won't—put any water in.

LAMPITO: Whew, that's the kind of aith I like!

LYSISTRATA: A cup and a wine-jar, somebody!

[*These are brought. Both are of enormous size.*]

CALONICE: My dears, isn't it a whopper? It cheers you up even to touch it!

LYSISTRATA: Put the cup down, and take up the sacrificial jar.

[*The attendant elevates the jar, and* LYSISTRATA *stretches out her hands towards it and prays.*]

O holy Goddess of Persuasion, and thou, O Lady of the Loving Cup, receive with favour this sacrifice from your servants the women of Greece. Amen.

[*The attendant begins to pour the wine into the cup.*]

CALONICE: What lovely red blood! And how well it flows!

LAMPITO: And how sweet it smells forby, by Castor!

MYRRHINE [*pushing to the front*]: Let me take the oath first!

CALONICE: Not unless you draw the first lot, you don't!

LYSISTRATA: Lampito and all of you, take hold of the cup. One of you repeat the oath after me, and everybody else signify assent.

[*All put their hands on the cup.* CALONICE *comes forward; and as she repeats each line of the following oath, all the others bow their heads.*]

LYSISTRATA: I will not allow either boyfriend or husband—

CALONICE: I will not allow either boyfriend or husband—

LYSISTRATA: —to approach me in an erect condition. Go on!

CALONICE: —to approach me in an—erect—condition—help, Lysistrata, my knees are giving way! [*She nearly faints, but recovers herself.*]

LYSISTRATA: And I will live at home without any sexual activity—

CALONICE: And I will live at home without any sexual activity—

LYSISTRATA: —wearing my best make-up and my most seductive dresses—

CALONICE: —wearing my best make-up and my most seductive dresses—

LYSISTRATA: —to inflame my husband's ardour.

CALONICE: —to inflame my husband's ardour.

LYSISTRATA: But I will never willingly yield to his desires.

CALONICE: But I will never willingly yield to his desires.

LYSISTRATA: And should he force me against my will—

CALONICE: And should he force me against my will—

LYSISTRATA: I will be wholly passive and unresponsive.
CALONICE: I will be wholly passive and unresponsive.
LYSISTRATA: I will not raise my legs towards the ceiling.
CALONICE: I will not raise my legs towards the ceiling.
LYSISTRATA: I will not take up the lion-on-a-cheese-grater position.
CALONICE: I will not take up the lion-on-a-cheese-grater position.
LYSISTRATA: As I drink from this cup, so will I abide by this oath.
CALONICE: As I drink from this cup, so will I abide by this oath.
LYSISTRATA: And if I do not abide by it, may the cup prove to be filled with water.
CALONICE: And if I do not abide by it, may the cup prove to be filled with water.
LYSISTRATA [*to the others*]: Do you all join in this oath?
ALL: We do.

EXPLANATORY NOTES

1. The Greek text names him as Eucrates; it seems he was suspected of intriguing with the enemy.
2. Still in Athenian hands.
3. For an Athenian, this meant Demeter and her daughter Persephone.
4. The highest mountain in Laconia.
5. After the capture of Troy, when he had intended to kill her for her infidelity.
6. A contemporary comic poet.
7. From *The Seven against Thebes*—except that in that play it was bull's blood that was used. That would have been too masculine for Lysistrata.
8. An attempt to disguise the fact that she was proposing to use wine instead of the regulation blood.

ANNA COMNENA

Byzantium Meets the Crusaders

Anna Comnena (1083–1153) was the highly educated and ambitious daughter of a successful Byzantine emperor, Alexius Comnenus (who ruled from 1081–1118). Raised at the court, she studied literature and philosophy and developed a real understanding of military matters. When she was very young, she was engaged to the son of a former emperor who was next in line for the throne. When Alexius had a son, however, Anna's hopes were replaced by bitterness. After her husband's early death, Anna married an aristocrat, Nicephorus Bryennius, who wrote a history of his own times. When Nicephorus was also named Caesar, second only to the emperor, it seemed that Anna might after all become an empress, but her hated brother John Comnenus (who ruled from 1118–1143) succeeded. After Anna was involved in two plots to murder him, she was exiled to a monastery, where she spent the last decades of her life, much of it devoted to writing a history in praise of her father. Her work stresses the campaigns of Alexius and reveals the highly negative Byzantine view of the Crusaders who passed through his empire.

This selection gives the Byzantines' first impressions of the unwelcome arrival of the crusading forces.

He had no time to relax before he heard a rumour that countless Frankish armies were approaching. He dreaded their arrival, knowing as he did their uncontrollable passion, their erratic character and their irresolution, not to mention the other peculiar traits of the Kelt, with their inevitable consequences: their greed for money, for example, which always led them, it seemed, to break their own agreements without scruple for any chance reason. He had consistently heard this said of them and it was abundantly justified. So far from despairing, however, he made every effort to prepare for war if need arose. What actually happened was more far-reaching and terrible than rumour suggested, for the whole of the west and all the barbarians who lived between the Adriatic and the Straits of Gibraltar migrated in a body to Asia, marching across Europe country by country with all their households. The reason for this mass-movement is to be found more or less in the following events. A certain Kelt, called Peter, with the surname Koukoupetros,[1] left to worship at the Holy Sepulchre and after suffering much ill-treatment at the hands of the Turks and Saracens who were plundering the whole of Asia, he returned home with difficulty. Unable to admit defeat, he wanted to make a second attempt by the same route, but realizing the folly of trying to do this alone (worse things might happen to him) he worked out a clever scheme. He decided to preach in all the Latin countries. A divine voice, he said, commanded him to proclaim to all the counts in France that all should depart from their homes, set out to worship at the Holy Shrine and with all their soul and might strive to liberate Jerusalem from the Agarenes.[2] Surprisingly, he was successful. It was as if he had inspired every heart with some divine oracle. Kelts assembled from all parts, one after another, with arms and horses and all the other equipment for war. Full of enthusiasm and ardour they thronged every highway, and with these warriors came a host of civilians, outnumbering the sand of the sea shore or the stars of heaven, carrying palms and bearing crosses on their shoulders. There were women and children, too, who had left their own countries. Like tributaries joining a river from all directions they streamed towards us in full force, mostly through Dacia. The arrival of this mighty host was preceded by locusts, which abstained from the wheat but made frightful inroads on the vines. The prophets of those days interpreted this as a sign that the Keltic army would refrain from interfering in the affairs of Christians but bring dreadful affliction on the barbarian Ishmaelites, who were the slaves of drunkenness and wine and Dionysos. The Ishmaelites are indeed dominated by Dionysos and Eros; they indulge readily in every kind of sexual licence, and if they are circumcised in the flesh they are certainly not so in their passions. In fact, the Ishmaelites are nothing more than slaves—trebly slaves—of the vices of Aphrodite[3]. Hence they reverence and worship Astarte and Ashtaroth, and in their land the figure of the moon and the golden image of Chobar[4] are considered of major importance. Corn, because it is not heady and at the same time is most nourishing, has been accepted as the symbol of Christianity. In the light of this the diviners interpreted the references to vines and wheat. So much for the prophecies. The incidents of the barbarians' advance followed in the order I have given and there was something strange about it, which intelligent people at least would notice. The multitudes did not arrive at the same moment, nor even by the same route—how could they cross the Adriatic *en masse* after setting out from different countries in such great numbers?—but they made the voyage in separate groups, some first, some in a second party and others after them in order, until all had arrived, and then they began their march across Epirus. Each army as I have said, was preceded by a plague of locusts, so that everyone, having observed the phenomenon several times, came to recognize locusts as the forerunners of Frankish battalions. They had already begun to cross the Straits of Lombardy in small groups when the emperor summoned certain leaders of the Roman forces and sent them to the area round Dyrrachium and Avlona, with instructions to receive the voyagers kindly and export from all countries abundant supplies for them along their route; then to watch them carefully and follow, so that if they saw them making raids or running off to plunder the neighbouring districts, they could check them by light skirmishes. These officers were accompanied by interpreters who understood the Latin language; their duty was to quell any incipient trouble between natives and pilgrims.

EXPLANATORY NOTES

1. Steven Runciman suggests that *chtou* or *kiokio* (Picard words) meaning 'little' may be the origin of this name. He was known to his contemporaries as Peter the Little but we know him as Peter the Hermit.
2. Another name (like Ishmaelites) for the Turks, i.e. descendants of Hagar.
3. Anna is unfair to the Mohammedans, but other authors accuse them of excessive wine-bibbing. She seems to be unaware that Aphrodite, Astarte and Ashtaroth are identical goddesses of love.
4. Chobar (or Chabar), meaning 'The Great', was the name given by the Saracens to the goddess of love. 'Moon' should perhaps be supplanted by 'star' (the Greek *astron* may refer to Lucifer). . . .

GREGORY OF TOURS

The Life of Clovis

Gregory of Tours was an important bishop and one of the best-known historians of the early Middle Ages. Born around 539 in the Auvergne region of what is now France, Gregory came from a distinguished, aristocratic family whose members included wealthy landowners and Roman senators on both his mother's and father's side. The rise of Christianity added ecclesiastical prestige to the family's political and economic status, and Gregory could claim all but five of his eighteen predecessors as bishop of Tours as blood relatives. Attaining the rank of bishop in 573, Gregory spent the remaining twenty-one years of his life presiding over the ecclesiastical welfare of Tours and surrounding cities. Although he probably never left his native Gaul, Gregory traveled widely within its limits, while his office and family connections ensured his place in the tangled web of contemporary Merovingian politics. But Gregory is best known today as the author of The History of the Franks, *the longest and most important of his written works; beyond history, these include saints' lives, miracle stories, a biblical commentary, and a treatise on church offices.*

Gregory began to write his History *soon after he became bishop. Its ten books remain one of the most important sources for the history of the Frankish kingdom, and Gregory's detailed narrative of events in his own era (Books 5–10) is an unparalleled source for sixth century Merovingian Gaul. Earlier books in the* History *rely on disparate sources for their information, yet all parts of the work reveal the author's concern for historical accuracy, narrative flair, and a direct, even plain, literary style. The violent and shifting world of contemporary politics permeates the* History's *last six books, though Gregory included numerous holy men and their miracles along with his kings, queens, and warriors. And if he frequently condemned the anarchic brutality he found around him, Gregory seems to have expected some violence as a matter of course from those who wielded secular power. The present selection, taken from Gregory's account of Clovis I, founder of the Frankish kingdom, describes the great king's momentous conversion from paganism to Christianity at the urging of his wife, Clotild. The importance of Clovis's conversion is difficult to overestimate, especially since he became a Catholic, rather than an Arian, Christian and*

*thus helped ensure Rome's eventual triumph in the Germanic kingdoms of
the West.*

---

27.   The next thing which happened was that Childeric died. His son
Clovis replaced him on the throne. In the fifth year of his reign Syagrius,
the King of the Romans[1] and the son of Aegidius, was living in the city
of Soissons, where Aegidius himself used to have his residence. Clovis
marched against him with his blood-relation Ragnachar, who also had
high authority, and challenged him to come out to fight. Syagrius did not
hesitate to do so, for he was not afraid of Clovis. They fought each other
and the army of Syagrius was annihilated. He fled and made his way as
quickly as he could to King Alaric II in Toulouse. Clovis summoned
Alaric to surrender the fugitive, informing him that he would attack him
in his turn for having given Syagrius refuge. Alaric was afraid to incur
the wrath of the Franks for the sake of Syagrius and handed him over
bound to the envoys, for the Goths are a timorous race. When Clovis
had Syagrius in his power he ordered him to be imprisoned. As soon as
he had seized the kingdom of Syagrius he had him killed in secret.

   At that time many churches were plundered by the troops of Clovis,
for he still held fast to his pagan idolatries. The soldiers had stolen an
ewer of great size and wondrous workmanship, together with many
other precious objects used in the church service. The bishop of the
church in question sent messengers to the King to beg that, even if he
would not hand back any of the other sacred vessels, this ewer at least
might be restored to the church. The King listened to them and replied:
'Follow me to Soissons, where all the objects which we have seized are
to be distributed. If this vessel for which your bishop is asking falls to
my share, I will meet his wishes.' They came to Soissons and all the
booty was placed in a heap before them. King Clovis addressed his men
as follows, pointing to the vessel in question: 'I put it to you, my lusty
freebooters, that you should agree here and now to grant me that ewer
over and above my normal share.' They listened to what he said and the
more rational among them answered: 'Everything in front of us is yours,
noble King, for our very persons are yours to command. Do exactly as
you wish, for there is none among us who has the power to say you nay.'
As they spoke one of their number, a feckless fellow, greedy and prompt
to anger, raised his battle-axe and struck the ewer. 'You shall have none
of this booty,' he shouted, 'except your fair share.' All present were
astounded at his words. The King hid his chagrin under a pretence of

long-suffering patience. He took the vessel and handed it over to the envoy of the church; but in his heart he resented what had happened. At the end of that year he ordered the entire army to assemble on the parade-ground, so that he could examine the state of their equipment. The King went round inspecting them all and came finally to the man who had struck the ewer. 'No other man has equipment in such a bad state as yours,' said he. 'Your javelin is in a shocking condition, and so are your sword and your axe!' He seized the man's axe and threw it on the ground. As the soldier bent forward to pick up his weapon, King Clovis raised his own battle-axe in the air and split his skull with it. 'That is what you did to my ewer in Soissons,' he shouted. The man fell dead. Clovis ordered the others to dismiss. They were filled with mighty dread at what he had done. Clovis waged many wars and won many victories. In the tenth year of his reign he invaded the Thuringians and subjected them to his rule.

28.   The King of the Burgundes was called Gundioc: he was of the family of that King Athanaric who persecuted the Christians and about whom I have told you. He had four sons: Gundobad, Godigisel, Chilperic and Gundomar. Gundobad killed his brother Chilperic and drowned Chilperic's wife after tying a stone round her neck. He drove Chilperic's two daughters into exile: the elder, whose name was Chroma, became a religious, and the younger was called Clotild. Clovis often sent envoys to Burgundy and they saw the girl Clotild. They observed that she was an elegant young woman and clever for her years, and they discovered that she was of the blood royal. They reported all this to Clovis and he immediately sent more messengers to Gundobad to ask for her hand in marriage. Gundobad was afraid to refuse and he handed Clotild over to them. They took her back with them, and presented her to their King. Clovis already had a son called Theuderic by one of his mistresses, but he was delighted when he saw Clotild and made her his wife.

29.   The first child which Clotild bore for Clovis was a son. She wanted to have her baby baptized, and she kept on urging her husband to agree to this. 'The gods whom you worship are no good,' she would say. 'They haven't even been able to help themselves, let alone others. They are carved out of stone or wood or some old piece of metal. The very names which you have given them were the names of men, not of gods. Take your Saturn, for example, who ran away from his own son to avoid being exiled from his kingdom, or so they say; and Jupiter, that obscene perpetrator of all sorts of mucky deeds, who couldn't keep his hands off

other men, who had his fun with all his female relatives and couldn't even refrain from intercourse with his own sister,

'... Jovisque
Et soror et coniunx,'[2]

to quote her own words. What have Mars and Mercury ever done for anyone? They may have been endowed with magic arts, but they were certainly not worthy of being called divine. You ought instead to worship Him who created at a word and out of nothing heaven, and earth, the sea and all that therein is,[3] who made the sun to shine, who lit the sky with stars, who peopled the water with fish, the earth with beasts, the sky with flying creatures, at whose nod the fields became fair with fruits, the trees with apples, the vines with grapes, by whose hand the race of man was made, by whose gift all creation is constrained to serve in deference and devotion the man He made.' However often the Queen said this, the King came no nearer to belief. 'All these things have been created and produced at the command of *our* gods,' he would answer. 'It is obvious that *your* God can do nothing, and, what is more, there is no proof that he is a God at all.'

The Queen, who was true to her faith, brought her son to be baptized. She ordered the church to be decorated with hangings and curtains, in the hope that the King, who remained stubborn in the face of argument, might be brought to the faith by ceremony. The child was baptized; he was given the name Ingomer; but no sooner had he received baptism than he died in his white robes. Clovis was extremely angry. He began immediately to reproach his Queen. 'If he had been dedicated in the name of my gods,' he said, 'he would have lived without question; but now that he has been baptized in the name of your God he has not been able to live a single day!' 'I give thanks to Almighty God,' replied Clotild, 'the Creator of all things, who has not found me completely unworthy, for He has deigned to welcome to His kingdom a child conceived in my womb. I am not at all cast down in my mind because of what has happened, for I know that my child, who was called away from this world in his white baptismal robes, will be nurtured in the sight of God.'

Some time later Clotild bore a second son. He was baptized Chlodomer. He began to ail and Clovis said: 'What else do you expect? It will happen to him as it happened to his brother: no sooner is he baptized in the name of your Christ than he will die!' Clotild prayed to the Lord and at His command the baby recovered.

30.   Queen Clotild continued to pray that her husband might recognize the true God and give up his idol-worship. Nothing could persuade him

to accept Christianity. Finally war broke out against the Alamanni and in this conflict he was forced by necessity to accept what he had refused of his own free will. It so turned out that when the two armies met on the battlefield there was great slaughter and the troops of Clovis were rapidly being annihilated. He raised his eyes to heaven when he saw this, felt compunction in his heart and was moved to tears. 'Jesus Christ,' he said, 'you who Clotild maintains to be the Son of the living God, you who deign to give help to those in travail and victory to those who trust in you, in faith I beg the glory of your help. If you will give me victory over my enemies, and if I may have evidence of that miraculous power which the people dedicated to your name say that they have experienced, then I will believe in you and I will be baptized in your name. I have called upon my own gods, but, as I see only too clearly, they have no intention of helping me. I therefore cannot believe that they possess any power, for they do not come to the assistance of those who trust in them. I now call upon you. I want to believe in you, but I must first be saved from my enemies.' Even as he said this the Alamanni turned their backs and began to run away. As soon as they saw that their King was killed, they submitted to Clovis. 'We beg you,' they said, 'to put an end to this slaughter. We are prepared to obey you.' Clovis stopped the war. He made a speech in which he called for peace. Then he went home. He told the Queen how he had won a victory by calling on the name of Christ. This happened in the fifteenth year of his reign.

31.   The Queen then ordered Saint Remigius, Bishop of the town of Rheims, to be summoned in secret. She begged him to impart the word of salvation to the King. The Bishop asked Clovis to meet him in private and began to urge him to believe in the true God, Maker of heaven and earth, and to forsake his idols, which were powerless to help him or any-one else. The King replied: 'I have listened to you willingly, holy father. There remains one obstacle. The people under my command will not agree to forsake their gods. I will go and put to them what you have just said to me.' He arranged a meeting with his people, but God in his power had preceded him, and before he could say a word all those pres-ent shouted in unison: 'We will give up worshipping our mortal gods, pious King, and we are prepared to follow the immortal God about whom Remigius preaches.' This news was reported to the Bishop. He was greatly pleased and he ordered the baptismal pool to be made ready. The public squares were draped with coloured cloths, the churches were adorned with white hangings, the baptistry was prepared, sticks of incense gave off clouds of perfume, sweet-smelling candles gleamed bright and the

holy place of baptism was filled with divine fragrance. God filled the hearts of all present with such grace that they imagined themselves to have been transported to some perfumed paradise. King Clovis asked that he might be baptized first by the Bishop.[4] Like some new Constantine he stepped forward to the baptismal pool, ready to wash away the sores of his old leprosy and to be cleansed in flowing water from the sordid stains which he had borne so long. As he advanced for his baptism, the holy man of God addressed him in these pregnant words: 'Bow your head in meekness, Sicamber.[5] Worship what you have burnt, burn what you have been wont to worship.'

Saint Remigius was a bishop of immense learning and a great scholar more than anything else, but he was also famous for his holiness and he was the equal of Saint Silvester for the miracles which he performed. We still have an account of his life, which tells how he raised a man from the dead. King Clovis confessed his belief in God Almighty, three in one. He was baptized in the name of the Father, the Son and the Holy Ghost, and marked in holy chrism with the sign of the Cross of Christ. More than three thousand of his army were baptized at the same time. His sister Albofled was baptized, but she soon after died and was gathered to the Lord. The King grieved over her death, but Saint Remigius sent him a consoling letter which began with these words:

> I am greatly distressed and I share your grief at the loss of your sister of pious memory. We can take consolation in this, that she has met her death in such a way that we can look up to her instead of mourning for her.[6]

Another sister of Clovis, called Lanthechild, was converted at the same time. She had accepted the Arian heresy, but she confessed the tri-une majesty of the Father, the Son and the Holy Ghost, and received the holy chrism.

EXPLANATORY NOTES

1. Syagrius was not King; he was probably Master of the Soldiers.
2. *Aeneid*, 1, 46–7: 'at once sister and wife of Jupiter'.
3. 43. Psalms 146, 6.
4. A.D. 496.
5. The Merovingians claimed to be descended from the Sicambri.
6. The text of this letter still exists.

BEDE

Augustine of Canterbury

The Venerable Bede (672–735) was an Anglo-Saxon monk, scholar, and
theologian who achieved his most lasting fame as the author of the Ecclesiastical History of the English People. The scope and success of this pioneer-
ing work, completed in 731, have earned him the epithet "Father of English
History." Throughout the Middle Ages, however, Bede was better known for
his many scriptural commentaries, covering nearly every book in the Bible.
Dedicated to the monastic life at the age of seven, Bede spent virtually all of
his life at the Northumbrian monasteries of Wearmouth and Jarrow. He
devoted himself to a wide range of scholarship, encompassing not just scripture and theology but also grammar, chronology, and computation. A lifelong champion of the Roman method for calculating the date of Easter,
Bede's Ecclesiastical History and chronological treatises also made the system of reckoning dates according to "the year of our Lord," or A.D., widely
popular. His command of language and literature, along with his skills as a
historian, made him the greatest scholar of his day in the Latin West.
    Bede's modern reputation rests chiefly on the Ecclesiastical History,
though his other works have begun to receive more attention. Covering
English history from Roman times to his own day, the work's five books are
an indispensable source for the conversion of the Anglo-Saxons to Christianity, and indeed for early English history in general. Astonishing miracles
and incredible biographies of holy men and women coexist peacefully with
more conventional historical narrative, for Bede's purpose was a moral one,
tracing the hand of God in unifying the disparate peoples of Britain under
the banner of Catholic (i.e., Roman) Christianity. Like other scholars of his
age Bede wrote in Latin, but he hailed vernacular poets like Caedmon
(d. 680) who helped spread Christianity among the illiterate. Key events and
themes in the Ecclesiastical History include the arrival of Christianity in
England, the mission of St. Augustine of Canterbury (the "Apostle of England"), the Synod of Whitby in 664 (at which the Roman dating of Easter
prevailed over Celtic custom), and the celebration of local miracles and
saints. The present selection describes Augustine of Canterbury's missionary

and organizational activities, from his commissioning by Pope Gregory the Great, to his death in the first decade of the seventh century.

BOOK 1
CHAPTER 23: THE HOLY POPE GREGORY SENDS AUGUSTINE AND OTHER MONKS TO PREACH TO THE ENGLISH NATION, AND ENCOURAGES THEM IN A LETTER TO PERSEVERE IN THEIR MISSION [A.D. 596]

In the year of our Lord 582, Maurice, fifty-fourth in succession from Augustus, became Emperor, and ruled for twenty-one years. In the tenth year of his reign, Gregory, an eminent scholar and administrator, was elected Pontiff of the apostolic Roman see, and ruled it for thirteen years, six months, and ten days. In the fourteenth year of this Emperor, and about the one hundred and fiftieth year after the coming of the English to Britain, Gregory was inspired by God to send his servant Augustine with several other God-fearing monks to preach the word of God to the English nation.[1] Having undertaken this task in obedience to the Pope's command and progressed a short distance on their journey, they became afraid, and began to consider returning home. For they were appalled at the idea of going to a barbarous, fierce, and pagan nation, of whose very language they were ignorant. They unanimously agreed that this was the safest course, and sent back Augustine—who was to be consecrated bishop in the event of their being received by the English—so that he might humbly request the holy Gregory to recall them from so dangerous, arduous, and uncertain a journey. In reply, the Pope wrote them a letter of encouragement, urging them to proceed on their mission to preach God's word, and to trust themselves to his aid. . . .

CHAPTER 25: AUGUSTINE REACHES BRITAIN, AND FIRST PREACHES IN THE ISLE OF THANET BEFORE KING ETHELBERT, WHO GRANTS PERMISSION TO PREACH IN KENT [A.D. 597]

Reassured by the encouragement of the blessed father Gregory, Augustine and his fellow-servants of Christ resumed their work in the word of God, and arrived in Britain. At this time the most powerful king there was Ethelbert, who reigned in Kent and whose domains extended northwards to the river Humber, which forms the boundary between the north and south Angles. To the east of Kent lies the large island of

Thanet, which by English reckoning is six hundred hides in extent; it is separated from the mainland by a waterway about three furlongs broad called the Wantsum, which joins the sea at either end and is fordable only in two places. It was here that God's servant Augustine landed with companions, who are said to have been forty in number. At the direction of blessed Pope Gregory, they had brought interpreters from among the Franks, and they sent these to Ethelbert, saying that they came from Rome bearing very glad news, which certainty assured all who would receive it of eternal joy in heaven and an everlasting kingdom with the living and true God. On receiving this message, the king ordered them to remain in the island where they had landed, and gave directions that they were to be provided with all necessaries until he should decide what action to take. For he had already heard of the Christian religion, having a Christian wife of the Frankish royal house named Bertha, whom he had received from her parents on condition that she should have freedom to hold and practise her faith unhindered with Bishop Liudhard, whom they had sent as her helper in the faith.

After some days, the king came to the island and, sitting down in the open air, summoned Augustine and his companions to an audience. But he took precautions that they should not approach him in a house; for he held an ancient superstition that, if they were practisers of magical arts, they might have opportunity to deceive and master him. But the monks were endowed with power from God, not from the Devil, and approached the king carrying a silver cross as their standard and the likeness of our Lord and Saviour painted on a board. First of all they offered prayer to God, singing a litany for the eternal salvation both of themselves and of those to whom and for whose sake they had come. And when, at the king's command, they had sat down and preached the word of life to the king and his court, the king said: 'Your words and promises are fair indeed; but they are new and uncertain, and I cannot accept them and abandon the age-old beliefs that I have held together with the whole English nation. But since you have travelled far, and I can see you are sincere in your desire to impart to us what you believe to be true and excellent, we will not harm you. We will receive you hospitably and take care to supply you with all that you need; nor will we forbid you to preach and win any people you can to your religion.' The king then granted them a dwelling in the city of Canterbury, which was the chief city of all his realm, and in accordance with his promise he allowed them provisions and did not withdraw their freedom to preach. Tradition says that as they approached the city, bearing the holy cross and the likeness of our great King and Lord Jesus Christ as was their custom, they sang in unison this litany: 'We pray Thee,

O Lord, in all Thy mercy, that Thy wrath and anger may be turned away from this city and from Thy holy house, for we are sinners. Alleluia.'

CHAPTER 26: THE LIFE AND DOCTRINE OF THE PRIMITIVE CHURCH ARE FOLLOWED IN KENT: AUGUSTINE ESTABLISHES HIS EPISCOPAL SEE IN THE KING'S CITY

As soon as they had occupied the house given to them they began to emulate the life of the apostles and the primitive Church. They were constantly at prayer; they fasted and kept vigils; they preached the word of life to whomsoever they could. They regarded worldly things as of little importance, and accepted only the necessities of life from those they taught. They practised what they preached, and were willing to endure any hardship, and even to die for the truth which they proclaimed. Before long a number of heathen, admiring the simplicity of their holy lives and the comfort of their heavenly message, believed and were baptized. On the east side of the city stood an old church, built in honour of Saint Martin during the Roman occupation of Britain, where the Christian queen of whom I have spoken went to pray. Here they first assembled to sing the psalms, to pray, to say Mass, to preach, and to baptize, until the king's own conversion to the Faith gave them greater freedom to preach and to build and restore churches everywhere.

At length the king himself, among others, edified by the pure lives of these holy men and their gladdening promises, the truth of which they confirmed by many miracles, believed and was baptized. Thenceforward, great numbers gathered each day to hear the word of God, forsaking their heathen rites and entering the unity of Christ's holy Church as believers. While the king was pleased at their faith and conversion, it is said that he would not compel anyone to accept Christianity; for he had learned from his instructors and guides to salvation that the service of Christ must be accepted freely and not under compulsion. Nevertheless, he showed greater favour to believers, because they were fellow-citizens of the kingdom of heaven. And it was not long before he granted his teachers in his capital of Canterbury a place of residence appropriate to their station, and gave them possessions of various kinds to supply their wants. . . .

CHAPTER 29: GREGORY SENDS AUGUSTINE THE PALLIUM, A LETTER, AND SEVERAL CLERGY [A.D. 601]

Hearing from Bishop Augustine that he had a rich harvest but few to help him gather it, Pope Gregory sent with his envoys several colleagues and clergy, of whom the principal and most outstanding were Mellitus, Justus, Paulinus, and Rufinianus. They brought with them everything necessary for the worship and service of the Church, including sacred vessels, altar coverings, church ornaments, vestments for priests and clergy, relics of the holy Apostles and martyrs, and many books. Gregory also sent a letter to Augustine, telling him that he had dispatched the *pallium* to him, and giving him directions on the appointment of bishops in Britain. This letter runs as follows:

'To our most reverend and holy brother and fellow-bishop Augustine: Gregory, servant of the servants of God.

'While Almighty God alone can grant His servants the ineffable joys of the kingdom of heaven, it is proper that we should reward them with earthly honours, and encourage them by such recognition to devote themselves to their spiritual labours with redoubled zeal. And since the new Church of the English has now, through the goodness of God and your own efforts, been brought to the grace of God, we grant you the privilege of wearing the *pallium* in that Church whenever you perform the solemnities of the Mass. You are to consecrate twelve bishops in different places, who will be subject to your jurisdiction: the bishop of the city of London will thenceforward be consecrated by his own synod, and will receive the honour of the *pallium* from this apostolic See which, by divine decree, we at present occupy. We wish you also to send a bishop of your own choice to the city of York, and if that city with the adjoining territory accepts the word of God, this bishop is to consecrate twelve other bishops, and hold the dignity of Metropolitan. If we live to see this, we intend to grant him the *pallium* also, but he is to remain subject to your authority. After your death, however, he is to preside over the bishops whom he has consecrated and to be wholly independent of the Bishop of London. Thenceforward, seniority of consecration is to determine whether the Bishop of London or York takes precedence; but they are to consult one another and take united action in all matters concerning the Faith of Christ, and take and execute all decisions without mutual disharmony.

'You, my brother, are to exercise authority in the Name of our Lord and God Jesus Christ both over those bishops whom you shall consecrate, and any who shall be consecrated by the Bishop of York, and also over all the British bishops. Let Your Grace's words and example show them a pattern of right belief and holy life, so that they may execute their office in right belief and practice and, when God wills, attain the kingdom of heaven. God keep you safe, most reverend brother.

'Dated the twenty-second of June, in the nineteenth year of our most pious Lord and Emperor Maurice Tiberius Augustus, and the nineteenth after his Consulship: the fourth indiction.'

...

BOOK 2
CHAPTER 3: AUGUSTINE CONSECRATES MELLITUS AND JUSTUS AS BISHOPS: HIS OWN DEATH [A.D. 604]

In the year of our Lord 604, Augustine, Archbishop of Britain, consecrated two bishops, Mellitus and Justus. Mellitus was appointed to preach in the province of the East Saxons, which is separated from Kent by the river Thames, and bounded on the east by the sea. Its capital is the city of London, which stands on the banks of the Thames, and is a trading centre for many nations who visit it by land and sea. At this time Sabert, Ethelbert's nephew through his sister Ricula, ruled the province under the suzerainty of Ethelbert, who, as already stated, governed all the English peoples as far north as the Humber. When this province too had received the faith through the preaching of Mellitus, King Ethelbert built a church dedicated to the holy Apostle Paul in the city of London, which he appointed as the episcopal see of Mellitus and his successors. Augustine also consecrated Justus as bishop of a Kentish city which the English call Hrofescaestir[2] after an early chieftain named Hrof. This lies nearly twenty-four miles west of Canterbury, and a church in honour of Saint Andrew the Apostle was built here by King Ethelbert, who made many gifts to the bishops of both these churches as well as to Canterbury; he later added lands and property for the maintenance of the bishop's household.

When our father Augustine, the beloved of God, died, his body was laid to rest just outside the church of the holy Apostles Peter and Paul, since the church was not yet completed or consecrated. But as soon as it was dedicated, his body was brought inside and buried in the north chapel with great honour. This is also the last resting-place of all succeeding archbishops except Theodore and Bertwald, whose bodies lie inside the church, no space remaining in the chapel. Almost in the centre of the church stands an altar dedicated in honour of blessed Pope Gregory, at which a priest of the place says solemn mass in their memory each Saturday. On the tomb of Augustine is inscribed this epitaph:

'Here rests the Lord Augustine, first Archbishop of Canterbury, who, having been sent here by blessed Gregory, Pontiff of the City of Rome, and supported by God with miracles, guided King Ethelbert and his people from the worship of idols to the Faith of Christ. He ended the days of his duty in peace, and died on the twenty-sixth day of May in the above King's reign.'[3]

EXPLANATORY NOTES

1. Although earlier chapters provide the general context, this one marks the 'real subject' (Plummer) of Bede's work. Its Kentish inspiration is certain. Some or all of the letters of Gregory used by Bede were inserted at a late stage; but it should be noted that Bede did not use or did not have access to *all* of Gregory's letters which relate to England. These still provide a useful check on, and supplement to Bede: their author died over a century before Bede wrote.
2. Rochester.
3. Bede gives the day of the month, but not the year of Augustine's death, which was between 604 and 609.

FROISSART

Tournament at Saint-Inglevert

Jean Froissart (c. 1337–c. 1410) was a poet, scholar, and author who has also been called "the historian of the Hundred Years War." Born in Valenciennes, in what is now northeast France, Froissart came from a family of businessmen and moneylenders. His talent for poetry, however, soon helped him gain entrance to court life, first in his native county of Hainault and eventually in England and throughout the Netherlands. Froissart first went to England in 1361, where he joined the household of Philippa, Edward III's queen, as a kind of court poet and chronicler. Over the following decades he traveled extensively in Britain and on the Continent, accompanying royal dignitaries on missions of state and diplomacy. When Queen Philippa died in 1369 Froissart was in Brussels, and he spent most of the rest of his life in the Netherlands. While Froissart's career brought him into contact with literary men as eminent as Petrarch and Chaucer, it also offered opportunities to observe firsthand the military and diplomatic battles of the Hundred Years War between England and France. Begun in 1369, Froissart's Chronicles cover the war in some detail, along with many other aspects of European political and social life, and they have ensured his lasting fame.

The scope of the Chronicles is enormous, covering not only the Hundred Years War but all the important events that occurred in England and on the European continent during Froissart's lifetime and a bit before. Froissart made great use of interviews and eyewitnesses to enrich the Chronicles with an extraordinary level of detail, although he also attempted to take a bird's-eye view as an analyst of events and their broader significance. It is not always easy to decide where the facts stop and Froissart's imagination begins, for his interest in character and a good story betrays the outlook of a poet and an author above all; if Froissart was the first great war journalist, he might also be counted among Europe's great historical novelists. Interested above all in acts of daring, chivalry, and courtesy, Froissart's sympathies clearly lay with the elite classes of Europe, their military prowess, their tournaments, and their feasts. This attention to pageantry, daring, and chivalrous behavior is on full display in the present selection, which

---

describes a medieval tournament of the kind that has since captured the western imagination. For this, Froissart himself is largely responsible.

———————

While Charles VI was in the south of France, three French knights, Bouci-caut the younger, Regnault de Roye and Jean de Sempy, had issued a challenge inviting all comers to meet them in a friendly trial of arms near Calais. The challenge was directed particularly at England, with which country a three-year truce had recently been concluded. Part of the formal invitation ran:

'. . . and we beg all those noble knights and foreign squires who are willing to come not to imagine for a moment that we are doing this out of pride, hatred or malice, but in order to have the honour of their company and to get to know them better, a thing which we desire with our whole hearts. And none of our shields shall be covered with iron or steel, nor shall the shields of those who come to joust against us. Nor shall there be any other unfair advantage, fraud, trickery or evil design, nor anything not approved by those appointed by both sides to guard the lists.'

At the beginning of the merry month of May, the three young knights of France named above were fully prepared for the trial of arms they were to hold at Saint-Inglevert and which had been announced in France, England and Scotland. They came first to Boulogne-sur-mer, where they stayed for a certain number of days, and then went on to the Abbey of Saint-Inglevert. There they were delighted to learn that a large number of knights and squires had come across from England to Calais. In order to hurry things forward and let the English know they were ready, they had three large and luxurious crimson tents set up in due form at a spot between Calais and Saint-Inglevert. At the entrance to each tent were hung two shields emblazoned with the arms of the particular knight, one a shield of peace and the other a shield of war.[1] The understanding was that whoever wished to run a course against any of them should touch one of the shields, or send someone to touch it, or both shields if he liked. He would then be provided with the opponent and the choice of joust he had asked for. . . .

On 21 May, in accordance with the proclamation which had been made, the three French knights were in readiness, with their horses saddled and equipped, as the rules of the tournament required. On the same day, all those knights and squires who wished to joust, or to watch the jousting, set out from Calais and rode to the appointed spot, where they drew up on one side of the lists. It was a wide and spacious stretch of ground with a level surface of good grass.

Sir John Holland (Earl of Huntingdon) began by sending one of his squires to knock on the war shield of my lord Boucicaut. Boucicaut came out of his tent in full armour, mounted his horse, and took up a shield and then a stout lance with a good steel point. The two knights rode to their separate ends and, having eyed each other carefully, they clapped spurs to their horses and came together at full speed. Boucicaut hit the Earl of Huntingdon in such a way that he pierced his shield and slid the point of his lance right over his arm without wounding him. Both knights rode on and stopped neatly at the end of their course. This joust was much admired. At the second lance they hit each other slightly, but did no damage, and at the third the horses refused.

The Earl of Huntingdon, who was jousting with relish and had warmed to the work, rode back to his mark and waited for Boucicaut to take up his lance again; but he did not do so and made it clear that he had finished jousting for that day so far as the Earl was concerned. Seeing this, the Earl sent a squire to knock on the war shield of the Lord of Sempy. He, who would never have refused a challenge, immediately came out of his tent, mounted his horse and took up his shield and lance. When the Earl saw that he was ready and eager to joust, he clapped his spurs to his horse, while Sempy did the same. They lowered their lances and came straight at one another, but just as they met, the horses crossed. They hit each other nevertheless, but because of the unfortunate crossing, the Earl was unhelmed. He returned to his own men and was quickly rehelmed and handed his lance. The two knights spurred forward and met this time with straight lances, hitting each other clean and hard on their shields. Both were nearly knocked to the ground, but they gripped their horses with their legs and stayed on. Each went back to his own end to rest a little and get his breath back. Sir John Holland, always eager to perform with honour in the lists, took up his lance again and gripped his shield tight and spurred his horse on. When Sempy saw him coming, he did not hold back but rode towards him in the straightest possible line. The two knights hit each other with their war lances on the steel helms, striking them so clean and hard that sparks flew from them. In this clash Sempy was unhelmed. The two knights passed very briskly on, then rode back each to his own end.

This joust was very highly applauded, and both French and English said that all three knights, the Earl of Huntingdon, my lord Boucicaut and the Lord Sempy, had jousted admirably, without either sparing themselves or causing each other an injury. The Earl of Huntingdon asked to be allowed to run another lance for the love of his lady, but this was not permitted him.

Froissart goes on to describe the whole of the rest of the tournament, encounter by encounter and lance by lance, using very similar terms throughout. In the four days over which the jousts lasted, more than forty challengers measured themselves against the three French knights, who remained unbeaten. In all one hundred and thirty-six lances are described, of which the following are a small further selection.

Next, a gallant knight of great spirit, John of Beaumont in England, came forward and sent a squire to rap on my lord Boucicaut's shield. That night was not slow to respond, for he was already mounted on his horse, having jousted a short time before with Sir Lewis Clifford. He took his shield and his lance and placed himself in position for jousting. The two knights spurred their horses hotly forward and came at each other. Lord Beaumont did not handle his lance well and struck Boucicaut a glancing blow, but Boucicaut struck him squarely on the middle of his shield and knocked him off his horse and then passed on. The English knight got up and, with the help of his men, was put back on his horse. The Lord Sempy then came forward to joust with him. They ran two lances very prettily without hurting one another.

Next came forward Sir Godfrey Seton, a gallant knight and a good jouster. He showed plainly, by the way he sat on his horse holding his lance, that he was eager to joust. He sent one of his squires to rap on the war shield of Sir Regnault de Roye. That knight responded, for he was ready mounted on his horse, with his shield at his neck. He took his lance and put himself in good jousting posture. The two knights spurred forward simultaneously and came together as squarely as they knew how, striking a violent blow on each other's shields. Their lances were stout and did not break, but curved up, and the powerful thrusts by strong arms stopped the horses dead in their tracks. Both knights then went back to their own ends, without dropping their lances, which they carried freely in front of them before putting them again in the rests. Then they spurred their horses, which were good, strong and tough. They came again at each other, but crossed just as they met, through the fault of the horses, not of the riders. As they passed by each other to ride round to their own ends again, they dropped their lances. They were picked up by ready hands and given back to them. When they had them, they put them in the rests and spurred their horses, showing that they did not mean to spare themselves, for they had warmed to the work. The English knight hit Sir Regnault de Roye very hard near the top of his helm, but did no other damage to him; Sir Regnault hit him on the shield with such a firm, powerful thrust, delivered with so strong an arm—for he was one of the strongest and toughest jousters in France at that time and also he was truly in love with a gay and beautiful young lady, and this contributed greatly to his success in all his undertakings—that his lance pierced the left-hand side of the English knight's shield and went straight into his arm. As it did so, the lance broke, the longer part falling to the ground and the shorter part remaining in the shield with the steel point in the arm. Nevertheless, the Englishman completed his ride round and came back very briskly to his own end. His friends attended to him. The lance head was pulled out and the wound staunched and bound up, while Sir Regnault de Roye went back to his people and waited there, leaning on another lance which they had given him.

For this joust Sir Regnault was greatly admired by his own side, and equally by the English. Although he had wounded the other knight, not a single abusive remark was made to him, for such are the hazards of arms. One man comes off well, the other badly. And also they were jousting with the full armament.

An English squire and good jouster called John Savage came forward; he was a squire of honour of the bodyguard of the Earl of Huntingdon. He sent a man to rap on the war shield of Sir Regnault. The knight, who was waiting ready armed inside his tent, came out eager to joust and mounted his horse. His shield was buckled on, he took his lance and placed it in the rest. Both men spurred at full speed towards each other until they met. They hit each other full on the centre of their shields, with such force that one or both must have fallen if the shields had not split.

This was a fine and dangerous encounter, although the jousters suffered no injury. After piercing the shields, their lances glanced off sideways, breaking off about one foot from the blades, which remained fixed in the shields, while the two men passed on with the broken shafts. The onlookers feared that they had wounded each other badly, and each side hurried to their man, but were glad to find that neither had suffered harm. They were told that they had done enough for that day, but John Savage was not satisfied by this, saying that he had not crossed the sea merely to run one lance. When this remark was repeated to Sir Regnault de Roye, he said 'He is quite right. It is proper for him to be fully satisfied either by me or my companions-in-arms.' They were got ready again and given new shields and lances. When each was in position on his mark, they eyed one another and clapped spurs to their horses simultaneously. They lowered their lances as they approached and expected to meet squarely, but were prevented by their horses running across. So they missed with their second lance, to their great annoyance, and returned each to his own end. Their lances, which they had thrown down in disgust, were handed back to them, and they put them in the rests, looked carefully at one another and spurred their horses forward. This time they hit each other on the helms, straight on the eye-slits; the points caught there in such a way that they unhelmed each other as they rode past. It was a fine thrust which all admired. Each returned to his own end. The English went up to John Savage and told him once more that he had done enough for that day and could leave off with honour, and that others besides himself must be given a chance to practise arms. He yielded to this advice, put down his shield and lance and, getting off his courser, mounted a rounsey to watch the others jousting.

Next there came forward a knight from Bohemia, belonging to the Queen of England's personal guard, whose name was Herr Hans. He was considered a good jouster, strong and tough. His arms were argent, three gryphons' feet sable with azure claws. When he came into the lists, he was asked which of the three knights he wished to joust against. He said, Boucicaut. An English squire was sent, as the rules required, to knock on my lord Boucicaut's war shield. This knight, being ready armed and mounted, duly responded to the challenge. His shield was buckled on, he took his lance and placed it in the rest, and looked carefully at the Bohemian knight, who was also in jousting posture with his shield at his neck and his lance in his hand. They spurred their horses hard forward and came together, expecting to hit each other squarely, but this they failed to do. The Bohemian knight dealt a foul blow which was strongly condemned, for he struck my lord Boucicaut's helm with an ugly sideways thrust before riding on. The English saw clearly that he was at fault and knew that he had forfeited his horse and armour if the French insisted on it. The French and English held a long discussion together about that improper thrust, but finally the three knights excused him, from a desire to please the English.

Herr Hans begged to be allowed to run just one more lance and was asked whom he wished to challenge. He sent a squire to rap on the war shield of Sir Regnault de Roye. This knight, who was in his tent and had not yet jousted that day, came out fully armed and said that he would be glad to satisfy him, since such was the agreed procedure. His shield was buckled on, his lance was handed to him. He took it and put it in the rest and looked long and carefully ahead of him, so as to hit the Bohemian fair and square. Both spurred their horses. As they neared each other, they lowered their lances and struck one another full on their shields. Sir Reg-nault de Roye, who was one of the strongest and toughest jousters in France at that time, hit him so hard that he lifted him right out of the saddle and sent him flying to the ground with such force that they thought he was killed. The French knight passed on and rode round to return to his mark. Herr Hans's men got him up with great difficulty and took him back among them. The English were very pleased that he had suffered this defeat, because of the unchivalrous way in which he had jousted on his first course. And need I say that he had no mind to joust again that day?[2]

The jousts ended for that day (Thursday) and no one else came forward from the English side. So the Earl of Huntingdon, the Earl Marshal, Sir Lewis Clifford, Lord Beaumont, Sir John Clynton, Sir Jean d'Aubrecicourt, Sir Thomas Sherborne and all the knights who had jousted during the four days went in a company to the French knights and thanked them warmly for the sport they had had, saying:

'All the knights and squires in our company who wish to joust have done so, so we take our leave of you, for we are returning to Calais and thence to England. We are well aware that anyone else wishing to make a trial of arms against you will find you here for the remainder of the thirty days mentioned in your challenge. Once we are back in England, we assure you that we will inform all the knights and squires whom we meet of this tournament and will request them to come and find you here.'

'Many thanks,' the three knights replied, 'they will be cordially welcomed and provided with a trial of arms, as you have been. And with that we thank you greatly for the courtesy which you have shown us.'

On that peaceful and friendly note the English left the French at the lists of Saint-Inglevert and went back to Calais.

It may be added that, after the English company had taken leave of the French knights, the King of France and the Lord of Garencières, who had been present at the jousts *incognito*, went back for the night to Marquise. Early the next day, Friday, they left there to return to France, riding continually until they reached Creil on the river Oise, where the Queen of France was staying. Very few people except his personal attendants knew where the King had been.

EXPLANATORY NOTES

1. The 'peace' arms sometimes used in tournaments were lighter and less lethal than those used in actual war. This applied particularly to the lance, which

in its 'peace' form had a head consisting of three blunt prongs in place of the sharp-pointed blade of the war lance.

2. The passages given above cover nearly all the incidents and variations of the joust as described by Froissart. A few additional details are contained in these extracts:

As they were nearing each other, both horses swerved away, preventing them from hitting each other with a full thrust. (Sempy and John Russell.)

My lord Boucicaut broke his lance, but the English knight kept his intact and used it well, for he knocked off Boucicaut's heim so violently that the blood gushed from his nose. My lord Boucicaut retired to his tent and did no more jousting that day, for it was getting towards evening. (Boucicaut and Sherborne.)

Sempy unhelmed him so violently that the buckle to which the helm was attached behind broke, and it fell on the grass. (Sempy and Blaket.)

The thrusts were good and much admired, for both were unhelmed, only their caps remaining on their heads. (Boucicaut and William Mascley.)

The force of the thrusts which they delivered on each other's shields lifted their horses' forelegs from the ground and both knights reeled in the saddle. Nevertheless, they rode on. . . . (R. de Roye and Jean d'Aubrecicourt.)

Swinnerton did very well not to fall off. It was quite surprising, for Sir Regnault hit him in such a way that he forced his spine right back on to his horse's crupper. He straightened up very nimbly as they passed by, but lost his lance. (R. de Roye and Swinnerton.)

SNORRI STURLUSON

Gylfaginning

Then spoke Gangleri: 'Have any greater events taken place among the Æsir? It was a very great exploit that Thor achieved on this expedition.'

High replied: 'There are events to be related that would have been thought more significant by the Æsir. And the beginning of this story is that Baldr the Good dreamed great dreams boding peril to his life. And when he told the Æsir the dreams they took counsel together and it was decided to request immunity for Baldr from all kinds of danger, and Frigg received solemn promises so that Baldr should not be harmed by fire and water, iron and all kinds of metal, stones, the earth, trees, diseases, the animals, the birds, poison, snakes. And when this was done and confirmed, then it became an entertainment for Baldr and the Æsir that he should stand up at assemblies and all the others should either shoot at him or strike at him or throw stones at him. But whatever they did he was unharmed, and they all thought this a great glory. But when Loki Laufeyiarson saw this he was not pleased that Baldr was unharmed. He went to Fensalir to Frigg and changed his appearance to that of a woman. Then Frigg asked this woman if she knew what the Æsir were doing at the assembly. She said that everyone was shooting at Baldr, and moreover that he was unharmed. Then said Frigg:

'"Weapons and wood will not hurt Baldr. I have received oaths from them all."

'Then the woman asked: "Have all things sworn oaths not to harm Baldr?"

'Then Frigg replied: "There grows a shoot of a tree to the west of Valhall. It is called mistletoe. It seemed young to me to demand the oath from."

'Straight away the woman disappeared. And Loki took mistletoe and plucked it and went to the assembly. Hod was standing at the edge of the circle of people, for he was blind. Then Loki said to him:

'"Why are you not shooting at Baldr?"

'He replied: "Because I cannot see where Baldr is, and secondly because I have no weapon."

'Then said Loki: "Follow other people's example and do Baldr honour like other people. I will direct you to where he is standing. Shoot at him this stick."

Excerpts from *Edda*, by Snorri Sturluson, translated by Anthony Faulkes, (2002), reprinted by permission of Everyman's Library.

'Hod took the mistletoe and shot at Baldr at Loki's direction. The missile flew through him and he fell dead to the ground, and this was the unluckiest deed ever done among gods and men. When Baldr had fallen, then all the Æsir's tongues failed them, as did their hands for lifting him up, and they all looked at each other and were all of one mind towards the one who had done the deed. But no one could take vengeance, it was a place of such sanctuary. When the Æsir tried to speak then what happened first was that weeping came out, so that none could tell another in words of his grief. But it was Odin who took this injury the hardest in that he had the best idea what great deprivation and loss the death of Baldr would cause the Æsir. And when the gods came to themselves then Frigg spoke, and asked who there was among the Æsir who wished to earn all her love and favour and was willing to ride the road to Hel and try if he could find Baldr, and offer Hel a ransom if she would let Baldr go back to Asgard. Hermod the Bold, Odin's boy, is the name of the one who undertook this journey. Then Odin's horse Sleipnir was fetched and led forward and Hermod mounted this horse and galloped away. So the Æsir took Baldr's body and carried it to the sea. Hringhorni was the name of Baldr's ship. It was the biggest of all ships. This the Æsir planned to launch and perform on it Baldr's funeral. But the ship refused to move. So they sent to Giantland for a giantess called Hyrrokkin. And when she arrived, riding a wolf and using vipers as reins, she dismounted from her steed, and Odin summoned four berserks to look after the mount, and they were unable to hold it without knocking it down. Then Hyrrokkin went to the prow of the boat and pushed it out with the first touch so that flame flew from the rollers and all lands quaked. Then Thor became angry and grasped his hammer and was about to smash her head until all the gods begged for grace for her. Then Baldr's body was carried out on to the ship, and when his wife Nanna Nep's daughter saw this she collapsed with grief and died. She was carried on to the pyre and it was set fire to. Then Thor stood by and consecrated the pyre with Miollnir. But a certain dwarf ran in front of his feet. His name was Lit. Thor kicked at him with his foot and thrust him into the fire and he was burned.

'This burning was attended by beings of many different kinds: firstly to tell of Odin, that with him went Frigg and valkyries and his ravens, while Freyr drove in a chariot with a boar called Gullinbursti or Slidrugtanni. But Heimdall rode a horse called Gulltopp, and Freyia her cats. There came also a great company of frost-giants and mountain-giants. Odin laid on the pyre a gold arm-ring called Draupnir. It afterwards had the property that every ninth night there dripped from it eight gold rings of the same weight. Baldr's horse was led on to the pyre with all its harness. But there is this to tell of Hermod that he rode for nine nights through valleys dark and deep so that he saw nothing until he came to the river Gioll and rode on to Gioll bridge. It is covered with glowing gold. There is a maiden guarding the bridge called Modgud. She asked him his name and lineage and said that the other day there had ridden over the bridge five battalions of dead men.

'"But the bridge resounds no less under just you, and you do not have the colour of dead men. Why are you riding here on the road to Hel?"

'He replied: "I am to ride to Hel to seek Baldr. But have you seen anything of Baldr on the road to Hel?"

'And she said that Baldr had ridden there over Gioll bridge, "but downwards and northwards lies the road to Hel."

'Then Hermod rode on until he came to Hel's gates. Then he dismounted from the horse and tightened its girth, mounted and spurred it on. The horse jumped so hard and over the gate that it came nowhere near. Then Hermod rode up to the hall and dismounted from his horse, went into the hall, saw sitting there in the seat of honour his brother Baldr; and Hermod stayed there the night. In the morning Hermod begged from Hel that Baldr might ride home with him and said what great weeping there was among the Æsir. But Hel said that it must be tested whether Baldr was as beloved as people said in the following way,

'"And if all things in the world, alive and dead, weep for him, then he shall go back to the Æsir, but be kept with Hel if any objects or refuses to weep."

'Then Hermod got up and Baldr went with him out of the hall and took the ring Draupnir and sent it to Odin as a keepsake, and Nanna sent Frigg a linen robe and other gifts too; to Fulla a finger-ring. Then Hermod rode back on his way and came to Asgard and told all the tidings he had seen and heard.

'After this the Æsir sent over all the world messengers to request that Baldr be wept out of Hel. And all did this, the people and animals and the earth and the stones and trees and every metal, just as you will have seen that these things weep when they come out of frost and into heat. When the envoys were travelling back having well fulfilled their errand, they found in a certain cave a giantess sitting. She said her name was Thanks. They bade her weep Baldr out of Hel. She said:

> "Thanks will weep dry tears for Baldr's burial. No good got I from the old one's son either dead or alive. Let Hel hold what she has."

'It is presumed that this was Loki Laufeyiarson, who has done most evil among the Æsir.'

Then spoke Gangleri: 'It was quite an achievement of Loki's when he brought it about first of all that Baldr was killed, and also that he was not redeemed from Hel. But was he punished at all for this?'

High said: 'He was requited for this in such a way that he will not soon forget it. The gods having become as angry with him as one might expect, he ran away and hid in a certain mountain, built a house there with four doors so that he could see out of the house in all directions. But in the daytime he often turned himself into the form of a salmon and hid in a place called Franangr waterfall. Then he pondered what sort of device the Æsir would be likely to think up to catch him in the waterfall. And as he sat in the house he took some linen thread and tied knots in it in the way in which ever since a net has been. A fire was burning in front of him. Then he noticed that the Æsir were only a short distance away from him, and Odin had seen where he was from Hlidskialf. He immediately jumped up and out into the river throwing the net down into the fire. And when the Æsir reached the house then the first to enter was the wisest of all, called Kvasir. And when he saw in the fire the shape in the ashes where the net had burned he realized that it must be a device to catch fish, and told the Æsir. After that they went and made themselves a net just like what they saw in the ashes that Loki had made. And when the net was finished the Æsir went to the river and threw the net into the waterfall. Thor held one end and all the Æsir held the other and they dragged the net. But Loki went along in front and lay down between two stones. They dragged the net over him and could tell there was something live there and went a second time up to the waterfall and threw out the net and weighted it down so heavily that nothing would be able to go underneath. Then Loki went along in front of the net, and when he saw that it was only a short way to the sea then he leaped up over the top of the net and slipped up into the waterfall. This time the Æsir saw where he went, they went back up to the waterfall and divided their party into two groups, and Thor waded along the middle of the river and thus they advanced towards the sea. And when Loki saw there were two alternatives—it was mortal danger to rush into the sea, but so it was also to leap again over the net—and this is what he did, leaped as swiftly as he could over the top of the net. Thor grabbed at him and got his hand round him and he slipped in his hand so that the hand caught hold at the tail. And it is for this reason that the salmon tapers towards the tail.

'Now Loki was captured without quarter and taken to a certain cave. Then they took three stone slabs and set them on edge and knocked a hole in each slab. Then Loki's sons Vali and Nari or Narfi were fetched. The Æsir turned Vali into the form of a wolf and he tore his brother Narfi to pieces. Then the Æsir took his guts and bound Loki with them across the three stones—one under his shoulders, one under his loins, the third under the backs of his knees—and these bonds turned to iron. Then Skadi got a poisonous snake and fixed it up over him so that the poison would drip from the snake into his face. But his wife Sigyn stands next to him holding a basin under the drops of poison. And when the basin is full she goes and pours away the poison, but in the meantime the poison drips into his face. Then he jerks away so hard that the whole earth shakes. That is what you call an earthquake. There he will lie in bonds until Ragnarok.'

Then spoke Gangleri: 'What information is there to be given about Ragnarok? I have not heard tell of this before.'

High said: 'There are many important things to be told about it. First of all that a winter will come called *fimbul*-winter [mighty or mysterious winter]. Then snow will drift from all directions. There will then be great frosts and keen winds. The sun will do no good. There will be three of these winters together and no summer between. But before that there will come three other winters during which there will be great battles throughout the world. Then brothers will kill each other out of greed and no one will show mercy to father or son in killing or breaking the taboos of kinship. Thus it says in *Voluspa*:

> Brothers will fight and kill each other, cousins will break the bonds of their relationship. It will be harsh for heroes, much depravity, age of axes, age of swords, shields cloven, age of winds, age of wolves, until the world is ruined.

Then something will happen that will be thought a most significant event, the wolf will swallow the sun, and people will think this a great disaster. Then the other wolf will catch the moon, and he also will cause much mischief. The stars will disappear from the sky. Then there will take place another event, the whole earth and mountains will shake so much that trees will become uprooted from the earth and the mountains will fall, and all fetters and bonds will snap and break. Then Fenriswolf will get free. Then the ocean will surge up on to the lands because the Midgard serpent will fly into a giant rage and make its way ashore. Then it will also happen that Naglfar will be loosed from its moorings, the ship of that name. It is made of dead people's nails, and it is worth taking care lest anyone die with untrimmed nails, since such a person contributes much material to the ship Naglfar which gods and men wish would take a long time to finish. And in this flood Naglfar will be carried along. There is a giant called Hrym who will captain Naglfar. But Fenriswolf will go with mouth agape and its upper jaw will be against the sky and its lower one against the earth. It would gape wider if there was room. Flames will burn from its eyes and nostrils. The Midgard serpent will spit so much poison that it will bespatter all the sky and sea, and it will be very terrible, and it will be on one side of the wolf. Amid this turmoil the sky will open and from it will ride the sons of Muspell. Surt will ride in front, and both before and behind him there will be burning fire. His sword will be very fine. Light will shine from it more brightly than from the sun. And when they ride over Bifrost it will break, as was said above. Muspell's lads will advance to the field called Vigrid. Then there will also arrive there Fenriswolf and the Midgard serpent. By then Loki will also have arrived there and Hrym and with him all the frost-giants, but with Loki will be all Hel's people. But Muspell's sons will have their own battle array; it will be very bright. The field Vigrid is a hundred leagues in each direction.

'And when these events take place, Heimdall will stand up and blow mightily on Giallarhorn and awaken all the gods and they will hold a parliament together. Then Odin will ride to Mimir's well and consult Mimir on his own and his people's behalf. Then the ash Yggdrasil will shake and nothing will then be unafraid in heaven or on earth. The Æsir will put on their war gear, and so will all the Einheriar, and advance on to the field. Odin will ride in front with golden helmet and fine coat of mail and his spear called Gungnir. He will make for Fenriswolf, and Thor will advance at his side and be unable to aid him because he will have his hands full fighting the Midgard serpent. Freyr will fight Surt and there will be a harsh conflict before Freyr falls. The cause of his death will be that he will be without the good sword that he gave Skirnir. Then will also have got free the dog Garm, which is bound in front of Gnipahellir. This is the most evil creature. He will have a battle with Tyr and they will each be the death of the other. Thor will be victorious over the Midgard serpent and will step away from it nine paces. Then he will fall to the ground dead from the poison which the serpent will spit at him. The wolf will swallow Odin. That will be the cause of his death. And immediately after Vidar will come forward and step with one foot on the lower jaw of the wolf. On this foot he will have a shoe for which the material has been being collected throughout all time: it is the waste pieces that people cut from their shoes at the toe and heel. Therefore anyone that is concerned to give assistance to the Æsir must throw these pieces away. With one hand he will grasp the wolf's upper jaw and tear apart its mouth and this will cause the wolf's death. Loki will have a battle with Heimdall and they will cause each other's death. After that Surt will fling fire over the earth and burn the whole world. Thus it is related in *Voluspa*:

> Loud blows Heimdall, his horn is aloft. Odin speaks with Mim's head. The ash Yggdrasil shakes as it stands, the ancient tree groans, and the giant gets free.

> What is it with the Æsir? What is it with the elves? All Giantland resounds. Æsir are in council. Dwarfs groan before rock doorways, frequenters of rock-walls. Know you yet, or what?

> Hrym drives from the east holding his shield before him, Iormungand writhes in a giant rage. The serpent churns the waves, the eagle will screech with joy, darkly pale it tears corpses, Naglfar is loosed.

> A bark sales from the east, across the sea will come Muspell's troops with Loki at the helm. All the monstrous brood are there with the wolf. In company with them is Byleist's brother.

> Surt travels from the south with the stick-destroyer [fire]. Shines from his sword the sun of the gods of the slain. Rock cliffs crash and troll-wives are abroad, heroes tread the road of Hel and heaven splits.

> Then Hlin's second sorrow come to pass as Odin goes to fight the wolf, and Beli's bright slayer against Surt. There shall fall Frigg's delight.

> Odin's son goes to fight the wolf, Vidar on his way against the slaughterous beast. With his hand he lets his blade pierce Hvedrung's son's heart. So is his father avenged.

> Goes the great son of Hlodyn, dying, to the serpent; who shrinks from no shame. All heroes shall leave the world when Midgard's protector strikes in wrath.

> The sun will go dark, earth sink in the sea. From heaven vanish bright stars. Steam surges and life's warmer [fire], high flame flickers against the very sky.

It also says here:

> There is a field called Vigrid where shall meet in battle Surt and the sweet gods. A hundred leagues each way it is; this field is marked out for them.'

Then spoke Gangleri: 'What will happen then after heaven and earth and all the world is burned and all the gods and all Einheriar and all mankind are dead? You said previously that everyone shall live in some world or other for ever and ever.'

Then said Third: 'There will then be many mansions that are good, and many that are bad. The best place to be in heaven then will be Gimle, and there will be plenty of good drink for those that take pleasure in it in the hall called Brimir. That is also in heaven. That is also a good hall which is situated on Nidafioll, built of red gold. It is called Sindri. In these halls shall dwell good and virtuous people. On Nastrands is a large and unpleasant hall, and its doors face north. It is also woven out of snakes' bodies like a wattled house, and the snakes' heads all face inside the house and spit poison so that rivers of poison flow along the hall, and wading those rivers are oathbreakers and murderers, as it says here:

> I know a hall that stands far from the sun on Nastrand. North face the doors. Poison drops flow in through the smoke-hole. This hall is woven from snakes' backs. There shall wade heavy streams men who are perjured and murderers.

But it is worst in Hvergelmir:

> There Nidhogg torments the bodies of the dead.'

Then spoke Gangleri: 'Will there be any gods alive then? And will there be any kind of earth or sky?'

High said: 'The earth will shoot up out of the sea and will then be green and fair. Crops will grow unsown. Vidar and Vali will be alive, the sea and Surt's fire not having harmed them, and they will dwell on Idavoll, where Asgard had been previously. And then Thor's sons Modi and Magni will arrive, bringing Miollnir. After that Baldr and Hod will arrive from Hel. Then they will all sit down together and talk and discuss their mysteries and speak of the things that had happened in former times, of the Midgard serpent and Fenriswolf. Then they will find in the grass the golden playing pieces that had belonged to the Æsir. Thus it is said:

> Vidar and Vali will dwell in the gods' holy places when Surt's flame goes dark. Modi and Magni shall have Miollnir when Vingnir fights no more.

And in a place called Hoddmimir's holt two people will lie hid during Surt's fire called Life and Leifthrasir, and their food will be the dews of morning. And from these people there will be descended such a great progeny that all the world will be inhabited. As it says here:

> Life and Leifthrasir, and they shall lie hid in Hoddmimir's holt. Dews of morning they shall have as their food, and from them shall grow mankind.

And this also will seem amazing to you, that the sun will have begotten a daughter no less fair than she is, and she shall follow the paths of her mother, as it says here:

A daughter shall Alfrodul bear before Fenrir catches her. She shall ride, when the powers die, the maiden, her mother's road.

And now if you know any more questions to ask further into the future, I do not know where you will find answers, for I have heard no one relate the history of the world any further on in time. And may the knowledge you have gained do you good.'

Next Gangleri heard great noises in every direction from him, and he looked out to one side. And when he looked around further he found he was standing out on open ground, could see no hall and no castle. Then he went off on his way and came back to his kingdom and told of the events he had seen and heard about. And from his account these stories passed from one person to another.

But the Æsir sat down to discuss and hold a conference and went over all these stories that had been told him, and assigned those same names that were mentioned above to the people and places that were there [in Sweden], so that when long periods of time had passed men should not doubt that they were all the same, those Æsir about whom stories were told above and those who were now given the same names. So someone there was given the name Thor—and this means the ancient Thor of the Æsir, that is Oku-Thor—and to him are attributed the exploits which Thor (Hec-tor) performed in Troy. And it is believed that the Turks told tales about Ulysses and that they gave him the name Loki, for the Turks were especially hostile to him.

THE KORAN

The Believer's Duties

The Koran, *according to Muslims, was not written by any human being, but is an eternal creation of God, revealed by him to the prophet Mohammed through the angel Gabriel. For them, it is the direct word of God, an unchangeable holy scripture. It consists of 114 chapters, or surahs, revealed over a long period beginning in 610 C.E., memorized and copied on perishable materials in the prophet's lifetime, and edited by the caliph Othman (644–656 C.E.). The chapters were arranged according to their length, not by subject or date of revelation. Some scholars believe the work actually passed through a long period of oral transmission and that it may have introduced confusion when it was finally written down perhaps a century or more after it was revealed. The prophet Mohammed (570–632 C.E.) was a native of Mecca in Arabia, the member of a poor branch of one of the ruling families. He became a merchant, visited Syria with caravans, and eventually married a rich widow. His travels acquainted him with Judaism and Christianity. In 610 C.E., he received his first revelation and began to preach a new religion, Islam. His success in his native city stirred the hostility of the ruling establishment and in 622 C.E. he was forced to take refuge in the city of Medina. Muslims count their era from the date of Mohammed's flight, or hegira. At Medina, he became both prophet and head of state, completely reorganizing society according to the revelations he constantly received, and expelling the Jews who refused to hearken to his call. Finally in 630 C.E., he gained control of his native Mecca, whose sacred shrine became, and has remained, the center of the new religion. Mohammed, who made no claims to miracle-working or immortality, died in Medina in 632 C.E.*

Reflecting the prophet's dual civil and religious role, The Koran bears a mixed message of religious texts, including revelations of God's will, references to prophets of the past (including many familiar from the Old Testament), descriptions of heaven and hell, as well as prescriptions, some quite precise, for running an entire society. The present selection deals with prime obligations of every Moslem regarding diet, retaliation, fasting, and pilgrimage, among others.

You people! Eat of what is lawful and wholesome on the 2:168
earth and do not walk in Satan's footsteps, for he is your invet-
erate foe. He enjoins on you evil and lewdness, and bids you
assert about God what you know not.

When they are told: 'Follow what God has revealed,' they
reply: 'We will follow what our fathers practised,' even though
their fathers understood nothing and had no guidance.

The unbelievers are like beasts which, call out to them as one
may, can hear nothing but a shout and a cry. Deaf, dumb, and
blind, they understand nothing.

Believers, eat of the wholesome things with which We have
provided you and give thanks to God, if it is Him you worship.

He has forbidden you carrion, blood, and the flesh of swine; 2:173
also any flesh that is consecrated other than in the name of
God. But whoever is driven by necessity, intending neither to
sin nor to transgress, shall incur no guilt. God is forgiving and
merciful.

Those that suppress any part of the Scriptures which God has 2:174
revealed in order to gain some paltry end shall swallow nothing
but fire into their bellies. On the Day of Resurrection God will
neither speak to them nor purify them. Woeful punishment
awaits them.

Such are those that barter guidance for error and forgiveness
for punishment. How steadfastly they seek the Fire! That is
because God has revealed the Book with the truth; those that
disagree about it are in extreme schism.

Righteousness does not consist in whether you face towards
the East or the West. The righteous man is he who believes in
God and the Last Day, in the angels and the Book and the
prophets; who, though he loves it dearly, gives away his wealth
to kinsfolk, to orphans, to the destitute, to the traveller in need
and to beggars, and for the redemption of captives; who attends
to his prayers and renders the alms levy; who is true to his
promises and steadfast in trial and adversity and in times of war.
Such are the true believers; such are the God-fearing.

Believers, retaliation is decreed for you in bloodshed: a free 2:178
man for a free man, a slave for a slave, and a female for a female.
He who is pardoned by his aggrieved brother shall be prosecuted
according to usage and shall pay him a liberal fine. This is a merciful dispensation from your Lord. He that transgresses thereafter
shall be sternly punished.

Men of understanding! In retaliation you have a safeguard for your lives; perchance you will guard yourselves against evil.

It is decreed that when death approaches, those of you that leave property shall bequeath it equitably to parents and kindred. This is a duty incumbent on the righteous. He that alters a will after hearing it shall be accountable for his crime. God hears all and knows all.

He that suspects an error or an injustice on the part of a testator and brings about a settlement among the parties incurs no guilt. God is forgiving and merciful.

2:182

Believers, fasting is decreed for you as it was decreed for those before you; perchance you will guard yourselves against evil. Fast a certain number of days, but if any one among you is ill or on a journey, let him fast a similar number of days later; and for those that cannot[1] endure it there is a penance ordained: the feeding of a poor man. He that does good of his own accord shall be well rewarded; but to fast is better for you, if you but knew it.

2:183

In the month of Ramadan the Koran was revealed, a book of guidance for mankind with proofs of guidance distinguishing right from wrong.[2] Therefore whoever of you is present in that month let him fast. But he who is ill or on a journey shall fast a similar number of days later on.

God desires your well-being, not your discomfort. He desires you to fast the whole month so that you may magnify God and render thanks to Him for giving you His guidance.

If My servants question you about Me, tell them that I am near. I answer the prayer of the suppliant when he calls to Me; therefore let them answer My call and put their trust in Me, that they may be rightly guided.

2:186

It is now lawful for you to lie with your wives on the night of the fast; they are a comfort to you as you are to them. God knew that you were deceiving yourselves. He has relented towards you and pardoned you. Therefore you may now lie with them and seek what God has ordained for you. Eat and drink until you can tell a white thread from a black one in the light of the coming dawn. Then resume the fast till nightfall and do not approach them, but stay at your prayers in the mosques.

These are the bounds set by God: do not approach them. Thus He makes known His revelations to mankind that they may guard themselves against evil.

Do not devour one another's property by unjust means, nor 2:188
bribe the judges with it in order that you may wrongfully and
knowingly usurp the possessions of other men.

They question you about the phases of the moon. Say: 'They 2:189
are seasons fixed for mankind and for the pilgrimage.'

Righteousness does not consist in entering your dwellings
from the back.³ The righteous man is he that fears God. Enter
your dwellings by their doors and fear God, so that you may
prosper.

Fight for the sake of God those that fight against you, but do
not attack them first. God does not love aggressors.

Slay them wherever you find them. Drive them out of the
places from which they drove you. Idolatry is more grievous
than bloodshed. But do not fight them within the precincts of
the Holy Mosque unless they attack you there; if they attack
you put them to the sword. Thus shall the unbelievers be
rewarded: but if they mend their ways, know that God is forgiving and merciful.

Fight against them until idolatry is no more and God's reli- 2:193
gion reigns supreme. But if they desist, fight none except the
evil-doers.

A sacred month for a sacred month: sacred things too are
subject to retaliation. If anyone attacks you, attack him as he
attacked you. Have fear of God, and know that God is with the
righteous.

Give generously for the cause of God and do not with your
own hands cast yourselves into destruction. Be charitable; God
loves the charitable.

Make the pilgrimage and visit the Sacred House for His sake. 2:196
If you cannot, send such offerings as you can afford and do not
shave your heads until the offerings have reached their destina-
tion. But if any of you is ill or suffers from an ailment of the
head, he must do penance either by fasting or by almsgiving or
by offering a sacrifice.

If in peacetime anyone among you combines the visit
with the pilgrimage, he must offer such gifts as he can afford;
but if he lacks the means let him fast three days during the pilgrimage and seven when he has returned; that is, ten days in
all. That is incumbent on him whose family are not present at
the Holy Mosque. Have fear of God: know that God is stern in
retribution.

Make the pilgrimage in the appointed months. He that intends   2:197
to perform it in those months must abstain from sexual intercourse, obscene language, and acrimonious disputes while on pilgrimage. God is aware of whatever good you do. Provide well for
yourselves: the best provision is piety. Fear Me, then, you that
are endowed with understanding.

It shall be no offence for you to seek the bounty of your
Lord. When you come running from 'Arafat[4] remember God as
you approach the sacred monument. Remember Him that gave
you guidance when you were in error. Then go out from the
place whence the pilgrims will go out and implore the forgiveness of God. God is forgiving and merciful. And when you have
fulfilled your sacred duties, remember God as you remember
your forefathers or with deeper reverence.

There are some who say: 'Lord, give us abundance in this   2:201
world.' These shall have no share in the world to come. But
there are others who say: 'Lord, give us what is good both in
this world and in the world to come, and keep us from the torment of the Fire.' These shall have a share, according to what
they did. Swift is God's reckoning.

Give glory to God on the appointed days. He that departs on
the second day incurs no sin, nor does he who stays on longer, if
he truly fears God. Have fear of God, then, and know that you
shall all be gathered before Him.

EXPLANATORY NOTES

1. Thus Al-Jalalayn; the negative being understood. Alternatively: '. . . and for those well able to fast there is a penance ordained.'
2. Alternatively: '. . . with proofs of guidance and *salvation.*'
3. It was the custom of pagan Arabs, on returning from pilgrimage, to enter their homes from the back.
4. Near Mecca.

PETER DAMIAN

The Monastic Ideal

---

*St. Peter Damian (1007–72) was an influential teacher and reformer of the
eleventh century. Born in Ravenna, he studied in a number of Italian cities
before becoming a monk in 1035. By all accounts he practiced a rigorous
form of monastic discipline and self-denial, eventually becoming prior of a
hermitage at Fonte Avella. In the middle decades of the eleventh century
he began to gain a formidable reputation as a preacher and reformer; his
activities also included the founding of new monasteries, and sharp criticism of clerical tendencies toward worldliness and simony. Swept along in
the broader reform movement of the eleventh century, he became a cardinal-
bishop in 1057 and continued to play an important role in ecclesiastical
affairs for the rest of his life. While Peter's emphasis on self-denial, poverty,
and the ideal apostolic life has led some to view him as a forerunner of
St. Francis of Assisi, he was also a renowned theologian in his own right,
and produced a large body of written work on many Christian themes.*

*The present selection offers a glimpse of his beliefs about the monastic
life and its proper pursuit. Peter was concerned not just with the rules, but
also with restoring the spirit of Benedictine monasticism, and his zeal for
"the perfection of the monks" reveals him as the product of an age of
reform, as well as one of its talented architects.*

ON CONTEMPT OF THE WORLD

For when we have renounced the world, we have constituted God as our
property and consequently we have become His property in such a way
that He has become our portion and we are His peculiar heritage. . . . If
then the omnipotent God Himself deigns to be our portion, what kind
of riches, I ask, will it avail anyone to acquire which could exceed in
merit this matchless treasure? For that treasure is such that even if it be
alone, all riches can truly be possessed in it. "In the heart of Jesus are
hidden all the treasures of wisdom and knowledge.". . .

How, O monk, do you mean to lay Christ up in your cell? First, cast out money, for Christ and money do not go well together in one place; if you shut them both up at the same time, you will find yourself the possessor of one without the other. The richer you may be in the poor lucre of this world, the more miserably lacking you are in true riches. Therefore if money is there, let it retire forthwith into other halls so that Christ may find vacant the cell of your heart. That great Guest seeks indeed to descend into the recesses of your lodging-place, and He wishes to dwell alone there, without any companions. For how can you try, in the poor corner of your cell, to put strange companions with that One whom the vastness of heaven and earth cannot contain? Let terrestrial wealth give way where celestial treasure is admitted! . . .

This treasure, then, namely Christ, our God and Lord, who was made for us as both redeemer and reward, He Himself both the promiser and the prize, who is both the life of man and the eternity of the angels—this, I say, store away with diligent care in the recesses of your heart. On Him cast the anxiety of any care whatsoever. In Him delight through the discourse of zealous prayer. In Him refresh yourself by the nightly feasts of holy meditation. Let Him be your food, and your clothing no less. If it should happen that you lack anything of external convenience, do not be uncertain, do not despair of His true promise in which He said, "Seek ye first the kingdom of God, and all things shall be added unto you.". . .

Nor do I deem it possible, dearest brother, to exclude this from your memory, that we have often grieved among ourselves in familiar intercourse about that baneful habit of the monks; we have suffered in fraternal love over the brothers who are restless and sinking to their ruin through the vice of roaming about. For there are some who, when they bore the burden of service in the world, were weary under this yoke of human servitude with running hither and thither, and therefore they resolved to go over to monastic peace through love of liberty. Now, however, they burn with such a great flame of pernicious restlessness that when no occasion of going to a distance presents itself, they seem to be shut in by the dark horror of prison confinement, which without doubt the astuteness of the old enemy is not ignorant of. For those whom that most evil rider drives to this, he urges on to the dangerous incitements of wandering so that they, returning to the vanity of the world, may perish and turn others away from seizing the path of true salvation. . . .

From this poisoned root of restlessness so many shoots of vices spring that whatever plant it is perceived in is stripped of all the fruit of monastic perfection like a withered tree. . . . For, to name only a few out of many, a monk while travelling is not able to fast because the hospitable kindness shown him does not permit it. He does not recite the psalms as he should because the loquacity of the moving company prevents him. He does not persist in nightly vigils because the privacy of isolation is lacking; he does not sweat on bended knees in prayer because the toil of travel does not agree with the zeal of holy devotion. He is in no way constrained by the rule of silence because frequently when occasions arise, though unwillingly, he gives way to much speaking. . . .

Whoever, therefore, as a monk hastens to attain the height of perfection, let him confine himself within the walls of his cloister, let him love spiritual quiet, let him have a horror of running about in the world, as he would of immersing himself in a pool of blood. For the world is more and more every day polluted by the contamination of so many crimes that any holy mind is corrupted by the mere consideration of it. . . .

ON THE MORTIFICATION OF THE FLESH

And so there is nothing but the love of God and the mortification of yourselves. For if the apostolic maxim lives in us, which says, "Always bearing the dying of Jesus in our body," because carnal love does not have wherewith to diffuse itself within us, by necessity all our joy transfers itself, raised on high, to God; and our fire, leaping up, lives there because within us it does not have room to spread. The man who is wise and earnestly intent on guarding his salvation watches always with such great solicitude to repress his vices that with the belt of perfect mortification he girds his loins and his reins, his belly as well as his flanks, on all sides. This indeed is then done, when the itching palate is repressed, when the bold tongue is restrained in silence, when the ear is closed to evil speaking, when the eye is forbidden to look at illicit things, when the hand is restrained lest it strike cruelly, the foot lest it go off wandering idly; when the heart is resisted lest it envy the good fortune of another's happiness, lest it desire through avarice that which is not its own, lest it cut itself off by wrath from fraternal love, lest it arrogantly praise itself above others, lest it yield to seductive luxury through pleasure, lest it sink immoderately into grief, or in joy open the way to the tempter.

Therefore, dearest brothers, seize the arms of all the virtues—sobriety, humility, patience, obedience, chastity, charity—and fight not on behalf of fields or cities, not for children or wives, but for your souls which rise above every emotion of relationship. Especially should you

221

fast, so that your youth may acquire strength, and pray, for the reason that fasting subdues the vigour of the flesh and prayer raises the soul to God. It should be known, however, that some, while they indiscriminately carry out the fast, do not receive the benefits of fasting; for whatever they deny themselves one day, the next they gorge on at will. And so it is that one day of fasting serves for the following day. . . .

That one fasts well who on the day of refreshment [after fasting] is content with the common fare, if, that is, while he does not reject any kind of food, he does not also exceed the daily portion of those eating. Nevertheless, do not, ascribing too much importance to fasting, lose sight of obedience which is the golden road to heaven. . . .

Be content with garments mean and few. Accustom yourself to wearing light and scant clothing. This indeed is done at first not without travail but as habit grows, when it becomes natural, the discomfort of cold is easily assuaged. Moreover, the poverty of clothing and the scarcity of food forthwith drive out all avarice from the heart of a monk. For what should I long for that does not add either to food or clothing? Therefore, as beginners we shudder not without a certain dread at the bareness of feet, and scarcity of clothes, the hardness of bed, the harshness of food, the drink of water, imagining sauces and other such things; persevering and persisting for a long time, however, we find these things easy henceforth and bearable. Frequency indeed mitigates severity, and custom makes rigour agreeable. . . .

Come now, brother, what is this body which you clothe with such diligent care and nourish gently as if it were royal offspring? Is it not a mass of putrefaction, is it not worms, dust, and ashes? It is fit that the wise man consider not this which now is, but rather what it will be afterwards in the future, pus, slime, decay, and the filth of obscene corruption. What thanks will the worms render to you, who are about to devour the flesh you nourished so gently and tenderly? Come, I say, why did Christ suffer? That He should wash away His own sins and blot out the faults of His own transgression? But hear Peter on this, saying, "Who did no sin, neither was guile found in His mouth." For whom then did He suffer? Peter himself answers, "Christ suffered for us, leaving us an example that ye should follow in His steps.". . . Why then do we read that Christ suffered, unless we follow His example from His footsteps? . . . Let the holy mind not fear therefore to share the cross of Christ in scourging, let him not blush with shame at the nakedness of the body, since He says, "For whosoever shall be ashamed of Me and of My words, of him shall the Son of man be ashamed, when He shall come in His majesty.". . .

ON THE MORTIFICATION OF THE SPIRIT

Now let me speak with chagrin about those who follow after the rabble of the grammarians and who, abandoning spiritual studies, lust to learn the trifles of earthly art. Counting as little the Rule of Benedict they rejoice to apply themselves to the rules of Donatus. These, scorning the experience of ecclesiastical discipline, and panting after secular studies, what else do they seem to do but abandon the chaste spouse in the marriage bed of faith and descend to actresses and harlots? . . .

Moreover, the one who endeavoured to lead the troops of all the vices placed the desire for learning as head of the army, and so in her train brought all the crowds of iniquities into the unhappy world. What marvel, therefore, if in the daughter of Eve still vibrates that same spear which formerly the old enemy thrust into the same Eve? . . .

Moreover, tears which are from God approach the tribunal of divine grace confidently, and obtaining what they seek, are assured of certain remission of our sins. Tears are mediators in the peace to be negotiated between man and God, and truthful and learned masters in any uncertainty whatsoever of human ignorance. For when we doubt whether something is pleasing to God or not, never do we receive greater certainty than when we pray, truly weeping. . . .

O tears, spiritual delights, even above honey and the honeycomb, and sweeter than all nectar! how you refresh minds raised to God with the pleasant sweetness of secret savour, and water arid and wasting hearts in the inmost part with the draught of supernal grace.

ST. AUGUSTINE OF HIPPO

A Christian Critique of Pagan Ethics

St. Augustine of Hippo (354–430 C.E.) was the greatest theologian produced by the Western Church in Antiquity, and remains a leading authority of the Roman Catholic Church to the present day. The story of his spiritual journey and eventual conversion to Catholic Christianity, told in The Confessions *(397–398 C.E.), remains among the great autobiographies in Western literature. Born in Thagaste in North Africa to a pagan father and a Christian mother, Augustine was educated in classical literature and rhetoric, eventually becoming a professor of rhetoric in Milan. After his conversion he moved back to Africa where he organized a religious community, was ordained a priest, and in 396 C.E. was chosen bishop of Hippo, where he remained until the end of his life. He died in August of 430 C.E., as the Vandal tribes were besieging Hippo.*

The City of God, *a gigantic work in twenty-two books, was composed between 413 and 426 C.E., just a few decades after Christianity had become the official religion of the Roman Empire. The work was written as a defense of Christianity against pagan critics who argued that the triumph of the Christian faith had led to disaster for the Roman Empire and constituted a vulgar corruption of true spiritual life, represented by the great pagan philosophies. In the present selection Augustine argues that none of the ancient philosophies was capable of providing true, stable happiness, and that the only real hope of happiness lay in Christian salvation.*

---

4. THE CHRISTIAN VIEW OF THE SUPREME GOOD AND THE SUPREME EVIL, CONTRASTED WITH THAT OF THE PHILOSOPHERS WHO FOUND THE SUPREME GOOD IN THEMSELVES

If, therefore, we are asked what reply the City of God gives when asked about each of these points, and first what view it holds about the Ultimate

Good and the Ultimate Evil, the reply will be that eternal life is the Supreme Good, and eternal death the Supreme Evil, and that to achieve the one and escape the other, we must live rightly. That is why the Scripture says, 'The just man lives on the basis of faith.'[1] For we do not yet see our good, and hence we have to seek it by believing; and it is not in our power to live rightly, unless while we believe and pray we receive help from him who has given us the faith to believe that we must be helped by him. Whereas those who have supposed that the Ultimate Good and the Ultimate Evil are to be found in this life, placing the Supreme Good in the body, or in the soul, or in both (to put it more explicitly, in pleasure, or in virtue, or in both); in repose, or in virtue, or in both; in the combination of pleasure and repose, or in virtue, or in both; in the primary gifts of nature, or in virtue, or in both—all these philosophers have wished, with amazing folly, to be happy here on earth and to achieve bliss by their own efforts. The Truth ridiculed such people through the words of the prophet: 'The Lord knows the thoughts of men'[2]—or, as the apostle Paul quotes the passage, 'The Lord knows that the thoughts of wise men are foolish.'[3]

For who is competent, however torrential the flow of his eloquence, to unfold all the miseries of this life? Cicero lamented them, as best he could, in his *Consolation* on the death of his daughter.[4] But what did his best amount to? For, to tell the truth, when, where, how can the 'primary gifts of nature', so called, be in so flourishing a state in this life that they escape being tossed about at the mercy of chance and accident? For is there any pain, the opposite of pleasure, any disturbance, the contrary of repose, that cannot befall a wise man's body? Certainly the amputation or enfeeblement of a man's limbs makes havoc of his bodily soundness; ugliness despoils his beauty, sickness his health; weakness subdues his strength, lassitude or lethargy his mobility. And is there any of these which may not assault the wise man's physical frame? The attitudes and movements of the body, when they are graceful and harmonious, are reckoned among primary gifts of nature. But what if some illness makes the limbs shake and tremble? What if a man's spine is so curved as to bring his hands to the ground, turning the man into a virtual quadruped? Will not this destroy all beauty and grace of body whether in repose or in motion?

Then what about the primary goods, so called, of the mind itself? The two ranked first are sensation and understanding, because they lead to the apprehension and awareness of truth. But what kind of sensation is left, and how much of it, if a man becomes blind and deaf, not to mention other disabilities? And whither will reason and intelligence retire,

225

where will they slumber, if a man is rendered insane by some disease? Crazy people say and do many incongruous things, things for the most part alien to their intentions and their characters, certainly contrary to their good intentions and characters; and when we think about their words and actions, or see them with our eyes, we can scarcely—or possibly we cannot at all—restrain our tears, if we consider their situation as it deserves to be considered. And what am I to say of those subjected to the attacks of demons? Where is their intellect hidden away under cover, while the malignant spirit employs their soul and body to work his own will? Yet is anyone quite confident that such a disaster cannot happen to a wise man in this life? Again, what sort of awareness of truth is there, how much awareness is there when we are in this material flesh, when, as we read in the truth-telling Book of Wisdom, 'The perishable body weighs down the soul, and the earthly habitation presses down the mind as it ponders many questions'?[5] Moreover, the impulse or urge towards action (if this is the right way to express what the Greeks call *hormê*), which is also counted among the primary gifts of nature, is not this impulse responsible for the gestures and actions of the insane that move our pity, that make us shudder, when sensation is perverted and reason is asleep?

Then again, what of virtue itself, which is not one of the primary gifts, since it supervenes on them later, introduced by teaching? Although it claims the topmost place among human goods, what is its activity in this world but unceasing warfare with vices, and those not external vices but internal, not other people's vices but quite clearly our own, our very own? And this is the particular struggle of that virtue called in Greek *sôphrosynê*, which is translated 'temperance'—the virtue which bridles the lusts of the flesh to prevent their gaining the consent of the mind and dragging it into every kind of immorality. For it is never true, in this life, that vice does not exist, when, as the Apostle says, 'the desires of the flesh oppose the spirit'; but to this vice there is an opposing virtue, when, as the same Apostle says, 'the desires of the spirit oppose the flesh. For these two are in mutual opposition, so that you do not achieve what you want to achieve.'[6] But what in fact, do we want to achieve, when we desire to be made perfect by the Highest Good? It can, surely, only be a situation where the desires of the flesh do not oppose the spirit, and where there is in us no vice for the spirit to oppose with its desires. Now we cannot achieve this in our present life, for all our wishing. But we can at least, with God's help, see to it that we do not give way to the desires of the flesh which oppose the spirit by allowing our spirit to be overcome, and that we are not dragged to the perpetration of sin with our own consent. God forbid, then, that, so long as we are engaged in this internal strife, we should believe ourselves to have already attained that happiness, the end we desire to reach by our victory. And who has reached such a height of wisdom as to have no struggle to maintain against his lusts?

And what of that virtue called prudence? Does she not employ all her vigilance in distinguishing good from evil, so that in our pursuit of the good and our endeavour to shun the evil, no mistakes may creep in? And does not she herself thus testify that we are in the midst of evils, or rather that evils are in us? For she teaches us that it is an evil to consent in sinning, and a good to refuse to consent. But although prudence teaches us not to consent to that evil, and self-control causes us not to consent, neither prudence nor self-control removes that evil from this life. Consider the virtue of justice. The function of justice is to assign to each his due; and hence there is established in man himself a certain just order of nature, by which the soul is subordinated to God, and the body to the soul, and thus both body and soul are subordinated to God. Does not justice demonstrate, in performing this function, that she is still labouring at her task rather than resting after reaching its completion? For, we may be sure, the less the soul has God in mind in all its thinking, the less it is subordinated to God; and the more the desires of the flesh oppose the spirit, the less subordinate is the body to the soul. So long, therefore, as there is in us this weakness, this disease, this lethargy, how shall we dare to claim that we are saved? And if not saved, how shall we dare to assert that we are already blest with that final bliss? And then again, that virtue whose name is fortitude, however great the wisdom with which she is accompanied, bears most unmistakable witness to the fact of human ills; for it is just those ills that she is compelled to bear with patient endurance.

I am astounded at the effrontery of the Stoics in their contention that those ills are not ills at all, when they admit that if they should be so great that a wise man cannot or ought not to endure them, he is forced to put himself to death and to depart from this life.[7] Yet so great is the stupefying arrogance of those people who imagine that they find the Ultimate Good in this life and that they can attain happiness by their own efforts, that their 'wise man' (that is, the wise man as described by them in their amazing idiocy), even if he goes blind, deaf, and dumb, even if enfeebled in limb and tormented with pain, and the victim of every other kind of ill that could be mentioned or imagined, and thus is driven to do himself to death—that such a man would not blush to call that life of his, in the setting of all those ills, a life of happiness! What a life of bliss, that seeks the aid of death to end it! If this is happiness, let him continue in it! How can these circumstances fail to be evil which overcome the good of fortitude, and not only compel that same fortitude to give way to them, but to reach such a pitch of delirium as to call a life happy and in the same breath persuade a man that he should make his escape from it? Is anyone so blind as to fail to see that if it were a happy life it would not be a life to seek escape from? In fact the admission that it is a life to be escaped from is an open confession of weakness. Then what keeps the Stoics from humbling their stiff-necked pride and admitting that it is a life of misery? Was it by patient endurance that Cato took his own life?[8] Was it not rather through a lack of it? For he would not have so acted had he not been unable to endure Caesar's victory. What happened, then, to his fortitude? Why, it yielded; it succumbed. It was so thoroughly defeated that it abandoned this 'happy life'; it deserted and fled. Or was it a happy life no longer? If so, it was a wretched life. Then how can it be that those circumstances were not evil, if they made life a misery from which a man should escape?

This shows that those who acknowledged such things to be evils are talking in a more tolerable fashion; the Peripatetics, for example, and the members of the Old Academy—the sect supported by Varro. Even so, they also are guilty of a remarkable error, in contending that amid those evils, even if they are so grievous that a man who suffers them is right to seek escape by self-inflicted death, life is nevertheless happy. 'Bodily torments and agonies' says Varro 'are evils, and their evil increases in proportion to their severity. And to get free of them a man should escape from this life.' What life, pray? 'This life', he replies, 'which is burdened with such great evils.' It is certainly happy, I take it, amid those same evils which lead you to say that one should escape from it? Or is your reason for calling it happy the very fact that you have permission to withdraw from these evils by death? Then what if by some divine judgement you were beset by such evils and not permitted either to die or ever to be exempt from them? Surely in that case, at any rate, you would call such a life wretched? That implies that it does not fail to be wretched simply because it is quickly abandoned, seeing that, if it were everlasting, it would be wretched, even in your judgement. And so it ought not to be regarded as free from any misery, simply because the misery is short-lived; nor—for this would be even more nonsensical—should it be called a state of bliss, simply because of the brevity of the wretchedness.

There is a mighty force in the evils which compel a man, and, according to those philosophers, even a wise man, to rob himself of his existence as a man; although they say, and say with truth, that the first and greatest utterance of nature, as we may call it, is that a man should be reconciled to himself and for that reason should naturally shun death— that he should be his own friend, in that he should emphatically desire to continue as a living being and to remain alive in this combination of body and soul, and that this should be his aim. There is a mighty force in those evils which overpower this natural feeling which makes us employ all our strength in our endeavour to avoid death—which defeat this feeling so utterly that what was shunned is now wished and longed for, and, if it cannot come to him from some other source, is inflicted on a man by himself. There is a mighty force in those evils which make Fortitude a murderer—if indeed she is still to be called fortitude when she is so utterly vanquished by those evils that she not only cannot by her endurance keep guard over the man she has undertaken to govern and protect, but is herself compelled to go so far as to kill him. The wise man ought, indeed, to endure even death with a steadfastness, but a death that comes to him from outside himself. Whereas if he is compelled, as those philosophers say, to inflict it on himself, they must surely admit that these are not only evils, but intolerable evils, when they compel him to commit this crime.

It follows from this that the life weighed down by such great and grievous ills, or at the mercy of such chances, would never be called happy, if the men who so term it, and who, when overcome by the growing weight of ills, surrender to adversity in compassing their own death—if these people would bring themselves to surrender to the truth, when overcome by sound reasoning, in their quest for the happy life, and would give up supposing that the ultimate, Supreme Good is something to be enjoyed by them in this condition of mortality. For in this state the very virtues, which are certainly the best and most useful of man's endowments here below, bear reliable witness to man's miseries in proportion to their powerful support against man's perils, hardships and sorrows. In fact, if they are genuine virtues (and genuine virtues can exist only in those in whom true godliness is present) they do not profess to have the power to ensure that the people in whom they exist will not suffer any miseries; genuine virtues are not such liars as to advance such claims. But they do claim that though human life is compelled to be wretched by all the grievous evils of this world, it is happy in the expectation of the world to come, just as, in expectation, it is saved. For how can it be happy, if it is not yet saved? This point is also made by the apostle Paul. He is speaking not about men without prudence, without steadfastness, without self-control, without justice, but about those who lived by the standards of genuine godliness, whose virtues were therefore genuine virtues, and he says, 'It is in hope that we are saved. But when hope is seen fulfilled it is hope no longer: why should a man hope for what he already sees? But if we are hoping for something we do not yet see, then it is with steadfast endurance that we await it.'[9] As, therefore, we are saved in hope, it is in hope that we have been made happy; and as we do not yet possess a present salvation, but await salvation in the future, so we do not enjoy a present happiness, but look forward to happiness in the future, and we look forward 'with steadfast endurance'. We are beset by evils, and we have to endure them steadfastly until we reach those goods where there will be everything to supply us with delight beyond the telling, and there will be nothing any longer that we are bound to endure. Such is the salvation which in the world to come will also be itself the ultimate bliss. Yet these philosophers refuse to believe in this blessedness because they do not see it; and so they attempt to fabricate for themselves an utterly delusive happiness by means of a virtue whose falsity is in proportion to its arrogance.

EXPLANATORY NOTES

1. Hab. 2, 4; Rom. 1, 17; Gal. 3, 11; Hebr. 10, 38.
2. Ps. 94, 11.
3. 1 Cor. 3, 20.
4. Only fragments remain of Cicero's *Consolatio* on the death of Tullia in 45 B.C.
5. Wisd. 9, 15.
6. Gal. 5, 17.
7. cf. Bk I, 22n.
8. cf. Bk I, 5n.
9. Rom. 8, 24f.

BOETHIUS

True Happiness

Anicius Manlius Torquatus Severinus Boethius (c. 480–524) was the scion of a Christian senatorial family that first came to prominence in Rome during the Constantinian Age. Boethius enjoyed a distinguished career as public servant and as a friend and adviser to the Gothic king Theoderic. Theoderic ruled Italy in the early sixth century in the name of the Roman empire, and under his patronage Boethius rose to hold the title of consul in 510. But Boethius's deepest commitment was to the study of philosophy. He had had a philosophical education in his youth and dedicated his mature years to a great project, never completed, to translate into Latin the complete works of Plato and Aristotle. His own philosophical outlook was deeply colored by Platonism and Augustinianism. His work is a striking example of the fusion between Christian and classical culture that was characteristic of late Antiquity.

Around 524 Boethius became implicated, for reasons that remain unclear, in a court conspiracy and he fell from favor. He was imprisoned in a tower in Pavia, tortured, and finally put to death by bludgeoning. While in prison Boethius wrote what is by far his most famous work, The Consolation of Philosophy, *which became the most widely read philosophical work of the Middle Ages. It was translated into Anglo-Saxon by King Alfred and into Dutch, French, German, and Italian in the later Middle Ages; it inspired important philosophers and literary figures such as Thomas Aquinas, Dante, Chaucer, and Lorenzo de'Medici. The main themes of the book are the nature of true happiness, the justification of God's goodness despite the apparent existence of evil, and the reconciliation of human free will with Divine Providence. In the present selection Boethius explained why only God can be the true source of happiness, summarizing his views in a famous poem based on Plato's* Timaeus.

IX

'I have said enough to give a picture of false happiness, and if you can see that clearly, the next thing is to show what true happiness is like.'

"True Happiness," from *The Consolation of Philosophy,* by Boethius, revised edition, translated by Victor Watts, copyright © 1969, 1999 by Victor Watts, 63–68. Reprinted by permission of Penguin Books Ltd.

'I do indeed see that sufficiency has nothing to do with riches, or power with kingship, respect with honours, glory with fame, or happiness with pleasures.'

'But have you grasped the reasons for this?'

'I think I can see a glimmer of them, but I would like to learn of them more clearly from you.'

'The reason is very clear. That which is one and undivided is mistakenly subdivided and removed by men from the state of truth and perfection to a state of falseness and imperfection. Do you consider self-sufficiency as a state deficient in power?'

'Not at all.'

'Of course not; for if a being had some weakness in some respect, it would necessarily need the help of something else.'

I agreed.

'So that self-sufficiency and power are of one and the same nature.'

'So it seems.'

'Would you then consider a being of this kind beneath contempt, or on the contrary supremely worthy of veneration?'

'The latter, there is no doubt about it.'

'Then let us add the state of being revered to sufficiency and power, that we may judge all three to be one.'

'We must, if we care to admit the truth.'

'What do you think, then, would such a combination of unrecognized and unknown, or famous and renowned? Granted that it lacks nothing, possesses all power, and is supremely worthy of honour, ask yourself whether it would lack a glory which it cannot provide for itself and therefore whether it seems of qualified merit.'

'I can only say that in view of its nature it would be unsurpassed in fame and glory.'

'And consequently we may say that fame, glory, renown is nothing different from the three we already have.'

'Yes.'

'If there were, then, a being self-sufficient, able to accomplish everything from its own resources, glorious and worthy of reverence, surely it would also be supremely happy?'

'How any sorrow could approach such a being is inconceivable: it must be admitted that provided the other qualities are permanent, it will be full of happiness.'

'And for the same reason this conclusion, too, is inescapable; sufficiency, power, glory, reverence and happiness differ in name but not in substance.'

'Yes.'

'Human perversity, then, makes divisions of that which by nature is one and simple, and in attempting to obtain part of something which has no parts, succeeds in getting neither the part—which is nothing—nor the whole, which they are not interested in.'

'How does that happen?'

'If a man pursues wealth by trying to avoid poverty, he is not working to get power; he prefers being unknown and unrecognized, and even denies himself many natural pleasures to avoid losing the money he has got. But certainly no sufficiency is achieved this way, since he is lacking in power and vexed by trouble; he is of no account because of his low esteem, and is buried in obscurity. And if a man pursues only power, he expends wealth, despises pleasures and honour without power, and holds glory of no account. But you can see how much this man also lacks; at any one time he lacks the necessaries of life and is consumed by worry, from which he cannot free himself, so he ceases to be what he most of all wants to be, that is, powerful. A similar argument can be applied to honour, glory, and pleasures, for, since any one of them is the same as the others, a man who pursues one of them to the exclusion of the others, cannot even acquire the one he wants.'

'But suppose someone should want to obtain them all at one and the same time.'

'Then he would be seeking the sum of happiness. But do you think he would find it among these things which we have shown to be unable to confer what they promise?'

'No, I don't.'

'So that it is impossible to find happiness among these things which are thought to confer each of the desired states individually?'

'I agree, and no truer word could be spoken.'

'Then there you have both the nature and the cause of false happiness. Now turn your mind's eye in the opposite direction and you will immediately see the true happiness that I promised.'

'Even a blind man could see it,' I said, 'and you revealed it just now when you were trying to show the causes of false happiness. For unless I'm mistaken, true and perfect happiness is that which makes a man self-sufficient, strong, worthy of respect, glorious and joyful. And to show you that I have more than a superficial understanding, without a shadow of doubt I can see that happiness to be true happiness which, since they are all the same thing, can truly bestow any one of them.'

'You are blessed in this belief, my child, provided you add one thing.'

'What is that?'

'Do you think there is anything among these mortal and degenerate things which could confer such a state?'

'No, I don't, and you have proved it as well as anyone could wish.'

'Clearly, therefore, these things offer man only shadows of the true good, or imperfect blessings, and cannot confer true and perfect good.'

'Yes.'

'Since then you have realized the nature of true happiness and seen its false imitations, what remains now is that you should see where to find this true happiness.'

'Which is the very thing I have long and eagerly been waiting for.'

'But since in the *Timaeus* my servant Plato was pleased to ask for divine help even over small matters,[1] what do you think we ought to do now in order to be worthy of discovering the source of that supreme good?'

'We ought to pray to the Father of all things. To omit to do so would not be laying a proper foundation.'

'Right,' she said, and immediately began the following hymn.

'O Thou who dost by everlasting reason rule,
Creator of the planets and the sky, who time
From timelessness dost bring, unchanging Mover,
No cause drove Thee to mould unstable matter, but
The form benign of highest good within Thee set.   5
All things Thou bringest forth from Thy high archetype:
Thou, height of beauty, in Thy mind the beauteous world
Dost bear, and in that ideal likeness shaping it,
Dost order perfect parts a perfect whole to frame.
The elements by harmony Thou dost constrain,   10
That hot to cold and wet to dry are equal made,
That fire grow not too light, or earth too fraught with weight.
The bridge of threefold nature mad'st Thou soul, which spreads
Through nature's limbs harmonious and all things moves.
The soul once cut, in circles two its motion joins,   15
Goes round and to itself returns encircling mind,
And turns in pattern similar the firmament.
From causes like Thou bringst forth souls and lesser lives,
Which from above in chariots swift Thou dost disperse
Through sky and earth, and by Thy law benign they turn   20
And back to Thee they come through fire that brings them home.
Grant, Father, that our minds Thy august seat may scan,
Grant us the sight of true good's source, and grant us light
That we may fix on Thee our mind's unblinded eye.
Disperse the clouds of earthly matter's cloying weight;   25

Shine out in all Thy glory; for Thou art rest and peace
To those who worship Thee; to see Thee is our end,
Who art our source and maker, lord and path and goal.'[2]

EXPLANATORY NOTES

1. Before embarking on his account of how the universe began Timaeus says they must pray to all the gods and goddesses, for 'everyone with the least sense always calls on god at the beginning of any undertaking, small or great'. (Plato, *Timaeus* 27c, tr. H. D. P. Lee, Penguin Classics, p. 40.)

2. This poem, remarkable for the masterly succinctness of its majestic poetry, the literary climax and main turning point of the whole work, has long been regarded as a kind of epitome of the first part of Plato's *Timaeus,* and was especially dear to commentators of the early Middle Ages whose direct knowledge of Plato was otherwise confined to a translation of the *Timaeus* by Chalcidius. There are a number of points, however, in which the Boethian version differs from the *Timaeus* which cannot, therefore, be regarded as its only source. The epitome begins at line 4, and the following parallels with H. D. P. Lee's translation of the *Timaeus* are noteworthy: line 6, Lee, p. 42; 9, Lee, p. 44; 10–12, Lee, pp. 43–4; 13–14, Lee, pp. 49 and 46; 15–16, Lee, pp. 48, 45 and 49; 18, Lee, p. 57; 19, Lee, ibid; 20 and 21, Lee, pp. 57–8. For most of the passages for which there is no parallel in the *Timaeus* sources can be found in the writings of the Neoplatonists and especially Proclus's commentary on the *Timaeus.* The poem, in fact, is composed in the form of a Platonic hymn to God, and is full of phrases which echo the vocabulary of the Platonic hymns. There is also some influence from the Judaeo-Christian tradition, particularly in the movement of the final lines of the poem: the introduction of the particle *for* in line 26 parallels the construction of the *Gloria* in the liturgy of the Western church and the Lord's Prayer rather than the Platonic hymns. And no one can be deaf to the echo in the final line of St John's gospel.

The following phrases need a word of comment:

ll. 7–8. Nowhere does Plato say that God carries the model of the universe in his mind; this is part of the teaching of Neoplatonism.

l. 16. 'encircling mind'. Plato does not say that the soul encircles mind. Plotinus, however, uses the figure of the dance of the imperfect around the perfect, i.e. of created soul around the uncreated mind of God.

l. 17. 'in pattern similar'. Proclus speaks of Soul as set between Mind and Body; soul is moved by Mind, i.e. God, which in a similar way itself moves Body, i.e. corporeal and concrete nature—here the firmament.

l. 18. 'lesser lives'. Proclus commenting on *Timaeus* 41d holds that there are three different kinds of souls; the 'lesser lives' of this passage are either souls enclosed in earthly bodies, or lesser souls compared with the world soul described in lines 15–17.

ll. 19–21 contain a summary of Neoplatonic religion, the descent of the souls (figuratively spoken of as fixed in chariots in a formula taken over by the Neoplatonists from Plato himself) from God and their ultimate ascent and return through the purifying action of fire which returns them to God.

Even, therefore, in the part of Boethius' hymn which has been seen as an epitome of the *Timaeus,* Boethius is heavily influenced by the doctrine and sacred hymns of Neoplatonism. For details see Friedrich Klingner, *De Boethii Consolatione Philosophiae,* 2te Unveranderte Auflage, Weidmann, Zurich/Dublin, 1966, pp. 38–67. And for Boethius's use of Proclus' commentary on the *Timaeus,* H. R. Patch in *Speculum* VIII, 1933, pp. 41–51.

THOMAS AQUINAS

Thomas Aquinas on Natural Law

Thomas Aquinas (c. 1225–1274) was the greatest theologian of the medieval Catholic Church and an outstanding representative of scholasticism, the intellectual tradition associated with medieval universities. Aquinas was born in Roccasecca near Aquino, a town in Campania south of Rome. The son of a nobleman, he was educated at the abbey of Montecassino and at the University of Naples, where he became a member of the Dominican Order of Preachers. Aquinas later studied the newly revived philosophy of Aristotle at Cologne under Albert the Great and took the degree of Master of Theology at Paris in 1256. He spent the rest of his life teaching at Dominican study houses and universities in France and Italy, and died in 1274. He was canonized in 1323.

Aquinas's thought, known as Thomism, has historically constituted the most important theological tradition within Roman Catholicism. Broadly speaking, it attempts to reconcile the teachings of the best pagan philosophers, particularly Aristotle, with Christian doctrine, or (as Aquinas would have said) Reason with Faith. The present selection, written in 1271, is one of the most famous parts of the Summa Theologiae, *in which Thomas discusses his conception of natural law and its relationship to eternal law, divine law, and human law.*

Article 2: Is there some natural law in us?

It seems that there is not.

1. A man is sufficiently governed by eternal law, for Augustine says in *On Free Will* 1.6 that the eternal law is that by which it is just that all things are perfectly ordered. But nature does not abound in superfluities, just as it is not deficient in what is necessary. Therefore there is no natural law in man.

2. Moreover, by law a man's acts are ordered to the end, as was said above, but the ordering of human acts to the end is not by nature, as

happens in irrational creatures, which by natural appetite alone act for the sake of the end; man acts for the sake of the end through reason and will. Therefore, there is no natural law in man.

3. To the degree that one is free he is less subject to the law. But man is freer than the other animals, thanks to free will, which he has beyond the other animals. Therefore since other animals are not subject to natural law, neither should man be subject to any natural law.

ON THE CONTRARY:

On Romans 2.14, 'These having no law are a law unto themselves,' the Gloss says that although they do not have the written law, they have the natural law which each understands and is thereby conscious of what is good and what is evil.

RESPONSE:

It should be said that, as has been urged, law, since it is a rule and measure, can be in something in two ways: in one way, as in the one ruling and measuring, in another way, as in the ruled and measured, since insofar as they participate in something of the rule or measure, they are ruled and measured. Since all things subject to divine providence are ruled and measured by the eternal law, as is clear from what has been said, it is manifest that all things participate in some way in eternal law, insofar as by its impression they have inclinations to their proper acts and ends. Among others, however, the rational creature is subject to divine providence in a more excellent manner, insofar as he comes to be a participant in providence, providing for himself and others. Hence in him the eternal reason is participated in in such a way that he has a natural inclination to the fitting act and end. Such a participation in eternal law in the rational creature is called natural law. Hence when the Psalmist says in Psalm 4.6, 'Offer sacrifices of righteousness, and hope in the Lord,' he adds as if in response to someone asking what the works of justice are, 'Many say: "Who will show us good things?"' Replying to that question, he says, 'Lift up the light of thy countenance upon us, O Lord,' as if the natural light of reason, whereby we discern good and evil, which pertains to natural law, is nothing else than the impression of the divine light in us. Hence it is evident that natural law is nothing other than the participation in eternal law on the part of the rational creature.

Ad 1. It should be said that that argument would work if natural law were something different from eternal law. But it is nothing but a participation in it, as has been said.

Ad 2. It should be said that every act of reason and will in us is derived from that which is according to nature, as was said above, for all reasoning derives from principles naturally known, and every desire for the things which are for the sake of the end derives from the natural desire for the ultimate end. Thus it is necessary that the first direction of our acts to the end should come about through natural law.

Ad 3. It should be said that even the irrational animals participate in the eternal law in their fashion, as does the rational creature. But because the rational creature participates in it intellectually and rationally, the participation in eternal law by the rational creature is properly called law, for law is something of reason, as has been said. But in the irrational creature it is not participated in rationally, hence it can only be called law by way of similitude.

HILDEGARD OF BINGEN

Women and the Monastic Life

———————

*Hildegard of Bingen (1098–1179) is commonly considered the most promi-
nent and multitalented of medieval abbesses, some of whom headed all-
female convents and even double monasteries housing monks of both sexes.
Hildegard is well known for her mysticism, her musical compositions, her
scientific knowledge, and her medical advice. Hildegard came from a
prominent German family who backed her political and religious positions
and enabled her to remain independent from directions by local princes and
high church officials. The youngest of eight children, she entered a Benedictine convent when she was seven and took her vows at age fourteen, and
her visions started while she was still a teenager. When she reached age
thirty-two, in 1136, she became abbess at Dissem, and as the congregation
there grew, she moved the convent to Bingen. She also began her writing
career with* Scivias, *a varied work which included hymns, poetry, and a
religious play, devoted to a description of her visions. Musicologists identify
her as the earliest female composer for large audiences. Yet her interests
were not limited to religious, literary, and musical arenas; she also wrote
natural history works that included descriptions of elements, plants, and
animals and discussed medical issues such as blood circulation. She even
wrote some of the earliest commentaries on mental illness. In addition, she
produced a range of significant correspondence, giving advice to the Holy
Roman Emperor, local political figures, and church leaders including Pope
Eugenius III. She played an important role in building support for the Second Crusade. Few religious figures of her era, male or female, could match
her extraordinary range of learning and creative endeavor.*

In the present selection from her Letters, *Hildegard discussed various
issues of spirituality and monastic discipline with her correspondents.*

———————

MISTRESS TENGSWICH TO HILDEGARD

1148–50

To Hildegard, mistress of the brides of Christ, Tengswich, unworthy superior of the sisters at Andernach, with a prayer that she eventually be joined to the highest order of spirits in heaven.

The report of your saintliness has flown far and wide and has brought to our attention things wondrous and remarkable. And, insignificant as we are, these reports have highly commended the loftiness of your outstanding and extraordinary mode of religious life to us. We have learned from a number of people that an angel from above reveals many secrets of heaven for you to record, difficult as they are for mortal minds to grasp, as well as some things that you are to do, not in accordance with human wisdom, but as God himself instructs them to be done.

We have, however, also heard about certain strange and irregular practices that you countenance. They say that on feast days your virgins stand in the church with unbound hair when singing the psalms and that as part of their dress they wear white, silk veils, so long that they touch the floor. Moreover, it is said that they wear crowns of gold filigree, into which are inserted crosses on both sides and the back, with a figure of the Lamb on the front, and that they adorn their fingers with golden rings. And all this despite the express prohibition of the great shepherd of the Church, who writes in admonition: Let women comport themselves with modesty "not with plaited hair, or gold, or pearls, or costly attire" [I Tim 2.9]. Moreover, that which seems no less strange to us is the fact that you admit into your community only those women from noble, well-established families and absolutely reject others who are of lower birth and of less wealth. Thus we are struck with wonder and are reeling in confusion when we ponder quietly in our heart that the Lord himself brought into the primitive Church humble fishermen and poor people, and that, later, at the conversion of the gentiles, the blessed Peter said: "In truth, I perceive that God is no respecter of persons" [Acts 10.34; cf. Rom 2.11]. Nor should you be unmindful of the words of the Apostle in Corinthians: "Not many mighty, not many noble, but God hath chosen the contemptible and the ignoble things of this world" [I Cor 1.26–28]. We have examined as accurately as possible all the precedents laid down by the fathers of the Church, to which all spiritual people must conform, and we have found nothing in them comparable to your actions.

O worthy bride of Christ, such unheard-of practices far exceed the capacity of our weak understanding, and strike us with no little wonder.

And although we feeble little women wholeheartedly rejoice with all the esteem due your spiritual success, we still wish you to inform us on some points relative to this matter. Therefore, we have decided to send this humble little letter to you, saintly lady, asking by whose authority you can defend such practices, and we devoutly and meekly beseech, worthy lady, that you not disdain to write back to us as soon as possible. Farewell, and remember us in your prayers.

HILDEGARD TO THE CONGREGATION OF NUNS

1148–50

The Living Fountain says: Let a woman remain within her chamber so that she may preserve her modesty, for the serpent breathed the fiery danger of horrible lust into her. Why should she do this? Because the beauty of woman radiated and blazed forth in the primordial root, and in her was formed that chamber in which every creature lies hidden. Why is she so resplendent? For two reasons: on the one hand, because she was created by the finger of God and, on the other, because she was endowed with wondrous beauty. O, woman, what a splendid being you are! For you have set your foundation in the sun, and have conquered the world.

Paul the apostle, who flew to the heights but kept silent on earth so as not to reveal that which was hidden [cf. II Cor 12.2ff.], observed that a woman who is subject to the power of her husband [cf. Ephes 5.22ff; Col 3.18], joined to him through the first rib, ought to preserve great modesty, by no means giving or displaying her vessel to another man who has no business with her, for that vessel belongs to her husband [cf. I Thess 4.4]. And let her do this in accordance with the word spoken by the master of the earth in scorn of the devil: "What God hath joined together, let no man put asunder" [Matt 19.6].

Listen: The earth keeps the grass green and vital, until winter conquers it. Then winter takes away the beauty of that flower, and the earth covers over its vital force so that it is unable to manifest itself as if it had never withered up, because winter has ravaged it. In a similar manner, a woman, once married, ought not to indulge herself in prideful adornment of hair or person, nor ought she to lift herself up to vanity, wearing a crown and other golden ornaments, except at her husband's pleasure, and even then with moderation.

But these strictures do not apply to a virgin, for she stands in the unsullied purity of paradise, lovely and unwithering, and she always remains in the full vitality of the budding rod. A virgin is not commanded to cover up her hair, but she willingly does so out of her great humility, for a person will naturally hide the beauty of her soul, lest, on account of her pride, the hawk carry it off.

Virgins are married with holiness in the Holy Spirit and in the bright dawn of virginity, and so it is proper that they come before the great High Priest as an oblation presented to God. Thus through the permission granted her and the revelation of the mystic inspiration of the finger of God, it is appropriate for a virgin to wear a white vestment, the lucent symbol of her betrothal to Christ, considering that her mind is made one with the interwoven whole, and keeping in mind the One to whom she is joined, as it is written: "Having his name, and the name of his Father, written on their foreheads" [Apoc 14.1] and also "These follow the Lamb whithersoever he goeth" [Apoc 14.4].

God also keeps a watchful eye on every person, so that a lower order will not gain ascendancy over a higher one, as Satan and the first man did, who wanted to fly higher than they had been placed. And who would gather all his livestock indiscriminately into one barn—the cattle, the asses, the sheep, the kids? Thus it is clear that differentiation must be maintained in these matters, lest people of varying status, herded all together, be dispersed through the pride of their elevation, on the one hand, or the disgrace of their decline, on the other, and especially lest the nobility of their character be torn asunder when they slaughter one another out of hatred. Such destruction naturally results when the higher order falls upon the lower, and the lower rises above the higher. For God establishes ranks on earth, just as in heaven with angels, archangels, thrones, dominions, cherubim, and seraphim. And they are all loved by God, although they are not equal in rank. Pride loves princes and nobles because of their illusions of grandeur, but hates them when they destroy that illusion. And it is written that "God does not cast off the mighty, since He himself is mighty" [Job 36.5]. He does not love people for their rank but for their works which derive their savor from Him, just as the Son of God says: "My food is to do the will" of my Father [John 4.34]. Where humility is found, there Christ always prepares a banquet. Thus when individuals seek after empty honor rather than humility, because they believe that one is preferable to the other, it is necessary that they be assigned to their proper place. Let the sick sheep be cast out of the fold, lest it infect the entire flock.

God has infused human beings with good understanding so that their name will not be destroyed. It is not good for people to grab hold of a mountain which they cannot possibly move. Rather, they should stand in the valley, gradually learning what they are capable of.

These words do not come from a human being but from the Living Light. Let the one who hears see and believe where these words come from. . . .

HILDEGARD TO THE MONK HEINRICH

Before 1170

The Shadow of God's mysteries says: The wind blows, the air shifts, and clouds become so intermingled that sometimes they are stormy, sometimes black, sometimes white, and sometimes luminous. And you are just like that, O knight of God. For sometimes you have worldly sadness like the blowing wind, and sometimes you are caught up in the pleasure that the devil lays down as a trap like the shifting air, and sometimes you are morally astray like the mingling clouds, so that sometimes your morals are squalid in storms, sometimes terrified in darkness, sometimes sweet in whiteness, sometimes wholesome in luminosity.

Therefore, listen. A certain lord stood on a high mountain, and called his servants, saying: Pay your debt [cf Matt 18.34]. One of those servants was standing before him, and the other was seated. And the one who was standing answered: Lord, I have come as an exile from a far distant land, where I acquired an unstable character through my many vices and sins. O woe that I have broken all your precepts! Therefore, for fear of losing your love, I swear that I will repent with my whole heart. Moreover, I have always loved and honored your sun, moon, and stars. And his lord answered him: Good servant, I—an ever-turning wheel—accept your answer, saying: I, who live without beginning or end, will give you great honors above all that you have loved before, and I will not condemn you because you have called out to me in penitence. But the servant who was sitting answered with disdain: Your sun has burned me, your moon has oppressed me, your stars have beaten me down, your dew has drenched the hairs of my head, and your rains have inundated me. And so impeded by all of these, I could not look to you. Therefore, I do not know what I can say. And his lord answered him: Iniquitous servant [cf. Matt 18.32], when I established the sun, moon, and stars, did I need your help? And why do you not blush to respond to me so rashly? For such temerity you deserve to be bound hand and foot, and cast into outer darkness [cf. Matt 22.13] until you pay back everything.

Now, you, O knight of Christ, heed this parable. This lord is your God, Who keeps watch from the heights, because God ought to be invoked by all things. And God exhorts men with this admonition: You must be judged by your works. But some men labor in honor to the Divine, while others dawdle in the doldrums of tedium. Yet those who honor God say: By the instigation of the devil, we fell when Adam went astray, and we have contracted many vices in our works. But we tearfully lament that transgression, and for the glory of Your name, we promise that we desire to abstain from our sins. And in great love, we have venerated Your honor, Your justice, and the Scriptures that You have given us. And the Lord, Who is inscrutable, praises them, and gives them charge over many good things [cf. Matt 25.21ff], and He does not condemn them, because they invoked Him in penitence. But those who slumber in disregard of divine fear say: Your glory has afflicted us, Your justice has wounded us, the multitude of Your Scriptures has suffocated us, the viridity of Your Spirit has turned aside the desire of our mind, and the outpouring of Your zeal has tired us out so that we cannot look to You in joy, and we cannot excuse ourselves. And the Lord calls them iniquitous servants, declaring that He had no need of their aid in administering His justice. Moreover, He asks why they do not blush to assail Him with the temerity of their words. Therefore, they ought to be bound and punished until they get rid of all their vices.

Now, you, O knight of Christ, understand that all these things pertain to you. Indeed, the servant who was standing denotes you. For you did few good things when you were in secular life. But the admonition of the Holy Spirit struck you, and turned you to good. Yet beware lest you be like the sitting servant, that is, lest you say that you are burned by the Rule as by the sun, or lest you have contempt for governance as for the moon, or lest you grow tired of the communion of your brothers as of the stars, or lest you bring derision upon the admonition of the Holy Spirit as the dew, or lest you disdain correction as the rain. But always embrace God in good will and desire, and, by embracing, persevere in Him. Then you will live.

AN ABBESS TO HILDEGARD

Before 1173

To the lady Hildegard, sister dearest to her in Christ, N., abbess (although unworthy) of St. Glodesindis in Metz, with a prayer for salvation in the true Savior.

Because we greatly presume on your grace and your benevolence, we do not wish to hide from you that we are placed in great danger, since we are forced to govern the souls of many although we are not sufficient to the task. Thus we ask you, saintly lady, and earnestly beseech you by our Lord Jesus to strengthen our shaky ignorance, and take care to advise us in a letter what we ought to do: whether we should remain in our office or cede our place to another who might do better. Please inform us if the Lord Jesus deigns to reveal something to you about this matter.

Farewell, and for God's sake pray to God for me, and, if it please you, write back again to me quickly.

HILDEGARD TO THE ABBESS

Before 1173

Predictably, Hildegard argues that an administrator should not lightly set aside the duties of office, and continues to discuss the "plagues" of sin that mankind inherited from Adam.

Mt. Sion is high, and its shadow, stretching into the valleys, shows its great height. There are other mountains in the pilgrimage of this world, through which Mt. Sion is made strong, and which are beautiful for the people to look upon. Prelates and teachers, who are the firmament of the Church, are signified by the height of Sion and the other mountains, and their disciples are called the "daughters of Sion" [Cant 3.11; Is 3.16]. It would be a great shame if this mountain should fall, or if the others destroyed it.

Therefore, let anyone who holds the reins of governance beware of casting off his yoke, or allowing others to depose him. For just as the mountains serve as a defense for many against their enemies, so also administrators, through their learning and the power to command obedience that God grants them, defend many from the treachery of their enemies. Therefore, as long as he can offer words of doctrine, let no administrator cast aside the rod of correction that he has received from the hand of God, for often mud is cast off by mud, just as an administrator is cleansed by his subordinates, and the subordinates by the administrator. For out of fear for his subordinates, he will afflict himself, and he is punished by the tormentors of his unruly subordinates, and in this way he imitates the Great Master who preceded him. Then, he will say, I showed them your precepts, et cetera [Ex 18.16], and also: "He that hath ears to hear, let him hear" [Matt 11.15]. Therefore, learn from these things lest you flee because of the cloud of instability among your subordinates, or because of the tedium of your labor. For many flee from the tedium of the labor, more than from the fact that they cannot control their subordinates.

A clear day that is not overshadowed by a storm is full of joy. That is what Adam had before the Fall, but the first great deceiver overshadowed that day of his through temptation. From this come the seven plagues [cf. Apoc 15.1ff] that wound the spirit.

The first plague is vainglory, which gathers to itself what it neither sowed nor merited, and takes to itself what was never granted to it by God. The first deceiver taught this, for he acted in just this way. And so vainglory does not seek God.

The second plague is a person's awareness that he has the power to sin, and thus treasures the delight of the flesh, and, once he has tasted it, embraces and kisses it.

The third plague brings on great disaster and grief through filthy morals, so that a person lives as if he were dead to God and scarcely hopes that God knows him.

The fourth plague is that deceit through which a person excuses himself of the aforementioned sins, and defends himself, saying that those sins are not so perilous as he has been told. Thus he becomes so hateful toward his fellow man that he trusts no one.

The fifth plague is pride, which says that since a person cannot abstain from sin because of the flesh of his humanity, he should not have to deny his carnal desires. In its temerity, this is the law that pride adopts for itself, and so shows no respect to God.

The sixth plague manifests itself when a person seeks his salvation from another created thing, and demands it to show him everything, despising his Creator and seeking nothing from Him, as if He were unable to help him.

The seventh plague is enslavement to idolatry, which worships the devil and despises God.

These seven plagues have, as it were, an army under their control more numerous than the branches on a tree, because they all lay hidden in the transgression of the bite that Adam took. For God said to him: In the hour that "thou shalt eat of it, thou shalt die the death" [Gen 2.17]. God set this precept for him lest he should do as the devil did, that is, that he should not be free from His precepts, as the devil wanted to be. Thus no person can be secure in this life on account of the first temptation of the devil to which Adam succumbed.

Therefore, O daughter of God, gird yourself with the mighty armor of the seven gifts of the Holy Spirit, through which you can conquer these seven vices. Gird yourself lest, bewailing, you are wounded by them; and rise up and conquer them by strenuous war like a stalwart knight, so that you may live in eternity.

And so, O daughter, may God see you in the mirror of salvation. [...]

AN ABBOT TO HILDEGARD

Before 1173

Fearful of the turmoil of war, the abbot had postponed an intended visit to Hildegard, and writes this letter instead, seeking her consolation and advice.

To Hildegard, blessed and saintly woman, E., abbot (in name only) of the brothers of Neuenburg, may we both attain our mutual desire.

The widespread fame of your sanctity has greatly stimulated our spirit to see your face. Therefore, this past summer I prepared to make the trip to see you, but terrified by the storms of war threatening at that time, I did not dare to start out. Nevertheless, I sent a messenger to you with a letter, but he has not yet returned with an answer. And since this letter may be lost through the negligence of the messenger, I will repeat the contents of that letter.

First, I give thanks from the bottom of my heart that you met with a delegation of our brothers. Then, I beseech that through your prayers the Lord help me in these threatening dangers, for placed in a position of authority, I am buffeted by the storms of secular matters. Therefore, I flee to the harbor of your saintliness and prayer so that, no matter what, I will not give in to sin in these matters. And since I ask this in all earnestness, I beg especially that through your prayers I may merit salvation from the Lord, body and soul, when the course of my life has been completed. Amid all these pressures, one stands out above all the others, for which I beseech you to pray to the Lord. Through the present messenger, please send some token of salvation through which I may prosper and have a remembrance of you. My desire to visit with you will never leave me until—"if life accompany" [II Kings 4.16]—I have been able to do so.

Farewell.

HILDEGARD TO THE ABBOT

Before 1173

Hildegard exhorts the abbot to persevere in his office.

Your mind is like the sphere of the fixed stars, which moves those stars here and there. But frequently a cloud is stirred up by a whirlwind and by the darkness of fire and water until the sun penetrates all things with its fiery sphere.

In your doubt, you are weary, and you are unwilling to labor because of the multifarious wars of mankind's morals. Now, if a young knight, who rejoices to be called a knight in his youthful strength, should say when his enemies attack him, "I cannot conquer my enemies," and throws down his arms, he would be derided and called a fool because his weapons did not flash honorably in battle. Similarly, O master, you say that you are naked as a snake lying in its hole, because you do not strive to vanquish the storms assailing mankind with your armament.

This is not the way it will be. For in the first age the Lord established stewards and caretakers over all His possessions who were to render an account to Him [cf. Matt 25.14ff; Luke 16.1ff]. When a steward receives gifts, let him gather up his spears and arrows—spears to infuse the savage with Scriptures, arrows to infuse the impious, the crafty, and the furtive with the lessons from other writings. But if a great storm should arise with whirlwinds and black fire and water, with wrath and transgression or neglect of God's precepts, let him give way until the storm abates. Then let him offer medicine [cf. Ecclus 18.20] with the sun of Scriptures, as it is written, "I will have mercy and not sacrifice" [Matt 9.13; cf Hos 6.6].

Mercy demands prayer, which God loves. May the Holy Spirit make that prayer fiery between us, so that He may bring us into the heavenly Jerusalem [cf. Heb 12.22]. Amen.

AN ABBESS TO HILDEGARD

Before 1173

To Hildegard, beloved lady and mother, N., abbess (although unworthy) of the sisters at Neuss. Please accept this trifling prayer and service offered with complete devotion.

Because we have no doubt, blessed lady, that you have heard it noised abroad concerning our condition, how we have fallen back into our early state and, alas, abandoned our aspirations, we are all the more earnestly and insistently beseeching your prayers, so that we may be made aware for God's sake why our erratic spirit has been so burdened that we are buffeted here and there by various impulses and are forced to endure such distress.

We are fully aware that God is "terrible in his counsels over the sons of men" [Ps 65.5], and so, fearing the inscrutable (though not unjust) judgments of His chastisement, we commit fully the matter of our soul to you, whom we trust more than any other human being, and to your venerable sisters. We also long with our whole heart to receive a written response from you.

Farewell.

HILDEGARD TO THE ABBESS

Before 1173

O servant of God, run in the circle of the sun in the zeal of your heart, and sigh to God for your sins. Also, do good works before your day sets when you can no longer work [cf. John 9.4]. Heed that steward who was accused before his master and who lowered the amounts in his account book of those who were in debt to his master [cf. Luke 16.1ff].

Do likewise. For since you have not performed your duties well, help your daughters now with sound advice and be compassionate toward them, just as seasonable rain falls on the grass and brings forth luxuriant vegetation. In this way, through penitence and compassion you will be wiser than the sons of light [cf. Luke 16.8], that is, the fallen angels, who were unwilling to behave thus.

For when you do good works, those works will receive you "into everlasting dwellings" [Luke 16.9] after your death. For if you had plowed the earth properly and had seasonable rain, you would be fertile soil. But the dew that should have caused you to bring forth is lacking in you, and you are turning on the wheel which you call your salvation, but which is, in fact, full of ashes.

Now plow in your heart with the knowledge of sacred Scripture, receive the rain through sighs of earnest zeal, and in your felicitous way of life keep the dew of blessing through good works. Do this before the day of your death, and you will live forever.

A CERTAIN BROTHER TO HILDEGARD

Before 1173

To the lady Hildegard, his spiritual mother, Brother S., least of the brothers of the church at Otterberg and darkened with the filth of sin beyond all others, with a prayer that she serve the spiritual banquet with Martha, and sigh with Mary for the joys of life in heaven [cf. Luke 10.38ff].

I rejoice with joy [cf. Is 66.10; Matt 2.10], spiritual mother, that you have found grace in the sight of our Lord God, and that you have kept the lamp of your blessed soul kindled so far with the fire of the Holy Spirit in anticipation of His coming, and have not grown weary [cf. Matt 25.1ff].

O friend of God, because with the wise virgins you are strong in the integrity of chastity, and because you keep the eye of contemplation firmly fixed upon the divine brightness, my puny devotion prays that with your righteous prayers you will take pains on my behalf to appease the face of the Lord [cf. 1 Sam 13.12], which I have greatly offended with the fiery brand of my perversity. I am certain that our God, our refuge and strength, will gladly deign to hear your petition on my behalf [cf. Ps 6.10], and, for your sake, will not cause me, justified because of you, to founder forever [cf. Ps 54.23]. Surely, because He is righteous, He will not, once the spirit of blasphemy, which has for too long assailed my unhappy spirit, has been put to rout.

I also request this of your abundant goodness: Please, saintly lady, send me, puny creature that I am, a written response through the present messenger. And offer to your nuns, who follow the monastic way of life, as many greetings and prayers from me as there are dwellings in the eternal mansions of the Lord [cf. John 14.2].

Farewell.

HILDEGARD TO THE BROTHER

Before 1173

Your mind wheels like a bird, arranging and categorizing everything it encounters. Your beginning was consecrated because you have been so imbued with God's grace that you are able to lay hold of virtue and many other noble attributes.

Some people, however, have winds in their disposition, and because of the viridity and humidity of the earth, and the air and the waters, their minds are subject to sensuality. For God was pleased to say, "Let there be" [cf. Gen 1.3ff], at which word all creation came forth according to its kind, as it is written: "God hath spoken once, these two things have I heard, that power belongeth to God, and mercy to thee, O Lord; for thou wilt render to every man according to his works" [Ps 61.12–13]. For with his command God created all things, and He did this once for all time when He said, "Let there be." In this, two things are to be understood: that His power was great in giving man the law, and that He Who rules all things by mercy paid the ancient debt through His Incarnation, for He forgives the sin of all who see and understand these things through penitence. But He casts off those who will not see or learn, and He exacts righteous retribution from them according to their works.

God cast the first angel into the lake of misery because he had unrighteously exalted himself, and He cast the first man into the prison of this world because of his foolish vainglory. For God has established nothing in vain. The first angel had great knowledge and wisdom, but out of his great malice he would not render God His due honor, and thus he fell and has remained fallen. Man, however, fell because he tasted food, and for this reason the Son of God offered Himself as a sacrifice for his sin. Thus when a man recalls that he has greatly sinned through his knowledge of good and evil and sighs out to God, he is reborn in God through penitence [cf. John 3.3].

As for you, O son, keep learning day and night. So that you may live forever.

HILDEGARD TO THE ABBOT PHILIP

1170–73

O father, neglectful though you are, you fear God and love Him so that you sigh to Him in all your distress. Now, run to the fountain of living water [cf. Num 20.6; Jer 2.13] to wash yourself, and not only yourself but also others that you see weak and wounded. Never cease pouring the wine of penitence upon them and anointing them with the oil of mercy [cf. Luke 10.33–34].

In this way, you imitate the Living Fountain and Unbroken Wheel, Who receives sinners that run to Him for the aid of His mercy, and Who judges harshly the impious that gainsay Him. No mountain can match the circumference of this wheel, because its shadow towers over all things, nor can it be overshadowed by the depths, for it is exalted over all. God has life from nothing but Himself, and so He has neither beginning nor end. Therefore, whosoever runs to the aid of His grace will never fall from the bliss of eternal life, but the spark of salvation vitalizes him anew through the living God. For God does not wish the death of a sinner, but, rather, to have life through Him [cf. Ezech 18.23; 33.11].

Now, mild father, you who serve as Christ's representative, receive this woman Ida, who has not yet completely shown her hidden wounds, and diligently treat her, and all others running to you, with the medicine of penitence, so that you will live forever in the wheel of the true Trinity.

ANONYMOUS

Anglo-Saxon Heroism

———————

Beowulf *(eighth century C.E.) is an action-filled epic composed in Anglo-Saxon England but set in fifth century Scandinavia. The work was meant to be performed orally, and it is usually considered the first important piece of English literature. In it, the young hero, Beowulf, and his companions feast in their great hall and feud relentlessly. Beowulf kills the evil monster Grendel, and his mother, but loses his own life while dispatching a dragon that had been destroying his people.*

The work reveals the violence and rugged values of a warrior society.

———————

Then spoke Beowulf, son of Edgetheow:
'I thank my friend Unferth, who unlocks us this tale
of Breca's bragged exploit; the beer lends
eloquence to this tongue. But the truth is as I've said:
I had more sea-strength, outstaying Breca's,
and endured underwater a much worse struggle.

It was in early manhood that we undertook
with a public boast—both of us still
very young men—to venture our lives
on the open ocean; which we accordingly did.
Hard in our right hands we held each a sword
as we went through the sea, so to keep off
the whales from us. If he whitened the ocean,
no wider appeared the water between us.
He could not away from me; nor would I from him.
Thus stroke for stroke we stitched the ocean
five nights and days, drawn apart then
by cold storm on the cauldron of waters:
under lowering night the northern wind
fell on us in warspite: the waves were rough!

The unfriendliness was then aroused of the fishes of the deep.
Against sea-beasts my body-armour,
hand-linked and hammered, help me then,
this forge-knit battleshirt bright with gold,
decking my breast. Down to the bottom
I was plucked in rage by this reptile-fish,
pinned in this grip. But I got the chance
to thrust once at the ugly creature
with my weapon's point: war took off then
the mighty monster; mine was the hand did it.
Then loathsome snouts snickered by me,
swarmed at my throat. I served them out
with my good sword, gave them what they asked for:
those scaly flesh-eaters sat not down
to dine on Beowulf, they browsed not on me
in that picnic they'd designed in the dingles of the sea.
Daylight found them dispersed instead
up along the beaches where my blade had laid them
soundly asleep; since then they have never
troubled the passage of travellers over
that deep water-way. Day in the east grew,
God's bright beacon, and the billows sank
so that I then could see the headlands,
the windy cliffs. "Weird saves oft
the man undoomed if he undaunted be!" —
and it was my part then to put to the sword
seven sea-monsters, in the severest fight
by night I have heard of under heaven's vault;
a man more sorely pressed the seas never held.
I came with my life from the compass of my foes,
but tired from the struggle. The tide bore me
away on its currents to the coasts of the Lapps,
whelms of water.
No whisper has yet reached me
of sword-ambushes survived, nor such scathing perils
in connection with your name! Never has Breca,
nor you Unferth either, in open battle-play
framed such a deed of daring with your
shining swords—small as my action was.
You have killed only kindred, kept your blade
for those closest in blood; you're a clever man, Unferth,
but you'll endure hell's damnation for that.

It speaks for itself, my son of Edgelaf,
that Grendel had never grown such a terror,

this demon had never dealt your lord
such havoc in Heorot, had your heart's intention
been so grim for battle as you give us to believe.
He's learnt there's in fact not the least need
excessively to respect the spite of this people,
the scathing steel-thresh of the Scylding nation.
He spares not a single sprig of your Danes
in extorting his tribute, but treats himself proud,
butchering and dispatching, and expects no resistance
from the spear-wielding Scyldings.
                                    I'll show him Geatish
strength and stubbornness shortly enough now,
a lesson in war. He who wishes shall go then
blithe to the banquet when the breaking light
of another day shall dawn for men
and the sun shine glorious in the southern sky.'

Great then was the hope of the grey-locked Hrothgar,
warrior, giver of rings. Great was the trust
of the Shield of the Danes, shepherd of the people,
attending to Beowulf's determined resolve.

There was laughter of heroes, harp-music ran,
words were warm-hearted. *Wealhtheow* moved,
mindful of courtesies, the queen of Hrothgar,
glittering to greet the Geats in the hall,
peerless lady; but to the land's guardian
she offered first the flowing cup,
bade him be blithe at the beer-drinking,
gracious to his people; gladly the conqueror
partook of the banquet, tasted the hall-cup.
The Helming princess then passed about among
the old and the young men in each part of the hall,
bringing the treasure-cup, until the time came
when the flashing-armed queen, complete in all virtues,
carried out to Beowulf the brimming vessel;
she greeted the Geat, and gave thanks to the Lord
in words wisely chosen, her wish being granted
to meet with a man who might be counted on
for aid against these troubles. He took then the cup,
a man violent in war, at Wealhtheow's hand,
and framed his utterance, eager for the conflict.

Thus spoke Beowulf son of Edgetheow:
'This was my determination in taking to the ocean,
benched in the ship among my band of fellows,

that I should once and for all accomplish the wishes
of your adopted people, or pass to the slaughter,
viced in my foe's grip. This vow I shall accomplish,
a deed worthy of an earl; decided otherwise
here in this mead-hall to meet my ending-day!'

This speech sounded sweet to the lady,
the vaunt of the Geat; glittering she moved
to her lord's side, splendid folk-queen.

Then at last Heorot heard once more
words of courage, the carousing of a people
singing their victories; till the son of Healfdene
desired at length to leave the feast,
be away to his night's rest; aware of the monster
brooding his attack on the tall-gabled hall
from the time they had seen the sun's lightness
to the time when darkness drowns everything
and under its shadow-cover shapes do glide
dark beneath the clouds. The company came to its feet.

Then did the heroes, Hrothgar and Beowulf,
salute each other; success he wished him,
control of the wine-hall, and with this word left him:
'Never since I took up targe and sword
have I at any instance to any man beside,
thus handed over Heorot, as I here do to you.
Have and hold now the house of the Danes!
Bend your mind and your body to this task
and wake against the foe! There'll be no want of liberality
if you come out alive from this ordeal of courage.'
Then Hrothgar departed, the Protector of the Danes
passed from the hall at the head of his troop.
The war-leader sought Wealhtheow his queen,
the companion of his bed.
                          Thus did the King of Glory,
to oppose this Grendel, appoint a hall-guard
—so the tale went abroad—who took on a special
task at the court—to cope with the monster.
The Geat prince placed all his trust
in his mighty strength, his Maker's favour.

He now uncased himself of his coat of mail,
unhelmed his head, handed his attendant
his embellished sword, best of weapons,
and bade him take care of these trappings of war.

Beowulf then made a boasting speech,
the Geat man, before mounting his bed:
'I fancy my fighting-strength, my performance in combat,
at least as greatly as Grendel does his;
and therefore I shall not cut short his life
with a slashing sword—too simple a business.
He has not the art to answer me in kind,
hew at my shield, shrewd though he be
at his nasty catches. No, we'll at night play
without any weapons—if unweaponed he dare
to face me in fight. The Father in His wisdom
shall apportion the honours then, the All-holy Lord,
to whichever side shall seem to Him fit.'

Then the hero lay down, leant his head
on the bolster there; about him many
brave sea-warriors bowed to their hall-rest.
Not one of them thought he would thence be departing
ever to set eyes on his own country,
the home that nourished him, or its noble people;
for they had heard how many men of the Danes
death had dragged from that drinking-hall.
But God was to grant to the Geat people
the clue to war-success in the web of fate—
His help and support; so that they all did
overcome the foe—through the force of one
unweaponed man. The Almighty Lord
has ruled the affairs of the race of men
thus from the beginning.

DANTE ALIGHIERI

Dante Begins His Journey through Hell

Dante Alighieri is widely considered the greatest and most characteristic poet of the Middle Ages, but little is known about his life. Born in Florence in 1265, his early life coincided with the emergence of Florence as the major economic and military power in Tuscany. Dante played a minor role in Florence's great victory of Campaldino in 1289, which established her dominance in Tuscany. After a brief but disastrous career in politics, Dante was falsely accused of corruption and in 1302 he was banished from Florence. As an exile, he became progressively more alienated from the Florentine traditions of republicanism, pro-papalism, and commercialism and aligned himself with the forces of Florence's enemy, the German emperor Henry VII of Luxembourg. After the latter's death, Dante continued to live in exile and attached himself to the courts of petty lords in northern Italy. He died in Ravenna in 1321 without ever returning to Florence.

Before his exile Dante was the youngest member in a group of Florentine poets whose aim was to turn Tuscan into a literary language, to create a "sweet new style" (dolce stil novo) suitable for writing courtly poetry. Dante took this development one step further and during his exile developed a poetic language capable of treating with sustained elevation the most sublime and difficult subjects: the nature of God; the universe and human destiny; divine justice and forgiveness. Drawing on traditions of courtly love poetry and religious poetry as well as the example of Virgil and other ancient Latin poets, Dante created a new kind of poetry that is learned and mysterious, but also extremely vivid and sensuous. It is didactic poetry that also tells an absorbing story.

The Divine Comedy *tells the story of Dante's journey to the center of the Earth, through lowest Hell to Purgatory, located on the opposite side of the globe. At the top of the mountain of Purgatory is the Earthly Paradise, where the human race began, and from there Dante ascends to the height of Heaven and has a vision of the Blessed Virgin Mary and the Trinity. Indeed, the whole poem is a vision, an experience that Dante undergoes while in an elevated state of divine inspiration during the Easter Triduum,*

"Dante Begins His Journey through Hell," from cantos 1 and 2 in *The Divine Comedy,* vol. I: *The Inferno,* by Dante Alighieri, translated by Mark Musa, copyright © 1971 by Indiana University Press, 67–71, 79–83. Reprinted by permission of Penguin Books, a division of Penguin Putnam Inc.

*the three days before Easter in the church calendar. His vision brings Dante
to an understanding of the workings of Divine Providence in history and in
the lives of Christians and non-Christians. The purpose of the* Comedy *is
thus prophetic: It aims to rouse Dante's fellow Christians from spiritual
tepidity by showing them the ultimate consequences of their acts. But it is
also a supreme work of literary skill that, like most medieval poetry, can be
read on many levels at once, symbolically and allegorically as well as literally. In the present selection Dante describes the circumstances that started
him on his visionary journey, and he meets a guide in the person of Virgil,
the great Roman epic poet. The latter tells him how "three blessed
ladies"—the Blessed Virgin, St. Lucy, and Dante's courtly lover Beatrice—
took pity on Dante and provided Virgil as his guide.*

CANTO I

*HALFWAY through his life, DANTE THE PILGRIM wakes to find himself lost
in a dark wood. Terrified at being alone in so dismal a valley, he wanders
until he comes to a hill bathed in sunlight, and his fear begins to leave
him. But when he starts to climb the hill his path is blocked by three fierce
beasts: first a LEOPARD, then a LION, and finally a SHE-WOLF. They fill
him with fear and drive him back down to the sunless wood. At that
moment the figure of a man appears before him; it is the shade of VIRGIL,
and the Pilgrim begs for help. Virgil tells him that he cannot overcome
the beasts which obstruct his path; they must remain until a "GREY-
HOUND" comes who will drive them back to Hell. Rather by another
path will the Pilgrim reach the sunlight, and Virgil promises to guide him
on that path through Hell and Purgatory, after which another spirit,
more fit than Virgil, will lead him to Paradise. The Pilgrim begs Virgil to
lead on, and the Guide starts ahead. The Pilgrim follows.*

Midway along the journey of our life
   I woke to find myself in a dark wood,
   for I had wandered off from the straight path.   3

How hard it is to tell what it was like,
   this wood of wilderness, savage and stubborn
   (the thought of it brings back all my old fears),   6

a bitter place! Death could scarce be bitterer.
   But if I would show the good that came of it
   I must talk about things other than the good.   9

How I entered there I cannot truly say,
   I had become so sleepy at the moment
   when I first strayed, leaving the path of truth;   12

but when I found myself at the foot of a hill,
   at the edge of the wood's beginning, deep in the valley,
   where I first felt my heart plunged deep in fear,   15

I raised my head and saw the hilltop shawled
   in morning rays of light sent from the planet
   that leads men straight ahead on every road.   18

And then only did terror start subsiding
   in my heart's lake, which rose to heights of fear
   that night I spent in deepest desperation.   21

Just as a swimmer, still with panting breath,
   now safe upon the shore, out of the deep,
   might turn for one last look at the dangerous waters,   24

so I, although my mind was turned to flee,
   turned round to gaze once more upon the pass
   that never let a living soul escape.   27

I rested my tired body there awhile
   and then began to climb the barren slope
   (I dragged my stronger foot and limped along).   30

Beyond the point the slope begins to rise
   sprang up a leopard, trim and very swift!
   It was covered by a pelt of many spots.   33

And, everywhere I looked, the beast was there
   blocking my way, so time and time again
   I was about to turn and go back down.   36

The hour was early in the morning then,
   the sun was climbing up with those same stars
   that had accompanied it on the world's first day,   39

the day Divine Love set their beauty turning;
   so the hour and sweet season of creation
   encouraged me to think I could get past   42

that gaudy beast, wild in its spotted pelt,
   but then good hope gave way and fear returned
   when the figure of a lion loomed up before me,   45

and he was coming straight toward me, it seemed,
   with head raised high, and furious with hunger—
   the air around him seemed to fear his presence.   48

And now a she-wolf came, that in her leanness
   seemed racked with every kind of greediness
   (how many people she has brought to grief!).   51

This last beast brought my spirit down so low
   with fear that seized me at the sight of her,
   I lost all hope of going up the hill.   54

As a man who, rejoicing in his gains,
   suddenly seeing his gain turn into loss,
   will grieve as he compares his then and now,   57

so she made me do, that relentless beast;
   coming toward me, slowly, step by step,
   she forced me back to where the sun is mute.   60

While I was rushing down to that low place,
   my eyes made out a figure coming toward me
   of one grown faint, perhaps from too much silence.   63

And when I saw him standing in this wasteland,
   "Have pity on my soul," I cried to him,
   "whichever you are, shade or living man!"   66

"No longer living man, though once I was,"
   he said, "and my parents were from Lombardy,
   both of them were Mantuans by birth.   69

I was born, though somewhat late, *sub Julio*,
   and lived in Rome when good Augustus reigned,
   when still the false and lying gods were worshipped.   72

I was a poet and sang of that just man,
   son of Anchises, who sailed off from Troy
   after the burning of proud Ilium.   75

But why retreat to so much misery?
   Why not climb up this blissful mountain here,
   the beginning and the source of all man's joy?"   78

"Are you then Virgil, are you then that fount
   from which pours forth so rich a stream of words?"
   I said to him, bowing my head modestly.   81

"O light and honor of the other poets,
    may my long years of study, and that deep love
    that made me search your verses, help me now!   84

You are my teacher, the first of all my authors,
    and you alone the one from whom I took
    the noble style that was to bring me honor.   87

You see the beast that forced me to retreat;
    save me from her, I beg you, famous sage,
    she makes me tremble, the blood throbs in my veins."   90

"But you must journey down another road,"
    he answered, when he saw me lost in tears,
    "if ever you hope to leave this wilderness;   93

this beast, the one you cry about in fear,
    allows no soul to succeed along her path,
    she blocks his way and puts an end to him.   96

She is by nature so perverse and vicious,
    her craving belly is never satisfied,
    still hungering for food the more she eats.   99

She mates with many creatures, and will go on
    mating with more until the greyhound comes
    and tracks her down to make her die in anguish.   102

He will not feed on either land or money:
    his wisdom, love, and virtue shall sustain him;
    he will be born between Feltro and Feltro.   105

He comes to save that fallen Italy
    for which the maid Camilla gave her life
    and Turnus, Nisus, Euryalus died of wounds.   108

And he will hunt for her through every city
    until he drives her back to Hell once more,
    whence Envy first unleashed her on mankind.   111

And so, I think it best you follow me
    for your own good, and I shall be your guide
    and lead you out through an eternal place   114

where you will hear desperate cries, and see
    tormented shades, some old as Hell itself,
    and know what second death is, from their screams.   117

And later you will see those who rejoice
   while they are burning, for they have hope of coming,
   whenever it may be, to join the blessèd—   120

to whom, if you too wish to make the climb,
   a spirit, worthier than I, must take you;
   I shall go back, leaving you in her care,   123

because that Emperor dwelling on high
   will not let me lead any to His city,
   since I in life rebelled against His law.   126

Everywhere He reigns, and there He rules;
   there is His city, that is His high throne.
   Oh, happy the one He makes His citizen!"   129

And I to him: "Poet, I beg of you,
   in the name of God, that God you never knew,
   save me from this evil place and worse,   132

lead me there to the place you spoke about
   that I may see the gate Saint Peter guards
   and those whose anguish you have told me of."   135

Then he moved on, and I moved close behind him.

CANTO II

BUT THE PILGRIM begins to waver; he expresses to Virgil his misgivings about his ability to undertake the journey proposed by Virgil. His predecessors have been Aeneas and Saint Paul; and he feels unworthy to take his place in their company. But Virgil rebukes his cowardice, and relates the chain of events that led him to come to Dante. The VIRGIN MARY took pity on the Pilgrim in his despair and instructed SAINT LUCIA to aid him. The Saint turned to BEATRICE because of Dante's great love for her, and Beatrice in turn went down to Hell, into Limbo, and asked Virgil to guide her friend until that time when she herself would become his guide. The Pilgrim takes heart at Virgil's explanation and agrees to follow him.

The day was fading and the darkening air
   was releasing all the creatures on our earth
   from their daily tasks, and I, one man alone,   3

was making ready to endure the battle
   of the journey, and of the pity it involved,
   which my memory, unerring, shall now retrace.   6

O Muses! O high genius! Help me now!
 O memory that wrote down what I saw,
 here your true excellence shall be revealed!   9

Then I began: "O poet come to guide me,
 tell me if you think my worth sufficient
 before you trust me to this arduous road.   12

You wrote about young Sylvius's father,
 who went beyond, with flesh corruptible,
 with all his senses, to the immortal realm;   15

but if the Adversary of all evil
 was kind to him, considering who he was,
 and the consequence that was to come from him,   18

this cannot seem, to thoughtful men, unfitting,
 for in the highest heaven he was chosen
 father of glorious Rome and of her empire,   21

and both the city and her lands, in truth,
 were established as the place of holiness
 where the successors of great Peter sit.   24

And from this journey you celebrate in verse,
 Aeneas learned those things that were to bring
 victory for him, and for Rome, the Papal seat;   27

then later the Chosen Vessel, Paul, ascended
 to ring back confirmation of that faith
 which is the first step on salvation's road.   30

But why am I to go? Who allows me to?
 I am not Aeneas, I am not Paul,
 neither I nor any man would think me worthy;   33

and so, if I should undertake the journey,
 I fear it might turn out an act of folly—
 you are wise, you see more than my words express."   36

As one who unwills what he willed, will change
 his purpose with some new second thought,
 completely quitting what he first had started,   39

so I did, standing there on that dark slope,
 thinking, ending the beginning of that venture
 I was so quick to take up at the start.   42

"If I have truly understood your words,"
   that shade of magnanimity replied,
     "your soul is burdened with that cowardice   45

which often weighs so heavily on man,
   it turns him from a noble enterprise
     like a frightened beast that shies at its own shadow.   48

To free you from this fear, let me explain
   the reason I came here, the words I heard
     that first time I felt pity for your soul: 51

I was among those dead who are suspended,
   when a lady summoned me. She was so blessed
     and beautiful, I implored her to command me.   54

With eyes of light more bright than any star,
   in low, soft tones she started to address me
     in her own language, with an angel's voice: 57

'O noble soul, courteous Mantuan,
   whose fame the world continues to preserve
     and will preserve as long as world there is,   60

my friend, who is no friend of Fortune's, strays
   on a desert slope; so many obstacles
     have crossed his path, his fright has turned him back   63

I fear he may have gone so far astray,
   from what report has come to me in Heaven,
     that I may have started to his aid too late.   66

Now go, and with your elegance of speech,
   with whatever may be needed for his freedom,
     give him your help, and thereby bring me solace.   69

I am Beatrice, who urges you to go;
   I come from the place I am longing to return to;
     love moved me, as it moves me now to speak.   72

When I return to stand before my Lord,
   often I shall sing your praises to Him.'
     And then she spoke no more. And I began,   75

'O Lady of Grace, through whom alone mankind
   may go beyond all worldy things contained
     within the sphere that makes the smallest round,   78

your plea fills me with happy eagerness—
　　to have obeyed already would still seem late!
　　You needed only to express your wish.　　　　　　81

But tell me how you dared to make this journey
　　all the way down to this point of spacelessness,
　　away from your spacious home that calls you back.'　　84

'Because your question searches for deep meaning,
　　I shall explain in simple words,' she said,
　　'just why I have no fear of coming here.　　　　　　87

A man must stand in fear of just those things
　　that truly have the power to do us harm,
　　of nothing else, for nothing else is fearsome.　　　90

God gave me such a nature through His Grace,
　　the torments you must bear cannot affect me,
　　nor are the fires of Hell a threat to me.　　　　　　93

A gracious lady sits in Heaven grieving
　　for what happened to the one I send you to,
　　and her compassion breaks Heaven's stern decree.　　96

She called Lucia and making her request,
　　she said, "Your faithful one is now in need
　　of you, and to you I now command his soul."　　　　99

Lucia, the enemy of cruelty,
　　hastened to make her way to where I was,
　　sitting by the side of ancient Rachel,　　　　　　102

and said to me: "Beatrice, God's true praise,
　　will you not help the one whose love was such
　　it made him leave the vulgar crowd for you?　　　　105

Do you not hear the pity of his weeping,
　　do you not see what death it is that threatens him
　　along that river the sea shall never conquer?"　　108

There never was a wordly person living
　　More anxious to promote his selfish gains
　　than I was at the sound of words like these—　　　111

to leave my holy seat and come down here
　　and place my trust in you, in your noble speech
　　that honors you and all those who have heard it!'　　114

When she had finished reasoning, she turned
   her shining eyes away, and there were tears
   How eager then I was to come to you!   117

And I have come to you just as she wished,
   and I have freed you from the beast that stood
   blocking the quick way up the mount of bliss.   120

So what is wrong? Why, why do you delay?
   Why are you such a coward in your heart,
   why aren't you bold and free of all your fear,   123

when three such gracious ladies, who are blessed,
   watch out for you up there in Heaven's court,
   and my words, too, bring promise of such good?"   126

As little flowers from the frosty night
   are closed and limp, and when the sun shines down
   on them, they rise to open on their stem,   129

my wilted strength began to bloom within me,
   and such warm courage flowed into my heart
   that I spoke like a man set free of fear.   132

"O she, compassionate, who moved to help me!
   And you, all kindness, in obeying quick
   those words of truth she brought with her for you— 135

you and the words you spoke have moved my heart
   with such desire to continue onward
   that now I have returned to my first purpose.   138

Let us start, for both our wills, joined now, are one.
   You are my guide, you are my lord and teacher."
   These were my words to him and, when he moved,   141

I entered on that deep and rugged road.

GEOFFREY CHAUCER

A Group of Medieval Pilgrims

Geoffrey Chaucer was born in London around 1342. His father was a wine seller, and had once served as Butler to the King. He managed to place Geoffrey at court, as a page to King Edward III. Other than a brief stint as a soldier, Chaucer remained a courtier throughout his life. He served Edward as a valet, and later as a minor diplomat. In 1366 Chaucer married a woman named Philippa, who served in the queen's court. During his travels as a diplomat, Chaucer encountered the literary culture of Europe, and particularly that of Italy. Dante, Petrarch, and Boccaccio all influenced his themes and style. Chaucer's skills as a poet and translator seemed to have served him well at court, but he was not paid for his writing. In 1374 Chaucer became Comptroller of the Customs; in 1385 he became Justice of the Peace in Kent, and in 1386 he sat in Parliament. Chaucer was a man of many talents. He mastered several languages, was deeply versed in European literature, and had some skill as a mathematician and astronomer. He also executed an esteemed translation of Boethius's Consolation of Philosophy. *He died in 1400.*

Chaucer's twin masterpieces were The Canterbury Tales *(c. 1390) and* Troilus and Criseyde *(mid-1380s). The Canterbury Tales tells the story of a group of English pilgrims on their way to Canterbury. On their pilgrimage the diverse travelers tell a series of tales, and these tales provide the material for Chaucer's poem.* The Canterbury Tales *survives in a series of fragments. The "First Fragment" is the most polished. It contains Chaucer's prologue and four of his most famous tales (those of the Knight, the Miller, the Reeve, and the Cook). Many of the stories in* The Canterbury Tales *are comic, and all provide glimpses into the social world of medieval England.*

An asterisk, placed at the nearest point in the glosses, indicates a note immediately helpful to the reader.

his his, its   *shoures soote* sweet showers
droghte dryness*   *perced* pierced
veyne vein (of sap)   *swich licour* liquid such (that)
Of which vertu by its power   *flour* flower
5   *Zephirus* god of the west wind; breeze   *eek* also
Inspired breathed life into   *holt* grove   *heeth* field
croppes shoots, new leaves   *yonge* young*
Has run (the second) half of his course in Aries*
smale foweles little birds
10   *ye* eye
So much does Nature prick them in their hearts*
longen folk to goon people long to go
palmeres pilgrims*   *straunge strondes* foreign shores
To distant shrines known in various lands
15   *every shires ende* the corner of every county
wende make their way
blisful martir blessed martyr (St Thomas Becket)*   *seke* seek
hem hath holpen helped them*   *seeke* sick
Bifil it happened   *seson* season
20   *Southwerk* Southwark   *Tabard* Tabard Inn*   *lay* stayed

corage spirit

25   Of various sorts of people fallen by chance
felaweship fellowship
wolden wished to
chambres bedrooms   *wyde* spacious
And we were made very comfortable in the best way
30   *to reste* setting
hem everichon every one of them
That I became part of their company
made forward (we) made agreement
ther as as   *devyse* shall tell
35   *natheless* nonetheless
Er before   *pace* proceed
Me thynketh it it seems to me   *resoun* proper order
condicioun state, circumstances
ech of hem each one of them
40   And of what occupation and rank they were
eek also   *array* dress
than wol then will

GENERAL PROLOGUE

HERE BYGYNNETH THE BOOK OF THE TALES OF CAUNTERBURY.

Whan that Aprill with his shoures soote
The droghte of March hath perced to the roote,
And bathed every veyne in swich licour
of which vertu engendred is the flour;
5   Whan Zephirus eek with his sweete breeth
Inspired hath in every holt and heeth
The tendre croppes, and the yonge sonne
Hath in the Ram his half cours yronne,
and smale foweles maken melodye,
10   That slepen al the nyght with open ye
(So priketh hem nature in hir corages),
Thanne longen folk to goon on pilgrimages,
And palmeres for to seken straunge strondes,
To ferne halwes, kowthe in sondry londes;
15   And specially from every shires ende
Of Engelond to Caunterbury they wende,
The hooly blisful martir for to seke,
That hem hath holpen whan that they were seeke.
    Bifil that in that seson on a day,
20   In Southwerk at the Tabard as I lay
Redy to wenden on my pilgrymage
To Caunterbury with ful devout corage,
At nyght was come into that hostelrye
Wel nyne and twenty in a compaignye
25   Of sondry folk, by aventure yfalle
In felaweshipe, and pilgrimes were they alle,
That toward Caunterbury wolden ryde.
The chambres and the stables weren wyde,
And wel we weren esed atte beste.
30   And shortly, whan the sonne was to reste,
So hadde I spoken with hem everichon
That I was of hir felaweshipe anon,
And made forward erly for to ryse,
To take oure wey ther as I yow devyse.
35   But nathelees, whil I have tyme and space,
Er that I ferther in this tale pace,
Me thynketh it acordaunt to resoun
To telle yow al the condicioun
Of ech of hem, so as it semed me,
40   And which they weren, and of what degree,
And eek in what array that they were inne;
And at a knyght than wol I first bigynne.

KNYGHT knight*   *worthy* respected, brave

45   *riden out* go on campaign   *chivalrie* prowess
Trouthe integrity   *fredom* magnanimity
lordes werre the war of his feudal superior
ferre further
In Christendom as well as in heathen lands*
50   . . .

SQUIER (e)squire, beginner in knighthood*
80   *lovyere* lover   *lusty* zestful   *bacheler* aspirant to knighthood*
crulle curly   *presse* curler

of even lengthe well-proportioned
delyvere agile
85   *somtyme* for a time   *chyvachie* cavalry expedition
Flaundres Flanders*
born hym conducted himself   *space* space of time
his lady grace his lady's favour
Embrouded embroidered   *meede* meadow
90   *reede* red
floytynge playing the flute

koude knew how to
95   *endite* write (the words for a song)
Juste joust   *purtreye* draw
hoote passionately   *nyghtertale* night-time
sleep slept
lowely humble   *servysable* willing to serve
100   *carf* carved
YEMAN yeoman, free-born servant*   *he* the Knight   *namo* no more
hym liste it pleased him
he the Yeoman
pecok with flights made from peacock feathers
105   *bar ful thriftily* bore very properly
He knew well how to care for his equipment like a true yeoman
His arrows did not fall short with sagging feathers

not heed close-cropped head   *broun* dark brown
110

bracer archer's arm-guard
bokeler buckler, shield
gay bright
Harneised ornamented

272

A KNYGHT ther was, and that a worthy man,
That fro the tyme that he first bigan
45 To riden out, he loved chivalrie,
Trouthe and honour, fredom and curteisie.
Ful worthy was he in his lordes werre,
And therto hadde he riden, no man ferre,
As well in cristendom as in hethenesse,
50 And evere honoured for his worthynesse;
. . .

    With hym ther was his sone, a young SQUIER,
80 A lovyere and a lusty bacheler,
With lokkes crulle as they were leyd in presse.
Of twenty yeer of age he was, I gesse.
Of his stature he was of evene lengthe,
And wonderly delyvere, and of greet strengthe.
85 And he hadde been somtyme in chyvachie
In Flaundres, in Artoys, and Pycardie,
And born hym weel, as of so litel space,
In hope to stonden in his lady grace.
Embrouded was he, as it were a meede
90 Al ful of fresshe floures, whyte and reede.
Syngynge he was, or floytynge, al the day;
He was as fressh as is the month of May.
Short was his gowne, with sleves longe and wyde.
Wel koude he sitte on hors and faire ryde.
95 He koude songes make and wel endite,
Juste and eek daunce, and weel purtreye and write.
So hoote he lovede that by nyghtertale
He sleep namoore than dooth a nyghtyngale.
Curteis he was, lowely, and servysable,
100 And carf biforn his fader at the table.
    A YEMAN hadde he and servantz namo
At that tyme, for hym liste ride so,
And he was clad in cote and hood of grene.
A sheef of pecok arwes, bright and kene,
105 Under his belt he bar ful thriftily
(Wel koude he dresse his takel yemanly;
His arwes drouped noght with fetheres lowe),
and in his hand he baar a myghty bowe.
A not heed hadde he, with a broun visage.
110 Of wodecraft wel koude he al the usage.
Upon his arm he baar a gay bracer,
And by his syde a swerd and a bokeler,
And on that oother syde a gay daggere
Harneised wel and sharp as point of spere;

115   *Cristopher* image of St Christopher*   *sheene* bright
        bar bore   *bawdryk* baldrick, shoulder strap
        forster forester, gamekeeper   *soothly* truly
        PRIORESSE head of a priory of nuns*
        symple unaffected   *coy* shyly reserved
120   *ooth* oath   *but* only   *Seinte Loy* St Eloi, St Eligius*
        cleped called
        soong the service dyvyne sang the liturgy*
        Entuned intoned   *ful semely* in a most seemly manner
        fetisly gracefully
125   In the manner of Stratford at Bow*
        unknowe unknown
        At mete at table*   *with alle* indeed
        leet allowed

130   *koude* know how to   *kepe* take care
        fille fell
        She took great delight in courtly manners
        over upper
        hir coppe her cup   *ferthyng* spot the size of a farthing
135
        after hir mete she raughte she reached for her food
        sikerly certainly   *greet desport* fine deportment
        port bearing, manner
        And took pains to represent the manners
140   *estatlich* dignified*
        And to be held worthy of respect
        conscience moral sense
        pitous compassionate
        saugh saw

        chapeleyne assistant   *preestes thre**
        . . .

165   *MONK**   *a fair for the maistrie* a surpassingly fine one
        outridere a rider-out, supervisor   *venerie* hunting*
        A fine figure of a man, good enough to make an abbot
        deyntee fine
        rood was riding   *heere* hear
        . . .

270   *MARCHANT* merchant*
        mottelee cloth woven with a parti-coloured design   *hye* in a high saddle
        Flaundryssh Flemish   *bever* beaver
        fetisly neatly
        resons opinions   *solempnely* impressively

115 A Cristopher on his brest of silver sheene.
An horn he bar, the bawdryk was of grene;
A forster was he, soothly, as I gesse.
    Ther was also a Nonne, a PRIORESSE,
That of hir smylyng was ful symple and coy;
120 Hire gretteste ooth was but by Seinte Loy;
And she was cleped madame Eglentyne.
Ful weel she soong the service dyvyne,
Entuned in hir nose ful semely;
And Frenssh she spak ful faire and fetisly,
125 After the scole of Stratford atte Bowe,
For Frenssh of Parys was to hire unknowe.
At mete wel ytaught was she with alle;
She leet no morsel from hir lippes falle,
Ne wette hir fyngres in hir sauce depe;
130 Wel koude she carie a morsel and wel kepe
That no drope ne fille upon hire brest.
In curteisie was set ful muchel hir lest.
Hir over-lippe wyped she so clene
That in hir coppe ther was no ferthyng sene
135 Of grece, whan she dronken hadde hir draughte.
Ful semely after hir mete she raughte.
And sikerly she was of greet desport,
And ful plesaunt, and amyable of port,
And peyned hire to countrefete cheere
140 Of court, and to been estatlich of manere,
And to ben holden digne of reverence.
But for to speken of hire conscience,
She was so charitable and so pitous
She wolde wepe, if that she saugh a mous

    . . .

    Another NONNE with hire hadde she,
That was hir chapeleyne, and preestes thre.
165   A MONK ther was, a fair for the maistrie,
An outridere, that lovede venerie,
A manly man, to been an abbot able.
Ful many a deyntee hors hadde he in stable,
And whan he rood, men myghte his brydel heere

    . . .

270   A MARCHANT was ther with a forked berd,
In mottelee, and hye on horse he sat;
Upon his heed a Flaundryssh bever hat,
His bootes clasped faire and fetisly.
His resons he spak ful solempnely,

275

275   *Sownynge in* tending to   *wynning* profit
       He wanted the sea to be guarded at any price
       Middleburgh Dutch port   *Orewelle* Orwell, nr Ipswich*
       koude knew how to   *sheeldes* cus, units of exchange*
       bisette employed
280   *wight* creature*   *dette* debt*
       estatly dignified   *governaunce* conduct
       bargaynes lending and borrowing   *chevyssaunce* dealing*
       For sothe truly   *with alle* indeed
       noot (ne woot) do not know

       SERGEANT OF THE LAWE lawyer for the Crown*   *war* shrewd
310   *Parvys* the porch of St Paul's Cathedral*

       swich so
       Justice judge   *assise* (county) court of assizes
315   By open (royal) letter and with full jurisdiction
       science knowledge   *renoun* reputation
       fees and robes yearly grants*   *many oon* many a one
       purchasour buyer of land   *noon* not one
       fee symple unrestricted ownership*   *in effect* in the upshot
320   *been infect* be invalidated
       nas was not
       . . .

540   *propre swynk* own labour   *catel* posessions*
       tabard short sleeveless outer garment   *mere* mare
       REVE steward
       SOMNOUR summoner (to the church court)
       MAUNCIPLE buyer of provisions   *namo* no more
       . . .
715   *clause* short compass
       estaat condition

       highte was called   *faste* close   *Belle* Bell, an inn
720
       baren us behaved   *ilke* same
       alyght arrived
       wol will   *viage* journey
       remenaunt remainder

275 Sownynge alwey th'encrees of his wynnyng.
     He wolde the see were kept for any thyng
     Bitwixe Middelburgh and Orewelle.
     Wel koude he in eschaunge sheeldes selle.
     This worthy man ful wel his wit bisette:
280 Ther wiste no wight that he was in dette,
     So estatly was he of his governaunce
     With his bargaynes and with his chevyssaunce.
     For sothe he was a worthy man with alle,
     But, sooth to seyn, I noot how men hym calle.
         . . .
         A SERGEANT OF THE LAWE, war and wys,
310 That often hadde been at the Parvys,
     Ther was also, ful riche of excellence.
     Discreet he was and of greet reverence
     He semed swich, his wordes weren so wise.
     Justice he was ful often in assise,
315 By patente and by pleyn commissioun.
     For his science and for his heigh renoun,
     Of fees and robes hadde he many oon.
     So greet a purchasour was nowher noon:
     Al was fee symple to hym in effect;
320 His purchasyng myghte nat been infect.
     Nowher so bisy a man as he ther nas,
     And yet he semed bisier than he was.
         . . .
540 Bothe of his propre swynk and his catel.
     In a tabard he rood upon a mere.
         Ther was also a REVE, and a MILLERE,
     A SOMNOUR, and a PARDONER also,
     A MAUNCIPLE, and myself—ther were namo.
         . . .
715   Now have I toold you soothly, in a clause,
     Th'estaat, th'array, the nombre, and eek the cause
     Why that assembled was this compaignye
     In Southwerk at this gentil hostelrye
     That highte the Tabard, faste by the Belle.
720 But now is tyme to yow for to telle
     How that we baren us that ilke nyght,
     Whan we were in that hostelrie alyght;
     And after wol I telle of our viage
     and al the remenaunt of oure pilgrimage.

GIOVANNI BOCCACCIO

Nature's Revenge

Giovanni Boccaccio (1313–1375), poet, scholar, and writer of short stories, was one of the greatest writers of the Italian Renaissance. He was born in Tuscany, a bastard child of the general manager of the Bardi Bank of Florence, one of the greatest European banks of the day. When his father became director of the Naples branch of the bank in 1327, young Giovanni went along and there received an education in law, a subject for which he proved unsuited. Turning to literature and scholarship instead, the young Boccaccio established a reputation in the court of the Angevin Kings of Naples as an innovative poet, specializing in the transfer of popular poetic genres from French to Italian. In 1341 he was compelled to return to Florence where in 1348–9 he witnessed firsthand the effects of the Black Death, the most devastating plague in European history. In later life Boccaccio came under the influence of Francesco Petrarca, the first great humanist of the Renaissance, and spent the final decades of his life writing various learned compendia in Latin, including biographical collections of famous men and women, and erudite studies of classical mythology.

It was in the decade after the Black Death that Boccaccio composed what is by far his most famous work, The Decameron. *This work is a collection of one hundred short tales, purporting to be told by young noblemen and noblewomen to each other while in the country, seeking refuge from the plague. By turns witty, satirical, ribald, and moralizing, the tales reveal the attitudes of laymen of the Renaissance to the world of religious and social conformity that surrounded them. The bawdy tale excerpted here illustrates one of Boccaccio's central themes: that Christian asceticism is unnatural, and attempts to live according to ascetic norms end with Nature having her revenge.*

Alibech becomes a recluse, and after being taught by the monk, Rustico, to put the devil back in Hell, she is eventually taken away to become the wife of Neerbal.

Dioneo had been following the queen's story closely, and on perceiving that it was finished, knowing that he was the only speaker left, he smiled and began without waiting to be bidden:

Gracious ladies, you have possibly never heard how the devil is put back into Hell, and hence, without unduly straying from the theme of your discussions for today, I should like to tell you about it. By learning how it is done, there may yet be time perhaps for you to save our souls from perdition, and you will also discover that, even though Love is more inclined to take up his abode in a gay palace and a dainty bedchamber than in a wretched hovel, there is no denying that he sometimes makes his powers felt among pathless woods, on rugged mountains, and in desert caves; nor is this surprising, since all living things are subject to his way.

Now, to come to the point, there once lived in the town of Gafsa, in Barbary, a very rich man who had numerous children, among them a lovely and graceful young daughter called Alibech. She was not herself a Christian, but there were many Christians in the town, and one day, having on occasion heard them extol the Christian faith and the service of God, she asked one of them for his opinion on the best and easiest way for a person to 'serve God', as they put it. He answered her by saying that the ones who served God best were those who put the greatest distance between themselves and earthly goods, as happened in the case of people who had gone to live in the remoter parts of the Sahara.

She said no more about it to anyone, but next morning, being a very simple-natured creature of fourteen or thereabouts, Alibech set out all alone, in secret, and made her way towards the desert, prompted by nothing more logical than a strong adolescent impulse. A few days later, exhausted from fatigue and hunger, she arrived in the heart of the wilderness, where, catching sight of a small hut in the distance, she stumbled towards it, and in the doorway she found a holy man, who was astonished to see her in those parts and asked her what she was doing there. She told him that she had been inspired by God, and that she was trying, not only to serve Him, but also to find someone who could teach her how she should go about it.

On observing how young and exceedingly pretty she was, the good man was afraid to take her under his wing lest the devil should catch him unawares. So he praised her for her good intentions, and having given her a quantity of herb-roots, wild apples and dates to eat, and some water to drink, he said to her:

'My daughter, not very far from here there is a holy man who is much more capable than I of teaching you what you want to know. Go along to him.' And he sent her upon her way.

When she came to this second man, she was told precisely the same thing, and so she went on until she arrived at the cell of a young hermit, a very devout and kindly fellow called Rustico, to whom she put the same inquiry as she had addressed to the others. Being anxious to prove to himself that he possessed a will of iron, he did not, like the others, send her away or direct her elsewhere, but kept her with him in his cell, in a corner of which, when night descended, he prepared a makeshift bed out of palm-leaves, upon which he invited her to lie down and rest.

Once he had taken this step, very little time elapsed before temptation went to war against his willpower, and after the first few assaults, finding himself outmanoeuvred on all fronts, he laid down his arms and surrendered. Casting aside pious thoughts, prayers, and penitential exercises, he began to concentrate his mental faculties upon the youth and beauty of the girl, and to devise suitable ways and means for approaching her in such a fashion that she should not think it lewd of him to make the sort of proposal he had in mind. By putting certain questions to her, he soon discovered that she had never been intimate with the opposite sex and was every bit as innocent as she seemed; and he therefore thought of a possible way to persuade her, with the pretext of serving God, to grant his desires. He began by delivering a long speech in which he showed her how powerful an enemy the devil was to the Lord God, and followed this up by impressing upon her that of all the ways of serving God, the one that He most appreciated consisted in putting the devil back in Hell, to which the Almighty had consigned him in the first place.

The girl asked him how this was done, and Rustico replied:

'You will soon find out, but just do whatever you see me doing for the present.' And so saying, he began to divest himself of the few clothes he was wearing, leaving himself completely naked. The girl followed his example, and he sank to his knees as though he were about to pray, getting her to kneel directly opposite.

In this posture, the girl's beauty was displayed to Rustico in all its glory, and his longings blazed more fiercely than ever, bringing about the resurrection of the flesh. Alibech stared at this in amazement, and said:

'Rustico, what is that thing I see sticking out in front of you, which I do not possess?'

'Oh, my daughter,' said Rustico, 'this is the devil I was telling you about. Do you see what he's doing? He's hurting me so much that I can hardly endure it.'

'Oh, praise be to God,' said the girl, 'I can see that I am better off than you are, for I have no such devil to contend with.'

'You're right there,' said Rustico. 'But you have something else instead, that I haven't.'

'Oh?' said Alibech. 'And what's that?'

'You have Hell,' said Rustico. 'And I honestly believe that God has sent you here for the salvation of my soul, because if this devil continues to plague the life out of me, and if you are prepared to take sufficient pity upon me to let me put him back into Hell, you will be giving me marvellous relief, as well as rendering incalculable service and pleasure to God, which is what you say you came here for in the first place.'

'Oh, Father,' replied the girl in all innocence, 'if I really do have a Hell, let's do as you suggest just as soon as you are ready.'

'God bless you, my daughter,' said Rustico. 'Let us go and put him back, and then perhaps he'll leave me alone.'

At which point he conveyed the girl to one of their beds, where he instructed her in the art of incarcerating that accursed fiend.

Never having put a single devil into Hell before, the girl found the first experience a little painful, and she said to Rustico:

'This devil must certainly be a bad lot, Father, and a true enemy of God, for as well as plaguing mankind, he even hurts Hell when he's driven back inside it.'

'Daughter,' said Rustico, 'it will not always be like that.' And in order to ensure that it wouldn't, before moving from the bed they put him back half a dozen times, curbing his arrogance to such good effect that he was positively glad to keep still for the rest of the day.

During the next few days, however, the devil's pride frequently reared its head again, and the girl, ever ready to obey the call to duty and bring him under control, happened to develop a taste for the sport, and began saying to Rustico:

'I can certainly see what those worthy men in Gafsa meant when they said that serving God was so agreeable. I don't honestly recall ever having done anything that gave me so much pleasure and satisfaction as I get from putting the devil back in Hell. To my way of thinking, anyone who devotes his energies to anything but the service of God is a complete blockhead.'

She thus developed the habit of going to Rustico at frequent intervals, and saying to him:

'Father, I came here to serve God, not to idle away my time. Let's go and put the devil back in Hell.'

And sometimes, in the middle of their labours, she would say:

'What puzzles me, Rustico, is that the devil should ever want to escape from Hell. Because if he liked being there as much as Hell enjoys receiving him and keeping him inside, he would never go away at all.'

By inviting Rustico to play the game too often, continually urging him on in the service of God, the girl took so much stuffing out of him that he eventually began to turn cold where another man would have been bathed in sweat. So he told her that the devil should only be punished and put back in Hell when he reared his head with pride, adding that by the grace of Heaven, they had tamed him so effectively that he was pleading with God to be left in peace. In this way, he managed to keep the girl quiet for a while, but one day, having begun to notice that Rustico was no longer asking for the devil to be put back in Hell, she said:

'Look here, Rustico. Even though your devil has been punished and pesters you no longer, my Hell simply refuses to leave me alone. Now that I have helped you with my Hell to subdue the pride of your devil, the least you can do is to get your devil to help me tame the fury of my Hell.'

Rustico, who was living on a diet of herb-roots and water, was quite incapable of supplying her requirements, and told her that the taming of her Hell would require an awful lot of devils, but promised to do what he could. Sometimes, therefore, he responded to the call, but this happened so infrequently that it was rather like chucking a bean into the mouth of a lion, with the result that the girl, who felt that she was not serving God as diligently as she would have liked, was found complaining more often than not.

But at the height of this dispute between Alibech's Hell and Rustico's devil, brought about by a surplus of desire on the one hand and a shortage of power on the other, a fire broke out in Gafsa, and Alibech's father was burnt to death in his own house along with all his children and every other member of his household, so that Alibech inherited the whole of his property. Because of this a young man called Neerbal who had spent the whole of his substance in sumptuous living, having heard that she was still alive, set out to look for her, and before the authorities were able to appropriate her late father's fortune on the grounds that there was no heir, he succeeded in tracing her whereabouts. To the great relief of Rustico, but against her own wishes, he took her back to Gafsa and married her, thus inheriting a half-share in her father's enormous fortune.

Before Neerbal had actually slept with her, she was questioned by the women of Gafsa about how she had served God in the desert, and she replied that she had served Him by putting the devil back in Hell, and that Neerbal had committed a terrible sin by stopping her from performing so worthy a service.

'How do you put the devil back in Hell?' asked the women.

Partly in words and partly through gestures, the girl showed them how it was done, whereupon the women laughed so much that they are laughing yet; and they said:

'Don't let it worry you, my dear. People do the job every bit as well here in Gafsa, and Neerbal will give you plenty of help in serving the Lord.'

The story was repeated throughout the town, being passed from one woman to the next, and they coined a proverbial saying there to the effect that the most agreeable way of serving God was to put the devil back in Hell. The dictum later crossed the sea to Italy, where it survives to this day.

And so, young ladies, if you stand in need of God's grace, see that you learn to put the devil back in Hell, for it is greatly to His liking and pleasurable to the parties concerned, and a great deal of good can arise and flow in the process.

SIR THOMAS MALORY

Chivalric Justice

Sir Thomas Malory (fl. 1470) was most likely a knight from Warwickshire, but this is not certain. He seems to have been born in the early part of the fifteenth century and spent much of the last twenty years of his life in prison, either because he had committed violent crimes or because he had fought for the Lancastrians, the losing side in the Wars of the Roses in England; the latter explanation is the more likely. He observed what he considered the end of the age of chivalry, and regretted its passing deeply.

Le Morte D'Arthur (1470) is one of the greatest, most moving renditions of the Arthurian legend. William Caxton published it in 1485, making it one of the first books to be printed in England. The work concerns the life, deeds, and death of Arthur, the legendary king of Britain, who was killed in combat by his illegitimate son, Mordred. It also tells of the love affair between Lancelot and Guenever, the quest for the Holy Grail, Merlin's magic, and other famous stories.

BOOK XVIII

CHAPTER 1: *Of the joy King Arthur and the queen had of the achievement of the Sangrail; and how Launcelot fell to his old love again.*

So after the quest of the Sangrail was fulfilled, and all knights that were left alive were comen again unto the Table Round, as the Book of the Sangrail maketh mention, then was there great joy in the court; and in especial King Arthur and Queen Guenever made great joy of the remnant that were comen home, and passing glad was the king and the queen of Sir Launcelot and of Sir Bors, for they had been passing long away in the quest of the Sangrail.

Then, as the book saith, Sir Launcelot began to resort unto Queen Guenever again, and forgat the promise and the perfection that he made in the quest. For, as the book saith, had not Sir Launcelot been in his privy thoughts and in his minds so set inwardly to the queen as he was in seeming outward to God, there had no knight passed him in the quest of the Sangrail; but ever his thoughts were privily on the queen, and so they loved together more hotter than they did toforehand, and had such privy draughts together, that many in the court spake of it, and in especial Sir Agravain, Sir Gawain's brother, for he was ever open-mouthed.

So befell that Sir Launcelot had many resorts of ladies and damosels that daily resorted unto him, that besought him to be their champion, and in all such matters of right Sir Launcelot applied him daily to do for the pleasure of Our Lord, Jesu Christ. And ever as much as he might he withdrew him from the company and fellowship of Queen Guenever, for to eschew the slander and noise; wherefore the queen waxed wroth with Sir Launcelot.

And upon a day she called Sir Launcelot unto her chamber, and said thus:

'Sir Launcelot, I see and feel daily that thy love beginneth to slake,[1] for thou hast no joy to be in my presence, but ever thou art out of this court, and quarrels and matters thou hast nowadays for ladies and gentlewomen more than ever thou were wont to have aforehand.'

'Ah madam,' said Launcelot, 'in this ye must hold me excused for divers causes; one is, I was but late in the quest of the Sangrail; and I thank God of His great mercy, and never of my desert, that I saw in that my quest as much as ever saw any sinful man, and so was it told me. And if I had not had my privy thoughts to return to your love again as I do, I had seen as great mysteries as ever saw my son Galahad, other Percival, or Sir Bors; and therefore, madam, I was but late in that quest. Wit ye well, madam, it may not be yet lightly forgotten the high service in whom I did my diligent labour.

'Also, madam, wit ye well that there be many men speaken of our love in this court, and have you and me greatly in a-wait, as Sir Agravain and Sir Mordred; and madam, wit ye well I dread them more for your sake than for any fear I have of them myself, for I may happen to escape and rid myself in a great need, where ye must abide all that will be said unto you. And then if that ye fall in any distress through wilful folly, then is there none other remedy or help but by me and my blood.

'And wit ye well, madam, the boldness of you and me will bring us to great shame and slander; and that were me loth to see you dishonoured. And that is the cause I take upon me more for to do for damosels and maidens than ever I did tofore, that men should understand my joy and my delight is my pleasure to have ado for damosels and maidens.'

CHAPTER 2: *How the queen commanded Sir Launcelot to avoid the court, and of the sorrow that Launcelot made*

All this while the queen stood still and let Sir Launcelot say what he would. And when he had all said she brast out on weeping, and so she sobbed and wept a great while. And when she might speak she said, 'Launcelot, now I well understand that thou art a false recreant knight and a common lecher, and lovest and holdest other ladies, and by me thou hast disdain and scorn. For wit thou well,' she said, 'now I understand thy falsehood, and therefore shall I never love thee no more. And never be thou so hardy to come in my sight; and right here I discharge thee this court, that thou never come within it; and I forfend[2] thee my fellowship, and upon pain of thy head that thou see me no more.'

Right so Sir Launcelot departed with great heaviness, that unnethe he might sustain himself for great dole-making. Then he called Sir Bors, Sir Ector de Maris, and Sir Lionel, and told them how the queen had forfended him the court, and so he was in will to depart into his own country.

'Fair sir,' said Sir Bors de Ganis, 'ye shall not depart out of this land by mine advice. Ye must remember in what honour ye are renowned, and called the noblest knight of the world; and many great matters ye have in hand. And women in their hastiness will do ofttimes that sore repenteth them; and therefore by mine advice ye shall take your horse, and ride to the good hermitage here beside Windsor, that sometime was a good knight, his name is Sir Brastias, and there shall ye abide till I send you word of better tidings.'

'Brother,' said Sir Launcelot, 'wit ye well I am full loth to depart out of this realm, but the queen hath defended me so highly, that meseemeth she will never be my good lady as she hath been.'

'Say ye never so,' said Sir Bors, 'for many times or this time she hath been wroth with you, and after it she was the first that repented it.'

'Ye say well,' said Launcelot, 'for now will I do by your counsel, and take mine horse and my harness, and ride to the hermit, Sir Brastias, and there will I repose me until I hear some manner of tidings from you, but, fair brother, I pray you get me the love of my lady, Queen Guenever, and ye may.'

'Sir,' said Sir Bors, 'ye need not to move me of such matters, for well ye wot I will do what I may to please you.'

And then the noble knight, Sir Launcelot, departed with right heavy cheer suddenly, that none earthly creature wist of him, nor where he was become, but Sir Bors. So when Sir Launcelot was departed, the queen outward made no manner of sorrow in showing to none of his blood nor to none other. But wit ye well, inwardly, as the book saith, she took great thought, but she bare it out with a proud countenance as though she felt nothing nor danger.

CHAPTER 3: *How at dinner that the queen made there was a knight poisoned, which Sir Mador laid on the queen*

And then the queen let make a privy dinner in London unto the knights of the Round Table. And all was for to show outward that she had as great joy in all other knights of the Table Round as she had in Sir Launcelot. All only at that dinner she had Sir Gawain and his brethren, that is for to say Sir Agravain, Sir Gaheris, Sir Gareth, and Sir Mordred. Also there was Sir Bors de Ganis, Sir Blamor de Ganis, Sir Bleoberis de Ganis, Sir Galihud, Sir Galihodin, Sir Ector de Maris, Sir Lionel, Sir Palomides, Sir Safer his brother, Sir La Cote Male Taile, Sir Persant, Sir Ironside, Sir Brandiles, Sir Kay le Seneschal, Sir Mador de la Porte, Sir Patrise, a knight of Ireland, Aliduke, Sir Astamore, and Sir Pinel le Savage, the which was cousin to Sir Lamorak de Gales, the good knight that Sir Gawain and his brethren slew by treason.

And so these four and twenty knights should dine with the queen in a privy place by themself, and there was made a great feast of all manner of dainties. But Sir Gawain had a custom that he used daily at dinner and at supper, that he loved well all manner of fruit, and in especial apples and pears. And therefore whosomever dined or feasted Sir Gawain would commonly purvey for good fruit for him, and so did the queen for to please Sir Gawain; she let purvey for him all manner of fruit. For Sir Gawain was a passing hot knight of nature, and this Pinel hated Sir Gawain because of his kinsman Sir Lamorak de Gales; and therefore for pure envy and hate Sir Pinel enpoisoned certain apples for to enpoison Sir Gawain.

And so this was well unto the end of the meat; and so it befell by misfortune a good knight named Patrise, cousin unto Sir Mador de la Porte, to take a poisoned apple. And when he had eaten it he swelled so till he brast, and there Sir Patrise fell down suddenly dead among them. Then every knight leapt from the board ashamed, and araged for wrath, nigh out of their wits. For they wist not what to say; considering Queen Guenever made the feast and dinner, they all had suspicion unto her.

'My lady, the queen,' said Gawain, 'wit ye well, madam, that this dinner was made for me, for all folks that knowen my condition understand that I love well fruit, and now I see well I had near been slain; therefore, madam, I dread me lest ye will be shamed.'

Then the queen stood still and was sore abashed, that she nist not what to say.

'This shall not so be ended,' said Sir Mador de la Porte, 'for here have I lost a full noble knight of my blood; and therefore upon this shame and despite I will be revenged to the utterance.' And there openly Sir Mador appelled the queen of the death of his cousin, Sir Patrise.

Then stood they all still, that none would speak a word against him, for they all had great suspicion unto the queen because she let make that dinner. And the queen was so abashed that she could none other ways do, but wept so heartily that she fell in a swoon. With this noise and cry came to them King Arthur, and when he wist of that trouble he was a passing heavy man.

CHAPTER 4: *How Sir Mador appeached the queen of treason, and there was no knight would fight for her at the first time*

And ever Sir Mador stood still afore the king, and ever he appelled the queen of treason, for the custom was such that time that all manner of shameful death was called treason.

'Fair lords,' said King Arthur, 'me repenteth of this trouble, but the case is so I may not have ado in this matter, for I must be a rightful judge; and that repenteth me that I may not do battle for my wife, for as I deem this deed came never by her. And therefore I suppose she shall not be all distained,[3] but that some good knight shall put his body in jeopardy for my queen rather than she shall be burnt in a wrong quarrel. And therefore, Sir Mador, be not so hasty, for it may happen she shall not be all friendless; and therefore desire thou thy day of battle, and she shall purvey her of some good knight that shall answer you, or else it were to me great shame, and to all my court.'

'My gracious lord,' said Sir Mador, 'ye must hold me excused, for though ye be our king in that degree, ye are but a knight as we are, and ye are sworn unto knighthood as well as we; and therefore I beseech you that ye be not displeased, for there is none of the four and twenty knights that were bidden to this dinner but all they have great suspicion unto the queen. What say ye all, my lords?' said Sir Mador.

Then they answered by and by that they could not excuse the queen; for why she made the dinner, and other it must come by her or by her servants.

'Alas,' said the queen, 'I made this dinner for a good intent, and never for none evil, so Almighty God me help in my right, as I was never purposed to do such evil deeds, and that I report me unto God.'

'My lord, the king,' said Sir Mador, 'I require you as ye be a righteous king give me a day that I may have justice.'

'Well,' said the king, 'I give the day this day fifteen days that thou be ready armed on horseback in the meadow beside Winchester. And if it so fall that there be any knight to encounter with you, there mayest thou do the best, and God speed the right. And if it so fall that there be no knight at that day, then must my queen be burnt, and there she shall be ready to have her judgement.'

'I am answered,' said Sir Mador.

And every knight went where it liked them. So when the king and the queen were together the king asked the queen how this case befell.

The queen answered, 'So God me help, I wot not how nor in what manner.'

'Where is Sir Launcelot?' said King Arthur; 'And he were here he would not grudge to do battle for you.'

'Sir,' said the queen, 'I wot not where he is, but his brother and his kinsmen deem that he be not within this realm.'

'That me repenteth,' said King Arthur, 'for and he were here he would soon stint this strife. Then I will counsel you,' said the king, 'and unto Sir Bors: "That ye will do battle for her for Sir Launcelot's sake," and upon my life he will not refuse you. For well I see,' said the king, 'that none of these four and twenty knights that were with you at your dinner where Sir Patrise was slain, that will do battle for you, nor none of them will say well of you, and that shall be a great slander for you in this court.'

'Alas,' said the queen, 'and I may not do withal, but now I miss Sir Launcelot, for and he were here he would put me soon to my heart's ease.'

'What aileth you,' said the king, 'ye cannot keep Sir Launcelot upon your side? For wit ye well,' said the king, 'who that hath Sir Launcelot upon his part hath the most man of worship in the world upon his side. Now go your way,' said the king unto the queen, 'and require Sir Bors to do battle for you for Sir Launcelot's sake.'

CHAPTER 5: *How the queen required Sir Bors to fight for her, and how he granted upon condition; and how he warned Sir Launcelot thereof*

So the queen departed from the king, and sent for Sir Bors into her chamber. And when he was come she besought him of succour.

'Madam,' said he, 'what would ye that I did? For I may not with my worship have ado in this matter, because I was at the same dinner, for dread that any of those knights would have me in suspicion. Also, Madam,' said Sir Bors, 'now miss ye Sir Launcelot, for he would not have failed you neither in right nor in wrong, as ye have well proved when ye have been in danger; and now ye have driven him out of this country, by whom ye and all we were daily worshipped by; therefore, madam, I marvel how ye dare for shame require me to do any thing for you, in so much ye have chased him out of your country by whom we were borne up and honoured.'

'Alas, fair knight,' said the queen, 'I put me wholly in your grace, and all that is done amiss I will amend as ye will counsel me.' And therewith she kneeled down upon both her knees, and besought Sir Bors to have mercy upon her: 'Other I shall have a shameful death, and thereto I never offended.'

Right so came King Arthur, and found the queen kneeling afore Sir Bors; then Sir Bors pulled her up and said,

'Madam, ye do me great dishonour.'

'Ah, gentle knight,' said the king, 'have mercy upon my queen, courteous knight, for I am now in certain she is untruly defamed. And therefore, courteous knight,' said the king, 'promise her to do battle for her, I require you for the love of Sir Launcelot.'

'My lord,' said Sir Bors, 'ye require me the greatest thing that any man may require me; and wit ye well if I grant to do battle for the queen I shall wrath many of my fellowship of the Table Round. But as for that,' said Bors, 'I will grant my lord that for my lord Sir Launcelot's sake, and for you sake I will at that day be the queen's champion unless that there come by adventure a better knight than I am to do battle for her.'

'Will ye promise me this,' said the king, 'by your faith?'

'Yea sir,' said Sir Bors, 'of that I will not fail you, nor her both, but if there came a better knight than I am, and then shall he have the battle.'

Then was the king and the queen passing glad, and so departed, and thanked him heartily. So then Sir Bors departed secretly upon a day, and rode unto Sir Launcelot thereas he was the hermit, Sir Brastias, and told him of all their adventure.

'Ah Jesu,' said Sir Launcelot, 'this is come happily as I would have it, and therefore I pray you make you ready to do battle, but look that ye tarry till ye see me come, as long as ye may. For I am sure Mador is an hot knight when he is enchafed, for the more ye suffer him the hastier will he be to battle.'

'Sir,' said Bors, 'let me deal with him, doubt ye not ye shall have all your will.'

Then departed Sir Bors from him and came to the court again. Then was it noised in all the court that Sir Bors should do battle for the queen; wherefore many knights were displeased with him, that he would take upon him to do battle in the queen's quarrel; for there were but few knights in all the court but they deemed the queen was in the wrong, and that she had done that treason. So Sir Bors answered thus to his fellows of the Table Round:

'Wit ye well, my fair lords, it were shame to us all and we suffered to see the most noble queen of the world to be shamed openly, considering her lord and our lord is the man of most worship in the world, and most christened, and he hath ever worshipped us all in all places.'

Many answered him again: 'As for our most noble King Arthur, we love him and honour him as well as ye do, but as for Queen Guenever we love her not, because she is a destroyer of good knights.'

'Fair lords,' said Sir Bors, 'meseemeth ye say not as ye should say, for never yet in my days knew I never nor heard say that ever she was a destroyer of any good knight. But at all times as far as ever I could know she was a maintainer of good knights; and ever she hath been large and free of her goods to all good knights, and the most bounteous lady of her gifts and her good grace, that ever I saw or heard speak of. And therefore it were shame,' said Sir Bors, 'to us all to our most noble king's wife, and we suffered her to be shamefully slain. And wit ye well,' said Sir Bors, 'I will not suffer it, for I dare say so much, the queen is not guilty of Sir Patrise's death, for she owed him never none ill will, nor none of the four and twenty knights that were at that dinner; for I dare say for good love she bad us to dinner, and not for no mal engine, and that I doubt not shall be proved hereafter, for howsomever the game goeth, there was treason among us.'

Then some said to Sir Bors, 'We may well believe your words.'

And so some of them were well pleased, and some were not so.

CHAPTER 6: *How at the day Sir Bors made him ready for to fight for the queen; and when he should fight how another discharged him*

The day came on fast until the even that the battle should be. Then the queen sent for Sir Bors and asked him how he was disposed.

'Truly madam,' said he, 'I am disposed in likewise as I promised you, that is for to say I shall not fail you, unless by adventure there come a better knight than I am to do battle for you, then, madam, am I discharged for my promise.'

'Will ye,' said the queen, 'that I tell my lord Arthur thus?'

'Do as it shall please you, madam.'

Then the queen went unto the king and told him the answer of Sir Bors.

'Have ye no doubt,' said the king, 'of Sir Bors, for I call him now one of the best knights of the world, and the most profitliest man.'

And thus it passed on until the morn, and the king and the queen and all manner of knights that were there at that time drew them unto the meadow beside Winchester where the battle should be. And so when the king was come with the queen and many knights of the Round Table, then the queen was put there in the constable's ward, and a great fire made about an iron stake, that and Sir Mador de la Porte had the better, she should be burnt: such custom was used in those days, that neither for favour, neither for love nor affinity, there should be none other but righteous judgement, as well upon a king as upon a knight, and as well upon a queen as upon another poor lady.

So in this meanwhile came in Sir Mador de la Porte, and took his oath afore the king, that the queen did this treason until his cousin Sir Patrise, and unto his oath he would prove it with his body, hand for hand, who that would say the contrary.

Right so came in Sir Bors de Ganis, and said that 'as for Queen Guenever she is in the right, and that will I make good with my hands that she is not culpable of this treason that is put upon her.'

'Then make thee ready,' said Sir Mador, 'and we shall prove whether thou be in the right or I.'

'Sir Mador,' said Sir Bors, 'wit thou well I know you for a good knight. Notforthan I shall not fear you so greatly, but I trust to God I shall be able to withstand your malice. But thus much have I promised my lord Arthur and my lady the queen, that I shall do battle for her in this case to the uttermost, unless that there come a better knight than I am and discharge me.'

'Is that all?' said Sir Mador, 'other come thou off and do battle with me, or else say nay.'

'Take your horse,' said Sir Bors, 'and as I suppose, ye shall not tarry long but ye shall be answered.'

Then either departed to their tents and made them ready to horseback as they thought best. And anon Sir Mador came into the field with his shield on his shoulder and his spear in his hand; and so rode about the place crying unto Arthur: 'Bid your champion come forth and he dare.'

Then was Sir Bors ashamed and took his horse and came to the lists' end.

And then was he ware where came from a wood there fast by a knight all armed, upon a white horse, with a strange shield of strange arms; and he came riding all that he might run, and so he came to Sir Bors, and said thus:

'Fair knight, I pray you be not displeased, for here must a better knight than ye are have this battle, therefore I pray you withdraw you.

For wit ye well I have had this day a right great journey, and this battle ought to be mine, and so I promised you when I spake with you last, and with all my heart I thank you of your good will.'

Then Sir Bors rode unto King Arthur and told him how there was a knight come that would have the battle for to fight for the queen.

'What knight is he?' said the king.

'I wot not,' said Sir Bors, 'but such covenant he made with me to be here this day. Now my lord,' said Sir Bors, 'here am I discharged.'

CHAPTER 7: *How Sir Launcelot fought against Sir Mador for the queen, and how he overcame Sir Mador, and discharged the queen*

Then the king called to that knight, and asked him if he would fight for the queen.

Then he answered to the king, 'Therefore came I hither, and therefore, sir king,' he said, 'tarry me no longer, for I may not tarry. For anon as I have finished this battle I must depart hence, for I have ado many matters elsewhere. For wit you well,' said that knight, 'this is dishonour to you all knights of the Round Table, to see and know so noble a lady and so courteous a queen as Queen Guenever is, thus to be rebuked and shamed amongst you.'

Then they all marvelled what knight that might be that so took the battle upon him. For there was not one that knew him, but if it were Sir Bors.

Then said Sir Mador de la Porte unto the king, 'Now let me wit with whom I shall have ado withal.'

And then they rode to the lists' end, and there they couched their spears, and ran together with all their mights, and Sir Mador's spear brake all to pieces, but the other's spear held, and bare Sir Mador's horse and all backward to the earth a great fall. But mightily and suddenly he avoided his horse and put his shield afore him, and then drew his sword, and bad the other knight alight and do battle with him on foot.

Then that knight descended from his horse lightly like a valiant man, and put his shield afore him and drew his sword; and so they came eagerly unto battle, and either gave other many great strokes, tracing and traversing, rasing and foining, and hurtling together with their swords as it were wild boars. Thus were they fighting nigh an hour, for this Sir Mador was a strong knight, and mightily proved in many strong battles. But at the last this knight smote Sir Mador grovelling upon the earth, and the knight stepped near him to have pulled Sir Mador flatling upon the ground; and therewith suddenly Sir Mador arose, and in his rising he smote that knight through the thick of the thighs that the blood ran out fiercely.

And when he felt himself so wounded, and saw his blood, he let him arise upon his feet. And he gave him such a buffet upon the helm that he fell to the earth flatling, and therewith he strode to him to have pulled off his helm off his head. And then Sir Mador prayed that knight to save his life, and so he yielded him as overcome, and released the queen of his quarrel.

'I will not grant thee thy life,' said that knight, 'only that thou freely release the queen for ever, and that no mention be made upon Sir Patrise's tomb that ever Queen Guenever consented to that treason.'

'All this shall be done,' said Sir Mador, 'I clearly discharge my quarrel for ever.'

Then the knights parters of the lists took up Sir Mador, and led him to his tent, and the other knight went straight to the stairfoot where sat King Arthur; and by that time was the queen come to the king, and either kissed other heartily.

And when the king saw that knight, he stooped down to him, and thanked him, and in likewise did the queen' and the king prayed him to put off his helmet, and to repose him, and to take a sop of wine. And then he put off his helm to drink, and then every knight knew him that it was Sir Launcelot du Lake.

Anon as the king wist that, he took the queen in his hand, and yode unto Sir Launcelot, and said, 'Sir, gramercy of your great travail that ye have had this day for me and for my queen.'

'My lord,' said Sir Launcelot, 'wit ye well I ought of right ever to be in your quarrel, and in my lady the queen's quarrel, to do battle; for ye are the man that gave me the high order of knighthood, and that day my lady, your queen, did me great worship, and else I had been shamed; for that same day ye made me knight, through my hastiness I lost my sword, and my lady, your queen, found it, and lapped it in her train, and gave me my sword when I had need thereto, and else had I been shamed among all knights; and therefore, my lord Arthur, I promised her at that day ever to be her knight in right other in wrong.'

'Gramercy,' said the king, 'for this journey; and wit ye well,' said the king, 'I shall acquit your goodness.'

And ever the queen beheld Sir Launcelot, and wept so tenderly that she sank almost to the ground for sorrow that he had done to her so great goodness where she showed him great unkindness.

Then the knights of his blood drew unto him, and there either of them made great joy of other. And so came all the knights of the Table Round that were there at that time, and welcomed him. And then Sir Mador was had to leech craft, and Sir Launcelot was healed of his wound. And then there was made great joy and mirths in that court.

EXPLANATORY NOTES

1. *slake:* abate.
2. *forfend:* forbid.
3. *distained:* dishonoured.

ANONYMOUS

Everyman

Everyman.   O, to whom shall I make my moan
  For to go with me in that heavy journey?
  First *Fellowship* said he would with me gone;
  His words were very pleasant and gay,
  But afterward he left me alone.
  Then spake I to my kinsmen all in despair,
  And also they gave me words fair,
  They lacked no fair speaking,
  But all forsake me in the ending.
  Then went I to my *Goods* that I loved best,
  In hope to have comfort, but there had I least;
  For my *Goods* sharply did me tell
  That he bringeth many into hell.
  Then of myself I was ashamed,
  And so I am worthy to be blamed;
  Thus may I well myself hate.
  Of whom shall I now counsel take?
  I think that I shall never speed
  Till that I go to my *Good-Deed*,
  But alas, she is so weak,
  That she can neither go nor speak;
  Yet will I venture on her now.—
  My *Good-Deeds*, where be you?
Good-Deeds.   Here I lie cold in the ground;
  Thy sins hath me sore bound,
  That I cannot stir.
Everyman.   O, *Good-Deeds*, I stand in fear;
  I must you pray of counsel,
  For help now should come right well.
Good-Deeds.   *Everyman*, I have understanding
  That ye be summoned account to make

Excerpt from *Everyman*, by Anonymous, reprinted from *Everyman and Other Old Religious Plays*, (1909), J.M. Dent & Sons, Ltd.

Before *Messias,* of Jerusalem King;
    And you do by me that journey what you will I take.[30]
Everyman.   Therefore I come to you, my moan to make;
    I pray you, that ye will go with me.
Good-Deeds.   I would full fain, but I cannot stand verily.
Everyman. Why, is there anything on you fall?[31]
Good-Deeds.   Yea, sir, I may thank you of[32] all;
    If ye had perfectly cheered me,
    Your book of account now full ready had be.
    Look, the books of your works and deeds eke;[33]
    Oh, see bow they lie under the feet,
    To your soul's heaviness.
Everyman.   Our Lord *Jesus,* help me!
    For one letter here I can not see.
Good-Deeds.   There is a blind reckoning in time of distress!
Everyman.   *Good-Deeds,* I pray you, help me in this need,
    Or else I am for ever damned indeed;
    Therefore help me to make reckoning
    Before the redeemer of all thing,
    That king is, and was, and ever shall.
Good-Deeds.   *Everyman,* I am sorry of your fall,
    And fain would I help you, and I were able.
Everyman.   *Good-Deeds,* your counsel I pray you give me.
Good-Deeds.   That shall I do verily;
    Though that on my feet I may not go,
    I have a sister, that shall with you also,
    Called *Knowledge,* which shall with you abide,
    To help you to make that dreadful reckoning.
Knowledge.   *Everyman,* I will go with thee, and be thy guide,
    In thy most need to go by thy side.
Everyman.   In good condition I am now in every thing,
    And am wholly content with this good thing;
    Thanked be God my Creator.
Good-Deeds.   And when he hath brought thee there,
    Where thou shalt heal thee of thy smart,

---

30. *And you . . . I take.]* If you do as I say, I will take that journey with you.

31. *fall]* befallen.

32. *of]* for.

33. *eke]* also.

Then go you with your reckoning and your *Good-Deeds* together
For to make you joyful at heart
Before the blessed Trinity.

Everyman.   My *Good-Deeds*, gramercy;
I am well content, certainly,
With your words sweet.

Knowledge.   Now go we together lovingly,
To *Confession*, that cleansing river.

Everyman.   For joy I weep; I would we were there;
But, I pray you, give me cognition
Where dwelleth that holy man, *Confession.*

Knowledge.   In the house of salvation:
We shall find him in that place,
That shall us comfort by God's grace.
Lo, this is *Confession;* kneel down and ask mercy,
For he is in good conceit[34] with God almighty.

Everyman.   O glorious fountain that all uncleanness doth clarify,
Wash from me the spots of vices unclean,
That on me no sin may be seen;
I come with *Knowledge* for my redemption,
Repent with hearty and full contrition;
For I am commanded a pilgrimage to take,
And great accounts before God to make.
Now, I pray you, *Shrift,* mother of salvation,
Help my good deeds for my piteous exclamation.

Confession.   I know your sorrow well, *Everyman;*
Because with *Knowledge* ye come to me,
I will you comfort as well as I can,
And a precious jewel I will give thee,
Called penance, wise voider of adversity;
Therewith shall your body chastised be,
With abstinence and perseverance in God's service:
Here shall you receive that scourge of me,
Which is penance strong, that ye must endure,
To remember thy Saviour was scourged for thee
With sharp scourges, and suffered it patiently;
So must thou, or thou scape that painful pilgrimage;
Knowledge, keep him in this voyage,

---

34. *good conceit*] favorable opinion, i.e., highly esteemed by.

And by that time *Good-Deeds* will be with thee.
But in any wise, be sure of mercy,
For your time draweth fast, and ye will saved be;
Ask God mercy, and He will grant truly,
When with the scourge of penance man doth him bind,
The oil of forgiveness then shall he find.

Everyman.   Thanked be God for his gracious work!
For now I will my penance begin;
This hath rejoiced and lighted my heart,
Though the knots be painful and hard within.

Knowledge.   *Everyman*, look your penance that ye fulfil,
What pain that ever it to you be,
And *Knowledge* shall give you counsel at will,
How your accounts ye shall make clearly.

Everyman.   O eternal God, O heavenly figure,
O way of rightwiseness, O goodly vision,
Which descended down in a virgin pure
Because he would *Everyman* redeem,
Which *Adam* forfeited by his disobedience:
O blessed Godhead, elect and high-divine,
Forgive my grievous offence;
Here I cry thee mercy in this presence.
O ghostly treasure, O ransomer and redeemer
Of all the world, hope and conductor,
Mirror of joy, and founder of mercy,
Which illumineth heaven and earth thereby,
Hear my clamorous complaint, though it late be;
Receive my prayers; unworthy in this heavy life,
Though I be, a sinner most abominable,
Yet let my name be written in *Moses'* table;
O *Mary*, pray to the Maker of all thing,
Me for to help at my ending,
And save me from the power of my enemy,
For *Death* assaileth me strongly;
And, Lady, that I may by means of thy prayer
Of your Son's glory to be partaker,
By the means of his passion I it crave,
I beseech you, help my soul to save.—
Knowledge, give me the scourge of penance;
My flesh therewith shall give a quittance:
I will now begin, if God give me grace.

Knowledge. *Everyman,* God give you time and space:
Thus I bequeath you in the hands of our Saviour,
Thus may you make your reckoning sure.
Everyman. In the name of the Holy Trinity,
My body sore[35] punished shall be:
Take this body for the sin of the flesh;
Also thou delightest to go gay and fresh,
And in the way of damnation thou did me bring;
Therefore suffer now strokes and punishing.
Now of penance I will wade the water clear,
To save me from purgatory, that sharp fire.
Good-Deeds. I thank God, now I can walk and go;
And am delivered of my sickness and woe.
Therefore with *Everyman* I will go, and not spare;
His good works I will help him to declare.
Knowledge. Now, *Everyman,* be merry and glad;
Your *Good-Deeds* cometh now; ye may not be sad;
Now is your *Good-Deeds* whole and sound,
Going upright upon the ground.
Everyman. My heart is light, and shall be evermore;
Now will I smite faster than I did before.
Good-Deeds. *Everyman,* pilgrim, my special friend,
Blessed be thou without end;
For thee is prepared the eternal glory.
Ye have me made whole and sound,
Therefore I will bide by thee in every stound.[36]
Everyman. Welcome, my *Good-Deeds;* now I hear thy voice,
I weep for very sweetness of love.
Knowledge. Be no more sad, but ever rejoice,
God seeth thy living in his throne above;
Put on this garment to thy behove,[37]
Which is wet with your tears,
Or else before God you may it miss,
When you to your journey's end come shall.
Everyman. Gentle *Knowledge,* what do you it call?

---

35. *sore*] grievously.

36. *stound*] season.

37. *behove*] advantage.

Knowledge.   It is a garment of sorrow:
    From pain it will you borrow;
    Contrition it is,
    That getteth forgiveness;
    It pleaseth God passing well.
Good-Deeds.   *Everyman,* will you wear it for your heal?
Everyman.   Now blessed be *Jesu, Mary's* Son!
    For now have I on true contrition.
    And let us go now without tarrying;
    Good-Deeds, have we clear our reckoning?
Good-Deeds.   Yea, indeed I have it here.
Everyman.   Then I trust we need not fear;
    Now, friends, let us not part in twain.[38]
Knowledge.   Nay, Everyman, that will we not, certain.
Good-Deeds. Yet must thou lead with thee
    Three persons of great might.
Everyman.   Who should they be?
Good-Deeds.   *Discretion and Strength* they hight,[39]
    And thy *Beauty* may not abide behind.
Knowledge.   Also ye must call to mind
    Your *Five-wits* as for your counsellors.
Good-Deeds.   You must have them ready at all hours.
Everyman.   How shall I get them hither?
Knowledge.   You must call them all together,
    And they will hear you incontinent.[40]
Everyman.   My friends, come hither and be present
    Discretion, Strength, my *Five-wits,* and *Beauty.*
Beauty.   Here at your will we be all ready.
    What will ye, that we should do?
Good-Deeds.   That ye would with *Everyman* go,
    And help him in his pilgrimage,
    Advise you, will ye with him or not in that voyage?
Strength.   We will bring him all thither,
    To his help and comfort, ye may believe me.
Discretion.   So will we go with him all together.

---

38. *twain*] two.

39. *hight*] are called, named.

40. *incontinent*] immediately.

Everyman.   Almighty God, loved thou be,
I give thee laud that I have hither brought
Strength, Discretion, Beauty, and *Five-wits;* lack I nought;
And my *Good-Deeds,* with *Knowledge* clear,
All be in my company at my will here;
I desire no more to my business.
Strength.   And I, *Strength,* will by you stand in distress,
Though thou would in baffle fight on the ground.
Five-wits.   And though it were through the world round,
We will not depart for sweet nor sour.
Beauty.   No more will I unto death's hour,
Whatsoever thereof befall.
Discretion.   *Everyman,* advise you first of all;
Go with a good advisement and deliberation;
We all give you virtuous monition[41]
That all shall be well.
Everyman.   My friends, hearken what I will tell:
I pray God reward you in his heavenly sphere.
Now hearken, all that be here,
For I will make my testament
Here before you all present.
In alms half my good I will give with my hands twain
In the way of charity, with good intent,
And the other half still shall remain
In quiet to be returned there it ought to be.
This I do in despite of the fiend of hell
To go quite out of his peril
Ever after and this day.
Knowledge.   *Everyman,* hearken what I say;
Go to priesthood, I you advise,
And receive of him in any wise
The holy sacrament and ointment together;
Then shortly see ye turn again hither;
We will all abide you here.
Five-wits.   Yea, *Everyman,* hie you that ye ready were,
There is no emperor, king, duke, ne baron,
That of God hath commission,
As hath the least priest in the world being;

---

41. *monition*] warning

302

For of the blessed sacraments pure and benign,
He beareth the keys and thereof hath the cure
For man's redemption, it is ever sure;
Which God for our soul's medicine
Gave us out of his heart with great pine;
Here in this transitory life, for thee and me
The blessed sacraments seven there be,
Baptism, confirmation, with priesthood good,
And the sacrament of God's precious flesh and blood,
Marriage, the holy extreme unction, and penance;
These seven be good to have in remembrance,
Gracious sacraments of high divinity.

Everyman.　　Fain would I receive that holy body
And meekly to my ghostly father I will go.

Five-wits.　　*Everyman*, that is the best that ye can do:
God will you to salvation bring,
For priesthood exceedeth all other thing;
To us Holy Scripture they do teach,
And converteth man from sin heaven to reach;
God hath to them more power given,
Than to any angel that is in heaven;
With five words he may consecrate
God's body in flesh and blood to make,
And handleth his maker between his hands;
The priest bindeth and unbindeth all bands,
Both in earth and in heaven;
Thou ministers all the sacraments seven;
Though we kissed thy feet thou were worthy;
Thou art surgeon that cureth sin deadly:
No remedy we find under God
But all only priesthood.
Everyman, God gave priests that dignity,
And setteth them in his stead among us to be;
Thus be they above angels in degree.

Knowledge.　　If priests be good it is so surely;
But when Jesus hanged on the cross with great smart
There he gave, out of his blessed heart,
The same sacrament in great torment:
He sold them not to us, that Lord Omnipotent.
Therefore Saint Peter the apostle doth say
That Jesu's curse hath all they
Which God their Saviour do buy or sell,

Or they for any money do take or tell.
Sinful priests giveth the sinners example bad;
Their children sitteth by other men's fires, I have heard;
And some haunteth women's company,
With unclean life, as lusts of lechery:
These be with sin made blind.

Five-wits.   I trust to God no such may we find;
Therefore let us priesthood honour,
And follow their doctrine for our souls' succour;
We be their sheep, and they shepherds be
By whom we all be kept in surety.
Peace, for yonder I see *Everyman* come,
Which hath made true satisfaction.

Good-Deeds.   Methinketh it is he indeed.

Everyman.   Now Jesu be our alder speed.[42]
I have received the sacrament for my redemption,
And then mine extreme unction:
Blessed be all they that counselled me to take it!
And now, friends, let us go without longer respite;
I thank God that ye have tarried so long.
Now set each of you on this rod your hand,
And shortly follow me:
I go before, there I would be; God be our guide.

Strength.   *Everyman,* we will not from you go,
Till ye have gone this voyage long.

Discretion.   I, *Discretion,* will bide by you also.

Knowledge.   And though this pilgrimage be never so strong,
I will never part you fro:
Everyman, I will be as sure by thee
As ever I did by Judas Maccabee.

Everyman.   Alas, I am so faint I may not stand,
My limbs under me do fold;
Friends, let us not turn again to this land,
Not for all the world's gold,
For into this cave must I creep
And turn to the earth and there to sleep.

Beauty.   What, into this grave? alas!

Everyman.   Yea, there shall you consume[43] more and less.

---

42. *Now . . . speed.*] May Jesus be the helper of all.

43. *consume*] decay.

Beauty.   And what, should I smother here?
Everyman.   Yea, by my faith, and never more appear.
     In this world live no more we shall,
     But in heaven before the highest Lord of all.
Beauty.   I cross out all this; adieu by Saint *John;*
     I take my cap in my lap and am gone.
Everyman.   What, *Beauty,* whither will ye?
Beauty.   Peace, I am deaf; I look not behind me,
     Not and thou would give me all the gold in thy chest.
Everyman.   Alas, whereto may I trust?
     Beauty goeth fast away hie;
     She promised with me to live and die.
Strength.   *Everyman,* I will thee also forsake and deny;
     Thy game liketh me not at all.
Everyman.   Why, then ye will forsake me all.
     Sweet *Strength,* tarry a little space.
Strength.   Nay, sir, by the rood[44] of grace
     I will hie me from thee fast,
     Though thou weep till thy heart brast.[45]
Everyman.   Ye would ever bide by me, ye said.
Strength.   Yea, I have you far enough conveyed;
     Ye be old enough, I understand
     Your pilgrimage to take on hand;
     I repent me that I hither came.
Everyman.   *Strength,* you to displease I am to blame;
     Will you break promise that is debt?
Strength.   In faith, I care not;
     Thou art but a fool to complain,
     You spend your speech and waste your brain;
     Go thrust thee into the ground.
Everyman.   I had wend surer I should you have found.
     He that trusteth in his *Strength*
     She him deceiveth at the length.
     Both *Strength* and *Beauty* forsaketh me,
     Yet they promised me fair and lovingly.
Discretion.   *Everyman,* I will after *Strength* be gone,
     As for me I will leave you alone.

---

44. *rood*] cross.

45. *brast*] break.

Everyman.   Why, *Discretion,* will ye forsake me?
Discretion.   Yea, in faith, I will go from thee,
        For when *Strength* goeth before
        I follow after evermore.
Everyman.   Yet, I pray thee, for the love of the Trinity,
        Look in my grave once piteously.
Discretion.   Nay, so nigh will I not come.
        Farewell, every one!
Everyman.   O all thing faileth, save God alone;
        Beauty, Strength, and *Discretion;*
        For when *Death* bloweth his blast,
        They all run from me full fast.
Five-wits.   *Everyman,* my leave now of thee I take;
        I will follow the other, for here I thee forsake.
Everyman.   Alas! then may I wail and weep,
        For I took you for my best friend.
Five-wits.   I will no longer thee keep;
        Now farewell, and there an end.
Everyman.   O Jesu, help, all hath forsaken me!
Good-Deeds.   Nay, *Everyman,* I will bide with thee,
        I will not forsake thee indeed;
        Thou shalt find me a good friend at need.
Everyman.   Gramercy, *Good-Deeds;* now may I true friends see;
        They have forsaken me every one;
        I loved them better than my *Good-Deeds* alone.
        Knowledge, will ye forsake me also?
Knowledge.   Yea, *Everyman,* when ye to death do go:
        But not yet for no manner of danger.
Everyman.   Gramercy, *Knowledge,* with all my heart.
Knowledge.   Nay, yet I will not from hence depart,
        Till I see where ye shall be come.
Everyman.   Methinketh, alas, that I must be gone,
        To make my reckoning and my debts pay,
        For I see my time is nigh spent away.
        Take example, all ye that this do hear or see,
        How they that I loved best do forsake me,
        Except my *Good-Deeds* that bideth truly.
Good-Deeds.   All earthly things is but vanity:
        Beauty, Strength, and *Discretion,* do man forsake,
        Foolish friends and kinsmen, that fair spake,
        All fleeth save *Good-Deeds,* and that am I.

Everyman.   Have mercy on me, God most mighty;
  And stand by me, thou Mother and Maid, holy *Mary.*
Good-Deeds.   Fear not, I will speak for thee.
Everyman.   Here I cry God mercy.
Good-Deeds.   Short our end, and minish[46] our pain;
  Let us go and never come again.
Everyman.   Into thy hands, Lord, my soul I commend;
  Receive it, Lord, that it be not lost;
  As thou me boughtest, so me defend,
  And save me from the fiend's boast,
  That I may appear with that blessed host
  That shall be saved at the day of doom.
  In manus tuas[47]—of might's most
  For ever—*commendo spiritum meum.*[48]
Knowledge.   Now hath he suffered that we all shall endure;
  The *Good-Deeds* shall make all sure.
  Now hath he made ending;
  Methinketh that I hear angels sing
  And make great joy and melody,
  Where Everyman's soul received shall be.
Angel.   Come, excellent elect spouse to Jesu:
  Hereabove thou shalt go
  Because of thy singular virtue:
  Now the soul is taken the body fro;
  Thy reckoning is crystal-clear.
  Now shalt thou into the heavenly sphere,
  Unto the which all ye shall come
  That liveth well before the day of doom.
Doctor.   This moral men may have in mind;
  Ye hearers, take it of worth, old and young,
  And forsake pride, for he deceiveth you in the end,
  And remember *Beauty, Five-wits, Strength,* and *Discretion,*
  They all at the last do *Everyman* forsake,
  Save his *Good-Deeds,* there doth he take.
  But beware, and they be small
  Before God, he hath no help at all.

---

46. *minish*] diminish.

47. *In manus tuas*] "Into thy hands."

48. *commendo spiriturn meum.*] I commend my spirit.

None excuse may be there for *Everyman*:
Alas, how shall he do then?
For after death amends may no man make,
For then mercy and pity do him forsake.
If his reckoning be not clear when he do come,
God will say—*ite maledicti in ignem ætemum.*[49]
And he that hath his account whole and sound,
High in heaven he shall be crowned;
Unto which place God bring us all thither
That we may live body and soul together.
Thereto help the Trinity,
Amen, say ye, for saint *Charity.*

THUS ENDETH THIS MORALL PLAY OF EVERYMAN.

---

49. *ite . . . æternum*] "Depart, ye cursed, into everlasting fire" (Matthew 25:41).

FRANCESCO GUICCIARDINI

Meditations of a Renaissance Historian

A Florentine statesman, political thinker, and historian, Guicciardini was a member of one of the city's most illustrious patrician families and one of Machiavelli's closest friends, in spite of their differences of opinion on matters of state. His some two hundred and twenty-two maxims, collected as the Ricordi, *were written between 1513 and 1530, but were never published during his lifetime. They constitute one of the most interesting critiques of Machiavelli's central claims about the imitation of the ancients and the use of classical models for current political behavior. Guicciardini is best remembered for his monumental* History of Italy, *a book of European scope that deals with the momentous events occuring in Italy and Europe between 1492 and 1534, known collectively as "The Calamity of Italy." It was clearly the most popular and widely translated vernacular history during the entire Renaissance period, and its influence on Western European historical writing in the early modern period was profound.*

The present selection shows Guicciardini's secret thoughts about human nature, politics, and the corruption of the clergy.

---

6. It is a great mistake to speak of worldly affairs indiscriminately and absolutely, and to deal with them—so to speak—by the rule; for almost all of them are different and exceptional because of the variety of circumstances which cannot be grasped by one single measure; and such differences and exceptions are not to be found written in books but must be taught by discretion.[1]

10. No one should place so much trust in natural intelligence as to persuade himself that this is sufficient without the assistance of experience, for anyone who has managed affairs, even though he be most intelligent indeed, has been able to recognize that with experience, one succeeds in many things, the attainment of which is impossible with natural intelligence alone.

15. Like all men, I have desired honor and profit; and often I obtained more of both than I had desired or hoped; nevertheless, I never found in them the satisfaction which I had imagined; a very powerful reason, if one considers this carefully, for curbing the vain cupidity of men.

28. I do not know if there is anyone who hates the ambition, the avarice, and the soft living of the priests more than I do—both because each of these vices in itself is odious and because all of them are unsuitable for those who profess to lead a life dependent upon God, and furthermore, because they are such contradictory vices that they cannot exist together except within a very strange individual. Nevertheless, the position I have held under several Popes has forced me, in my own self-interest, to serve their greatness;[2] and if it were not for this consideration, I should have esteemed Martin Luther as much as myself: not in order to free myself from the laws of the Christian religion in the manner in which they are commonly interpreted and understood, but, rather, in order to see this bunch of scoundrels reduced to their proper position—that is, to be either without vices or without power.

32. Ambition is not to be condemned, nor are ambitious men to be vituperated who seek glory through honest and honorable means: on the contrary, it is such men who undertake great and excellent deeds, and men who lack this desire are cold-spirited and inclined more to laziness than to activity. Pernicious and detestable ambition is the kind which has grandeur for its sole goal, as is usually the case with princes, and when princes make grandeur their idol, they will level conscience, honor, humanity, and everything else in order to reach it.

35. How different theory is from practice! How many people there are who understand things well but who either do not remember them or do not know how to put them into practice! The intelligence of such men is useless, for it is like having a treasure stored in a strongbox without ever being able to take it out.

48. One cannot wield political power according to the dictates of one's conscience, since if one considers its origin, all governments are violent, except for republics within their own territories but not beyond: and I do not except the Emperor from this rule, and even less the priests, for their power is doubly violent, since they assault us with both temporal and spiritual arms.

60. An above-average intellect is bestowed upon men for their unhappiness and torment, since it serves only to keep them in a greater state of turmoil and anxiety than those men whose intellects are more limited.

66. Do not believe those who preach liberty so fervently, for almost all of them—no, probably all of them—have their own private interests as their goal. And experience often shows beyond a shadow of a doubt that if such people believed they would be better off under an absolute government, they would race in that direction as fast as they could.

76. Everything which has existed in the past and exists in the present will also exist in the future; but both the names and the appearances of things change in such a way that anyone lacking a discerning eye will not recognize them, nor will he know how to draw conclusions or form a judgment from such observations.

101. There is no rule or prescription which counts in saving oneself from a bestial or cruel tyrant except that which applies to the plague: run from him as far and as fast as you can.

110. How those who cite the Romans in their every word deceive themselves! One would have to have a city with conditions exactly like theirs and then to govern it according to their example. That model is as unsuitable for a city lacking the proper qualities as it would be unsuitable to hope for a jackass to race like a horse.[3]

117. It is completely erroneous to judge by examples, since if they are not exactly alike in each and every detail, they serve no purpose, as each small variation in the case can be the cause of the greatest variation in the results. And to discern these variations, when they are small, requires a good and perspicacious eye.

125. Philosophers, theologians, and all the others who scrutinize supernatural affairs or invisible things all speak a lot of nonsense; for men are, in fact, in the dark about such affairs, and their investigation has served and still serves more to exercise their wits than to discover the truth.

134. All men are inclined by nature more to good than to evil, and there are none who, all other things being equal, would not more gladly do good than evil; but the nature of man is so weak and the occasions which invite him to do evil are so numerous in the world that men easily allow

themselves to deviate from the good.[4] And therefore, wise legislators invented rewards and punishments, and this was for no other reason than to hold men firm in their natural inclination by the use of hope and fear.

141. Do not be amazed if you find that we are ignorant of things that happened in past ages, not to mention those which occur in the provinces or far-away places. If you think about it carefully, we do not possess accurate information about present affairs, not to mention the daily events which occur in the same city; and there is often a fog so dense or a wall so thick between the palace and the piazza that being impenetrable to the eye of man, the people know as much about what those who govern are doing or about their reasons for doing it as they do about the things which people are doing in India. And so, the world is easily filled with erroneous and vain opinions.

161. When I think of the infinite number of ways the life of man is subjected to accidents, dangers of infirmity, or chance, or violence, and how many things must coincide during a year in order to produce a good harvest, there is nothing which amazes me more than seeing an old man or a fertile year.

164. A man's good fortune is often the worst enemy he has, since it causes him to become mean, irresponsible, and insolent; therefore, a man's ability to resist good fortune is a far better test of his character than his ability to handle adversity.

174. Do everything you can to have good relations with princes and with the states that they rule; for even though you may be innocent and live quietly and in an orderly fashion, and you are disposed not to cause trouble, events can nevertheless occur which of necessity will deliver you into the hands of those who govern. And then, the mere belief that you are not acceptable will hurt you in infinite ways.

176. Pray to God always to find yourself on the winning side, because in that way you will be praised for things which you did nothing to bring about, just as, on the contrary, anyone who finds himself on the losing side is accused of countless things for which he is completely innocent.

179. As a young man, I made fun of knowing how to play, to dance, to sing, and similar frivolities. I even made fun of writing well, of knowing

how to ride, of knowing how to dress properly, and of all those matters which seem to be more decorative than substantial in a man. But later I wished I had done the opposite, for though it might not be wise to lose too much time in training young people in these matters, nevertheless I have observed through experience that such ornaments and knowing how to do everything well bestow dignity and reputation upon men who are *also* well qualified, and it may even be said that men who lack such attributes lack something of importance. Not to mention the fact that being well endowed with such talents opens the way to the favor of princes, and is sometimes the beginning or the reason for their great profit and exaltation, since princes are no longer made in the world as they should be but as they are.

186. One cannot in effect proceed according to a single general and fixed rule. If it is often unwise to speak too freely even with your friends—I am referring to matters which deserve to be kept secret—on the other hand, acting with your friends in a manner which makes them realize that you are being reserved with them is the way to guarantee that they also do the same with you, for nothing makes another person confide in you so much as the assumption that you are confiding in them; thus, if you do not speak to others, you lose the capacity to learn from others. So, in this and in many other matters, it is necessary to be able to distinguish the character of people, of circumstances, and of the times, and to do this discretion is required, but if nature has not given discretion to you, experience can teach you enough discretion only very rarely; and books never can.

187. Know that anyone who governs himself by chance will eventually be at the mercy of chance. The proper way is to think, to examine, to consider everything, even the tiniest detail; and even living in this manner, affairs are managed with the greatest of difficulty. Imagine how things go for people who allow themselves to be carried along by the current.

189. All cities, all states, all kingdoms are mortal; everything by nature or by accident ends and finishes sometime. And so a citizen who finds himself living at the final stage of his country's existence should not so much lament the misfortune of his fatherland and call it unlucky as he should lament his own misfortune, for what happened to his country was what had to happen, but his misfortune was to have been born in that period during which the disaster had to occur.

210. "Little and good," as the proverb says. It is impossible for any-one who says or writes many things not to include in all this a great deal of nonsense; but a few things can be well digested and concise. And so it would perhaps have been better to select the best of these maxims (*ricordi*) rather than to have accumulated so much material.[5]

216. In this world, no one can choose the rank into which one is born, nor the circumstances or the fate with which one must live; therefore, in praising or criticizing men, it is necessary not to examine the fortune they enjoy but how they manage with it; for praise or blame of men has to arise from their comportment, not from the condition in which they find themselves. Just as in a comedy or a tragedy, the actor who plays the role of the master or the king is not more laudable than the actor who plays the role of the servant, since we pay attention only to who is the best actor.

218. In this world, the men who handle their affairs well are those who always have their self-interest[6] in mind and measure all their actions with this goal in mind. But the mistake lies in those men who do not realize clearly where their interests lie, that is to say, in those men who believe that their self-interest always lies in some monetary advantage more than in honor, in knowing how to maintain their reputation and their good name.

EXPLANATORY NOTES

1. The contrast between Machiavelli's reliance upon classical examples taken from his beloved Latin masters, on the one hand, and Guicciardini's suspicion of any political advice not grounded in practical experience and common sense, on the other, is quite marked. "Discretion" is a key quality for Guicciardini, one learned only through long trial and error in the real world.

2. Guicciardini was named Governor of Modena by Pope Leo X in 1516, a post to which the governorship of Reggio was added in 1517. When Leo died in 1522, Guicciardini defended Parma, and in 1523, he was named President of Romagna by another Medici Pope, Clement VII. He became lieutenant general of papal forces in the ill-fated League of Cognac, which ended in the sack of Rome in 1527 and Pope Clement VII's defeat by the troops of Emperor Charles V. Later, after the Medici family returned to Florence in 1530, Guicciardini was given the task by Clement VII of removing all republican opposition. In 1533, Guicciardini presided, as Governor

of Bologna, over the meeting between Pope Clement VII and the Emperor Charles V. All his life, Guicciardini was involved with ruling the papal state territories for his Medici patrons.

3. This maxim, and the one which follows, aims directly at the cornerstone of Machiavelli's view of history—the belief that useful examples can be learned by a study of the classical past or our own times.

4. While Machiavelli believes man is essentially evil, he also expects that men can be persuaded or forced to achieve good and even great deeds. Guicciardini, on the other hand, defines man as naturally good but weak.

5. Guicciardini was quite conscious that the choice of the maxim form implied entirely different assumptions from those of a political theorist such as Machiavelli, who chose the treatise form. In a sense, Guicciardini's use of the pithy maxim underlines his cynical distrust of the abstract, bookish learning of Machiavelli. Rather than present a theory, incorporated in a polished literary form, Guicciardini offers us his practical wisdom in the unconnected pattern of commonsense rules that he collected over a period of several decades.

6. Guicciardini has often been attacked as a cynic for his reliance upon self-interest in his maxims. While Machiavelli viewed human nature as evil and fallen, he could nevertheless conceive of selfless actions in the service of some higher goal. Guicciardini more often saw behind the supposedly pure and idealistic motives of the master politicians, kings, and princes of his times, and what he saw was frequently pure self-interest.

GIORGIO VASARI

Michelangelo Paints the Sistine Ceiling

Giorgio Vasari (1511–1574) is best known today as the first real historian of art, the author of the famous Lives of the Most Excellent Painters, Sculptors and Architects, *usually known as the* Lives of the Artists *(1550, second edition 1568). He was born in Arezzo into the artisan class and was trained as a painter by various Florentine artists. In Florence he became a loyal client of the ruling Medici house and executed numerous artistic and architectural commissions for them, including the office building of the Tuscan state, the Uffizi, now a famous picture gallery. He also helped promote the founding (1563) of the Accademia del Disegno (Academy of Design), the first major academy for fostering the visual arts, modeled on the literary and philosophical academies of the time.*

Vasari's Lives of the Artists *in its definitive second edition covered more than 250 years of artistic history and included biographies of more than 142 artists. Following numerous precedents in humanist writers, Vasari saw the recent history of art as a rebirth of ancient skill at representing nature, after a period of decline between the fourth and the thirteenth centuries. The key figures in his interpretation are Giotto, the early thirteenth century artist who reintroduced naturalism as the goal of art, and Michelangelo, who brought naturalism to its highest perfection. In the present selection Vasari tells the story of Michelangelo's commission to paint the ceiling of the Sistine Chapel, which for Vasari was the greatest work of art in history.*

Meanwhile, the Pope had returned to Rome while Michelangelo remained in Bologna to finish the statue. In his absence Bramante was constantly plotting with Raphael of Urbino to remove from the Pope's mind the idea of having Michelangelo finish the tomb on his return. Bramante did this (being a friend and relation of Raphael and therefore no friend of Michelangelo's) when he saw the way his holiness kept praising and glorifying Michelangelo's work as a sculptor. He and Raphael suggested to Pope Julius that if the tomb were finished it would bring nearer the day of his death, and they said that it was bad luck to have one's tomb built while one was still alive. Eventually they persuaded his holiness to get Michelangelo on his return to paint, as a memorial for his uncle Sixtus, the ceiling of the chapel that he had built in the Vatican. In this way Bramante and Michelangelo's other rivals thought they would divert his energies from sculpture, in which they realized he was supreme. This, they argued, would make things hopeless for him, since as he had no experience of colouring in fresco he would certainly, they believed, do less creditable work as a painter. Without doubt, they thought, he would be compared unfavourably with Raphael, and even if the work were a success being forced to do it would make him angry with the Pope; and thus one way or another they would succeed in their purpose of getting rid of him. So when Michelangelo returned to Rome he found the Pope resolved to leave the tomb as it was for the time being, and he was told to paint the ceiling of the chapel. Michelangelo, being anxious to finish the tomb, and considering the magnitude and difficulty of the task of painting the chapel, and his lack of experience, tried in every possible way to shake the burden off his shoulders. But the more he refused, the more determined he made the Pope, who was a wilful man by nature and who in any case was again being prompted by Michelangelo's rivals, and especially Bramante. And finally, being the hot-tempered man he was, his holiness was all ready to fly into a rage.

However, seeing that his holiness was persevering, Michelangelo resigned himself to doing what he was asked. Then the Pope ordered Bramante to make the ceiling ready for painting, and he did so by piercing the surface, and supporting the scaffolding by ropes. When Michelangelo saw this he asked Bramante what he should do, when the painting was finished, to fill up the holes. Bramante said: 'We'll think of it when it's time.' And he added that there was no other way. Michelangelo realized that Bramante either knew nothing about the matter or else was no friend of his, and he went to the Pope and told him that the scaffolding was unsatisfactory and that Bramante had not known how to make it; and the Pope replied, in the presence of Bramante, that Michelangelo should do it himself in his own way. So he arranged to have the scaffolding erected on props which kept clear of the wall, a method for use with vaults (by which many fine works have been executed) which he subsequently taught to various people, including Bramante. In this instance he enabled a poor carpenter, who rebuilt the scaffolding, to dispense with so many of the ropes that when Michelangelo gave him what was over he sold them and made enough for a dowry for his daughter.

Michelangelo then started making the cartoons for the vaulting; and the Pope also decided that the walls that had been painted by previous artists in the time of Sixtus should be scraped clean and that Michelangelo should have fifteen thousand ducats for the cost of the work, the price being decided through Giuliano da Sangallo. Then being forced reluctantly, by the magnitude of the task, to take on some assistants, Michelangelo sent for help to Florence. He was anxious to show that his paintings would surpass the work done there earlier, and he was determined to show modern artists how to draw and paint. Indeed, the circumstances of this undertaking encouraged Michelangelo to aim very high, for the sake both of his own reputation and the art of painting; and in this mood he started and finished the cartoons. He was then ready to begin the frescoes, but he lacked the necessary experience. Meanwhile, some of his friends, who were painters, came to Rome from Florence in order to assist him and let him see their technique. Several of them were skilled painters in fresco, and they included Granaccio, Giuliano Bugiardini, Jacopo di Sandro, the elder Indaco, Angelo di Donnino, and Aristotile. Having started the work, Michelangelo asked them to produce some examples of what they could do. But when he saw that these were nothing like what he wanted he grew dissatisfied, and then one morning he made up his mind to scrap everything they had done. He shut himself up in the chapel, refused to let them in again, and would never let them see him even when he was at home. So, when they thought the joke was wearing thin, they accepted their dismissal and went back ashamed to Florence.

Thereupon, having arranged to do all the work by himself, Michelangelo carried it well on the way to completion; working with the utmost solicitude, labour, and study he refused to let anyone see him in case he would have to show what he was painting. As a result every day the people became more impatient.

Pope Julius himself was always keen to see whatever Michelangelo was doing, and so naturally be was more anxious than ever to see what was being hidden from him. So one day he resolved to go and see the work, but he was not allowed in, as Michelangelo would never have consented. (This was the cause of the quarrel described earlier, when Michelangelo had to leave Rome as he would not let the Pope see what he was painting.) Now when a third of the work was completed (as I found out from Michelangelo himself, to clear up any uncertainty) during the winter when the north wind was blowing several spots of mould started to appear on the surface. The reason for this was that the Roman lime, which is white in colour and made of travertine, does not dry very quickly, and when mixed with pozzolana,[1] which is a brownish colour, forms a dark mixture which is very watery before it sets; then after the wall has been thoroughly soaked, it often effloresces when it is drying. Thus this salt efflorescence appeared in many places, although in time the air dried it up. When Michelangelo saw what was happening he despaired of the whole undertaking and was reluctant to go on. However, his holiness sent Giuliano da Sangallo to see him and explain the reason for the blemishes. Sangallo explained how to remove the moulds and encouraged him to continue. Then, when the work was half finished, the Pope who had subsequently gone to inspect it several times (being helped up the ladders by Michelangelo) wanted it to be thrown open to the public. Being hasty and impatient by nature, he simply could not bear to wait until it was perfect and had, so to say, received the final touch.

As soon as it was thrown open, the whole of Rome flocked to see it; and the Pope was the first, not having the patience to wait till the dust had settled after the dismantling of the scaffolds. Raphael da Urbino (who had great powers of imitation) changed his style as soon as he had seen Michelangelo's work and straight away, to show his skill, painted the prophets and sibyls of Santa Maria della Pace; and Bramante subsequently tried to persuade the Pope to let Raphael paint the other half of the chapel. When Michelangelo heard about this he complained of Bramante and revealed to the Pope, without reserve, many faults in his life and in his architectural works. (He himself, as it happened, was later to correct the mistakes made by Bramante in the fabric of St Peter's.) However, the Pope recognized Michelangelo's genius more clearly every day and wanted him to carry on the work himself; and after he had seen it displayed he was of the opinion that Michelangelo would do the other half even better. And so in twenty months Michelangelo brought the project to perfect completion without the assistance even of someone to grind his colours. Michelangelo at times complained that because of the haste the Pope imposed on him he was unable to finish it in the way he would have liked; for his holiness was always asking him importunately when it would be ready. On one of these occasions Michelangelo retorted that the ceiling would be finished 'when it satisfies me as an artist'.

And to this the Pope replied: 'And we want you to satisfy us and finish it soon.'

Finally, the Pope threatened that if Michelangelo did not finish the ceiling quickly he would have him thrown down from the scaffolding. Then Michelangelo, who had good reason to fear the Pope's anger, lost no time in doing all that was wanted; and after taking down the rest of the scaffolding he threw the ceiling open to the public on the morning of All Saints' Day, when the Pope went into the chapel to sing Mass, to the satisfaction of the entire city.

Michelangelo wanted to retouch some parts of the painting *a secco,* as the old masters had done on the scenes below, painting backgrounds, draperies, and skies in ultramarine, and in certain places adding ornamentation in gold, in order to enrich and heighten the visual impact.[2] The Pope, learning that this ornamentation was lacking, and hearing the work praised so enthusiastically by all who saw it, wanted him to go ahead. However, he lacked the patience to rebuild the scaffolding, and so the ceiling stayed as it was. His holiness used to see Michelangelo often and he would ask him to have the chapel enriched with colours and gold, since it looked impoverished. And Michelangelo would answer familiarly:

'Holy Father, in those days men did not bedeck themselves in gold and those you see painted there were never very rich. They were holy men who despised riches.'

For this work Michelangelo was paid by the Pope three thousand crowns in several instalments, of which he had to spend twenty-five on colours. He executed the frescoes in great discomfort, having to work with his face looking upwards, which impaired his sight so badly that he could not read or look at drawings save with his head turned backwards; and this lasted for several months afterwards. I can talk from personal experience about this, since when I painted five rooms in the great apartments of Duke Cosimo's palace if I had not made a chair where I could rest my head and relax from time to time I would never have finished; even so this work so ruined my sight and injured my head that I still feel the effects, and I am astonished that Michelangelo bore all that discomfort so well. In fact, every day the work moved him to greater enthusiasm, and he was so spurred on by his own progress and improvements that he felt no fatigue and ignored all the discomfort.

The painting on the ceiling of the chapel is arranged with six pendentives on either side and one in the centre of the walls at the foot and the head; and on these Michelangelo painted prophets and sibyls, twelve feet high.[3] In the middle of the vault he depicted from the Creation up to the Flood and the Drunkenness of Noah; and in the lunettes he showed all the Ancestors of Jesus Christ. For the foreshortenings in these compartments he used no consistent rule of perspective, nor is there any fixed point of view. He accommodated the various compartments to the figures, rather than his figures to the compartments, for he was resolved to execute both the draped figures and the nudes so that they should demonstrate the perfect quality of his draughtsmanship. There is no other work to compare with this for excellence, nor could there be; and it is scarcely possible even to imitate what Michelangelo accomplished. The ceiling has proved a veritable beacon to our art, of inestimable benefit to all painters, restoring light to a world that for centuries had been plunged into darkness. Indeed, painters no longer need to seek new inventions, novel attitudes, clothed figures, fresh ways of expression, different arrangements, or sublime subjects, for this work contains every perfection possible under those headings. In the nudes, Michelangelo displayed complete mastery: they are truly astonishing in their perfect foreshortenings, their wonderfully rotund contours, their grace, slenderness, and proportion. And to show the vast scope of his art he made them of all ages, some slim and some full-bodied, with varied expressions and attitudes, sitting, turning, holding festoons of oak-leaves and acorns (to represent the emblem of Pope Julius and the fact that his reign marked the golden age of Italy, before the travail and misery of the present time). The nudes down the middle of the ceiling hold medallions painted like gold or bronze with subjects taken from the Book of Kings. Moreover, to show the perfection of art and the greatness of God, in the histories Michelangelo depicted God dividing Light from Darkness, showing him in all his majesty as he rests self-sustained with arms outstretched, in a revelation of love and creative power.

In the second history, with beautiful judgement and skill he showed the Creation of the Sun and the Moon, depicting God, supported by many *putti*, in an attitude of sublime power conveyed by the strong foreshortening of his arms and legs. In the same scene Michelangelo showed the Almighty after the Blessing of the Earth and the Creation of the Animals, when he is seen on the vaulting in the form of a foreshortened figure, flying through the air, which turns and changes direction as one walks about the chapel. The same happens in the next history, where God is dividing the Waters from the Earth. And both these figures are beautiful forms and refinements of genius that only the inspired hands of Michelangelo could create. Then he went on to the Creation of Adam, where he showed God being borne by a group of nude angels of tender age who appear to be bearing up not one figure alone but the weight of the world; and this effect is achieved by the venerable majesty of the Divine Form and the way in which he moves, embracing some of the *putti* with one arm, as if to support himself, while with the other he stretches out his right hand towards Adam, a, figure whose beauty, pose, and contours are such that it seems to have been fashioned that very moment by the first and supreme creator rather than by the drawing and brush of a mortal man. Beyond this in another scene he showed God taking our mother Eve from the side of Adam; and here we see the two nude figures, one so enslaved by sleep that it seems dead, and the other awakened to life by the divine benediction. The brush of this wonderfully ingenious craftsman arrestingly reveals the difference that there is between sleep and wakefulness and how the divine majesty can be portrayed in the firm and tangible terms that humans understand.

After this comes the scene when Adam, at the persuasion of a figure half woman and half serpent, brings death upon himself and upon us through the apple; and there again we see Adam and Eve, now being driven from Paradise by the angel who appears in sublime grandeur to execute the commands of a wrathful Lord. Adam displays his remorse at having sinned and his fear of death; and the woman also shows her shame, abasement, and desire for forgiveness, as she covers her breasts with her arms, pressing her hands palm to palm and sinking her neck on to her bosom, and turns her head towards the angel, showing more fear of the justice of God than hope of divine mercy. No less beautiful is the scene showing the sacrifice of Cain and Abel, where there are some figures bringing the wood, some bending down and blowing the fire, and others cutting the throat of the victim; and this Michelangelo executed as carefully and judiciously as the others. He displayed similar art and judgement in the history of the Flood, where there are depicted some dying men who are overwhelmed by terror and dismay at what has happened and in various ways are striving their utmost to find safety. For in the heads of these figures one sees life in prey to death, along with fear, dismay, and hopelessness. Michelangelo also showed the pious actions of many people who are helping one another to climb to safety to the top of a rock. Among them is a man who has clasped someone who is half dead and is striving his utmost to save him; and nothing better than this could be seen in living nature. Nor can I describe how well expressed is the story of Noah, who is shown drunk with wine and exposed, in the presence of one son who is laughing at him and two others who are covering him up: a scene of beautiful artistry that sets its own standards. Then, as if Michelangelo's genius were emboldened by what he had already done, it soared even higher and achieved even more in the five sibyls and seven prophets that are painted on the ceiling. These figures, each ten feet or more in height, are shown in varied attitudes, wearing a variety of vestments and beautiful draperies; they are all executed with marvellous judgement, and invention, and they appear truly inspired to whoever studies their attitudes and expressions.

Thus, Jeremiah can be seen with his legs crossed, holding one hand to his beard and resting an elbow on his knee; the other hand rests on his lap, and the manner in which he inclines his head clearly expresses his melancholy and anxious reflection, and the bitterness forced on him by his people. Equally fine are the two *putti* and the first sibyl beyond him, in the direction of the door. In this figure Michelangelo was anxious to express the spirit of old age itself; she is enveloped in draperies, to suggest that her blood had frozen with the passing of time. And since her sight has failed, Michelangelo depicted her holding the book she reads very close to her eyes. Beyond this figure follows the prophet Ezekiel, an old man, full of movement and grace, and holding in one hand a roll of prophecies while he raises the other and, as he turns his head, prepares to utter words of lofty significance. Behind him there are two *putti* holding his books.

Next to him there follows a sibyl who, in contrast to the Erythraean sibyl described above, is holding a book at some distance and is about to turn one of the pages, sitting deep in contemplation, with one leg over the other, while she ponders what she must write; and then a little boy behind her blows on a burning brand to light her lamp.[4] Many aspects of this figure are of exceptional loveliness: the expression of her face, her head-dress, and the arrangement of her draperies; and her arms, which are bared, are as beautiful as the rest. Beyond her Michelangelo painted the prophet Joel who, sunk within himself, has taken a scroll which he is reading with great attention and emotion; he looks like a living person who has applied his thoughts intently to the matter before him, and from his expression one can recognize that he is content with what he reads. Then over the door of the chapel Michelangelo placed the aged Zechariah who holds a book in which he is seeking something that he cannot find, crouching with one leg raised back and the other lower down, oblivious to the discomfort of this posture because of the intensity of his search. This is a figure marvellous in its old age, somewhat full in form and wearing beautiful draperies with a few folds. Then there is the (Delphic) sibyl, next towards the altar on the other side, who is displaying certain writings and who, with her little boys in attendance, is no less admirable than the others. And then beyond her we see the prophet Isaiah. He is lost in thought, and with his legs crossed he keeps one hand inside the pages of his book, to mark his place, while he rests the other elbow by the book and presses that hand to his cheek; he is called by one of the *putti* behind him, but stays motionless, turning only his head. Anyone who studies this figure, copied so faithfully from nature, the true mother of the art of painting, will find a beautifully composed work capable of teaching in full measure all the precepts to be followed by a good painter. Beyond him is the elderly (Cumaean) sibyl a seated figure of great beauty, in an attitude of extraordinary grace as she studies the pages of a book, with two beautiful *putti* at her side. Then comes the figure of a young man, representing Daniel, who is shown writing in a great book, copying things from certain other writings with eager intensity. As a support for the weight Michelangelo painted between Daniel's legs a *putto* who is supporting the book while he writes; and the brush of no other artist will ever paint a group as marvellous as this. The same holds true for the lovely figure of the Libyan sibyl who, having written a great volume drawn from many books, is about to rise to her feet in an attitude of womanly grace; and at one and the same time she makes as if to rise and to close the book, something most difficult, not to say impossible, for anyone but the master to have depicted.

What can I say of the four scenes in the corner-spandrels of the ceiling? In one of them, exerting all his boyish strength, there is David cutting off the head of Goliath, while some soldiers in the background look on in amazement. Just as astonishing are the beautiful attitudes of the figures in the scene at the corner opposite, where Michelangelo depicted the headless, writhing body of Holofernes and Judith placing the head on a shallow basket resting on the head of her serving-woman. This old woman is so tall that she has to stoop to allow her mistress to balance it properly; and using her hands to help support the burden and to cover it up, she turns her face towards the trunk of Holofernes which, though lifeless, draws up an arm and a leg and disturbs the silence inside the tent. This disturbance causes her terror and alarm, which are clearly seen in her expression. Altogether this is a picture composed with marvellous thought and care.

Even more beautiful and inspired than that and the other scenes is the story of the serpents of Moses, over the left-hand side of the altar. For here one sees the deadly havoc wrought by the rain of serpents as they bite and sting, and the brazen serpent itself that Moses placed upon a pole. Michelangelo vividly depicted the various deaths suffered by those who are doomed by the serpents' bites. The deadly poison is causing the death of countless men and women in terror and convulsion, not to mention the rigid legs and twisted arms of those who remain just as they were struck down, unable to move, and then again the beautifully executed heads shown shrieking and thrown back in despair. No less marvellously portrayed than the rest are those who keep their eyes fixed with heart-felt emotion on the serpent, the sight of which has already lessened their grief; among them is a woman who has been bitten and reduced to terror and who now in her great and obvious need is supported by another figure offering clear and welcome assistance.

There are more beautiful figures in the next scene, which shows Ahasuerus lying in bed and reading his chronicles. Thus, there are three men eating at a table, representing the council that was held to deliver the Jewish people and order the hanging of Haman. Haman himself was depicted in an extraordinary example of foreshortening, for Michelangelo painted the trunk that supports his person and the arm thrust forward so that they seem in living relief, the same effect being seen in the leg that Haman stretches out and the other parts of the body that bend inwards. Of the beautiful and difficult figures executed by Michelangelo this is certainly the most beautiful and the most difficult. It would take too long to describe the various wonderful gestures and poses that he employed to illustrate the story of the Ancestors of Christ, showing the genealogy of all the Fathers beginning with the sons of Noah. And it is impossible to describe adequately all the many features of the figures in this section of Michelangelo's work: the draperies, the expressions of the heads, and the innumerable original and extraordinary fancies, all most brilliantly conceived. Every detail reflects Michelangelo's genius; all the figures are skilfully and beautifully foreshortened; and every single feature is manifestly inspired and beyond praise.

Then who is not filled with admiration and amazement at the awesome sight of Jonah, the last figure in the chapel? The vaulting naturally springs forward, following the curve of the masonry; but through the force of art it is apparently straightened out by the figure of Jonah, which bends in the opposite direction; and thus vanquished by the art of design, with its lights and shades, the ceiling even appears to recede.

What a happy age we live in! And how fortunate are our craftsmen, who have been given light and vision by Michelangelo and whose difficulties have been smoothed away by this marvellous and incomparable artist! The glory of his achievements has won them honour and renown; he has stripped away the bandage that kept their minds in darkness and shown them how to distinguish the truth from the falsehoods that clouded their understanding. You artists should thank heaven for what has happened and strive to imitate Michelangelo in everything you do.

When the work was thrown open, the whole world came running to see what Michelangelo had done; and certainly it was such as to make everyone speechless with astonishment. Then the Pope, exalted by the results and encouraged to undertake even more grandiose enterprises, generously rewarded Michelangelo with rich gifts and money. Michelangelo used to say of the extraordinary favours he was shown that they proved that his holiness fully recognized his abilities; and if sometimes, arising out of their intimacy, the Pope did him some hurt, he would heal it with extraordinary gifts and favours. There was an instance of this when Michelangelo once asked the Pope's permission to go to Florence for the feast day of St John and wanted some money from him for the purpose, and the Pope said:

'Well, what about this chapel? When will it be finished?'

'When I can, Holy Father,' said Michelangelo.

Then the Pope struck Michelangelo with a staff he was holding and repeated:

'When I can! When I can! What do you mean? I will soon make you finish it.'

However, after Michelangelo had gone back to his house to prepare for the journey to Florence, the Pope immediately sent his chamberlain, Cursio, with five hundred crowns to calm him down, as he was afraid that he would react in his usual unpredictable way; and the chamberlain made excuses for his holiness, explaining that such treatment was meant as a favour and a mark of affection. Then Michelangelo, because he understood the Pope's nature and, after all, loved him dearly, laughed it off, seeing that everything redounded to his profit and advantage and that the Pope would do anything to keep his friendship.

. . .

EXPLANATORY NOTES

1. A volcanic dust found near Pozzuoli.
2. *Fresco secco*—as opposed to *buon fresco*—is painted on dry plaster and was rarely used, even for retouching, by Michelangelo's time.
3. In fact, five pendentives on either side. Vasari's description, however, is substantially accurate, though in describing the histories he follows the logical sequence of the frescoes rather than the order in which they were painted. Michelangelo started work on the ceiling in 1508, the frescoes were unveiled in the summer of 1511, and the project was completed in 1512, setting the seal on his reputation as the greatest living artist.
4. Vasari has transposed the two sibyls: the first is the Persian sibyl, and the second the Erythraean.

BENVENUTO CELLINI
Surpassing the Antique

Benvenuto Cellini (1500–1571), the great Italian sculptor, goldsmith, and medallist, was also the author of the most fascinating autobiography of the Renaissance. Born in Florence into a family of prosperous craftsmen, Cellini was apprenticed as a goldsmith and studied the flute. In 1516, following a brawl, Cellini was forced to leave Florence and began life as an itinerant artist, visiting Siena, Bologna, Pisa, and Rome. Returning home in the early 1520s, he was soon expelled again on a charge of sodomy, and fled to Rome. In Rome he began to build an international reputation and won the favor of the Medici pope Clement VII. After Clement's death, Cellini was charged with the murder of a fellow-goldsmith and, despite a pardon from Pope Paul III, he fled to Florence. After various wanderings and a dramatic escape from the Castel Sant' Angelo, where he had been imprisoned for murder, Cellini went to France where he became a favorite artist of Francis I. As goldsmith to the king of France he executed the famous Salt Cellar, the most famous work in gold of the Renaissance. In 1545, accused of embezzling some silver given to him by the king, Cellini fled once more back to Florence, where he spent his final years in the service of the Medici Grand Dukes. It was there that he created his most famous works in sculpture, including a bronze portrait bust of Duke Cosimo I and the Perseus with the Head of Medusa.

In his later years Cellini fell into disfavor with the Medici owing to his incorrigible habits of vice and petty thievery, and abandoned the figurative arts for literature. His autobiography, finished between 1558 and 1566 (but not published until 1728), contained a lively record of his career, revealing his near total self-absorption and egotism in addition to his murders, innumerable liaisons and acts of petty theft. Yet with all its inaccuracies and unreliability, it remains a vivid portrait of artistic life in the greatest courts of the sixteenth century. In the present anecdote, which occurred while he was working for Francis I, Cellini describes a

battle of wits with his enemy, Madame d'Itampes, mistress of Francis I;
and his successful rivalry with antique works of sculpture.

Meanwhile I gave all my attention to finishing the fine silver statue of Jupiter together with its gilded base, which I had placed on a wooden plinth. Only a part of the plinth was visible and I had fixed in it four small balls, made of hard wood, more than half concealed in their sockets, like the nut in a crossbow. These were so skilfully arranged that a small child could easily, without the slightest effort, push the statue of Jupiter backwards and forwards or turn it round on itself. When I had set everything up to my satisfaction I took it to Fontainebleau, where the King was staying.

By then Bologna had brought from Rome the statues I mentioned, and he had taken great pains in having them cast in bronze. I knew nothing of this, partly because he had kept his doings very secret, and partly because Fontainebleau is more than forty miles away from Paris: so I was kept completely in the dark. When I wanted to find out from the King where to place the Jupiter, Madame d'Étampes, who was present, told him that there was no place more suitable than his beautiful gallery. This is what we call in Tuscany a loggia, or, more accurately a corridor—a corridor, because a loggia is the name given to apartments open along one side.

Anyhow, this room was more than a hundred paces in length, was richly furnished, and was hung with a number of paintings from the hand of our splendid Florentine, Rosso; under the paintings were grouped a great many pieces of sculpture, some in the round and others in low relief. The room was about twelve paces across. Bologna had brought here all his antiques, beautifully cast in bronze, and had arranged them magnificently with each one raised on its own pedestal. And, as I said before, they were the most exquisite works of art, copied from the antiques of Rome. I brought in my Jupiter; and then, when I saw such a splendid spectacle with everything so skilfully set out, I said to myself: 'This is certainly running the gauntlet—now God help me.'

I put it in its place, positioning it as well as I could, and I waited for the arrival of the great King. In Jupiter's right hand I had placed his thunderbolt, so that it looked as if he were about to hurl it; and in his left I had placed a globe. Among the flames I had very neatly introduced a length of white taper.

Madame d'Étampes had managed to keep the King distracted till nightfall, with the intention of ensuring one of two unfortunate results for myself—either his not coming at all, or, because of the darkness, my work's being shown at a disadvantage: but, as God rewards those of us who trust in Him, quite the opposite happened, because seeing that it was growing dark I lit the taper that the Jupiter was holding, and as this was lifted a little way above the statue's head its light fell down from above, making the work appear much more beautiful than it would have done in daylight.

The King appeared on the scene along with his Madame d'Étampes, the Dauphin his son (today the King), the Dauphiness, his brother-in-law the King of Navarre, with Madame Marguerite his daughter, and several other great lords whom Madame d'Étampes had carefully instructed to speak against me. As soon as I saw the King come in I had my assistant, Ascanio, push the beautiful statue of Jupiter forward in his direction; he moved it very gently, and since I had done the job very skilfully and the figure was very well constructed this slight movement made the statue seem alive. The antique statues were left somewhat in the background, and so my work was the first to delight the spectators.

Straight away the King said: 'This is much more beautiful than anything that has ever been seen before: even though I'm a connoisseur I would never have come near imagining anything like this.'

As for those noblemen who were to speak against me, it seemed that they could not say enough in praise of my work.

Madame d'Étampes exclaimed fiercely: 'Have you lost your eyes? Don't you see how many beautiful bronze figures there are placed farther back? The true genius of sculpture resides in them, not in this modern rubbish.'

Then the King came forward, followed by the others. He glanced at those figures, which were not shown to any advantage since the light came from below, and he said:

'Whoever it was wanted to do this man a bad turn has done him a great favour: the comparison with these splendid works of art only serves to make it apparent that his is more impressive and beautiful by a long chalk. We must rate Benvenuto very highly indeed: his work not only rivals, it surpasses the antiques.'

At this Madame d'Étampes said that if my work were to be seen in the daylight it would not appear a thousandth part as beautiful as it did by night; besides, she added, they were to notice how I had put a veil on my statue in order to hide its faults. This, in fact, was a piece of fine gauze that I had placed with exquisite grace over the Jupiter to add to its majesty. When I heard what she said I took hold of it, lifting it from below to reveal the statue's fine genitals, and then, with evident annoyance, I tore it off completely. She thought that I had unveiled those parts in order to mock her. When the King saw how insulted she was and how I myself, overcome by passion, was trying to force out some words, like the wise man he was he said with deliberation in his own tongue:

'Benvenuto, I forbid you to say a word: keep quiet, and you'll be rewarded with a thousand times more treasure than you desire.'

Unable to say anything I writhed with fury—which made her growl even more angrily. Then the King left much sooner than he would have done, saying in a loud voice, to encourage me, that he had brought from Italy the greatest artist ever born.

. . .

MARTIN LUTHER

Against the Sale of Indulgences

Martin Luther (1483–1546), the greatest of the Protestant reformers, was born in Thuringian Saxony, the son of a successful foundry owner and mine operator. He was sent to the University of Erfurt to study law, but joined the order of the Augustinian Hermits instead and embarked on a course of theological and Biblical studies. Eventually he succeeded his teacher, Johann von Staupitz, in the chair of Biblical studies at the University of Wittenberg, the town where he spent most of his later life. In his early thirties he underwent a religious crisis that caused him to question the theological bases of practices central to the life of the medieval Catholic Church. Following the publication of the Ninety-five Thesis *in November 1517 (the traditional date for the beginning of the Protestant Reformation), Luther's critique of the Church and its authority became ever more radical and wide ranging. In 1520 he was finally condemned by the papal bull* Exsurge Domine. *Following this condemnation, Luther began to elaborate his own theological positions, most famously in three key treatises of 1520,* The Freedom of a Christian, The Pagan Servitude of the Church, *and* An Appeal to the Ruling Class of the German Nation. *These three treatises dealt, respectively, with Luther's theory of salvation (or soteriology), his theory of the Church (or ecclesiology), and his theory of the role of the secular power in the governance and reform of the Church. These three treatises, along with the enormous volume of tracts and broadsides that poured from the German presses, established Luther as the intellectual leader of the reform movement. After his heroic refusal to recant at the Diet of Worms, even under pressure from the emperor himself, Luther became the moral leader of the movement as well.*

Out of love and concern for the truth, and with the object of eliciting it, the following heads will be the subject of a public discussion at Wittenberg under the presidency of the reverend father, Martin Luther, Augustinian, Master of Arts and Sacred Theology, and duly appointed Lecturer on these subjects in that place. He requests that whoever cannot be present personally to debate the matter orally will do so in absence in writing.

1. When our Lord and Master, Jesus Christ, said "Repent",[1] He called for the entire life of believers to be one of penitence.

2. The word cannot be properly understood as referring to the sacrament of penance, i.e., confession and satisfaction, as administered by the clergy.

3. Yet its meaning is not restricted to penitence in one's heart; for such penitence is null unless it produces outward signs in various mortifications of the flesh.

4. As long as hatred of self abides (i.e., true inward penitence) the penalty of sin abides, viz., until we enter the kingdom of heaven.

5. The pope has neither the will nor the power to remit any penalties beyond those imposed either at his own discretion or by canon law.

6. The pope himself cannot remit guilt, but only declare and confirm that it has been remitted by God; or, at most, he can remit it in cases reserved to his discretion. Except for these cases, the guilt remains untouched.

7. God never remits guilt to anyone without, at the same time, making him humbly submissive to the priest, His representative.

8. The penitential canons apply only to men who are still alive, and, according to the canons themselves, none applies to the dead.

9. Accordingly, the Holy Spirit, acting in the person of the pope, manifests grace to us, by the fact that the papal regulations always cease to apply at death, or in any hard case.

10. It is a wrongful act, due to ignorance, when priests retain the canonical penalties on the dead in purgatory.

11. When canonical penalties were changed and made to apply to purgatory, surely it would seem that tares were sown while the bishops were asleep.

12. In former days, the canonical penalties were imposed, not after, but before absolution was pronounced; and were intended to be tests of true contrition.

13. Death puts an end to all the claims of the church; even the dying are already dead to the canon laws, and are no longer bound by them.

14. Defective piety or love in a dying person is necessarily accompanied by great fear, which is greatest where the piety or love is least.

15. This fear or horror is sufficient in itself, whatever else might be said, to constitute the pain of purgatory, since it approaches very closely to the horror of despair.

16. There seems to be the same difference between hell, purgatory, and heaven as between despair, uncertainty, and assurance.

17. Of a truth, the pains of souls in purgatory ought to be abated, and charity ought to be proportionately increased.

18. Moreover, it does not seem proved, on any grounds of reason or Scripture, that these souls are outside the state of merit, or unable to grow in grace;

19. Nor does it seem proved to be always the case that they are certain and assured of salvation, even if we are very certain of it ourselves.

20. Therefore the pope, in speaking of the plenary remission of all penalties, does not mean "all" in the strict sense, but only those imposed by himself.

21. Hence those who preach indulgences are in error when they say that a man is absolved and saved from every penalty by the pope's indulgences;

22. Indeed, he cannot remit to souls in purgatory any penalty which canon law declares should be suffered in the present life.

23. If plenary remission could be granted to anyone at all, it would be only in the cases of the most perfect, i.e., to very few.

24. It must therefore be the case that the major part of the people are deceived by that indiscriminate and high-sounding promise of relief from penalty.

25. The same power as the pope exercises in general over purgatory is exercised in particular by every single bishop in his bishopric and priest in his parish.

26. The pope does excellently when he grants remission to the souls in purgatory on account of intercessions made on their behalf, and not by the power of the keys (which he cannot exercise for them).

27. There is no divine authority for preaching that the soul flies out of purgatory immediately the money clinks in the bottom of the chest.

28. It is certainly possible that when the money clinks in the bottom of the chest avarice and greed increase; but when the church offers intercession, all depends on the will of God.

29. Who knows whether all souls in purgatory wish to be redeemed in view of what is said of St. Severinus[2] and St. Paschal?[3]

30. No one is sure of the reality of his own contrition, much less of receiving plenary forgiveness.

31. One who *bona fide* buys indulgences is as rare as a *bona fide* penitent man, i.e., very rare indeed.

32. All those who believe themselves certain of their own salvation by means of letters of indulgence, will be eternally damned, together with their teachers.

33. We should be most carefully on our guard against those who say that the papal indulgences are an inestimable divine gift, and that a man is reconciled to God by them.

34. For the grace conveyed by these indulgences relates simply to the penalties of the sacramental "satisfactions" decreed merely by man.

35. It is not in accordance with Christian doctrine to preach and teach that those who buy off souls, or purchase confessional licences, have no need to repent of their own sins.

36. Any Christian whatsoever, who is truly repentant, enjoys plenary remission from penalty and guilt, and this is given him without letters of indulgence.

37. Any true Christian whatsoever, living or dead, participates in all the benefits of Christ and the Church; and this participation is granted to him by God without letters of indulgence.

38. Yet the pope's remission and dispensation are in no way to be despised, for, as already said, they proclaim the divine remission.

39. It is very difficult, even for the most learned theologians, to extol to the people the great bounty contained in the indulgences, while, at the same time, praising contrition as a virtue.

40. A truly contrite sinner seeks out, and loves to pay, the penalties of his sins; whereas the very multitude of indulgences dulls men's consciences, and tends to make them hate the penalties.

41. Papal indulgences should only be preached with caution, lest people gain a wrong understanding, and think that they are preferable to other good works: those of love.

42. Christians should be taught that the pope does not at all intend that the purchase of indulgences should be understood as at all comparable with works of mercy.

43. Christians should be taught that one who gives to the poor, or lends to the needy, does a better action than if he purchases indulgences;

44. Because, by works of love, love grows and a man becomes a better man; whereas, by indulgences, he does not become a better man, but only escapes certain penalties.

45. Christians should be taught that he who sees a needy person, but passes him by although he gives money for indulgences, gains no benefit from the pope's pardon, but only incurs the wrath of God.

46. Christians should be taught that, unless they have more than they need, they are bound to retain what is necessary for the upkeep of their home, and should in no way squander it on indulgences.

47. Christians should be taught that they purchase indulgences voluntarily, and are not under obligation to do so.

48. Christians should be taught that, in granting indulgences, the pope has more need, and more desire, for devout prayer on his own behalf than for ready money.

49. Christians should be taught that the pope's indulgences are useful only if one does not rely on them, but most harmful if one loses the fear of God through them.

50. Christians should be taught that, if the pope knew the exactions of the indulgence-preachers, he would rather the church of St. Peter were reduced to ashes than be built with the skin, flesh, and bones of his sheep.

51. Christians should be taught that the pope would be willing, as he ought if necessity should arise, to sell the church of St. Peter, and give, too, his own money to many of those from whom the pardon-merchants conjure money.

52. It is vain to rely on salvation by letters of indulgence, even if the commissary, or indeed the pope himself, were to pledge his own soul for their validity.

53. Those are enemies of Christ and the pope who forbid the word of God to be preached at all in some churches, in order that indulgences may be preached in others.

54. The word of God suffers injury if, in the same sermon, an equal or longer time is devoted to indulgences than to that word.

55. The pope cannot help taking the view that if indulgences (very small matters) are celebrated by one bell, one pageant, or one ceremony, the gospel (a very great matter) should be preached to the accompaniment of a hundred bells, a hundred processions, a hundred ceremonies.

56. The treasures of the church, out of which the pope dispenses indulgences, are not sufficiently spoken of or known among the people of Christ.

57. That these treasures are not temporal is clear from the fact that many of the merchants do not grant them freely, but only collect them;

58. Nor are they the merits of Christ and the saints, because, even apart from the pope, these merits are always working grace in the inner man, and working the cross, death, and hell in the outer man.

59. St. Laurence said that the poor were the treasures of the church, but he used the term in accordance with the custom of his own time.

60. We do not speak rashly in saying that the treasures of the church are the keys of the church, and are bestowed by the merits of Christ;

61. For it is clear that the power of the pope suffices, by itself, for the remission of penalties and reserved cases.

62. The true treasure of the church is the Holy Gospel of the glory and the grace of God.

63. It is right to regard this treasure as most odious, for it makes the first to be the last.

64. On the other hand, the treasure of indulgences is most acceptable, for it makes the last to be the first.

65. Therefore the treasures of the gospel are nets which, in former times, they used to fish for men of wealth.

66. The treasures of the indulgences are the nets to-day which they use to fish for men of wealth.

67. The indulgences, which the merchants extol as the greatest of favours, are seen to be, in fact, a favourite means for money-getting;

68. Nevertheless, they are not to be compared with the grace of God and the compassion shown in the Cross.

69. Bishops and curates, in duty bound, must receive the commissaries of the papal indulgences with all reverence;

70. But they are under a much greater obligation to watch closely and attend carefully lest these men preach their own fancies instead of what the pope commissioned.

71. Let him be anathema and accursed who denies the apostolic character of the indulgences;

72. On the other hand, let him be blessed who is on his guard against the wantonness and licence of the pardon-merchants' words.

73. In the same way, the pope rightly excommunicates those who make any plans to the detriment of the trade in indulgences.

74. It is much more in keeping with his views to excommunicate those who use the pretext of indulgences to plot anything to the detriment of holy love and truth.

75. It is foolish to think that papal indulgences have so much power that they can absolve a man even if he has done the impossible and violated the mother of God.

76. We assert the contrary, and say that the pope's pardons are not able to remove the least venial of sins as far as their guilt is concerned.

77. When it is said that not even St. Peter, if he were now pope, could grant a greater grace, it is blasphemy against St. Peter and the pope.

78. We assert the contrary, and say that he, and any pope whatever, possesses greater graces, viz., the gospel, spiritual powers, gifts of healing, etc., as is declared in I Corinthians 12 [:28].

79. It is blasphemy to say that the insignia of the cross with the papal arms are of equal value to the cross on which Christ died.

80. The bishops, curates, and theologians, who permit assertions of that kind to be made to the people without let or hindrance, will have to answer for it.

81. This unbridled preaching of indulgences makes it difficult for learned men to guard the respect due to the pope against false accusations, or at least from the keen criticisms of the laity;

82. They ask, e.g.: Why does not the pope liberate everyone from purgatory for the sake of love (a most holy thing) and because of the supreme necessity of their souls? This would be morally the best of all reasons. Meanwhile he redeems innumerable souls for money, a most perishable thing, with which to build St. Peter's church, a very minor purpose.

83. Again: Why should funeral and anniversary masses for the dead continue to be said? And why does not the pope repay, or permit to be repaid, the benefactions instituted for these purposes, since it is wrong to pray for those souls who are now redeemed?

84. Again: Surely this is a new sort of compassion, on the part of God and the pope, when an impious man, an enemy of God, is allowed to pay money to redeem a devout soul, a friend of God; while yet that devout and beloved soul is not allowed to be redeemed without payment, for love's sake, and just because of its need of redemption.

85. Again: Why are the penitential canon laws, which in fact, if not in practice, have long been obsolete and dead in themselves,—why are they, to-day, still used in imposing fines in money, through the granting of indulgences, as if all the penitential canons were fully operative?

86. Again: Since the pope's income to-day is larger than that of the wealthiest of wealthy men, why does he not build this one church of St. Peter with his own money, rather than with the money of indigent believers?

87. Again: What does the pope remit or dispense to people who, by their perfect penitence, have a right to plenary remission or dispensation?

88. Again: Surely greater good could be done to the church if the pope were to bestow these remissions and dispensations, not once, as now, but a hundred times a day, for the benefit of any believer whatever.

89. What the pope seeks by indulgences is not money, but rather the salvation of souls; why then does he not suspend the letters and indulgences formerly conceded, and still as efficacious as ever?

90. These questions are serious matters of conscience to the laity. To suppress them by force alone, and not to refute them by giving reasons, is to expose the church and the pope to the ridicule of their enemies, and to make Christian people unhappy.

91. If, therefore, indulgences were preached in accordance with the spirit and mind of the pope, all these difficulties would be easily overcome, and, indeed, cease to exist.

92. Away, then, with those prophets who say to Christ's people, "Peace, peace," where there is no peace.

93. Hail, hail to all those prophets who say to Christ's people, "The cross, the cross," where there is no cross.

94. Christians should be exhorted to be zealous to follow Christ, their Head, through penalties, deaths, and hells;

95. And let them thus be more confident of entering heaven through many tribulations rather than through a false assurance of peace.

EXPLANATORY NOTES

1. This quotation from Matt. 4:17 was known throughout Europe in its Latin form: *poenitentiam agite*. Unfortunately, the phrase was capable of two meanings: repent; and, do penance.
2. Pope, 638–40, successor to Honorius I.
3. Paschal I, pope 817–24. The legend is that he and Severinus were willing to endure the pains of purgatory for the benefit of the faithful.

JOHN CALVIN

Free Will and Predestination

John Calvin (1509–64), who after Luther was the most important of the
Protestant Reformers, was born in Picardy in Northern France and studied
theology at the University of Paris with the intention of pursuing an eccle-
siastical career. Later he studied law at Orleans and Bourges. In 1533 he
converted to Protestantism and in 1535 fled to Switzerland to escape Fran-
cis I's persecution of Protestants in France. From 1536 he preached and
taught in Geneva, but was expelled from the town in 1538. In 1541
Geneva was taken over by the Protestants, and its Catholic prince-bishop
was expelled. Calvin was recalled, and spent the next fourteen years estab-
lishing a theocratic regime in the city, outlined in his Ecclesiastical Ordi-
nances, *which was the model for Calvinist and Puritan regimes throughout*
Europe and in New England for the next century.

Calvin's influence as a theologian also spread widely in Europe. His
famous Institutes of the Christian Religion *(first edition, 1536) was consid-*
ered a kind of summa of Protestant theology and was widely adopted by
many if not most non-Lutheran reformed churches. The present selection
contains Calvin's treatment of the problem of free will and predestination,
one of the key issues of Reformation theology, and an issue that distinguished
not only Catholic from Protestant, but also Lutheran from Calvinist.

Since we have seen that the domination of sin, from the time of its subju-
gation of the first man,[1] not only extends over the whole race, but also
exclusively possesses every soul; it now remains to be more closely
investigated, whether we are despoiled of all freedom, and, if any particle
of it yet remain, how far its power extends. But that we may the more
easily discover the truth of this question, I will first set up by the way a
mark, by which our whole course must be regulated. The best method of
guarding against error is to consider the dangers which threaten us on
every side. For when man is declared to be destitute of all rectitude, he

immediately makes it an occasion of slothfulness; and because he is said to have no power of himself for the pursuit of righteousness, he totally neglects it, as though it did not at all concern him. On the other hand, he cannot arrogate anything to himself, be it ever so little, without God being robbed of His honour, and himself being endangered by presumptuous temerity. Therefore to avoid striking on either of these rocks, this will be the course to be pursued: that man, being taught that he has nothing good left in his possession, and being surrounded on every side with the most miserable necessity, should nevertheless be instructed to aspire to the good of which he is destitute, and to the liberty of which he is deprived; and should be roused from indolence with more earnestness than if he were supposed to be possessed of the greatest strength. The necessity of the latter is obvious to everyone. The former, I perceive, is doubted by more than it ought to be. For this being placed beyond all controversy, that man must not be deprived of anything that properly belongs to him, it ought also to be manifest how important it is that he should be prevented from false boasting. For if he was not even then permitted to glory in himself, when by the divine beneficence he was decorated with the noblest ornaments, how much ought he now to be humbled, when on account of his ingratitude he has been hurled from the summit of glory to the abyss of ignominy? At that time, I say, when he was exalted to the most honourable eminence, the Scripture attributes nothing to him, but that he was created after the image of God; which, certainly implies that his happiness consisted not in any goodness of his own, but in a participation of God. What then remains for him now, deprived of all glory, but that he acknowledge God, to whose beneficence he could not be thankful when he abounded in the riches of His favour? And that he now at least by a confession of his poverty glorify Him, whom he glorified not by an acknowledgement of His blessings? It is also no less conducive to our interest than to the divine glory that all the praise of wisdom and strength be taken away from us; so that they join sacrilege to our fall, who ascribe to us anything more than truly belongs to us. For what else is the consequence, when we are taught to contend in our own strength, but that we are lifted into the air on a reed, which being soon broken, we fall to the ground. Though our strength is placed in too favourable a point of view, when it is compared to a reed. For it is nothing but smoke, whatever vain men have imagined and pretend concerning it. Wherefore it is not without reason that that remarkable sentence is so frequently repeated by Augustine,[2] that free will is rather overthrown than established even by its own advocates. It was necessary to premise these things for the sake of some who, when they hear that human power is completely subverted in order that the power of God may be established in man, inveterately hate this whole argument, as dangerous and unprofitable: which yet appears to be highly useful to us, and essential to true religion. . . .

Now when I assert that the will, being deprived of its liberty, is necessarily drawn or led into evil, I should wonder if anyone considered it as a harsh expression, since it has nothing in it absurd, nor is it unsanctioned by the custom of good men. It offends those who know not how to distinguish between necessity and compulsion. But if anyone should ask them whether God is not necessarily good, and whether the devil is not necessarily evil, what answer will they make? For there is such a close connection between the goodness of God and His divinity that His deity is not more necessary than His goodness. But the devil is by his fall so alienated from communion with all that is good that he can do nothing but what is evil. But if anyone should sacrilegiously object that little praise is due to God for His goodness, which He is constrained to preserve, shall we not readily reply that His inability to do evil arises from His infinite goodness and not from the impulse of violence? Therefore if a necessity of doing well impairs not the liberty of the divine will in doing well; if the devil, who cannot but do evil, nevertheless sins voluntarily; who then will assert that man sins less voluntarily, because he is under a necessity of sinning? This necessity Augustine everywhere maintains, and even when he was pressed with the cavils of Celestius,[3] tried to throw an odium on this doctrine, he confidently expressed himself in these terms: 'By means of liberty it came to pass that man fell into sin; but now the penal depravity consequent on it, instead of liberty, has introduced necessity.' And whenever the mention of this subject occurs, he hesitates not to speak in this manner of the necessary servitude of sin. We must therefore observe this grand point of distinction, that man, having been corrupted by his fall, sins voluntarily, not with reluctance or constraint; with the strongest propensity of disposition, not with violent coercion; with the bias of his own passions, and not with external compulsion: yet such is the pravity of his nature that he cannot be excited and biased to anything but what is evil. . . . From these passages the reader clearly perceives that I am teaching no novel doctrine, but what was long ago advanced by Augustine with the universal consent of pious men, and which for nearly a thousand years after was confined to the cloisters of monks. But [Peter] Lombard,[4] for want of knowing how to distinguish necessity from coaction, gave rise to a pernicious error. . . .

It has now, I apprehend, been sufficiently proved that man is so enslaved by sin as to be of his own nature incapable of an effort or even an aspiration towards that which is good. We have also laid down a distinction between coaction and necessity, from which it appears that while he sins necessarily, he nevertheless sins voluntarily. But since, while he is devoted to the servitude of the devil, he seems to be actuated by his will rather than by his own, it remains for us to explain the nature of both kinds of influence. There is also this question to be resolved, whether anything is to be attributed to God in evil actions, in which the Scripture intimates that some influence of His is concerned. Augustine somewhere compares the human will to a horse, obedient to the direction of his rider: and God and the devil he compares to riders. 'If God rides it, He, like a sober and skilful rider, manages it in a graceful manner: stimulates its tardiness, restrains its immoderate celerity, represses its wantonness and wildness, tames its perverseness, and conducts it into the right way. But if the devil has taken possession of it, he, like a foolish and wanton rider, forces it through pathless places, hurries it into ditches, drives it down over precipices, and excites it to obstinacy and ferocity.' With this similitude, as no better occurs, we will at present be content. When the will of a natural man is said to be subject to the power of the devil, so as to be directed by it, the meaning is, not that it resists and is compelled to a reluctant submission, as masters compel slaves to an unwilling performance of their commands; but that, being fascinated by the fallacies of Satan, it necessarily submits itself to all his directions. For those whom the Lord does not favour with the government of His Spirit, He abandons in righteous judgement to the influence of Satan. . . .

The covenant of life not being equally preached to all, and among those to whom it is preached not always finding the same reception, this diversity discovers the wonderful depth of the divine judgement. Nor is it to be doubted that this variety also follows, subject to the decision of God's eternal election. If it be evidently the result of the divine will that salvation is freely offered to some and others are prevented from attaining it, this immediately gives rise to important and difficult questions, which are incapable of any other explication than by the establishment of pious minds in what ought to be received concerning election and predestination: a question, in the opinion of many, full of perplexity; for they consider nothing more unreasonable than that of the common mass of mankind some should be predestinated to salvation and others to destruction. But how unreasonably they perplex themselves will afterwards appear from the sequel of our discourse. Besides, the very obscurity which excites such dread not only displays the utility of this doctrine, but shows it to be productive of the most delightful benefit. We shall never be clearly convinced as we ought to be, that our salvation flows from the

fountain of God's free mercy, till we are acquainted with his eternal election, which illustrates the grace of God by this comparison, that He
adopts not all promiscuously to the hope of salvation, but gives to some
what He refuses to others. Ignorance of this principle evidently detracts
from the divine glory and diminishes real humility. But, according to
Paul, what is so necessary to be known never can be known, unless God,
without any regard to works, chooses those whom He has decreed. 'At
this present time also, there is a remnant according to the election of
grace. And if by grace, then it is no more of works: otherwise, grace is no
more grace. But if it be of works, then it is no more grace: otherwise,
work is no more work' [Romans 11:5]. If we need to be recalled to the
origin of election to prove that we obtain salvation from no other source
than the mere goodness of God, they who desire to extinguish this principle do all they can to obscure what ought to be magnificently and
loudly celebrated, and to pluck up humility by the roots. In ascribing the
salvation of the remnant of the people to the election of grace, Paul
clearly testifies that it is then only known that God saves whom He will
of His mere good pleasure, and does not dispense a reward to which there
can be no claim. They who shut the gates to prevent anyone from pre-
suming to approach and taste this doctrine do no less injury to man than
to God; for nothing else will be sufficient to produce in us suitable humility, or to impress us with a due sense of our great obligations to God. Nor
is there any other basis for solid confidence, even according to the
authority of Christ, who, to deliver us from all fear, and render us invincible amidst so many dangers, snares, and deadly conflicts, promises to preserve in safety all whom the Father hath committed to His care. Whence
we infer that they who know not themselves to be God's peculiar people
will be tortured with continual anxiety; and therefore that the interest of
all the faithful, as well as their own, is very badly consulted by those who,
blind to the three advantages we have remarked, would wholly remove
the foundation of our salvation. And hence the Church rises to our view;
which otherwise, as Bernard justly observes,[5] could neither be discovered
nor recognized among creatures, being in two respects wonderfully concealed in the bosom of a blessed predestination, and in the mass of a miserable damnation. But before I enter on the subject itself, I must address
some preliminary observations to two sorts of persons. The discussion of
predestination, a subject of itself rather intricate, is made very perplexed,
and therefore dangerous, by human curiosity, which no barriers can
restrain from wandering into forbidden labyrinths and soaring beyond its
sphere, as if determined to leave none of the divine secrets unscrutinized
or unexplored. As we see multitudes everywhere guilty of this arrogance

343

and presumption, and among them some who are not censurable in other respects, it is proper to admonish them of the bounds of their duty on this subject. First, then: let them remember that when they inquire into predestination they penetrate the inmost recesses of divine wisdom, where the careless and confident intruder will obtain no satisfaction to his curiosity, but will enter a labyrinth from which he will find no way to depart. For it is unreasonable that man should scrutinize with impunity those things which the Lord hath determined to be hidden in Himself; and investigate, even from eternity, that sublimity of wisdom which God would have us to adore and not comprehend, to promote our admiration of His glory. The secrets of His will which He determined to reveal to us He discovers in His Word; and these are all that He foresaw would concern us, or conduce to our advantage. . . .

Predestination, by which God adopts some to the hope of life and adjudges others to eternal death, no one, desirous of the credit of piety, dares absolutely to deny. But it is involved in many cavils, especially by those who make foreknowledge the cause of it. We maintain that both belong to God; but it is preposterous to represent one as dependent on the other. When we attribute foreknowledge to God, we mean that all things have ever been, and perpetually remain, before His eyes, so that to His knowledge nothing is future or past, but all things are present: and present in such a manner that He does not merely conceive of them from ideas formed in His mind, as things remembered by us appear present to our minds, but really beholds and sees them as if actually placed before Him. And this foreknowledge extends to the whole world and to all the creatures. Predestination we call the eternal decree of God, by which He hath determined in Himself what He would have to become of every individual of mankind. For they are not all created with a similar destiny; but eternal life is foreordained for some, and eternal damnation for others. Every man, therefore, being created for one or the other of these ends, we say, he is predestinated either to life or to death.

EXPLANATORY NOTES

1. Adam.
2. St Augustine of Hippo, A.D. 354–430, a Father of the early Church. His later years were occupied by the Pelagian controversy, in which he adopted a predestinarian stance.
3. Celestius was a fifth-century British heretic who, while in Rome, allied with Pelagius to preach the doctrine of free will. Celestius thought men responsible for their own actions and even went so far as to deny the existence of original sin.

4. Peter Lombard (d. Aug. 21/22 1160) was Bishop of Paris. His *Four Books of Sentences* (1148–51) was the standard medieval theological text. He was known as the Master of the Sentences. Book I dealt with God, the Trinity, Divine Guidance, evil and predestination.

5. St Bernard of Clairvaux (1090–1153), whose thought was heavily influenced by Augustine.

GIOVANNI PICO DELLA MIRANDOLA

The Dignity of Man

Giovanni Pico della Mirandola (1463–1494), a child prodigy, was the most famous philosopher of the Renaissance. The scion of wealthy, noble, and famous heirs to the tiny principality of Mirandola, Pico studied at the universities of Ferrara, Bologna, Padua, and Paris and was taught informally by Marsilio Ficino, the Platonist philosopher, in Florence. He mastered Hebrew, Greek, Arabic, and Latin in addition to his native Italian and gathered a large collection of esoteric writings in Asian languages. While the Christian Latin tradition provided the frame of reference for all his work, Pico came to believe that all religious and philosophical traditions spread across time and geography participated in a single universal theology, and that pagan and Hebrew occult traditions such as Hermetism and Kabbalah gave unique access to that theology. Pico spent most of his short life trying to work out a concord of all theologies, though only a short section of this planned work was ever finished, a treatise On Being and the One *(1491), which attempted to reconcile Plato and Aristotle on a fundamental metaphysical issue.*

Pico's first attempt at concord was launched in 1486, when he published nine hundred theses and offered, after the manner of university exercises of the day, to defend them at a grand disputation to be held in Rome; Pico even offered to pay the traveling expenses of the scholars invited to attend. It was for the opening of this debate that he wrote the Oration on the Dignity of Man, *from which the opening pages are excerpted here. But the actual debate never took place, for when Pope Innocent VIII had a commission investigate Pico's theses, they condemned thirteen propositions as heretical. Pico then became involved in a controversy with Church authorities and was obliged to flee to France, where he was arrested. He was returned to Italy on parole in the custody of Lorenzo de'Medici, and he remained in Florence until his death.*

The brief section of Pico's Oration *excerpted here has become famous in modern accounts of the Renaissance as the finest expression of the optimism believed to be characteristic of Italian humanism. More recent research emphasizes the traditional elements in Pico's celebration of human free*

---

*will, and sees the work rather as an example of the new Renaissance inter-
est in Christianizing the Kabbalah.*

I have read in the ancient annals of the Arabians, most reverend Fathers,
that when asked what on the world's stage could be considered most
admirable, Abdala the Saracen answered that there is nothing more
admirable to be seen than man. In agreement with this opinion is the
saying of Hermes Trismegistus: "What a great miracle, O Asclepius, is
man!"

When I had thought over the meaning of these maxims, the many reasons for the excellence of man advanced by many men failed to satisfy
me—that man is the intermediary between the creatures, the intimate of
the higher beings and the lord of those below him; the interpreter of
nature by the sharpness of his senses, by the discernment of his reason,
and by the light of his intellect; the intermediate point between fixed
eternity and fleeting time; and, as the Persians say, the bond or rather the
marriage song of the world, but little lower than the angels according to
David's testimony. These are weighty reasons, indeed, but they are not
the principal reasons, that is, those which should be accorded boundless
admiration. For why should we not admire more the angels themselves
and the most blessed choirs of heaven?

At last, it seems to me that I have understood why man is the most
fortunate living thing worthy of all admiration and precisely what rank
is his lot in the universal chain of being, a rank to be envied not only by
the brutes but even by the stars and by minds beyond this world. It is a
matter past faith and extraordinary! Why should it not be so? For it is
upon this account that man is justly considered and called a great miracle
and a truly admirable being. But hear, Fathers, exactly what man's rank
is, and as friendly listeners by virtue of your humanity, forgive any defi-
ciencies in this, my work.

God the Father, the supreme Architect, had already built this cosmic
home which we behold, this most majestic temple of divinity, in accordance with the laws of a mysterious wisdom. He had adorned the region
above the heavens with intelligences, had quickened the celestial spheres
with eternal souls and had filled the vile and filthy parts of the lower
world with a multitude of animals of every kind. But when the work was
completed, the Maker kept wishing that there were someone who could
examine the plan of so great an enterprise, who could love its beauty,
who could admire its vastness. On that account, when everything was

completed, as Moses and Timaeus both testify, He finally took thought of creating man. However, not a single archetype remained from which he might fashion this new creature, not a single treasure remained which he might bestow upon this new son, and not a single seat remained in the whole world in which the contemplator of the universe might sit. All was now complete; all things had been assigned to the highest, the middle, and the lowest orders. But it was not in the nature of the Father's power to fail in this final creative effort, as though exhausted; nor was it in the nature of His wisdom to waver in such a crucial matter through lack of counsel; and it was not in the nature of His Beneficent Love that he who was destined to praise God's divine generosity in regard to others should be forced to condemn it in regard to himself. At last, the Supreme Artisan ordained that the creature to whom He could give nothing properly his own should share in whatever He had assigned individually to the other creatures. He therefore accepted man as a work of indeterminate nature, and placing him in the center of the world, addressed him thus:

"O Adam, we have given you neither a place nor a form nor any ability exclusively your own, so that according to your wishes and your judgment, you may have and possess whatever place, form, or abilities you desire. The nature of all other beings is limited and constrained in accordance with the laws prescribed by us. Constrained by no limits, in accordance with your own free will, in whose hands we have placed you, you shall independently determine the bounds of your own nature. We have placed you at the world's center, from where you may more easily observe whatever is in the world. We have made you neither celestial nor terrestrial, neither mortal nor immortal, so that with honor and freedom of choice, as though the maker and molder of yourself, you may fashion yourself in whatever form you prefer. You shall have the power to degenerate into the inferior forms of life which are brutish; you shall have the power, through your soul's judgment, to rise to the superior orders which are divine."

O supreme generosity of God the Father! O highest and most admirable felicity of man to whom it is granted to have whatever he chooses, to be whatever he wills! From the moment of their birth, or as Lucilius says, from their mother's womb, the beasts bring with them all that they will ever possess. The highest spirits, either from the beginning of time or soon thereafter, become what they are to be throughout eternity. In man alone, at the moment of his creation, the Father placed the seeds of all kinds and the germs of every way of life. Whatever seeds each man cultivates will mature and bear their own fruit in him; if vegetative, he will be like a plant; if sensitive, he will become a brute; if rational, he will become a celestial being; if intellectual, he will be an angel and the son of God. And if content with the lot of no creature he withdraws into the center of his own unity, his spirit, made one with God, in the solitary darkness of the Father who is placed above all things, will surpass them all.

Who would not admire this our chameleon? Or who could admire any other being more greatly than man? Asclepius the Athenian justly says that man was symbolized in the mysteries by the figure of Proteus, because of his ability to change his character and transform his nature. This is the origin of those metamorphoses or transformations celebrated among the Hebrews and the Pythagoreans. For the occult theology of the Hebrews sometimes transforms the holy Enoch into an angel of divinity and sometimes transforms other people into other divinities. The Pythagoreans transform impious men into beasts and, if Empedocles is to be believed, even into plants. Echoing this, Mohammed often had this saying on his lips: "He who deviates from divine law becomes a beast," and he was right in saying so. For it is not the bark that makes the plant but its dumb and insentient nature; neither is it the hide that makes the beast of burden but its irrational and sensitive soul; neither is it the spherical form which makes the heavens, but their undeviating order; nor is it the freedom from a body which makes the angel but its spiritual intelligence.

If you see one abandoned to his appetites crawling along the earth on his belly, it is a plant, not a man, which you see; if you see one enchanted by the vain illusions of fancy, as if by the spells of Calypso, and seduced by these tempting wiles, a slave to his own senses, it is a beast and not a man you see. However, if you see a philosopher who discerns all things by means of right reason, you will venerate him: he is a celestial, not an earthly being. If you see a pure contemplator, unmindful of the body and wholly withdrawn into the inner reaches of the mind, he is neither a terrestrial nor a celestial being; he is a higher spirit clothed in mortal flesh and most worthy of respect.

Are there any who will not admire man? In the sacred Mosaic and Christian writings, man, not without reason, is sometimes described by the name of "all flesh" and sometimes by that of "every creature," since man molds, fashions, and transforms himself according to the form of all flesh and the character of every creature. For this reason, the Persian Evantes, in describing Chaldean theology, writes that man does not have an inborn and fixed image of himself but many which are external and foreign to him; whence comes the Chaldean saying: "Man is a being of varied, manifold, and inconstant nature."

But why do we reiterate all these things? To the end that from the moment we are born into the condition of being able to become whatever we choose, we should be particularly certain that it may never be said of us that, although born to a privileged position, we failed to realize it and became like brutes and mindless beasts of burden, but that the saying of Asaph the prophet might be repeated: "You are all gods and the sons of the Most High." Otherwise, abusing the most indulgent generosity of the Father, we shall make that freedom of choice which He has given to us into something harmful rather than something beneficial.

Let some holy ambition invade our souls, so that, dissatisfied with mediocrity, we shall eagerly desire the highest things and shall toil with all our strength to obtain them, since we may if we wish. Let us disdain earthly things, despise heavenly things, and finally, esteeming less all the things of this world, hasten to that court beyond the world which is nearest to the Godhead. There, as the sacred mysteries relate, Seraphim, Cherubim, and Thrones occupy the first places. Let us emulate their dignity and glory, intolerate of a secondary position for ourselves and incapable of yielding to them the first. If we have willed it, we shall be inferior to them in nothing.

But how shall we proceed and what in the end shall we do? Let us observe what they do, what sort of lives they live. For if we also come to live like them, and we are able to do so, we shall then equal their destiny.

NICCOLÒ MACHIAVELLI

Whether It Is Better to be Loved than Feared

Niccolò Machiavelli (1469–1527), the most famous of all Renaissance polit-
ical writers, is also the most controversial. He has been called the founder
of the social sciences, the originator of the theory of "power politics" in
international relations, the greatest Renaissance representative of "civic
humanism," a great theorist of republican liberty, as well as many less com-
plimentary names. He was born into an old but declining Florentine family
and received a standard humanistic education in the Greek and Latin clas-
sics. In his twenties he witnessed the expulsion of the Medici from Florence
and the ascendency of Fra Girolamo Savonarola, who temporarily turned
Florence into a kind of theocracy. From 1498 to 1512 he was employed as
the Second Chancellor (or under-secretary of state) to Florence's republican
regime, and became a close confidant ("lapdog," said his enemies) of Piero
Soderini, the Florentine head of state. In this period Machiavelli also served
as secretary to the emergency war commission, secretary of the civic board
governing the militia, and served as an ambassador and envoy on some
thirty-five diplomatic missions, including several to important leaders such
as King Louis XII of France, Cesare Borgia, Pope Julius II, and the
emperor Maximilian I. He had a much more extensive acquaintance with
men and affairs than most political theorists.

In 1512 the Soderini regime fell and the Medici returned to power.
Machiavelli was removed from office, and briefly imprisoned and tortured.
Yet he was still eager to serve the new regime and wrote The Prince *(1513,*
printed in 1531) in part to give the new Medici rulers proof of his political
acumen. Eventually he was commissioned by Cardinal Giulio de'Medici to
write a history of Florence. After his initial rejection by the Medici, Machi-
avelli sought to curry favor with leading oligarchs of the old republic, spec-
ulating on the possibility of their return to power. With this end in view he
composed The Discourses on the First Ten Books of Titus Livy *(1513–17,*
printed 1531). The dialogues on The Art of War, *written around 1520 and*
printed in 1521, display Machiavelli's credentials as an expert on military
matters. All of Machiavelli's works were on the papal Index of Prohibited
Books from 1557 until 1850.

In this selection from chapter XVII of The Prince, *Machiavelli explained that the prince's power and success must always trump lesser considerations such as his reputation for compassion and the love of the people.*

XVII. CRUELTY AND COMPASSION; AND WHETHER IT IS BETTER TO BE LOVED THAN FEARED, OR THE REVERSE

Taking others of the qualities I enumerated above, I say that a prince must want to have a reputation for compassion rather than for cruelty: none the less, he must be careful that he does not make bad use of compassion. Cesare Borgia was accounted cruel; nevertheless, this cruelty of his reformed the Romagna, brought it unity, and restored order and obedience. On reflection, it will be seen that there was more compassion in Cesare than in the Florentine people, who, to escape being called cruel, allowed Pistoia to be devastated.[1] So a prince must not worry if he incurs reproach for his cruelty so long as he keeps his subjects united and loyal. By making an example or two he will prove more compassionate than those who, being too compassionate, allow disorders which lead to murder and rapine. These nearly always harm the whole community, whereas executions ordered by a prince only affect individuals. A new prince, of all rulers, finds it impossible to avoid a reputation for cruelty, because of the abundant dangers inherent in a newly won state. Vergil, through the mouth of Dido, says:

> Res dura, et regni novitas me talia cogunt
> Moliri, et late fines custode tueri.[2]

None the less, a prince must be slow to believe allegations and to take action, and must watch that he does not come to be afraid of his own shadow; his behaviour must be tempered by humanity and prudence so that over-confidence does not make him rash or excessive distrust make him unbearable.

From this arises the following question: whether it is better to be loved than feared, or the reverse. The answer is that one would like to be both the one and the other; but because it is difficult to combine them, it is far better to be feared than loved if you cannot be both. One can make this generalization about men: they are ungrateful, fickle, liars, and deceivers, they shun danger and are greedy for profit; while you treat them well, they are yours. They would shed their blood for you, risk their property, their lives, their sons, so long, as I said above, as danger is remote; but when you are in danger they turn away. Any prince who has come to depend entirely on promises and has taken no other precautions ensures his own ruin; friendship which is bought with money and not with greatness and nobility of mind is paid for, but it does not last and it yields nothing. Men worry less about doing an injury to one who makes himself loved than to one who makes himself feared. For love is secured by a bond of gratitude which men, wretched creatures that they are, break when it is to their advantage to do so; but fear is strengthened by a dread of punishment which is always effective.

The prince must none the less make himself feared in such a way that, if he is not loved, at least he escapes being hated. For fear is quite compatible with an absence of hatred; and the prince can always avoid hatred if he abstains from the property of his subjects and citizens and from their women. If, even so, it proves necessary to execute someone, this is to be done only when there is proper justification and manifest reason for it. But above all a prince must abstain from the property of others; because men sooner forget the death of their father than the loss of their patrimony. It is always possible to find pretexts for confiscating someone's property; and a prince who starts to live by rapine always finds pretexts for seizing what belongs to others. On the other hand, pretexts for executing someone are harder to find and they are sooner gone.

However, when a prince is campaigning with his soldiers and is in command of a large army then he need not worry about having a reputation for cruelty; because, without such a reputation, no army was ever kept united and disciplined. Among the admirable achievements of Hannibal is included this: that although he led a huge army, made up of countless different races, on foreign campaigns, there was never any dissension, either among the troops themselves or against their leader, whether things were going well or badly. For this, his inhuman cruelty was wholly responsible. It was this, along with his countless other qualities, which made him feared and respected by his soldiers. If it had not been for his cruelty, his other qualities would not have been enough. The historians, having given little thought to this, on the one hand admire what Hannibal achieved, and on the other condemn what made his achievements possible.

That his other qualities would not have been enough by themselves can be proved by looking at Scipio, a man unique in his own time and through all recorded history. His armies mutinied against him in Spain, and the only reason for this was his excessive leniency, which allowed his soldiers more licence than was good for military discipline. Fabius Maximus reproached him for this in the Senate and called him a corrupter of the Roman legions. Again, when the Locrians were plundered by one of Scipio's officers, he neither gave them satisfaction nor punished his officer's insubordination; and this was all because of his being too lenient by nature.[3] By way of excuse for him some senators argued that many men were better at not making mistakes themselves than at correcting them in others. But in time Scipio's lenient nature would have spoilt his fame and glory had he continued to indulge it during his command; when he lived under orders from the Senate, however, this fatal characteristic of his was not only concealed but even brought him glory.

So, on this question of being loved or feared, I conclude that since some men love as they please but fear when the prince pleases, a wise prince should rely on what he controls, not on what he cannot control. He must only endeavour, as I said, to escape being hated.

EXPLANATORY NOTES

1. Pistoia was a subject-city of Florence, which forcibly restored order there when conflict broke out between two rival factions in 1502–2. Machiavelli was concerned with this business at first hand.
2. 'Harsh necessity, and the newness of my kingdom, force me to do such things and to guard my frontiers everywhere.' *Aeneid* i, 563.
3. Locri Epizephyrii was in Calabria. Machiavelli liked to make comparisons—elaborated in the *Discorsi*—between Hannibal and Publius Cornelius Scipio, called Scipio Africanus Major (326–182 B.C.), who defeated Hannibal during the Punic wars at Zama in 202 B.C.

THOMAS MORE

Imagining the Ideal Community

Thomas More (1477/8–1535) had the unusual distinction of combining the roles of humanist, lawyer, statesman, knight, and Catholic saint. He was the son of Sir John More, a successful London lawyer, and received a humanist education in London and Oxford; he also served as a page in the household of John Morton, archbishop of Canterbury (who is mentioned favorably in the Utopia). About 1494 he began to study law, after which he embarked on a career as a politician and royal servant. He served as a member of Parliament in 1504 and 1523 (when he was elected speaker of the house); as under-sheriff of London (1510–19); as royal counselor (after 1517); as well as in a number of other important offices, culminating in his appointment in 1529 as Lord Chancellor. In the early 1530s King Henry VIII's policy of bringing the Church of England under royal control alienated More, a pious Roman Catholic, from government service, and he resigned as Lord Chancellor in 1532. He refused to subscribe to a new oath required by the Act of Succession in 1534, and was named in a bill of attainder. After being examined by the King's Council, More was imprisoned in the Tower of London and eventually found guilty of treason on the basis of perjured testimony. He was beheaded on July 6, 1535, after pronouncing the famous last words, "I am the king's good servant, but God's first."

More's career as a humanist was influenced decisively by his friendship with the great Dutch humanist Erasmus of Rotterdam as well as by his Greek studies with William Grocyn and Thomas Linacre. More wrote a number of humanistic literary works, including a history of Richard III, an English translation of the life of Giovanni Pico della Mirandola, and a small body of Latin poetry, but his most famous and enduring work by far was the Utopia. Begun while on an embassy to Flanders in 1515, the work captures the atmosphere of hope and new possibilities that pervaded humanist circles in the early years of Henry VIII's reign. It also documents brilliantly the impact on the European imagination of the exploration of the New World. The Utopia (from the Greek ou-topos, no place) is inspired in part by Plato's Republic and other ancient writings, but gave rise to an entirely new genre of Utopian literature that flourished in western countries down to the twentieth century. In the present selection,

More's main interlocutor, Raphael Nonsenso, describes the geography, physical layout, economy, social customs, and political system of Utopia.

BOOK TWO

RAPHAEL: Well, the island is broadest in the middle, where it measures about two hundred miles across. It's never much narrower than that, except towards the very ends, which gradually taper away and curve right round, just as if they'd been drawn with a pair of compasses, until they almost form a circle five hundred miles in circumference. So you can picture the island as a sort of crescent, with its tips divided by a strait approximately eleven miles wide. Through this the sea flows in, and then spreads out into an enormous lake—though it really looks more like a vast standing pool, for, as it's completely protected from the wind by the surrounding land, the water never gets rough. Thus practically the whole interior of the island serves as a harbour, and boats can sail across it in all directions, which is very useful for everyone.

The harbour mouth is alarmingly full of rocks and shoals. One of these rocks presents no danger to shipping, for it rises high out of the water, almost in the middle of the gap, and has a tower built on it, which is permanently garrisoned. But the other rocks are deadly, because you can't see them. Only the Utopians know where the safe channels are, so without a Utopian pilot it's practically impossible for a foreign ship to enter the harbour. It would be risky enough even for the local inhabitants, if it weren't for certain landmarks erected on the shore—and by simply shifting these landmarks they could lure any number of enemy warships to destruction. Of course, there are plenty of harbours on the other side of the island, but they're all so well fortified, either naturally or artificially, that a handful of men could easily prevent a huge invading force from landing at any of them.

They say, though, and one can actually see for oneself, that Utopia was originally not an island but a peninsula. However, it was conquered by somebody called Utopos, who gave it its present name—it used to be called Sansculottia—and was also responsible for transforming a pack of ignorant savages into what is now, perhaps, the most civilized nation in the world. The moment he landed and got control of the country, he immediately had a channel cut through the fifteen-mile isthmus connecting Utopia with the mainland, so that the sea could flow all round it. Fearing it might cause resentment if he made the local inhabitants do all the work, he put his whole army on the job as well. With this colossal labour force, he got it done incredibly quickly, to the great surprise and terror of the people on the mainland, who'd begun by making fun of the whole idea.

There are fifty-four splendid big towns on the island, all with the same language, laws, customs, and institutions. They're all built on the same plan, and, so far as the sites will allow, they all look exactly alike. The minimum distance between towns is twenty-four miles, and the maximum, no more than a day's walk.

Each town sends three of its older and more experienced citizens to an annual meeting at Aircastle, to discuss the general affairs of the island. Aircastle is regarded as the capital, because of its central position, which makes it easy to get at from every part of the country. The distribution of land is so arranged that the territory of each town stretches for at least twenty miles in every direction, and in one direction much farther—that is, where the distance between towns reaches its maximum. No town has the slightest wish to extend its boundaries, for they don't regard their land as property but as soil that they've got to cultivate.

At regular intervals all over the countryside there are houses supplied with agricultural equipment, and town dwellers take it in turns to go and live in them. Each house accommodates at least forty adults, plus two slaves who are permanently attached to it, and is run by a reliable, elderly married couple, under the supervision of a District Controller, who's responsible for thirty such houses. Each year twenty people from each house go back to town, having done two years in the country, and are replaced by twenty others. These new recruits are then taught farming by the ones who've had a year on the land already, and so know more about the job. Twelve months later the trainees become the instructors, and so on. This system reduces the risk of food shortages, which might occur if the whole agricultural population were equally inexperienced.

Two years is the normal period of work on the land, so that no one's forced to rough it for too long, but those who enjoy country life—and many people do—can get special permission to stay there longer. Land-workers are responsible for cultivating the soil, raising livestock, felling timber, and transporting it to the towns, either by land or sea, whichever is more convenient. They breed vast numbers of chickens by a most extraordinary method. Instead of leaving the hens to sit on the eggs, they hatch out dozens at a time by applying a steady heat to them—with the result that, when the chicks come out of the shells, they regard the poul-tryman as their mother, and follow him everywhere!

They keep very few horses, and no really tame ones, as they only use them for riding practice. Ploughing and pulling carts is done by oxen.

Admittedly they can't go as fast as horses, but the Utopians say they're tougher and subject to fewer diseases. They're also less trouble and less expensive to feed, and, when they're finally past work, they're still useful as meat.

Corn is used solely for making bread, for they drink no beer, only wine, cider, perry, or water—sometimes by itself, but often flavoured with honey or liquorice, which are both very plentiful. The authorities of each town work out very accurately the annual food consumption of their whole area, but they always grow corn and breed livestock far in excess of their own requirements, so that they've plenty to spare for their neighbours.

Any necessary equipment which is not available in the country is got from one's home town—for there's a holiday once a month, when most people go there. You simply ask an official for what you want, and he hands it over, without any sort of payment.

Just before harvest-time District Controllers notify the urban authorities how much extra labour they'll need. So exactly that number of harvesters turns up punctually on the right day, and, if the weather's good, gets the whole job done in something like twenty-four hours.

But I must tell you some more about the towns. Well, when you've seen one of them, you've seen them all, for they're as nearly identical as local conditions will permit. So I'll just give you one example—it doesn't much matter which. However, the obvious choice is Aircastle, for the fact that Parliament meets there gives it a special importance, and it's the one I know best, having lived there for five years.

Aircastle is built on a gently sloping hill-side, and its groundplan is practically square. It stretches from just below the top of the hill to the River Nowater, two miles away, and extends for two miles and a bit along the river-bank.

The source of the Nowater is quite a small spring eighty miles further inland, but it's joined by several tributaries, two of them pretty big ones, so by the time it gets to Aircastle it's already more than fifty yards wide. It then keeps on growing wider, until it reaches the sea sixty miles away. Right up to the town, and for several miles beyond it, there are strong tidal currents which change direction every six hours. At high tide the sea comes thirty miles inland, filling the whole river-bed and forcing the river back. The water turns brackish for some distance further upstream, but after that the taste of salt gradually disappears, and the water which flows past Aircastle is absolutely fresh. At low tide the river chases the sea back, and continues pure and uncontaminated practically all the way to the coast.

The town is connected with the other bank of the river by a splendid arched bridge, with stone piers—not just wooden ones. That's at the land-ward end, so that ships can have unobstructed access to one whole side of the town. There's also another river, not very big, but delightfully calm and peaceful. It gushes out of the hill on which Aircastle is built, and flows down through the middle of it to join the Nowater. The fountain-head is just outside the town, but they've brought it within the circuit of the city wall, so that in case of invasion the enemy couldn't either cut off, divert, or poison their water supply. From that point water is run off to the lower districts of the town through a system of brickwork pipes. Where this method won't work, they have huge cisterns to collect rainwater—which serves the purpose equally well.

The town is surrounded by a thick, high wall, with towers and block-houses at frequent intervals. On three sides of it there's also a moat, which contains no water, but is very broad and deep, and obstructed by a thorn-bush entanglement. On the fourth side the river serves as a moat. The streets are well designed, both for traffic and for protection against the wind. The buildings are far from unimpressive, for they take the form of terraces, facing one another and running the whole length of the street. The fronts of the houses are separated by a twenty-foot carriage-way. Behind them is a large garden, also as long as the street itself, and completely enclosed by the backs of other streets. Each house has a front door leading into the street, and a back door into the garden. In both cases they're double swing-doors, which open at a touch, and close auto-matically behind you. So anyone can go in and out—for there's no such thing as private property. The houses themselves are allocated by lot, and changed round every ten years.

They're extremely fond of these gardens, in which they grow fruit, including grapes, as well as grass and flowers. They keep them in won-derful condition—in fact, I've never seen anything to beat them for beauty or fertility. The people of Aircastle are keen gardeners not only because they enjoy it, but because there are inter-street competitions for the best-kept garden. Certainly it would be hard to find any feature of the town more calculated to give pleasure and profit to the commu-nity—which makes me think that gardening must have been one of the founder's special interests.

By the founder I mean Utopos himself, who is said to have designed the whole layout of the town right from the start. However, he left pos-terity to embellish it and add the finishing touches, which he realized would take more than a single lifetime. According to their historical records, which cover a period of 1,760 years from the Conquest, and have always been most carefully written up, the original houses were merely small huts or cottages, built hurriedly with the first timber that came to hand. The walls were plastered with mud, the roofs ridged and thatched. But nowadays every house is an imposing three-storey structure. The walls are faced with flint or some other hard stone, or else with bricks, and lined with roughcast. The sloping roofs have been raised to the horizontal, and covered with a special sort of concrete which costs next to nothing, but is better than lead for resisting bad weather conditions, and is also fireproof. They keep out draughts by glazing the windows—oh yes, they use a great deal of glass there—or sometimes by fitting screens of fine linen treated with clear oil or amber, which has the effect of making it more transparent and also more airtight.

Now for their system of local government. The population is divided into groups of thirty households, each of which elects an official called a Styward every year. Styward is the Old Utopian title—the modern one is District Controller. For every ten Stywards and the households they represent there is a Bencheater, or Senior District Controller.

Each town has two hundred Stywards, who are responsible for electing the Mayor. They do it by secret ballot, after solemnly swearing to vote for the man that they consider best qualified, He has to be one of four candidates nominated by the whole electorate—for each quarter of the town chooses its own candidate and submits his name to the Council of Bencheaters. The Mayor remains in office for life, unless he's suspected of wanting to establish a dictatorship. Bencheaters are elected annually, but they're not normally changed. All other municipal appointments are for one year only.

Every three days, or more often if necessary, the Bencheaters have a meeting with the Mayor, at which they discuss public affairs, and promptly settle any private disputes—though these are very rare. They always invite two Stywards, a different pair each day, to attend their meetings, and there's a rule that no question affecting the general public may be finally decided until it has been debated for three days. It's a capital crime to discuss such questions anywhere except in the Council or the Assembly. Apparently this is to discourage the Mayor and Bencheaters from plotting to override the people's wishes and change the constitution. For the same reason any major issue is referred to the Assembly of Stywards, who explain it to all their households, talk it over among themselves, and then report their views to the Council. Occasionally the matter is referred to Parliament.

There's also a rule in the Council that no resolution can be debated on the day that it's first proposed. All discussion is postponed until the next well-attended meeting. Otherwise someone's liable to say the first thing that comes into his head, and then start thinking up arguments to justify what he has said, instead of trying to decide what's best for the community. That type of person is quite prepared to sacrifice the public to his own prestige, just because, absurd as it may sound, he's ashamed to admit that his first idea might have been wrong—when his first idea *should* have been to think before he spoke.

And now for their working conditions. Well, there's one job they all do, irrespective of sex, and that's farming. It's part of every child's education. They learn the principles of agriculture at school, and they're taken for regular outings into the fields near the town, where they not only watch farm-work being done, but also do some themselves, as a form of exercise.

Besides farming which, as I say, is everybody's job, each person is taught a special trade of his own. He may be trained to process wool or flax, or he may become a stonemason, a blacksmith, or a carpenter. Those are the only trades that employ any considerable quantity of labour. They have no tailors or dressmakers, since everyone on the island wears the same sort of clothes—except that they vary slightly according to sex and marital status—and the fashion never changes. These clothes are quite pleasant to look at, they allow free movement of the limbs, they're equally suitable for hot and cold weather—and the great thing is, they're all home-made. So everybody learns one of the other trades I mentioned, and by everybody I mean the women as well as the men— though the weaker sex are given the lighter job, like spinning and weaving, while the men do the heavier ones.

Most children are brought up to do the same work as their parents, since they tend to have a natural feeling for it. But if a child fancies some other trade, he's adopted into a family that practises it. Of course, great care is taken, not only by the father, but also by the local authorities, to see that the foster-father is a decent, respectable type. When you've learned one trade properly, you can, if you like, get permission to learn another—and when you're an expert in both, you can practise whichever you prefer, unless the other one is more essential to the public.

The chief business of the Stywards—in fact, practically their only business—is to see that nobody sits around doing nothing, but that everyone gets on with his job. They don't wear people out, though, by keeping them hard at work from early morning till late at night, like cart-horses. That's just slavery—and yet that's what life is like for the working classes nearly everywhere else in the world. In Utopia they have a six-hour working day—three hours in the morning, then lunch— then a two-hour break—then three more hours in the afternoon, followed by supper. They go to bed at 8 P.M., and sleep for eight hours. All the rest of the twenty-four they're free to do what they like—not to waste their time in idleness or self-indulgence, but to make good use of if in some congenial activity. Most people spend these free periods on further education, for there are public lectures first thing every morning. Attendance is quite voluntary, except for those picked out for academic training, but men and women of all classes go crowding in to hear them—I mean, different people go to different lectures, just as the spirit moves them. However, there's nothing to stop you from spending this extra time on your trade, if you want to. Lots of people do, if they haven't the capacity for intellectual work, and are much admired for such public-spirited behaviour.

After supper they have an hour's recreation, either in the gardens or in the communal dining-halls, according to the time of year. Some people practise music, others just talk. They've never heard of anything so silly and demoralizing as dice, but they have two games rather like chess. The first is a sort of arithmetical contest, in which certain numbers 'take' others. The second is a pitched battle between virtues and vices, which illustrates most ingeniously how vices tend to conflict with one another, but to combine against virtues. It also shows which vices are opposed to which virtues, how much strength vices can muster for a direct assault, what indirect tactics they employ, what help virtues need to overcome vices, what are the best methods of evading their attacks, and what ultimately determines the victory of one side or the other.

But here's a point that requires special attention, or you're liable to get the wrong idea. Since they only work a six-hour day, you may think there must be a shortage of essential goods. On the contrary, those six hours are enough, and more than enough to produce plenty of everything that's needed for a comfortable life. And you'll understand why it is, if you reckon up how large a proportion of the population in other countries is totally unemployed. First you have practically all the women—that gives you nearly fifty per cent for a start. And in countries where the women *do* work, the men tend to lounge about instead. Then there are all the priests, and members of so-called religious orders—how much work do they do? Add all the rich, especially the landowners, popularly known as nobles and gentlemen. Include their domestic staffs—I mean those gangs of armed ruffians that I mentioned before. Finally, throw in all the beggars who are perfectly hale and hearty, but pretend to be ill as an excuse for being lazy. When you've counted them up, you'll be surprised to find how few people actually produce what the human race consumes.

And now just think how few of these few people are doing essential work—for where money is the only standard of value, there are bound to be dozens of unnecessary trades carried on, which merely supply luxury goods or entertainment. Why, even if the existing labour force were distributed among the few trades really needed to make life reasonably comfortable, there'd be so much over-production that prices would fall too low for the workers to earn a living. Whereas, if you took all those engaged in non-essential trades, and all who are too lazy to work—each of whom consumes twice as much of the products of other people's labour as any of the producers themselves—if you put the whole lot of them on to something useful, you'd soon see how few hours' work a day would be amply sufficient to supply all the necessities and comforts of life—to which you might add all real and natural forms of pleasure.

But in Utopia the facts speak for themselves. There, out of all the able-bodied men and women who live in a town, or in the country round it, five hundred at the most are exempted from ordinary work. This includes the Stywards, who, though legally exempt, go on working voluntarily to set a good example. It also includes those who are permanently relieved of other duties so that they can concentrate on their studies. This privilege is only granted on the recommendation of the priests, confirmed by the Stywards in a secret ballot—and, if such a student produces disappointing results, he's sent back to the working class. On the other hand, it's not at all unusual for a manual worker to study so hard in his spare time, and make such good progress, that he's excused from practising his trade, and promoted to the intelligentsia.

This is the class from which the diplomats, priests, Bencheaters, and of course mayors are recruited. The old-fashioned word for a mayor, by the way, is *Barzanes,* though nowadays he's usually called a Nopeople. As hardly any other member of the population is either unemployed or non-productively employed, you can guess how much good work they get done in a few hours. Their labour problem is also reduced by the fact that they tackle essential jobs with more economy of effort than we do. For instance, the reason why the building trade usually absorbs so much labour is that people put up houses which their improvident heirs allow to tumble down. So the next generation has to start building all over again, which costs infinitely more than it would have cost to keep the original houses standing. In fact, what often happens is this: A builds a very expensive house, which then fails to satisfy B's fastidious taste. B therefore neglects it so badly that it's soon in ruins, and builds himself an equally expensive house elsewhere. But in Utopia, where everything's under state control, houses are very seldom built on entirely new sites, and repairs are carried out immediately they become necessary, if not before. Thus they achieve maximum durability with the minimum of labour, which means that builders sometimes have practically nothing to do. On such occasions they're sent home to saw up planks and get stones ready squared, so that if they do have to build anything it can go up all the faster.

Then think how much labour they save on clothes. Their working clothes are just loose-fitting leather overalls, which last for at least seven years. When they go about in public, they cover these rough garments with a sort of cloak, which is always the same colour—the natural colour of wool. Thus not only is their consumption of woollen fabric the lowest in the world, but so are their production costs for this material. Linen is even easier to produce, and therefore more often used—but, as long as the linen is white and the wool is clean, they don't care how fine or coarse the thread is. So whereas in other countries you won't find any-one satisfied with less than five or six suits and as many silk shirts, while dressy types want over ten of each, your Utopian is content with a single piece of clothing every two years. For why should he want more? They wouldn't make him any warmer—or any better looking.

With everybody doing useful work, and with such work reduced to a minimum, they build up such large reserves of everything that from time to time they can release a huge labour force to mend any roads which are in bad condition. And quite often, if there's nothing of that sort to be done, the authorities announce a shorter working day. They never force people to work unnecessarily, for the main purpose of their whole econ-omy is to give each person as much time free from physical drudgery as the needs of the community will allow, so that he can cultivate his mind—which they regard as the secret of a happy life.

Now I'd better explain their social arrangements—how society is organized, how they behave towards one another, how goods are dis-tributed, and so on. Well, the smallest social unit is the household, which is virtually synonymous with the family. When a girl grows up and gets married, she joins her husband's household, but the boys of each genera-tion stay at home, under the control of their oldest male relative—unless he becomes senile, in which case the next oldest takes over.

Each town consists of six thousand households, not counting the country ones, and to keep the population fairly steady there's a law that no household shall contain less than ten or more than sixteen adults—as they can't very well fix a figure for children. This law is observed by sim-ply moving supernumerary adults to smaller households. If the town as a whole gets too full, the surplus population is transferred to a town that's comparatively empty. If the whole island becomes overpopulated, they tell off a certain number of people from each town to go and start a colony at the nearest point on the mainland where there's a large area that hasn't been cultivated by the local inhabitants. Such colonies are governed by the Utopians, but the natives are allowed to join in if they want to. When this happens, natives and colonists soon combine to form a single community with a single way of life, to the great advantage of both parties—for, under Utopian management, land which used to be thought incapable of producing anything for one lot of people produces plenty for two.

If the natives won't do what they're told, they're expelled from the area marked out for annexation. If they try to resist, the Utopians declare war—for they consider war perfectly justifiable, when one country denies another its natural right to derive nourishment from any soil which the original owners are not using themselves, but are merely holding on to as a worthless piece of property.

Should any town become so depopulated that it can't be brought up to strength by transfers from elsewhere on the island, without reducing the population of some other town below the prescribed minimum—a thing which is said to have happened only twice in their history, each time as the result of a violent epidemic—they recall colonists to fill the gap, on the principle that it's better to lose a colony than to weaken any part of Utopia itself.

But let's get back to their social organization. Each household, as I said, comes under the authority of the oldest male. Wives are subordinate to their husbands, children to their parents, and younger people generally to their elders. Every town is divided into four districts of equal size, each with its own shopping centre in the middle of it. There the products of every household are collected in warehouses, and then distributed according to type among various shops. When the head of a household needs anything for himself or his family, he just goes to one of these shops and asks for it. And whatever he asks for, he's allowed to take away without any sort of payment, either in money or in kind. After all, why shouldn't he? There's more than enough of everything to go round, so there's no risk of his asking for more than he needs—for why should anyone want to start hoarding, when he knows he'll never have to go short of anything? No living creature is naturally greedy, except from fear of want—or in the case of human beings, from vanity, the notion that you're better than people if you can display more superfluous property than they can. But there's no scope for that sort of thing in Utopia.

ERASMUS

The Empire of Folly

Desiderius Erasmus (c. 1469–1536) was the most famous humanist scholar of his day. This master of Greek, Latin, rhetoric, and theology was born and educated in the Netherlands. He traveled extensively, studying and teaching in Paris and visiting England and Italy. Believing firmly in the value of education, he wrote several works of biting, brilliant satire for the benefit of his pupils. He attacked both scholars' arrogance and the common man's credulity. He was critical of state and church, of princes and popes alike. He produced the first published Greek edition of the New Testament, which Martin Luther used to make his translation of the Bible into German. Erasmus maintained a vast correspondence, writing hundreds of letters to friends, fellow scholars, and princes. He engaged in numerous debates with the leading scholars of his day, including Martin Luther. But while the Protestant Reformation took flame around Erasmus, he refused to desert the Catholic church, despite his many objections to its practices.

The Praise of Folly *(1509) is perhaps Erasmus's most popular work, though he claimed to have written it as a joke. The text displays the wide range of his humanist scholarship, including a vast number of references to works of classical Greek and Latin literature. It makes a thorough critique of European society in the early sixteenth century, in the best of good humor.*

Folly speaks:
Whatever is generally said of me by mortal men, and I'm quite well aware that Folly is in poor repute even amongst the greatest fools, still, I am the one—and indeed, the only one—whose divine powers can gladden the hearts of gods and men. Proof enough of this is in the fact that as soon as I stepped forward to address this crowded assembly, every face immediately brightened up with a new, unwonted gaiety and all your frowns were smoothed away. You laughed and applauded with such delightfully happy smiles that as I look at you all gathered round me I

could well believe you are tipsy with nectar like the Homeric gods, with a dash of nepenthe too, though a moment ago you were sitting looking as gloomy and harassed as if you had just come up from Trophonius' cave. Now, when the sun first shows his handsome golden visage upon earth or after a hard winter the newborn spring breathes out its mild west breezes, it always happens that a new face comes over everything, new colour and a kind of youthfulness return; and so it only takes the mere sight of me to give you all a different look. For great orators must as a rule spend time preparing long speeches and even then find it difficult to succeed in banishing care and trouble from your minds, but I've done this at once—and simply by my looks.

Why have I appeared today in this unaccustomed garb? Well, you shall hear the reason if you have no objection to lending me your ears— no, not the ones you use for preachers of sermons, but the ears you usually prick up for mountebanks, clowns, and fools, the sort of ears that once upon a time our friend Midas listened with to Pan. I've a fancy to play the sophist before you, and I don't mean by that one of the tribe today who cram tiresome trivialities into the heads of schoolboys and teach them more than feminine obstinacy in disputation—no, I shall follow the ancients who chose the name sophist in preference to the damaging title of wise men. Their concern was to provide eulogies in praise of gods and heroes, so it's a eulogy you are going to hear now, though not one of Hercules or Solon. It's in praise of myself, namely, Folly.

Now, I don't think much of those wiseacres who maintain it's the height of folly and conceit if anyone speaks in his own praise; or rather, it can be as foolish as they like, as long as they admit it's in character. What could be more fitting than for Folly to trumpet her own merits abroad and 'sing her own praises'. Who could portray me better than I can myself? Unless, of course, someone knows me better than I know myself. Yet in general I think I show a good deal more discretion than the general run of gentry and scholars, whose distorted sense of modesty leads them to make a practice of bribing some sycophantic speaker or babbling poet hired for a fee so that they can listen to him praising their merits, purely fictitious though these are. The bashful listener spreads his tail-feathers like a peacock and carries his head high, while the brazen flatterer rates this worthless individual with the gods and sets him up as the perfect model of all the virtues— though the man himself knows he is nowhere near that; 'infinity doubled' would not be too far away. Thus the wretched crow is decked out in borrowed plumage, the 'Ethiopian washed white', and 'elephant created out of a gnat'. Finally, I follow that well-worn popular proverb which says that a man does right to praise himself if he can't find anyone else to praise him.

. . .

And I may as well speak more frankly to you in my usual way. What is it, I ask you, which begets gods or men—the head, the face, the breast, hand, or ear, all thought of as respectable parts of the body? No, it's not. The propagator of the human race is that part which is so foolish and absurd that it can't be named without raising a laugh. There is the true sacred fount from which everything draws its being, not the quarternion of Pythagoras. Just tell me, please, what man would be willing to offer his neck to the halter of matrimony if he applied the usual practice of the wise man and first weighed up its disadvantages as a way of life? Or what woman would ever agree to take a husband if she knew or thought about the pains and dangers of childbirth and the trouble of bringing up children? So if you owe your existence to wedlock, you owe the fact of wedlock to madness, my attendant '*Anoia*', and can see how much in fact you owe to me. And if a woman has once had this experience, would she be willing to repeat it without the divine aid of '*Lethe*', who helps her to forget? Venus herself, whatever Lucretius says, would never deny that she would be weakened and shorn of her power if my own divinity didn't come to her aid. Thus from that game of mine, drunken and absurd as it is, spring haughty philosophers, and their present-day successors who are popularly called monks, kings in their purple, pious priests, and thrice-holy pontiffs; and finally, the whole assembly of the poets' gods, now so numerous that Olympus itself, for all its spaciousness, can scarcely hold such a crowd.

But I shouldn't claim much by saying that I'm the seed and source of existence unless I could also prove that whatever advantages there are all throughout life are all provided by me. What would this life be, or would it seem worth calling life at all, if its pleasure was taken away? I hear your applause, and in fact I've always felt sure that none of you was so wise or rather so foolish—no, I mean so wise—as to think it could. Even the stoics don't despise pleasure, though they are careful to conceal their real feelings, and tear it to pieces in public with their incessant outcry, so that once they have frightened everyone else off they can enjoy it more freely themselves. I'd just like them to tell me if there's any part of life which isn't dreary, unpleasant, graceless, stupid, and tedious unless you add pleasure, the seasoning of folly. I've proof enough in Sophocles, a poet who can never be adequately praised, who pays me a really splendid tribute in the line

For ignorance provides the happiest life.

But now let's take the facts one by one.

First of all, everyone knows that by far the happiest and universally enjoyable age of man is the first. What is there about babies which makes us hug and kiss and fondle them, so that even an enemy would give them help at that age? Surely it's the charm of folly, which thoughtful Nature has taken care to bestow on the newly born so that they can offer some reward of pleasure to mitigate the hard work of bringing them up and win the liking of those who look after them. Then follows adolescence, which everyone finds delightful, openly supports, and warmly encourages, eagerly offering a helping hand. Now whence comes the charm of youth if not from me? I've seen to it that youth has so little wisdom and hence so few frowns. It's a fact that as soon as the young grow up and develop the sort of mature sense which comes through experience and education, the bloom of youthful beauty begins to fade at once, enthusiasm wanes, gaiety cools down, and energy slackens. The further anyone withdraws from me the less and less he's alive, until 'painful age' comes on, that is, 'old age with its troubles' unwelcome not only to others but just as much to itself. This too would be intolerable to man if I weren't at his elbow out of pity for all he has to bear. Just as the gods of fiction often come to the aid of the dying with some metamorphosis, so do I recall people who are on the brink of the grave, as far as possible, to childhood once again. Hence the aptitude of the popular expression, 'second childhood'. And if any of you are interested in my method of transformation, I'm quite willing to tell you. The spring belonging to my nymph *Lethe* has its source in the Islands of the Blest, and what flows through the underworld is only a trickle of a stream. There I take them, so that once they have drunk deep draughts of forgetfulness the cares of the mind are gradually washed away and they recover their youth. I know they're called silly and foolish, as indeed they are, but that is exactly what it means to become a child again.

What else in childhood but silliness and foolishness? Its utter lack of sense is what we find so delightful. Everybody hates a prodigy, detests an old head on young shoulders; witness the oft-repeated saying 'I hate a small child who's too wise for his years.' And who could carry on doing business or having dealings with an old man if his vast experience of affairs was still matched by a vigorous mind and keen judgement?

So I see to it that the old man is witless, and this sets him free meanwhile from all those wretched anxieties which torment the man in his senses. He is also pleasant company for a drink, and doesn't feel the boredom with life which a more robust age can scarcely endure. There are times when, like the old man in Plautus, he goes back to those three special letters AMO, but he'd be anything but happy if he still had his wits. Meanwhile, thanks to what I do for him, he's happy, popular with his friends, even a welcome guest to bring life to a party. In Homer, the speech of old Nestor flows from his lips sweeter than honey, while that of Achilles is bitter, and the old men sitting on the walls of Troy speak in 'lily-sweet' voices. On this reckoning old age surpasses even childhood, for that is pleasant but inarticulate, and lacks the chief amusement in life—talk and still more talk. Add the fact that old people are always particularly delighted by children, and children by them—

For thus the god always brings like to like

—and there really is no difference between them except the old man's wrinkles and the number of birthdays he has counted. Otherwise they are exactly alike: white hair, toothless mouth, short stature, liking for milk, babbling, chattering, silliness, forgetfulness, thoughtlessness, everything in fact. The nearer people approach old age the closer they return to a semblance of childhood, until the time comes for them to depart this life, again like children, neither tired of living nor aware of death.

Anyone who likes can go and compare this service of mine with the changes made by other gods. What they did in anger, I'd rather not recount, but even when they're particularly well-disposed to people, they have a habit of turning them into a tree, a bird, a grasshopper, or even a snake—as if becoming something else were not just the same as dying. Now I restore a man unchanged to the best and happiest time of his life. But if mortals would henceforth have no truck with wisdom and spend all their time with me, there would be no more old age and they could be happy enjoying eternal youth.

You must have seen those soured individuals who are so wrapped up in their philosophic studies or some other serious, exacting affairs that they are old before they were ever young; I suppose it's because their preoccupations and the unremitting strain of their keen concentration gradually sap their spirit and vitality. By contrast my morons are plump, sleek, and glossy, typical 'Acarnanian porkers', as they say, and never likely to know any of the disadvantages of old age unless they pick up some infection from the wise. However, man isn't permitted to be happy every bit of his life.

. . .

But I don't think the female sex is so foolish as to be angry with me for attributing folly to them, seeing that I *am* Folly, and a woman myself. If they look at the matter in the right way they must see that it's entirely due to folly that they are better off than men in many respects. In the first place they have the gift of beauty, which they rightly value above everything else, for it ensures their power to tyrannize over tyrants themselves. Besides, that unkempt look, rough skin, bush beard, and all the marks of old age in a man can only come from the corrupting influence of wisdom, seeing that a woman always has smooth cheeks, gentle voice, soft skin, and a look of perpetual youth. Next, what else do women desire in this life but to give maximum pleasure to men? Isn't this the purpose of all their attention to their persons, all that make-up, bathing, hairdressing, and all those ointments and perfumes, as well as so many arts of arranging, painting, and disguising face, eyes, and skin? Now, does anything count more in winning them men's favour than their folly? There's nothing men won't permit to women, and for no other return than pleasure, but it's women's folly which makes them delight men. No one will deny the truth of this who considers the nonsense a man talks with a woman and the silly things he does whenever he wants to enjoy the pleasure she gives. So there you have the source of life's first and foremost delight.

However, there are some men, especially old men, who are more given to wine than to women, and find their greatest pleasure in drinking parties. Now whether a party can have much success without a woman present I must ask others to decide, but one thing is certain, no party is any fun unless seasoned with folly. In fact, if there's no one there to raise a laugh with his folly, genuine or assumed, they have to bring on a 'jester', one who's paid for the job, or invite some absurd hanger-on whose laughable, that is, foolish, remarks will banish silence and gloom from the company. What was the point of loading the stomach with all those delicacies, fancy dishes, and titbits if the eyes and ears and the whole mind can't be fed as well on laughter, jokes, and wit? But when it comes to that sort of confectionery, I'm the only mistress of the art. And all the usual rituals of banquets, drawing lots for a king, throwing dice, drinking healths, 'passing round the cup', singing with a myrtle branch, dancing, miming—none of them was discovered for the benefit of the human race by the Seven Sages of Greece, but by me. The very nature of all things of this sort is that the more folly they have, the more they enrich man's life, for if that is joyless it seems scarcely worth calling life at all. But it can't fail to end up joyless unless you can find diversions of this kind to remove the boredom inseparable from it.

. . .

Then there are the theologians, a remarkably supercilious and touchy lot. I might perhaps do better to pass over them in silence without 'stirring the mud of Camarina' or grasping that noxious plant, lest they marshal their forces for an attack with innumerable conclusions and force me to eat my words. If I refuse they'll denounce me as a heretic on the spot, for this is the bolt they always loose on anyone to whom they take a dislike.

Now there are none so unwilling to recognize my good services to them, and yet they're under obligation to me on several important counts, notably for their happiness in their self-love, which enables them to dwell in a sort of third heaven, looking down from aloft, almost with pity, on all the rest of mankind as so many cattle crawling on the face of the earth. They are fortified meanwhile with an army of <schoolmen's definitions>, conclusions, and corollaries, and propositions both explicit and implicit. They boast of so many 'bolt holes' that the meshes of Vulcan's net couldn't stop them from slipping out by means of the distinctions they draw, with which they can easily cut any knot (a double axe from Tenedos wouldn't do better), for they abound in newly coined expressions and strange-sounding words.

In addition, they interpret hidden mysteries to suit themselves: how the world was created and designed; through what channels the stain of sin filtered down to posterity; by what means, in what measure, and how long Christ was formed in the Virgin's womb; how, in the Eucharist, accidents can subsist without a domicile. But this sort of question has been discussed threadbare. There are others more worthy of great and enlightened theologians (as they call themselves) which can really rouse them to action if they come their way. What was the exact moment of divine generation? Are there several filiations in Christ? Is it a possible proposition that God the Father could hate his Son? Could God have taken on the form of a woman, a devil, a donkey, a gourd, or a flintstone? If so, how could a gourd have preached sermons, performed miracles, and been nailed to the cross? And what would Peter have consecrated <if he had consecrated> when the body of Christ still hung on the cross? Furthermore, at that same time could Christ have been called a man? Shall we be permitted to eat and drink after the resurrection? We're taking due precaution against hunger and thirst while there's time.

. . .

You may suppose that I'm saying all this by way of a joke, and that's not surprising, seeing that amongst the theologians themselves there are some with superior education who are sickened by these theological minutiae, which they look upon as frivolous. Others too think it a damnable form of sacrilege and the worst sort of impiety for anyone to speak of matters so holy, which call for reverence rather than explanation, with a profane tongue, or to argue with the pagan subtlety of the heathen, presume to offer definitions, and pollute the majesty of divine theology with words and sentiments which are so trivial and even squalid.

Yet those who do so are so happy in their self-satisfaction and self-congratulation, and so busy night and day with these enjoyable tomfooleries, that they haven't even a spare moment in which to read the Gospel or the letters of Paul even once through. And while they're wasting their time in the schools with this nonsense, they believe that just as in the poets Atlas holds up the sky on his shoulders, they support the entire church on the props of their syllogisms and without them it would collapse. Then you can imagine their happiness when they fashion and re-fashion the Holy Scriptures at will, as if these were made of wax, and when they insist that their conclusions, to which a mere handful of scholastics have subscribed, should carry more weight than the laws of Solon and be preferred to papal decrees.

They also set up as the world's censors, and demand recantation of anything which doesn't exactly square with their conclusions, explicit and implicit, and make their oracular pronouncements: "This proposition is scandalous; this is irreverent; this smells of heresy; this doesn't ring true." As a result, neither baptism nor the gospel, neither Paul, Peter, St Jerome, Augustine, or even Thomas, 'the greatest' of Aristotelians', can make a man Christian unless these learned bachelors have given their approval, such is the refinement of their judgement. For who could have imagined, if the savants hadn't told him, that anyone who said that the two phrases "chamber-pot you stink" and "the chamber-pot stinks", or "the pots boil" and "that the pots boils" are equally correct can't possibly be a Christian? Who could have freed the church from the dark error of its ways when no one would ever have read about these if they hadn't been published under the great seals of the schools?

And aren't they perfectly happy doing all this? They are happy too while they're depicting everything in hell down to the last detail, as if they'd spent several years there, or giving free rein to their fancy in fabricating new spheres and adding the most extensive and beautiful of all in case the blessed spirits lack space to take a walk in comfort or give a dinner-party or even play a game of ball. Their heads are so stuffed and swollen with these absurdities, and thousands more like them, that I don't believe even Jupiter's brain felt so burdened when he begged for Vulcan's axe to help him give birth to Athene. And so you mustn't be surprised if you see them at public disputations with their heads carefully bound up in all those fillets—it's to keep them from bursting apart.

For myself, I often have a good laugh when they particularly fancy themselves as theologians if they speak in a specially uncouth and slovenly style, and while they mumble so haltingly as to be unintelligible except to a fellow-stammerer, they refer to their powers of perception, which can't be attained by the common man. They insist that it detracts from the grandeur of sacred writing if they're obliged to obey the rules of grammar. It seems a most peculiar prerogative of theologians, to be the only people permitted to speak ungrammatically; however, they share this privilege with a lot of working men. Finally, they think themselves nearest to the gods whenever they are reverently addressed as "our masters", a title which holds as much meaning for them as the 'tetragram' does for the Jews. Consequently, they say it's unlawful to write MAGISTER NOSTER except in capital letters, and if anyone inverts the order and says, *"noster magister"*, he destroys the entire majesty of the theologians' title at a single blow.

BALDESAR CASTIGLIONE

The Courtier's True Purpose

The Book of the Courtier *by Baldesar Castiglione ranks as one of the supreme expressions of the Italian Renaissance. First published in 1528 in the full glory of the High Renaissance, the book encapsulates more than a century of humanistic discussions concerning the ways to perfect human nature. Though formally confined to one particular way of life — the life of courtiers at princely courts — the dialogue in fact is a virtual compendium of themes central to Italian Renaissance thought: themes such as virtue and good manners, spiritual and sensual love, religion, the nature of beauty, true nobility, the correct use of language, the active and contemplative lives, the status of women, the ideal form of the polity, and the respective truths of arms, letters, and the arts. These subjects are laid out in the form of imaginary dialogues among the most distinguished Italian noblemen and noblewomen of the day, gathered together at the famous Renaissance court in the Duchy of Urbino.*

The author of the dialogues, Baldesar Castiglione (1478–1529), was a humanist, soldier, and diplomat who spent most of his career in the service of the dukes of Urbino. In 1524 he was appointed papal nuncio to Spain and died in Toledo of the plague in 1529. The Courtier *is his only important work, but it is one of surpassing literary artistry that represents the Urbino of his youth as a model of Renaissance ideals. In the present selection from Book IV, Castiglione's interlocutor Ottaviano Fregoso describes the true purpose of the courtier, which is to serve as an example of virtue and speak truth to the powerful.*

'In my opinion, therefore, the end of the perfect courtier (which we have so far left untouched) is, by means of the accomplishments attributed to him by these gentlemen, so to win for himself the mind and favour of the prince he serves that he can and always will tell him the truth about all he needs to know, without fear or risk of displeasing him. And, if he knows that his prince is of a mind to do something unworthy, he should be in a position to dare to oppose him, and make courteous use of the favour his good qualities have won to remove every evil intention and persuade him to return to the path of virtue. Thus if the courtier is endowed with the goodness these gentlemen have attributed to him, as well as being quick-witted and charming, prudent and scholarly and so forth, he will always have the skill to make his prince realize the honour and advantages that accrue to him and his family from justice, liberality, magnanimity, gentleness and all the other virtues befitting a ruler, and on the other hand, the infamy and loss that result from practising the vices opposed to these virtues. Therefore I consider that just as music, festivities, games and other agreeable accomplishments are, so to speak, the flower of courtiership, so its real fruit is to encourage and help his prince to be virtuous and to deter him from evil. Then we must consider that the merit of good deeds consists in two principal things: to choose a truly virtuous end for our intentions, and to know how to find convenient and suitable means for its attainment. And so it necessarily follows that a man who strives to ensure that his prince is not deceived by anyone, does not listen to flatterers or slanderers or liars, and distinguishes between good and evil, loving the one and detesting the other, aims at the best end of all.

'It seems to me also that the accomplishments these gentlemen have attributed to the courtier can be a good means of attaining the end I have in mind; and this is because of the many faults we see in our present-day rulers the greatest are ignorance and conceit. And the root of these two evils is nothing other than falsehood, which is a vice rightly detestable to God and man and more harmful to princes than any other. For princes lack most of all what they must have in the fullest measure, namely, someone to tell them the truth and remind them of what is right. For those who are hostile to the prince are not prompted by affection to perform these offices; on the contrary, they prefer to have him live wickedly and never correct his faults. And then again, they dare not criticize the prince openly for fear of being punished. Meanwhile, among the prince's friends there are few who have free access to him, and these few are wary of reproaching him for his faults as freely as they reproach ordinary people, and often in order to win grace and favour they think only of suggesting things that are agreeable and diverting, even though they may be dishonourable and wicked. In this way, from being friends they become flatterers, and to benefit from their intimacy they always speak and act in order to gratify, and they mostly proceed by telling lies that foster ignorance in the prince's mind not only of the world around but of himself. And this can be said to be the greatest and most disastrous falsehood of all, for an ignorant mind deceives itself and lies to itself.

'The result of this is that apart from never hearing the truth of anything, princes become drunk with the power they wield, and abandoned to pleasure-seeking and amusements they become so corrupted in mind that (seeing themselves always obeyed and almost adored, with so much reverence and praise and never a hint of censure or contradiction) they pass from ignorance to extreme conceit. In consequence, they never accept anyone else's advice or opinion; and, believing that it is very easy to know how to rule and that successful government requires no art or training other than brute force, they devote all their mind and attention to maintaining the power they have and they believe that true happiness consists in being able to do what one wants. Therefore there are some princes who hate reason and justice because they think these would act as a bridle to their desires, reduce them to servitude, and if followed, rob them of the pleasures and satisfactions of their rule; and they suppose that their power would be neither perfect nor complete if they were constrained to obey the call of duty and honour, since they believe that no one who obeys is a true ruler. Therefore following on these beginnings, and letting themselves be carried away by self-conceit, they grow arrogant, and with imperious countenance and stern ways, with sumptuous dress, gold and gems, and rarely letting themselves be seen in public, they think to gain authority among men and to be regarded as gods. But these princes, to my mind, are like the giant figures that were made in Rome last year on the day of the festival in Piazza d'Agone and which outwardly looked like great men and horses in a triumph but inside were stuffed with rags and straw. However, princes of this sort are worse still. For the giant figures were held upright by their own great weight, whereas, since they are badly balanced within and out of proportion in relation to their base, the downfall of these rulers is caused by their own weight, and from one error they fall into countless others. For their ignorance and their false belief that they can do no wrong, and that their power springs from their own wisdom, prompt them to use all and every means, just or not, to usurp states whenever they have the chance.

'But if they decided to know and follow what they ought to do, then they would strive to rule in quite other ways than they do now; for they would realize how outrageous and pernicious it is when subjects, who must be governed, are wiser than the rulers who must govern them. You will agree that there is no harm in not knowing how to play music, or dance, or ride; nevertheless, a man who is not a musician is ashamed and does not dare to sing in the presence of others, or dance if he doesn't know how, or ride if he cannot sit his horse well. Yet ignorance of how to govern peoples gives rise to so many evils, so much death, destruction, burning and ruination, that it may be said to be the deadliest plague of all; and despite that some rulers who know absolutely nothing about government are not ashamed to set about the task of governing before the eyes not of a small group of men but rather of the entire world, seeing that they are so exalted in rank that all eyes are turned towards them and hence not only their great but even their slightest defects are always observed. Thus it is recorded that Cimon was censured for loving wine, Scipio for loving sleep and Lucullus for loving banquets. But would to God that the princes of our own time accompanied their sins with as many virtues as did these rulers of the ancient world, who, if they went wrong in some things, yet did not ignore the counsels and teachings of anyone who seemed capable of correcting their mistakes; on the contrary, they took meticulous care in ordering their lives on the pattern of exceptional men: as did Epaminondas on that of Lysias the Pythagorean, Agesilaus on that of Xenophon, Scipio on that of Panaetius and so on without number. But if some of our rulers were to be confronted by a strict philosopher, or indeed anyone at all who openly and candidly might wish to show them the awesome face of true virtue, teach them a good way of life and how a good prince should conduct himself, I am sure that as soon as he appeared they would loathe him as if he were a serpent or mock at him as if he were dirt.

'I maintain, therefore, that since nowadays rulers are so corrupted by evil living, by ignorance and by false conceit, and it is so difficult to give them an insight into the truth and lead them to virtue, and since men seek to win their favour through lies and flattery and other wicked means, the courtier easily can and should seek to gain the goodwill of his prince by means of the noble qualities given to him by Count Lodovico and Federico. Through these, he should so win over the mind of his prince that he may go to him freely whenever he wishes to discuss any subject without hindrance. And, if he is as has been described, he will succeed in this purpose without great effort and thus he will always be able to reveal the true facts on any subject very promptly. Moreover, he will gradually be able to instil virtue into his mind, to teach him continence, fortitude, justice and temperance, and enable him to relish the sweet fruit which lies under the slight bitterness first tasted by one who is struggling against his vices, which are always as harmful, offensive and notorious as the virtues are beneficial, agreeable and universally praised. And he will be able to incite his prince to virtue by the example of those famous captains and other outstanding men of whom it was customary in the ancient world to make statues of bronze and marble, and sometimes of gold, and to erect them in public places, both to honour the great and to inspire others to work to achieve the same glory through worthy emulation.

'In this way, the courtier will be able to lead his prince along the stern path of virtue, adorning it, however, with shady fronds and strewing it with gay flowers to lessen the tedium of an arduous journey for one whose endurance is slight; and so now with music, now with arms and horses, at other times with verse or with conversations about love, and with all the means these gentlemen have suggested, he will be able to keep the prince continually absorbed in innocent pleasures, while also, as I have said, always accompanying these beguilements with emphasis on some virtuous habit, and in that way practising a healthy deception like a shrewd doctor who often spreads some sweet liquid on the rim of a cup when he wants a frail and sickly child to take a bitter medicine. Thus, under the cloak of pleasure, no matter what the time, or place, or pursuit, the courtier will always achieve his objective, and for this he will deserve far greater praise and reward than for any other good work he could possibly do. For there is nothing so advantageous to mankind as a good prince, and nothing so harmful as an evil one; and it follows that no matter how cruel and atrocious, no punishment can be enough for those courtiers who turn gentle and charming manners and noble qualities to evil ends, and by these means seek to ingratiate themselves with their prince in order to corrupt him and make him stray from the path of virtue into vice. For of these it can be said that they contaminate with deadly poison not a single cup used by one person but the public fountain at which everyone must drink.'

EDMUND SPENSER

A Dragon Slain

_____

Edmund Spenser was born in 1552 in London. He was schooled at Pembroke College, Cambridge, and received his master of arts in 1576. Thereafter he served as secretary to a series of important figures in church and state. In 1580 he traveled to Ireland, where he remained for almost the rest of his life. There he served as secretary to the Lord Deputy of Ireland, and became friends with the great explorer and writer Sir Walter Raleigh. Spenser's career as a poet began shortly after his university days. His Shepheardes Calender *appeared in 1579, and was an important work in helping to revive the ancient tradition of pastoral poetry. Spenser published other works during his life, and he was a particular master of the sonnet, but without doubt the most beloved of Spenser's works was his magnificent* The Faerie Queene. The Faerie Queene *is a massive poem in six books, written between 1590 and 1596. The poem was designed as a tribute to Queen Elizabeth, and was the most famous work in the so-called "cult of Elizabeth" that captured the imagination of writers and courtiers during the late sixteenth century. It was the first epic poem ever composed in English; the work was also a romance, and it celebrated the medieval virtues of chivalry and courtly love. The poem colorfully narrates the exploits of a series of knights, all of whom serve a reigning empress, "Gloriana." Each of the books contains dramatic tales that were meant allegorically to embody various moral virtues such as temperance and chastity.* The Faerie Queene *borrows phrases and modes of expression from Italian literature, and it is often viewed as the greatest literary production of Renaissance England. As a tribute to Elizabeth, the work was a success and earned Spenser a pension. In 1598 Spenser lost his Irish estate in a rebellion. He fled to London, where he died the next year.*

*   The Faerie Queene *opens dramatically, with the story of a "gentle" knight sent by Gloriana to slay a dragon. The tale evokes Arthurian legend and the themes of medieval romances, and is a tribute to the virtue of bravery.*

_____

"A Dragon Slain," from Book 1, canto 1 in *The Faerie Queene*, by Edmund Spenser, edited by Thomas P. Roche, Jr., copyright © 1978 by Thomas P. Roche, Jr., 41–49. Reprinted by permission of Penguin Books Ltd.

1 A Gentle Knight was pricking on the plaine,
    Y cladd in mightie armes and siluer shielde,
    Wherein old dints of deepe wounds did remaine,
    The cruell markes of many a bloudy fielde;
    Yet armes till that time did he neuer wield:
    His angry steede did chide his foming bitt,
    As much disdayning to the curbe to yield:
    Full iolly knight he seemd, and faire did sitt,
As one for knightly giusts and fierce encounters fitt.

2 But on his breast a bloudie Cross he bore,
    The deare remembrance of his dying Lord,
    For whose sweete sake that glorious badge he wore,
    And dead as liuing euer him ador'd:
    Vpon his shield the like was also scor'd,
    For soueraine hope, which in his helpe he had:
    Right faithfull true he was in deede and word,
    But of his cheere did seeme too solemne sad,
Yet nothing did he dread, but euer was ydrad.

3 Vpon a great aduenture he was bound,
    That greatest *Gloriana* to him gaue,
    That greatest Glorious Queene of *Faerie* lond,
    To winne him worship, and her grace to haue,
    Which of all earthly things he most did craue;
    And euer as he rode, his hart did earne
    To proue his puissance in battell braue
    Vpon his foe, and his new force to learne;
Vpon his foe, a Dragon horrible and stearne.

4 A louely Ladie rode him faire beside,
    Vpon a lowly Asse more white then snow,
    Yet she much whiter, but the same did hide
    Vnder a vele, that wimpled was full low,
    And ouer all a blacke stole she did throw,
    As one that inly mournd: so was she sad,
    And heauie sat vpon her palfrey slow;
    Seemed in heart some hidden care she had,
And by her in a line a milke white lambe she lad.

5 So pure an innocent, as that same lambe,
    She was in life and euery vertuous lore,
    And by descent from Royall lynage came
    Of ancient Kings and Queenes, that had of yore
    Their scepters stretcht from East to Westerne shore,

And all the world in their subiection held;
Till that infernall feend with foule vprore
Forwasted all their land, and them expeld:
Whom to auenge, she had this Knight from far compeld.

6   Behind her farre away a Dwarfe did lag,
     That lasie seemd in being euer last,
     Or wearied with bearing of her bag
     Of needments at his backe. Thus as they past,
     The day with cloudes was suddeine ouercast,
     And angry *Ioue* an hideous storme of raine
     Did poure into his Lemans lap so fast,
     That euery wight to shrowd it did constrain,
And this fair couple eke to shroud themselues were fain.
     . . .

8   And foorth they passe, with pleasure forward led,
     Ioying to heare the birdes sweete harmony,
     Which therein shrouded from the tempest dred,
     Seemd in their song to scorne the cruell sky.
     Much can they prayse the trees so straight and hy,
     The sayling Pine, the Cedar proud and tall,
     The vine-prop Elme, the Poplar neuer dry,
     The builder Oake, sole king of forrests all,
The Aspine good for staues, the Cypresse funerall.
     . . .

11 At last resoluing forward still to fare,
     Till that some end they finde or in or out,
     That path they take, that beaten seemd most bare,
     And like to lead the labyrinth about;
     Which when by tract they hunted had throughout,
     At length it brought them to a hollow caue,
     Amid the thickest woods. The Champion stout
     Eftsoones dismounted from his courser braue,
And to the Dwarfe a while his needlesse spere he gaue.

12 Be well aware, quoth then that Ladie milde,
     Least suddaine mischiefe ye too rash prouoke:
     The danger hid, the place vnknowne and wilde,
     Breedes dreadfull doubts: Oft fire is without smoke,
     And perill without show: therefore your stroke
     Sir knight with-hold, till further triall made.
     Ah Ladie (said he) shame were to reuoke
     The forward footing for an hidden shade:
Vertue giues her selfe light, through darkenesse for to wade.

13 Yea but (quoth she) the perill of this place
    I better wot then you, though now too late,
    To wish you backe returne with foule disgrace,
    Yet wisedome warnes, whilest foot is in the gate,
    To stay the steppe, ere forced to retrate.
    This is the wandring wood, this *Errours den*,
    A monster vile, whom God and man does hate:
    Therefore I read beware. Fly fly (quoth then
The fearefull Dwarfe:) this is no place for liuing men.

14 But full of fire and greedy hardiment,
    The youthfull knight could not for ought be staide,
    But forth vnto the darksome hole he went,
    And looked in: his glistring armor made
    A litle glooming light, much like a shade,
    By which he saw the vgly monster plaine,
    Halfe like a serpent horribly displaide,
    But th'other halfe did womans shape retaine,
Most lothsom, filthie, foule, and full of vile disdaine.

15 And as she lay vpon the durtie ground,
    Her huge long taile her den all ouerspred,
    Yet was in knots and many boughtes vpwound,
    Pointed with mortall sting. Of her there bred
    A thousand yong ones, which she dayly fed,
    Sucking vpon her poisonous dugs, eachone
    Of sundry shapes, yet all ill fauored:
    Soone as that vncouth light vpon them shone,
Into her mouth they crept, and suddain all were gone.

16 Their dam vpstart, out of her den effraide,
    And rushed forth, hurling her hideous taile
    About her cursed head, whose folds displaid
    Were stretcht now forth at length without entraile.
    She lookt about, and seeing one in mayle
    Armed to point, sought backe to turne againe;
    For light she hated as the deadly bale,
    Ay wont in desert darknesse to remaine,
Where plaine none might her see, nor she see any plaine.

17 Which when the valiant Elfe perceiu'ed, he lept
    As Lyon fierce vpon the flying pray,
    And with his trenchand blade her boldly kept
    From turning backe, and forced her to stay:
    Therewith enrag'd she loudly gan to bray,
    And turning fierce, her speckled taile aduaunst,

Threatning her angry sting, him to dismay:
Who nought aghast, his mightie hand enhaunst:
The stroke down from her head vnto her shoulder glaunst.

18 Much daunted with that dint, her sence was dazd,
    Yet kindling rage, her selfe she gathered round,
    And all attonce her beastly body raizd
    With doubled forces high aboue the ground:
    Tho wrapping vp her wrethed sterne arownd,
    Lept fierce vpon his shield, and her huge traine
    All suddenly about his body wound,
    That hand or foot to stirre he stroue in vaine:
God helpe the man so wrapt in *Errours* endlesse traine.

19 His Lady sad to see his sore constraint,
    Cride out, Now now Sir knight, shew what ye bee,
    Add faith vnto your force, and be not faint:
    Strangle her, else she sure will strangle thee.
    That when he heard, in great perplexitie,
    His gall did grate for griefe and high disdaine,
    And knitting all his force got one hand free,
    Wherewith he grypt her gorge with so great paine
That soone to loose her wicked bands did her constraine.

20 Therewith she spewd out of her filthy maw
    A floud of poyson horrible and blacke,
    Full of great lumpes of flesh and gobbets raw,
    Which stunck so vildly, that it forst him slacke
    His grasping hold, and from her turne him backe:
    Her vomit full of bookes and papers was,
    With loathly frogs and toades, which eyes did lacke,
    And creeping sought way in the weedy gras:
Her filthy parbreake all the place defiled has.

21 As when old father *Nilus* gins to swell
    With timely pride aboue the *Aegyptian* vale,
    His fattie waues do fertile slime outwell,
    And ouerflow each plaine and lowly dale:
    But when his later spring gins to auale,
    Huge heapes of mudd he leaues, wherein there breed
    Ten thousand kindes of creatures, partly male
    And partly female of his fruitfull seed;
Such vgly monstrous shapes elswhere may no man reed.

22 The same so sore annoyed has the knight,
    That welnigh choked with the deadly stinke,
    His forces faile, ne can no longer fight.

Whose corage when the feend perceiu'd to shrinke,
She poured forth out of her hellish sinke
Her fruitfull cursed spawne of serpents small,
Deformed monsters, fowle, and blacke as inke,
Which swarming all about his legs did crall,
And him encombred sore, but could not hurt at all.

23 As gentle Shepheard in sweete euen-tide,
　When ruddy *Phœbus* gins to welke in west,
　High on an hill, his flocke to vewen wide,
　Markes which do byte their hasty supper best;
　A cloud of combrous gnattes do him molest,
　All striuing to infixe their feeble stings,
　That from their noyance he no where can rest,
　But with his clownish hands their tender wings
He brusheth oft, and oft doth mar their murmurings.

24 Thus ill bestedd, and fearefull more of shame,
　Then of the certaine perill he stood in,
　Halfe furious vnto his foe he came,
　Resolv'd in minde all suddenly to win,
　Or soone to lose, before he once would lin;
　And strooke at her with more then manly force,
　That from her body full of filthie sin
　He raft her hatefull head without remorse;
A streame of cole black bloud forth gushed from her corse.

25 Her scattred brood, soone as their Parent deare
　They saw so rudely falling to the ground,
　Groning full deadly, all with troublous feare,
　Gathred themselues about her body round,
　Weening their wonted entrance to haue found
　At her wide mouth: but being there withstood
　They flocked all about her bleeding wound,
　And sucked vp their dying mothers blood,
Making her death their life, and eke her hurt their good.

26 That detestable sight him much amazde,
　To see th'vnkindly Impes of heauen accurst,
　Deuoure their dam; on whom while so he gazd,
　Hauing all satisfide their bloudy thurst
　Their bellies swolne he saw with fulnesse burst,
　And bowels gushing forth: well worthy end
　Of such as drunke her life, the which them nurst;
　Now needeth him no lenger labour spend,
His foes haue slaine themselues, with whom he should
　　　　　　　　　　　　　　　　　　　[contend.

385

27 His Ladie seeing all, that chaunst, from farre
    Approcht in hast to greet his victorie,
    And said, Faire knight, borne vnder happy starre,
    Who see your vanquisht foes before you lye:
    Well worthy be you of that Armorie,
    Wherein ye haue great glory wonne this day,
    And proou'd your strength on a strong enimie,
    Your first aduenture: many such I pray,
And henceforth euer wish, that like succeed it may.

28 Then mounted he vpon his Steede againe,
    And with the Lady backward sought to wend;
    That path he kept, which beaten was most plaine,
    Ne euer would to any by-way bend,
    But still did follow one vnto the end,
    The which at last out of the wood them brought.
    So forward on his way (with God to frend)
    He passeth forth, and new aduenture sought;
Long way he trauelled, before he heard of ought.

29 At length they chaunst to meet vpon the way
    An aged Sire, in long blacke weedes yclad,
    His feete all bare, his beard all hoarie gray,
    And by his belt his booke he hanging had;
    Sober he seemde, and very sagely sad,
    And to the ground his eyes were lowly bent,
    Simple in shew, and voyde of malice bad,
    And all the way he prayed, as he went,
And often knockt his brest, as one that did repent.

30 He faire the knight saluted, louting low,
    Who faire him quited, as that courteous was:
    And after asked him, if he did know
    Of straunge aduentures, which abroad did pas.
    Ah my deare Sonne (quoth he) how should, alas,
    Silly old man, that liues in hidden cell,
    Bidding his beades all day for his trespas,
    Tydings of warre and worldly trouble tell?
With holy father sits not with such things to mell.

31 But if of daunger which hereby doth dwell,
    And homebred euill ye desire to heare,
    Of a straunge man I can you tidings tell,
    That wasteth all this countrey farre and neare.
    Of such (said he) I chiefly do inquere,
    And shall you well reward to shew the place,
    In which that wicked wight his dayes doth weare:

For to all knighthood it is foule disgrace,
That such a cursed creature liues so long a space.

32 Far hence (quoth he) in wastfull wildernesse
His dwelling is, by which no liuing wight
May euer passe, but thorough great distresse.
Now (sayd the Lady) draweth toward night,
And well I wote, that of your later fight
Ye all forwearied be: for what so strong,
But wanting rest will also want of might?
The Sunne that measures heauen all day long
At night doth baite his steedes the *Ocean* waues emong.

33 Then with the Sunne take Sir, your timely rest,
And with new day new worke at once begin:
Vntroubled night they say giues counsell best.
Right well Sir knight ye haue aduised bin,
(Quoth then that aged man;) the way to win
Is wisely to aduise: now day is spent;
Therefore with me ye may take vp your In
For this same night. The knight was well content:
So with that godly father to his home they went.

34 A little lowly Hermitage it was,
Downe in a dale, hard by a forests side,
Far from resort of people, that did pas
In trauell to and froe: a little wyde
There was an holy Chappell edifyde,
Wherein the Hermite dewly wont to say
His holy things each morne and euentyde:
Thereby a Christall streame did gently play,
Which from a sacred fountaine welled forth alway.

35 Arriued there, the little house they fill,
Ne looke for entertainement, where none was:
Rest is their feast, and all things at their will;
The noblest mind the best contentment has.
With faire discourse the euening so they pas:
For that old man of pleasing wordes had store,
And well could file his tongue as smooth as glas;
He told of Saintes and Popes, and euermore
He strowd an *Aue-Mary* after and before.

EXPLANATORY NOTES

1 2   Spenser in the *Letter to Ralegh* identifies Redcross's armour as that
described by Paul in Ephesians 6.11–17:

> Put on the whole armour of God, that ye may be able to stand against the assaults of the devil . . . For this cause take unto you the whole armour of God that ye may be able to resist in the evil day, and having finished all things, stand fast. Stand therefore, and your loins gird about with verity, and having on the breastplate of righteousness, And your feet shod with the preparation of the Gospel of peace. Above all, take the shield of faith, wherewith ye may quench all the fry darts of the wicked. And take the helmet of salvation and the sword of the spirit, which is the word of God.

All quotations from Genevan Bible, 1560, spelling modernized. A red cross on a white field forms the arms of St George, patron saint of England, with whom Redcross is identified in I.2.11.9 and 10.61 ff.

1	9	giusts: jousts.
2	5	scor'd: marked.
4	9	in a line: on a lead.
5	9	compeld: summoned.
6	1	Dwarfe: some editors allegorize the Dwarf as reason, prudence, or common sense.
8	6ff	Spenser's catalogue of trees imitates Chaucer, *Parlement of Foules* 176–82, who was following the tradition established by Ovid, *Met.* 10.90 ff, Statius, *Thebaid* 6.98 ff, and Boccaccio, *Teseida* 11.22–4, a source which Chaucer also used in 'The Knight's Tale', ll.29221 ff. The epithets describing the trees are intended to show the use to which society puts each tree (e.g., 'sayling Pine' because ships' masts were made of pine). The catalogue gives a picture in miniature of a world in which the diversity of choices can make man lose his way as Redcross and Una do, and relates this wood to the dark wood (*selva oscura*) in which Dante finds himself lost at the beginning of the *Divine Comedy*.
11	5	tract: traces.
12	7	shame were: it would be shame to.
12	8	forward footing for: i.e., going forward for fear of.
14	1	hardiment: courage, boldness.
15	3	boughtes: coils.
16	1	dam: mother.
16	4	without entraile: without coiling.
16	5	mayle: armour.
16	6	Armed to point: fully armed.
16	7	bale: death and conflagration (*OED* 1 and 3).
17	1	Elfe: inhabitant of Faeryland.
17	3	trenchand: sharp.
17	8	enhaunst: raised.
19	3	force: not merely physical force but fortitude as in French *force*. See R. Tuve, *Allegorical Imagery*, p. 120 ff. Cf. I. 1.3.8 and 1.24.6.
19	8	gorge: throat.

20 1 maw: stomach.

20 3 gobbets: lumps.

20 6 bookes and papers: theological books, tracts, and pamphlets, debating often violently the nature of the one, true Church, that is, theological controversy which involves men in Error's den.

20 7 frogs: Rev. 16.13: 'And I saw three unclean spirits like frogs come out of the mouth of the dragon, and out of the mouth of the beast, and out of the mouth of the false prophet.' Cf. Exodus 8.2–7.

20 9 parbreake: vomit.

21 1 *Nilus:* the river Nile. Spenser often uses the Latin forms of proper names as here.

21 9 reed: to see, only in Spenser (*OED*, 'read' 7). Cf. III.9.2.3.

23 2 *Phœbus:* sun.
       welke: fade.

23 8 clownish: rustic.

24 1 bestedd: situated.

26 2 vnkindly Impes: unnatural children.

27 5 Armorie: armour.

28 7 to frend: as friend.

29 2 weedes: garments; cf. *OF* 2.12–13, where Angelica meets the hypocritical old hermit.

29 9 knockt his brest: in reciting the *confiteor*, the act of confession in the Roman Mass, the pious would touch the right hand to the heart thrice as a sign of penitence at the words *'mea culpa, mea culpa, mea maxima culpa'* (through my fault, through my fault, through my most grievous fault).

30 2 faire him quited: responded similarly.

30 7 Bidding his beades: saying his rosary beads, prayers.
       trespas: sins.

30 9 sits not: is not proper.

32 1 wastfull: like a waste.

32 5 later: recent.

32 9 baite: refresh.

34 4 a little wyde: a little apart.

34 5 edifyde: built.

34 7 holy things: the prayers for matins and evensong, or perhaps more specifically the monastic offices of Roman Catholicism.

35 3 Rest is their feast, and all things at their will: i.e., rest is entertainment to them, and because they desire nothing, they have 'all things at their will'.

35 7 file his tongue: i.e., make his words persuasive.

35 9 *Aue-Mary:* 'Hail, Mary', the salutation of the archangel Gabriel to Mary announcing the conception of Christ (Luke 1.26 ff). The salutation was adopted as a prayer by the Roman Church and became the principal prayer in the Rosary.

FRANÇOIS RABELAIS

A Grotesque Flirtation

_____

François Rabelais (c. 1494–1553) was a contradictory figure in a turbulent age. The son of a wealthy lawyer, he was well educated in his youth and headed for a career in the church. In his twenties he became a Franciscan friar and devoted himself to learning Greek, but he was forced to abandon his studies in accordance with a general ban on teaching Greek in France, following the publication of Erasmus's Greek New Testament and his controversial commentary on Luke's Gospel. Rabelais left the friars and joined the more tolerant Benedictine monks. In 1528 he came to Paris, where he encountered the new humanist learning and proponents of Protestantism. He abandoned the Benedictines, and took orders as a secular priest. Obtaining a bachelor's degree in medicine, in 1532 he established a medical practice in Lyons. There he translated medical texts from the original Greek, corresponded with the great humanist scholar, Erasmus, and wrote satirical works about old scholastic learning, the universities, and the ecclesiastical establishment. His writings were wildly popular despite frequent condemnations from various authorities. Powerful supporters defended him, and arranged employment and protection for him in various parts of France and Italy, where he continued to publish controversial books. He died in Paris in 1553.

Gargantua and Pantagruel (1534), by far the most famous of his books, was condemned for its obscenity. In it Rabelais repeatedly mocked scholars and medieval learning, frequently relating their abstruse thought to bodily functions sexual, digestive, and excretory. He also derided doctors, lawyers, religious figures, and women. His writings, filled with references, puns, and inside jokes, present a sardonic depiction of the confused and uncertain age of the Renaissance and Reformation. The passage presented here illustrates the grotesque humor of the age and its attitudes to women and marriage.

_____

CHAPTER 21: HOW PANURGE FELL IN
LOVE WITH A GREAT PARISIAN LADY

Panurge began to gain a reputation in the city of Paris by this disputation in which he beat the Englishman, and from that time he made great use of his codpiece; which he caused to be decorated with embroidery in the Romanesque style. The world was loud in his praise. Indeed, a song was made about him, which the children sang when gathering mustard, and he was welcome in all companies of ladies and gentlewomen. He finally became so presumptuous, in fact, that he set out to conquer one of the great ladies of the city.

So, omitting the mass of long prologues and protestations habitually made by doleful and contemplative lent-lovers who never tamper with the flesh, he said to her one day: 'Madam, it would be most beneficial to the whole state, delightful for you, and an honour to your progeny, as it is a necessity to me, that you should be covered and breed from me. You must believe what I say, for experience will prove me right.'

At these words the lady pushed him back more than three hundred miles, and said: 'What right have you, you miserable idiot, to make such proposals to me? Whom do you think you are talking to? Go away, and never come near me again! But for one small thing, I'd have your arms and legs cut off.'

'Well,' he said, 'it would be all the same to me to have my arms and legs cut off, provided you and I had a bout of fun together, at the up-and-down game. For' (showing his long codpiece) 'here's Master John Thursday, who will play you a jig that you'll feel in the very marrow of your bones. He's a sprightly fellow, and he is so good at finding all the cracks and quirks and special spots in the carnal trap that after him there is no need of a broom.'

To which the lady replied: 'Go away, you wretch, go away! If you say one word more, I'll call the people and have you beaten on the spot.'

'Ho,' said he, 'you're not as bad as you say, or I am very much deceived by your face. For sooner shall the earth ascend into the heavens, the high heavens descend into the abyss, and the whole order of nature be perverted, than there could be one drop of gall or malice in such beauty and grace as yours. It's a true saying that hardly ever

Does one see a woman fair
Who's not difficult as well.

But that is said of mere common beauties. Your beauty is so transcendent, however, so singular, and so celestial that I believe Nature has made you for her paragon, so that we may understand how much she can do if she chooses to employ her full powers and her entire wisdom. There is nothing in you that is not honey, that is not sugar, that is not heavenly manna. It is to you that Paris should have awarded the golden apple, not to Venus, oh dear no; nor to Juno, nor to Minerva. For there was never such magnificence in Juno, such wisdom in Minerva, or such grace in Venus, as there is in you. O ye celestial gods and goddesses, how happy will be the man to whom you grant the favour of embracing this woman, of kissing her, and rubbing his bacon with her. By God, I shall be that man, as well I see, for already she loves me entirely; I am sure of it. I was predestined for this by the fairies. Therefore, to spare time, let's to and fro and at it.'

And he would have embraced her, had she not struggled to get to the window and call on the neighbours for help.

At this Panurge departed hurriedly, saying to her as he ran out: 'Wait for me here, madam. I'll go and fetch them for you. Don't trouble yourself.'

Next day he was at the church at the hour when she went to Mass, and in the porch he offered her the holy water, making a deep bow before her. After this he knelt close beside her most familiarly and said: 'Madam, I must tell you that I am so amorous of you that I can neither piss nor shit for love. I don't know what you think. But if some harm were to befall me, it would be a very dreadful thing!'

'Go away,' she said, 'go away. That is no affair of mine. Leave me alone to say my prayers.'

'But,' he said, 'what does *A Beaumont le Vicomte* remind you of?'

'I have no idea,' she replied.

'Of, "*A beau cont le vit monte.*"[1] But as for that, pray God to grant me what your noble heart desires, and be so kind as to give me those beads.'

'Take them,' she said, 'and don't bother me any more.'

As she spoke she tried to take off her rosary, which was of lemon-wood, with large gold beads at intervals of ten. But Panurge promptly drew out one of his knives, cut them neatly, and took them off to the pawnshop, saying to her as he went: 'Would you like my knife?'

'No, no,' said she.

'All the same,' he replied, 'it's very much at your service, body and goods, tripe and bowels.'

However, the lady was not very pleased about her beads, for they helped to keep her in countenance in church. 'This fine babbler,' she thought to herself, 'is a giddy fool from some strange country. I shall never get my rosary back. What will my husband say to that? He will be cross with me. But I'll tell him that some thief cut it off me in church, which he will easily believe, when he sees the end of the ribbon on my girdle.'

After dinner Panurge went to see her, carrying in his sleeve a great purse full of palace-tokens and counters, and he began by saying: 'Which of us two loves the other best, you me, or I you?'

To which she replied: 'For my part, I do not hate you. For, as God commands us to, I love all the world.'

'But to the point,' he replied. 'Aren't you in love with me?'

'I have already told you very many times,' she answered, 'not to use such words to me. If you speak to me like that again I'll show you that I'm not the woman to be addressed in this indecent way. Get out of here, and give me back my rosary, in case my husband asks me for it.'

'What, madam,' said he, 'your rosary? I'll do no such thing, I swear. But I'll willingly give you a new one. Now which would you like? One of well-enamelled gold in the shape of great round knobs, or of true love-knots, or all solid like great ingots? Or would you prefer one of ebony, or of large jacinths, or of great cut garnets, with every tenth stone a fine turquoise or a magnificent sapphire or a spider-ruby, and with the biggest beads of diamonds with twenty-eight facets? But no, no, that's too poor. I know of a beautiful rosary of fine emeralds, with every tenth bead of rounded amber, and at the clasp a Persian pearl as a big as an orange, and it costs no more than twenty-five thousand ducats. I should like to make you a present of that. I have enough ready money.'

And as he spoke he made his counters jingle, as if they were Sun-crowns.

'Would you like a piece of violet-crimson velvet, dyed in the grain, or a piece of embroidered satin, or of crimson perhaps? Would you like chains, gold ornaments, headbands, rings? You have only to say yes. Up to fifty thousand ducats; it is nothing to me.'

By virtue of these words he made her mouth water. Nevertheless she replied: 'I thank you, no. I want nothing to do with you.'

'By God,' said he, 'I certainly want something to do with you, though. But it is something that will cost you nothing, and you won't be the worse off for it. Look,' said he, pointing to his long codpiece. 'Here's Master John Owl, who wants a nest.'

At this he tried to embrace her. But she began to shout, although not very loud. Whereupon Panurge put off his disguise, and said to her: 'So you won't let me do a little business, then? A turd for you! You have no title to such a favour, not to such an honour. But, by God, I'll make the dogs ride you.'

And with this he ran away fast for fear of a beating, of which he was afraid by nature.

CHAPTER 22: HOW PANURGE PLAYED A
TRICK ON THE PARISIAN LADY WHICH
WAS NOT AT ALL TO HER ADVANTAGE

Now you must know that the next day was the great feast of Corpus Christi, on which all women wear their best clothes; and for that occasion this lady was dressed in a very fine gown of crimson satin, and a very costly white velvet bodice.

On the vigil of that day, Panurge hunted in all directions for a hot sheep-dog bitch; and when he had secured her with his belt, he took her to his room and fed her very well on that day and all the next night. In the morning he killed her and removed that part which the Greek necromancers know. This he cut into the smallest possible pieces, which he took away well wrapped up. Then he went to the church where the lady must go to follow the procession, as is the custom on this festival; and when she came in, he gave her the holy water, bowing to her most courteously. A little while later, after she had said her prayer, he sat down beside her on the same bench, and gave her this rondel, written out and running as follows:

> Just for this once, when I declared my mind,
> And you, most lovely dame, proved so unkind
> And sent me packing hopeless of return,
> Who never any wrong to you had done
> In word or deed, in slander or in slight,
> Since you disliked my suit, I think you might
> Have said to me, without wound or offence:
> 'My friend, be kind enough to go from hence
>   Just for this once.'
> I wrong you not if I my thoughts reveal,
> Saying how the beauty that your clothes conceal
> Is like a spark that sets afire my heart.
> I only ask that you then, for your part,
> Will be a saddle and will let me ride,
>   Just for this once.

And as she was opening this paper to see what was in it, Panurge deftly sprinkled the drug that he was carrying on to various parts of her, chiefly on the pleats of her sleeves and her dress.

Then he said to her: 'Madam, poor lovers are not always at peace. For myself, I hope that the sleepless nights, the evils and despites which I suffer from the love of you will earn me a deduction of so much pain in purgatory. But at least pray God to give me patience in my suffering.'

Panurge had no sooner spoken than all the dogs in the church ran up to the lady, attracted by the smell of the drug he had sprinkled on her.

Small and great, big and little, all came, lifting their legs, smelling her and pissing all over her. It was the most dreadful thing in the world.

Panurge made a show of driving them off, then took leave of her and retired into a chapel to see the fun. For these beastly dogs pissed over all her clothes, a great greyhound wetting her on the head, others on her sleeves, others on her backside; and the little ones pissed on her shoes; so that all the women who were thereabouts had great difficulty in saving her.

At this Panurge burst out laughing, and said to some of the gentlemen of the city: 'I think that woman's on heat, or else she has recently been covered by a greyhound.'

And when he saw all the dogs snarling around her as they do round a hot bitch, he went off to fetch Pantagruel. Everywhere on the way when he saw a dog, he gave it a kick and said: 'Aren't you going to join your mates at the wedding? Get on, get on, devil take you! Get along with you now!'

Then, having got to their lodgings, he said to Pantagruel: 'Master, I beg of you, come and see all the dogs, come and see all the dogs of this land, flocking round a lady. She is the most beautiful lady in the town, and they want to roger her.'

Pantagruel very gladly accepted this invitation and went to see the show, which he found very fine and original. But the best of it all was the procession, in which more than six hundred thousand and fourteen dogs were seen all around her, bothering her greatly, and everywhere she passed fresh hosts of dogs followed her trail, pissing in the road where her gown had touched it.

Everyone stopped to see the show, gazing with admiration at the dogs, who leapt as high as her neck and spoiled all her fine clothes. For this she could find no other remedy but to retire into her mansion. So she ran to hide, with the dogs after her and all the chambermaids laughing. But once she was inside and the door closed behind her, all the dogs ran up from two miles around, and pissed so hard against the gate of the house, that they made a stream with their urine big enough for the ducks to swim in. And it is this stream which now passes by Saint Victor, in which Madame Gobelin dyes her scarlet, thanks to the specific virtue of those piss-hounds, as our Master Dungpowder once proclaimed in a public sermon. So, God help you, a mill could have ground corn by it; but not so much as do the mills of Bazacle at Toulouse.

EXPLANATORY NOTE

1. A most indelicate pun, quite untranslatable.

MIGUEL DE CERVANTES

Don Quixote Becomes a Knight

Cervantes was born in Spain in 1547. His father was a doctor. At the age of twenty-one Cervantes became a soldier, and he served in Italy. In 1571 he was present at the naval battle of Lepanto (off the coast of Greece), where the fleet of the Ottoman Turks was defeated by the Holy League. Cervantes was wounded, and saw action in other naval battles. In 1575 he was captured by pirates and sold as a slave. After several unsuccessful efforts to escape, Cervantes was freed in 1580 and returned to Spain. His lifelong efforts to parlay his military service into a government post were unsuccessful. Cervantes wrote several plays in the 1580s, but in general he was plagued by poverty and was imprisoned several times. In 1604, however, Cervantes published the first part of his masterpiece, Don Quixote*. The work was immediately popular and widely translated. In 1613, by now well known, Cervantes published a collection of stories called* The Exemplary Novels. *Finally, in 1614 he published the second part of* Don Quixote. *In the following year he died.*

Don Quixote *remains one of the best known prose works of the seventeenth century. It is also the most famous work in the rich but neglected tradition of Spanish literature. The work is a parody, detailing the comic adventures of a delusional "knight errant" named Don Quixote, and his "squire" Sancho Panza. The story is based on a traditional Spanish ballad, but is vastly expanded and embellished by Cervantes. The work is in part a parody of the Medieval chivalric romances; it also has stylistic similarities with the popular pastoral literature of the period.* Don Quixote *is most enduringly a hilarious and entertaining adventure story, based on the exploits of one of literature's great characters.*

CHAPTER I. WHICH TREATS OF THE QUALITY AND WAY OF LIFE OF THE FAMOUS KNIGHT DON QUIXOTE DE LA MANCHA.

In a certain village in La Mancha, which I do not wish to name, there lived not long ago a gentleman—one of those who have always a lance in the rack, an ancient shield, a lean hack and a greyhound for coursing. His habitual diet consisted of a stew, more beef than mutton, of hash most nights, boiled bones on Saturdays, lentils on Fridays, and a young pigeon as a Sunday treat; and on this he spent three-quarters of his income. The rest of it went on a fine cloth doublet, velvet breeches and slippers for holidays, and a homespun suit of the best in which he decked himself on weekdays. His household consisted of a housekeeper of rather more than forty, a niece not yet twenty, and a lad for the field and market, who saddled his horse and wielded the pruning-hook.

Our gentleman was verging on fifty, of tough constitution, lean-bodied, thin-faced, a great early riser and a lover of hunting. They say that his surname was Quixada or Quesada—for there is some difference of opinion amongst authors on this point. However, by very reasonable conjecture we may take it that he was called Quexana. But this does not much concern our story; enough that we do not depart by so much as an inch from the truth in the telling of it.

The reader must know, then, that this gentleman, in the times when he had nothing to do—as was the case for most of the year—gave himself up to the reading of books of knight errantry; which he loved and enjoyed so much that he almost entirely forgot his hunting, and even the care of his estate. So odd and foolish, indeed, did he grow on this subject that he sold many acres of cornland to buy these books of chivalry to read, and in this way brought home every one he could get. And of them all he considered none so good as the works of the famous Feliciano de Silva. For his brilliant style and those complicated sentences seemed to him very pearls, especially when he came upon those love-passages and challenges frequently written in the manner of: 'The reason for the unreason with which you treat my reason, so weakens my reason that with reason I complain of your beauty'; and also when he read: 'The high heavens that with their stars divinely fortify you in your divinity and make you deserving of the desert that your greatness deserves.'

These writings drove the poor knight out of his wits; and he passed sleepless nights trying to understand them and disentangle their meaning, though Aristotle himself would never have unravelled or understood them, even if he had been resurrected for that sole purpose. He did not much like the wounds that Sir Belianis gave and received, for he imagined that his face and his whole body must have been covered with scars and marks, however skilful the surgeons who tended him. But, for all that, he admired the author for ending his book with the promise to continue with that interminable adventure, and often the desire seized him to take up the pen himself, and write the promised sequel for him. No doubt he would have done so, and perhaps successfully, if other greater and more persistent preoccupations had not prevented him.

Often he had arguments with the priest of his village, who was a scholar and a graduate of Siguenza, as to which was the better knight—Palmerin of England or Amadis of Gaul. But Master Nicholas, the barber of that village, said that no one could compare with the Knight of the Sun. Though if anyone could, it was Sir Galaor, brother of Amadis of Gaul. For he had a very accommodating nature, and was not so affected nor such a sniveller as his brother, though he was not a bit behind him in the matter of bravery.

In short, he so buried himself in his books that he spent the nights reading from twilight till daybreak and the days from dawn till dark; and so from little sleep and much reading, his brain dried up and he lost his wits. He filled his mind with all that he read in them, with enchantments, quarrels, battles, challenges, wounds, wooings, loves, torments and other impossible nonsense; and so deeply did he steep his imagination in the belief that all the fanciful stuff he read was true, that to his mind no history in the world was more authentic. He used to say that the Cid Ruy Diaz must have been a very good knight, but that he could not be compared to the Knight of the Burning Sword, who with a single backstroke had cleft a pair of fierce and monstrous giants in two. And he had an even better opinion of Bernardo del Carpio for slaying the enchanted Roland at Roncesvalles, by making use of Hercules' trick when he throttled the Titan Antaeus in his arms.

He spoke very well of the giant Morgante; for, though one of that giant brood who are all proud and insolent, he alone was affable and well-mannered. But he admired most of all Reynald of Montalban, particularly when he saw him sally forth from his castle and rob everyone he met, and when in heathen lands overseas he stole that idol of Mahomet, which history says was of pure gold. But he would have given his housekeeper and his niece into the bargain, to deal the traitor Galaon a good kicking.

In fact, now that he had utterly wrecked his reason he fell into the strangest fancy that ever a madman had in the whole world. He thought it fit and proper, both in order to increase his renown and to serve the state, to turn knight errant and travel through the world with horse and armour in search of adventures, following in every way the practice of the knights errant he had read of, redressing all manner of wrongs, and exposing himself to chances and dangers, by the overcoming of which he might win eternal honour and renown. Already the poor man fancied himself crowned by the valour of his arm, at least with the empire of Trebizond; and so, carried away by the strange pleasure he derived from these agreeable thoughts, he hastened to translate his desires into action.

The first thing that he did was to clean some armour which had belonged to his ancestors, and had lain for ages forgotten in a corner, eaten with rust and covered with mould. But when he had cleaned and repaired it as best as he could, he found that there was one great defect: the helmet was a simple head-piece without a visor. So he ingeniously made good this deficiency by fashioning out of pieces of pasteboard a kind of half-visor which, fitted to the helmet, gave the appearance of a complete head-piece. However, to see if it was strong enough to stand up to the risk of a sword-cut, he took out his sword and gave it two strokes, the first of which demolished in a moment what had taken him a week to make. He was not too pleased at the ease with which he had destroyed it, and to safeguard himself against this danger, reconstructed the visor, putting some strips of iron inside, in such a way as to satisfy himself of his protection; and, not caring to make another trial of it, he accepted it as a fine jointed headpiece and put it into commission.

Next he went to inspect his hack, but though, through leanness, he had more quarters than there are pence in a groat, and more blemishes than Gonella's horse, which was nothing but skin and bone, he appeared to our knight more than the equal of Alexander's Bucephalus and the Cid's Babieca. He spent four days pondering what name to give him; for, he reflected, it would be wrong for the horse of so famous a knight, a horse so good in himself, to be without a famous name. Therefore he tried to fit him with one that would signify what he had been before his master turned knight errant, and what he now was; for it was only right that as his master changed his profession, the horse should change his name for a sublime and high-sounding one, befitting the new order and the new calling he professed. So, after many names invented, struck out and rejected, amended, cancelled and remade in his fanciful mind, he finally decided to call him Rocinante, a name which seemed to him grand and sonorous, and to express the common horse he had been before arriving at his present state: the first and foremost of all hacks in the world.

Having found so pleasing a name for his horse, he next decided to do the same for himself, and spent another eight days thinking about it. Finally he resolved to call himself Don Quixote. And that is no doubt why the authors of this true history, as we have said, assumed that his name must have been Quixada and not Quesada, as other authorities would have it. Yet he remembered that the valorous Amadis had not been content with his bare name, but had added the name of his kingdom and native country in order to make it famous, and styled himself Amadis of Gaul. So, like a good knight, he decided to add the name of his country to his own and call himself Don Quixote de la Mancha. Thus, he thought, he very clearly proclaimed his parentage and native land and honoured it by taking his surname from it.

Now that his armour was clean, his helmet made into a complete head-piece, a name found for his horse, and he confirmed in his new title, it struck him that there was only one more thing to do: to find a lady to be enamoured of. For a knight errant without a lady is like a tree without leaves or fruit and a body without a soul. He said to himself again and again: 'If I for my sins or by good luck were to meet with some giant hereabouts, as generally happens to knights errant, and if I were to over-throw him in the encounter, or cut him down the middle or, in short, con-quer him and make him surrender, would it not be well to have someone to whom I could send him as a present, so that he could enter and kneel down before my sweet lady and say in tones of humble submission: "Lady, I am the giant Caraculiambro, lord of the island of Malindrania, whom the never-sufficiently-to-be-praised knight, Don Quixote de la Mancha, conquered in single combat and ordered to appear before your Grace, so that your Highness might dispose of me according to your will"?' Oh, how pleased our knight was when he had made up this speech, and even gladder when he found someone whom he could call his lady. It happened, it is believed, in this way: in a village near his there was a very good-looking farm girl, whom he had been taken with at one time, although she is supposed not to have known it or had proof of it. Her name was Aldonza Lorenzo, and she it was he thought fit to call the lady of his fancies; and, casting around for a name which should not be too far away from her own, yet suggest and imply a princess and great lady, he resolved to call her Dulcinea del Toboso—for she was a native of El Toboso—, a name which seemed to him as musical, strange and signif-icant as those others that he had devised for himself and his possessions.

CHAPTER II. WHICH TREATS OF THE
FIRST EXPEDITION WHICH THE INGENIOUS
DON QUIXOTE MADE FROM HIS VILLAGE.

Once these preparations were completed, he was anxious to wait no longer before putting his ideas into effect, impelled to this by the thought of the loss the world suffered by his delay, seeing the grievances there were to redress, the wrongs to right, the injuries to amend, the abuses to correct, and the debts to discharge. So, telling nobody of his intention, and quite unobserved, one morning before dawn—it was on one of those sweltering July days—he armed himself completely, mounted Rocinante, put on this badly-mended headpiece, slung on his shield, seized his lance and went out into the plain through the back gate of his yard, pleased and delighted to see with what ease he had started on his fair design. But scarcely was he in open country when he was assailed by a thought so terrible that it almost made him abandon the enterprise he had just begun. For he suddenly remembered that he had never received the honour of knighthood, and so, according to the laws of chivalry, he neither could nor should take arms against any knight, and even if he had been knighted he was bound, as a novice, to wear plain armour without a device on his shield until he should gain one by his prowess. These reflections made him waver in his resolve, but as his madness outweighed any other argument, he made up his mind to have himself knighted by the first man he met, in imitation of many who had done the same, as he had read in the books which had so influenced him. As to plain armour, he decided to clean his own, when he had time, till it was whiter than ermine. With this he quieted his mind and went on his way, taking whatever road his horse chose, in the belief that in this lay the essence of adventure.

As our brand-new adventurer journeyed along, he talked to himself, saying: 'Who can doubt that in ages to come, when the authentic story of my famous deeds comes to light, the sage who writes of them will say, when he comes to tell of my first expedition so early in the morning: "Scarce had the ruddy Apollo spread the golden threads of his lovely hair over the broad and spacious face of the earth, and scarcely had the forked tongues of the little painted birds greeted with mellifluous harmony the coming of the rosy Aurora who, leaving the soft bed of her jealous husband, showed herself at the doors and balconies of the Manchegan horizon, when the famous knight, Don Quixote de la Mancha, quitting the slothful down, mounted his famous steed Rocinante and began to journey across the ancient and celebrated plain of Montiel"?' That was, in fact, the road that our knight actually took, as he went on: 'Fortunate the age and fortunate the times in which my famous deeds shall come to light, deeds worthy to be engraved in bronze, carved in marble and painted on wood, as a memorial for posterity. And you, sage enchanter, whoever you may be, to whose lot it falls to be the chronicler of this strange history, I beg you not to forget my good Rocinante, my constant companion on all my rides and journeys!' And presently he cried again, as if he had really been in love: 'O Princess Dulcinea, mistress of this captive heart! You did me great injury in dismissing me and inflicting on me the cruel rigour of your command not to appear in your beauteous presence. Deign, lady, to be mindful of your captive heart, which suffers such griefs for love of you.'

MICHEL DE MONTAIGNE

A Brief Description of the Customs of Cannibals

Michel de Montaigne (1553–1592) was the son of a noble landowner in southern France. He trained as a lawyer and served as a counselor to the Parlement of Bordeaux, a town of which he was later twice elected mayor. Montaigne inherited his father's estates, retired from legal practice, and spent the better part of his adult life in leisured study. He was a melancholy man, having witnessed the death of his best friend and that of his much admired father, and his marriage failed to produce a male heir to continue the family's name. To relieve his sadness, Montaigne took to writing essays based upon his own experiences and self-reflection but illuminated by the wisdom he had attained through his prodigious reading. The Essays (1580) was the first example of a work of literature based upon the reflections of an individual. It was extremely influential for subsequent generations of French thinkers and writers. Montaigne died at his estate in 1592, having twice revised his Essays.

The discovery of the New World and its peoples was a decisive event in the intellectual life of Europe. Many travelers' accounts were published, some based on eyewitness reports, others on fears and fantasies. There was no more commonly imagined native stereotype than the cannibal. Montaigne uses an account of native Brazilians as a jumping-off point for reflections on the morals and values of his own countrymen.

. . . I find (from what has been told me) that there is nothing savage or barbarous about those peoples, but that every man calls barbarous anything he is not accustomed to; it is indeed the case that we have no other criterion of truth or right-reason than the example and form of the opinions and customs of our own country. There we always find the perfect religion, the perfect polity, the most developed and perfect way of doing anything! Those 'savages' are only wild in the sense that we call fruits

---

wild when they are produced by Nature in her ordinary course: whereas it is fruit which we have artificially perverted and misled from the common order which we ought to call savage. It is in the first kind that we find their true, vigorous, living, most natural and most useful properties and virtues, which we have bastardized in the other kind by merely adapting them to our corrupt tastes. [C] Moreover, there is a delicious savour which even our taste finds excellent in a variety of fruits produced in those countries without cultivation: they rival our own. [A] It is not sensible that artifice should be reverenced more than Nature, our great and powerful Mother. We have so overloaded the richness and beauty of her products by our own ingenuity that we have smothered her entirely. Yet wherever her pure light does shine, she wondrously shames our vain and frivolous enterprises:

> [B]   *Et veniunt ederæ sponte sua melius,*
> *Surgit et in solis formosior arbutus antris,*
> *Et volucres nulla dulcius arte canunt.*

[Ivy grows best when left untended; the strawberry tree flourishes more beautifully in lonely grottoes, and birds sing the sweeter for their artlessness.][1]

[A] All our strivings cannot even manage to reproduce the nest of the smallest little bird, with its beauty and appropriateness to its purpose; we cannot even reproduce the web of the wretched spider. [C] Plato says that all things are produced by nature, fortune or art, the greatest and fairest by the first two, the lesser and least perfect by the last.[2]

[A] Those peoples, then, seem to me to be barbarous only in that they have been hardly fashioned by the mind of man, still remaining close neighbours to their original state of nature. They are still governed by the laws of Nature and are only very slightly bastardized by ours; but their purity is such that I am sometimes seized with irritation at their not having been discovered earlier, in times when there were men who could have appreciated them better than we do. It irritates me that neither Lycurgus nor Plato had any knowledge of them, for it seems to me that what experience has taught us about those peoples surpasses not only all the descriptions with which poetry has beautifully painted the Age of Gold[3] and all its ingenious fictions about Man's blessed early state, but also the very conceptions and yearnings of philosophy. They could not even imagine a state of nature so simple and so pure as the one we have learned about from experience; they could not even believe that societies of men could be maintained with so little artifice, so little in the way of human solder. I would tell Plato that those people have no trade of any kind, no acquaintance with writing, no knowledge of numbers, no terms for governor or political superior, no practice of subordination or of riches or poverty, no contracts, no inheritances, no divided estates, no occupation but leisure, no concern for kinship—except such as is common to them all—no clothing, no agriculture, no metals, no use of wine or corn. Among them you hear no words for treachery, lying, cheating, avarice, envy, backbiting or forgiveness. How remote from such perfection would Plato find that Republic which he thought up— [C] *'viri a diis recentes'* [men fresh from the gods].[4]

[B] *Hos natura modos primum dedit.*

[These are the ways which Nature first ordained.][5]

[A] In addition they inhabit a land with a most delightful countryside and a temperate climate, so that, from what I have been told by my sources, it is rare to find anyone ill there;[6] I have been assured that they never saw a single man bent with age, toothless, blear-eyed or tottering. They dwell along the sea-shore, shut in to landwards by great lofty mountains, on a stretch of land some hundred leagues in width. They have fish and flesh in abundance which bear no resemblance to ours; these they eat simply cooked. They were so horror-struck by the first man who brought a horse there and rode it that they killed him with their arrows before they could recognize him, even though he had had dealings with them on several previous voyages. Their dwellings are immensely long, big enough to hold two or three hundred souls; they are covered with the bark of tall trees which are fixed into the earth, leaning against each other in support at the top, like some of our barns where the cladding reaches down to the ground and acts as a side. They have a kind of wood so hard that they use it to cut with, making their swords from it as well as grills to cook their meat. Their beds are woven from cotton and slung from the roof like hammocks on our ships; each has his own, since wives sleep apart from their husbands. They get up at sunrise and have their meal for the day as soon as they do so; they have no other meal but that one. They drink nothing with it, [B] like those Eastern peoples who, according to Suidas,[7] only drink apart from meals. [A] They drink together several times a day, and plenty of it. This drink is made from a certain root and has the colour of our claret. They always drink it lukewarm; it only keeps for two or three days; it tastes a bit sharp, is in no ways heady and is good for the stomach; for those who are not used to it it is laxative but for those who are, it is a very pleasant drink. Instead of bread they use a certain white product resembling coriander-cakes. I have tried some: it tastes sweet and somewhat insipid.

They spend the whole day dancing; the younger men go off hunting with bow and arrow. Meanwhile some of the women-folk are occupied in warming up their drink: that is their main task. In the morning, before their meal, one of their elders walks from one end of the building to the other, addressing the whole barnful of them by repeating one single phrase over and over again until he has made the rounds, their building being a good hundred yards long. He preaches two things only: bravery before their enemies and love for their wives. They never fail to stress this second duty, repeating that it is their wives who season their drink and keep it warm. In my own house, as in many other places, you can see the style of their beds and rope-work as well as their wooden swords and the wooden bracelets with which they arm their wrists in battle, and the big open-ended canes to the sound of which they maintain the rhythm of their dances. They shave off all their hair, cutting it more cleanly than we do, yet with razors made of only wood or stone. They believe in the immortality of the soul: souls which deserve well of the gods dwell in the sky where the sun rises; souls which are accursed dwell where it sets. They have some priests and prophets or other, but they rarely appear among the people since they live in the mountains. When they do appear they hold a great festival and a solemn meeting of several villages—each of the barns which I have described constituting a village situated about one French league distant from the next. The prophet then addresses them in public, exhorting them to be virtuous and dutiful, but their entire system of ethics contains only the same two articles: resoluteness in battle and love for their wives. He foretells what is to happen and the results they must expect from what they undertake; he either incites them to war or deflects them from it, but only on condition that if he fails to divine correctly and if things turn out other than he foretold, then—if they can catch him—he is condemned as a false prophet and hacked to pieces. So the prophet who gets it wrong once is seen no more.

[C] Prophecy is a gift of God.[8] That is why abusing it should be treated as a punishable deceit. Among the Scythians, whenever their soothsayers got it wrong they were shackled hand and foot and laid in ox-carts full of bracken where they were burned.[9] Those who treat subjects under the guidance of human limitations can be excused if they have done their best; but those who come and cheat us with assurances of powers beyond the natural order and then fail to do what they promise, should they not be punished for it and for the foolhardiness of their deceit?

[A] These peoples have their wars against others further inland beyond their mountains; they go forth naked, with no other arms but their bows and their wooden swords sharpened to a point like the blades of our pig-stickers. Their steadfastness in battle is astonishing and always ends in killing and bloodshed: they do not even know the meaning of fear or flight. Each man brings back the head of the enemy he has slain and sets it as a trophy over the door of his dwelling. For a long period they treat captives well and provide them with all the comforts which they can devise; afterwards the master of each captive summons a great assembly of his acquaintances; he ties a rope to one of the arms of his prisoner [C] and holds him by it, standing a few feet away for fear of being caught in the blows, [A] and allows his dearest friend to hold the prisoner the same way by the other arm: then, before the whole assembly, they both hack at him with their swords and kill him. This done, they roast him and make a common meal of him, sending chunks of his flesh to absent friends. This is not as some think done for food—as the Scythians used to do in antiquity—but to symbolize ultimate revenge. As a proof of this, when they noted that the Portuguese who were allied to their enemies practised a different kind of execution on them when taken prisoner—which was to bury them up to the waist, to shoot showers of arrows at their exposed parts and then to hang them—they thought that these men from the Other World, who had scattered a knowledge of many a vice throughout their neighbourhood and who were greater masters than they were of every kind of revenge, which must be more severe than their own; so they began to abandon their ancient method and adopted that one. It does not sadden me that we should note the horrible barbarity in a practice such as theirs: what does sadden me is that, while judging correctly of their wrong-doings we should be so blind to our own. I think there is more barbarity in eating a man alive than in eating him dead; more barbarity in lacerating by rack and torture a body still fully able to feel things, in roasting him little by little and having him bruised and bitten by pigs and dogs (as we have not only read about but seen in recent memory, not among enemies in antiquity but among our fellow-citizens and neighbours—and, what is worse, in the name of duty and religion) than in roasting him and eating him after his death.

Chrysippus and Zeno, the leaders of the Stoic school, certainly thought that there was nothing wrong in using our carcasses for whatever purpose we needed, even for food—as our own forebears did when, beleaguered by Caesar in the town of Alesia, they decided to relieve the hunger of the besieged with the flesh of old men, women and others who were no use in battle:

[B]   *Vascones, fama est, alimentis talibus usi*
Produxere animas.

[By the eating of such food it is notorious that the Gascons prolonged
their lives.][10]

EXPLANATORY NOTES

1. Propertius, I, ii, 10–12.
2. Plato, *Laws*, X, 888A–B.
3. Cf. Elizabeth Armstrong, *Ronsard and the Age of Gold*, Cambridge, 1968.
4. Seneca, *Epist. moral.*, XC, 44. (This epistle is a major defence of the innocence of natural man before he was corrupted by philosophy and progress.)
5. Virgil, *Georgics*, II, 208.
6. One of Montaigne's sources was Simon Goulart's *Histoire du Portugal*,
   Paris, 1587, based on a work by Bishop Jeronimo Osorio (da Fonseca) and
   others.
7. Suidas, *Historica, caeteraque omnia quae ad cognitionem rerum spectant*,
   Basle, 1564.
8. Cf. Cicero, *De divinatione*, I, i.1; I Peter 1:2; I Corinthians 12:20; 13:2.
9. Herodotus, *History*, IV, lxix.
10. Sextus Empiricus, *Hypotyposes*, III, xxiv; Caesar, *Gallic Wars*, VII, lvii–lviii;
    Juvenal, *Satires*, XV, 93–4.

FRANCESCO PETRARCH

The Scholar-Poet and His Love

Petrarch (1304–1374), Italy's greatest humanist and most influential lyric poet, was born in Arezzo, a provincial town in Tuscany. He spent much of his youth in the city of Avignon in Provence, where his father, a political exile from Florence, worked as a notary. After an unsuccessful career as a law student, Petrarch returned to Avignon and entered the service of the powerful Colonna family. It was on Good Friday of 1327 in a church in Avignon that Petrarch claimed to have seen for the first time his beloved Laura, the inspiration for his famous Canzoniere, *a collection of lyric poems in various metrical forms. This* Songbook *(as translates* Canzoniere) *was the model for romantic and other lyric poetry in various European vernacular languages for the next three hundred years. Petrarch is also famous as the first major Renaissance humanist, the man who more than any other inspired the Renaissance movement to revive classical literature. Petrarch tried to revive both the language of classical Latin and the genres of ancient literature including the epic, bucolic poetry, and the biography. He also compiled several large collections of his Latin correspondence, and worked to rediscover and restore lost, fragmentary, or corrupt copies of ancient literary works. All these activities were to become typical of the humanist movement during the Renaissance.*

Not only was Petrarch a brilliant and inspiring writer, but he also displayed a quite extraordinary self-awareness as an individual who struggled with the desire for love and fame while trying to respond to the claims of religion. The poems from the Canzoniere *excerpted here set the fashion for introspective love poetry that focused more on the emotions of the poet than upon the beloved.*

SELECTED POEMS FROM THE CANZONIERE

264
     I'm always thinking, and I'm caught in thought
by such abundant pity for myself
that often I am led
to weeping for a different kind of grief:
for seeing every day the end come closer,
a thousand times I begged God for those wings
with which our intellect
can soar to Heaven from this mortal jail.[1]
     But until now I have received no help,
no matter how I plead or sigh or weep,
and it is only just that it be so—
if he who can walk straight chooses to fall,
then he deserves to lie upon the ground.
Those arms stretched out in mercy[2]
in which I trust are open to me still,
but I still fear to think
how others ended, and I dread my state
and am spurred on, and it could be too late.

     A thought speaks to the mind and it declares:
"You're longing still? What help do you expect?
You poor thing, don't you see
with what dishonor time is passing by?
Make up your mind now, wisely, and decide
to pull out of your heart every last root
of pleasure that can never
bring happiness, nor will it let you breathe.
     Since you have long been tired and disgusted
by that false sweetness of a fleeting good,
a gift the treacherous world bestows on some,
why do you still place hope in such a thing
devoid of all peace and stability?
While life is in your body
you have the rein of all thoughts in your hands.
Hold tight now while you can,
for, as you know, delay is dangerous,
and now is not too early to begin.

     How well you know the great amount of sweetness
your eyes have taken from the sight of her,
the one I wish now were

still to be born, that we may have more peace.
You certainly remember, as you must,
the image of her rushing down into
your heart, there where, perhaps,
the flame of other torches could not enter.

    She set it burning, and if the false flame
has lasted many years waiting the day
that for our own salvation never comes,
now raise yourself to a more blessed hope,
by gazing on the heavens whirling round you,
beautiful and immortal:
if here desire, happy in its ills,
achieves its satisfaction
by a mere glance, a word or two, a song,
what will that joy be like, if this is great?"

    There is another thought that's bittersweet
with difficult and yet delightful weight
sitting within my soul
which fills my heart with need and feeds it hope;
only for love of glorious, kindly fame
it does not feel the times I freeze or burn
or if I'm pale or thin;
and killing it makes it grow back the stronger.

    This,[3] from the day I slept in baby clothes,
has been growing with me all of my days,
and I fear both of us will share one grave;
for when my soul is naked of its body,
glory's desire cannot accompany it.
If Latin or Greek tongues[4]
praise me when I am dead, it is all wind;
and since I fear to be
always hoarding what in a moment scatters,
I would embrace the truth,[5] and leave the lies.

    But then that other passion filling me
seems to block out all others born around it;
meanwhile time flies while I
with no concern for self write for another;
the radiance of those lovely eyes melting me
mellifluously in warmth of clarity
has hold of me with reins
against which neither wit nor might avails.

    So then what good is it for me to oil
my boat when it is caught upon a reef
and still tied up so tight by those two knots?[6]

411

You,[7] who from other knots that bind the world
in different ways have liberated me,
my Lord, why do you not,
once and for all, wipe from my face this shame?
For like a man who dreams
I seem to see Death standing there before me,
and I would fight for life, and have no weapons.

 I know myself, and I am not deceived
by a mistaken truth; I'm forced by Love
who blocks the path of honor
for anyone who trusts too much in him;
I feel enter my heart from time to time
a virtuous disdain, harsh and severe,
which pulls all hidden thoughts
up to my brow for everyone to see.
 To love a mortal thing with such great faith,
the kind that should be placed in God alone,
is less becoming the more one looks for honor.
And this[8] in a loud voice also calls back
my reason which went wandering with the senses;
but though it hears and means
to come back home, bad habit drives it further
and paints before my eyes
the one born only so that I may die
because she pleased me, and herself, too much.

 Nor do I know how much space Heaven gave me
when I was newly brought upon the earth
to suffer that harsh war
that I managed to start against myself;
nor can I through my body's veil foresee
the day that must arrive to close my life;
but I see my hair changing
and within me all of my desires aging.
 Now that I feel the time for my departure
approaches—it cannot be far away—
as he whose loss makes him wary and wise,
I think back to the point it was I left
the right road leading to the port of good:
on one side[9] I am pierced
by shame and sorrow, and they turn me back:
the other[10] will not free me
from pleasure which through time has grown so strong
that it dares bargain now with Death itself.

Song, this is how I live and my heart is
colder with fear than snow that's turned to ice,
feeling for certain that I am perishing;
in trying to decide I've wound the spool
by now with a good length of my short thread;[11]
never was there a weight
heavier than the one I carry now,
for with Death at my side
I seek new rules by which to lead my life,
and see the best, but still cling to the worst.

EXPLANATORY NOTES

1. Although this poem was probably written in 1348 while Laura was still alive, Petrarch places it at the beginning of the poems on Laura's death.
2. The arms of Christ upon the cross.
3. "This" refers to the thought described in the preceding stanza.
4. Latin and Greek were considered the most noble languages by Renaissance humanists. Although the study of Latin was widespread, Greek was hardly known in Petrarch's day.
5. A reference to God.
6. The "two knots" are Petrarch's love for Laura and his desire for worldly fame, which keep him from devoting his entire life to God. He debates his "two chains" with St. Augustine in the *Secretum*.
7. The poet addresses God directly until the end of the stanza.
8. "This" refers back to "virtuous disdain" in line 96.
9. The side of reason is afflicted.
10. This "other" is the side of the appetite or passion.
11. Metaphors for a man's life.

WILLIAM SHAKESPEARE

Sonnets

William Shakespeare is uniformly regarded as the greatest playwright and literary figure in the history of Britain. Born in Stratford-on-Avon in 1564 into a moderately prosperous family, his education was a product of local English schooling. He did not attend university nor did he have formal training in the literary arts. He was drawn to an acting company and made his way to London in his early twenties. There he served as actor, stage-hand, director, producer, and writer of plays that during the 1590s enjoyed a remarkable revival at court and on the southern bank of the Thames where rival theater groups competed for audiences and royal favor. Shake-speare wrote in all of the styles available to English playwrights, producing a cycle of history plays that celebrated the York and Tudor monarchies, a number of farce-like comedies of mistaken identity and unrequited love, and a comet tail of brilliant tragedies that continue to enthrall audiences wherever the English language is spoken. He died in 1616.

None of his plays were published during his lifetime. Stage copies were collected for the First Folio edition of 1623. Beyond his success in the the-ater, Shakespeare also considered himself a poet and he wrote several long dramatic poems early in his career including Venus and Adonis *and* The Rape of Lucrece. *Among his poetic works was a set of sonnets, the classic form of love poetry in the English Renaissance.*

19

Devouring time blunt thou the Lyons pawes,
And make the earth devoure her owne sweet brood,
Plucke the keene teeth from the fierce Tygers yawes,
And burne the long liv'd Phænix in her blood,
Make glad and sorry seasons as thou fleet'st,   5
And do what ere thou wilt swift-footed time
To the wide world and all her fading sweets:

"Sonnets," by William Shakespeare, from *The Penguin Book of Renaissance Verse*, edited by H. R. Woudhuysen, copyright © 1992 by David Norbrook and H. R. Woudhuysen, 304–315.

But I forbid thee one most hainous crime,
O carve not with thy howers my loves faire brow,
Nor draw noe lines there with thine antique pen, 10
Him in thy course untainted doe allow,
For beauties patterne to succeding men.
　　Yet doe thy worst ould Time; dispight thy wrong,
　　My love shall in my verse ever live young.

20

A womans face with natures owne hand painted,
Haste thou the Master Mistris of my passion,
A womans gentle hart but not acquainted
With shifting change as is false womens fashion,
An eye more bright then theirs, lesse false in rowling: 5
Gilding the object where-upon it gazeth,
A man in hew all *Hews* in his controwling,
Which steales mens eyes and womens soules amaseth.
And for a woman wert thou first created,
Till nature as she wrought thee fell a dotinge, 10
And by addition me of thee defeated,
By adding one thing to my purpose nothing.
　　But since she prickt thee out for womens pleasure,
　　Mine be thy love and thy loves use their treasure.

29

When in disgrace with Fortune and mens eyes,
I all alone beweepe my out-cast state,
And trouble deafe heaven with my bootlesse cries,
And looke upon my selfe and curse my fate.
Wishing me like to one more rich in hope, 5
Featur'd like him, like him with friends possest,
Desiring this mans art, and that mans skope,
With what I most injoy contented least,
Yet in these thoughts my selfe almost despising,
Haplye I thinke on thee, and then my state, 10
(Like to the Larke at breake of daye arising)
From sullen earth sings himns at Heavens gate,
　　For thy sweet love remembred such welth brings,
　　That then I skorne to change my state with Kings.

35

No more bee greev'd at that which thou hast done,
Roses have thornes, and silver fountaines mud,

Cloudes and eclipses staine both Moone and Sunne,
And loathsome canker lives in sweetest bud.
All men make faults, and even I in this,   5
Authorizing thy trespas with compare,
My selfe corrupting salving thy amisse,
Excusing thy sins more then thy sins are:
For to thy sensuall fault I bring in sence,
Thy adverse party is thy Advocate,   10
And gainst my selfe a lawfull plea commence,
Such civill war is in my love and hate,
   That I an accessary needs must be,
    To that sweet theefe which sourely robs from me.

36

Let me confesse that we two must be twaine,
Although our undevided loves are one:
So shall those blots that do with me remaine,
Without thy helpe, by me be borne alone.
In our two loves there is but one respect,   5
Though in our lives a seperable spight,
Which though it alter not loves sole effect,
Yet doth it steale sweet houres from loves delight,
I may not ever-more acknowledge thee,
Least my bewailed guilt should do thee shame,   10
Nor thou with publike kindnesse honour me,
Unlesse thou take that honour from thy name:
   But doe not so, I love thee in such sort,
    As thou being mine, mine is thy good report.

55

Not marble, nor the guilded monuments
Of Princes shall out-live this powrefull rime,
But you shall shine more bright in these contents
Then unswept stone, besmeer'd with sluttish time.
When wastefull warre shall *Statues* over-turne,   5
And broiles roote out the worke of masonry,
Nor *Mars* his sword, nor warres quick fire shall burne
The living record of your memory.
Gainst death, and all oblivious enmity
Shall you pace forth, your praise shall stil finde roome,   10
Even in the eyes of all posterity
That weare this world out to the ending doome.
   So til the judgement that your self arise,
    You live in this, and dwell in lovers eies.

56

Sweet love renew thy force, be it not said
Thy edge should blunter be then apetite,
Which but too daie by feeding is alaied,
To morrow sharpned in his former might.
So love be thou, although too daie thou fill   5
Thy hungrie eies, even till they winck with fulnesse,
Too morrow see againe, and doe not kill
The spirit of Love, with a perpetual dulnesse:
Let this sad *Intrim* like the Ocean be
Which parts the shore, where two contracted new,   10
Come daily to the banckes, that when they see
Returne of love, more blest may be the view.
   As cal it Winter, which being ful of care,
    Makes Sommers welcome, thrice more wish'd, more rare.

66

Tyr'd with all these for restfull death I cry,
As to behold desert a begger borne,
And needie Nothing trimd in jollitie,
And purest faith unhappily forsworne,
And gilded honor shamefully misplast,   5
And maiden vertue rudely strumpeted,
And right perfection wrongfully disgrac'd,
And strength by limping sway disabled,
And arte made tung-tide by authoritie,
And Folly (Doctor-like) controuling skill,   10
And simple-Truth miscalde Simplicitie,
And captive-good attending Captaine ill.
   Tyr'd with all these, from these would I be gone,
    Save that to dye, I leave my love alone.

74

But be contented when that fell arest,
With out all bayle shall carry me away,
My life hath in this line some interest,
Which for memoriall still with thee shall stay.
When thou revewest this, thou doest revew,   5
The very part was consecrate to thee,
The earth can have but earth, which is his due,
My spirit is thine the better part of me,
So then thou hast but lost the dregs of life,

The pray of wormes, my body being dead,   10
The coward conquest of a wretches knife,
To base of thee to be remembred,
   The worth of that, is that which it containes,
   And that is this, and this with thee remaines.

94

They that have powre to hurt, and will doe none,
That doe not do the thing, they most do showe,
Who moving others, are themselves as stone,
Unmooved, could, and to temptation slow:
They rightly do inherrit heavens graces,   5
And husband natures ritches from expence,
They are the Lords and owners of their faces,
Others, but stewards of their excellence:
The sommers flowre is to the sommer sweet,
Though to it selfe, it onely live and die,   10
But if that flowre with base infection meete,
The basest weed out-braves his dignity:
   For sweetest things turne sowrest by their deedes,
   Lillies that fester, smell far worse then weeds.

121

Tis better to be vile then vile esteemed,
When not to be, receives reproach of being,
And the just pleasure lost, which is so deemed,
Not by our feeling, but by others seeing.
For why should others false adulterat eyes   5
Give salutation to my sportive blood?
Or on my frailties why are frailer spies;
Which in their wils count bad what I think good?
Noe, I am that I am, and they that levell
At my abuses, reckon up their owne,   10
I may be straight though they them-selves be bevel.
By their rancke thoughtes, my deedes must not be shown
   Unlesse this generall evill they maintaine,
   All men are bad and in their badnesse raigne.

124

Yf my deare love were but the childe of state,
It might for fortunes basterd be unfathered,

As subject to times love, or to times hate,
Weeds among weeds, or flowers with flowers gatherd.
No it was buylded far from accident, 5
It suffers not in smilinge pomp, nor falls
Under the blow of thralled discontent,
Whereto th'inviting time our fashion calls:
It feares not policy that *Heriticke*,
Which workes on leases of short numbred howers, 10
But all alone stands hugely pollitick,
That it nor growes with heat, nor drownes with showres.
  To this I witnes call the foles of time,
    Which die for goodnes, who have liv'd for crime.

129

Th'expence of Spirit in a waste of shame
Is lust in action, and till action, lust
Is perjurd, murdrous, blouddy full of blame,
Savage, extreame, rude, cruell, not to trust,
Injoyd no sooner but dispised straight, 5
Past reason hunted, and no sooner had
Past reason hated as a swollowed bayt,
On purpose layd to make the taker mad.
Made In pursut and in possession so,
Had, having, and in quest to have, extreame, 10
A blisse in proofe and proud a very wo,
Before a joy proposd behind a dreame,
  All this the world well knowes yet none knowes well,
    To shun the heaven that leads men to this hell.

135

Who ever hath her wish, thou hast thy *Will*,
And *Will* too boote, and *Will* in over-plus,
More then enough am I that vexe thee still,
To thy sweet will making addition thus.
Wilt thou whose will is large and spatious, 5
Not once vouchsafe to hide my will in thine,
Shall will in others seeme right gracious,
And in my will no faire acceptance shine:
The sea all water, yet receives raine still,
And in aboundance addeth to his store, 10
So thou beeing rich in *Will* adde to thy *Will*,
One will of mine to make thy large *Will* more.

Let no unkinde, no faire beseechers kill,
Thinke all but one, and me in that one *Will*.

138

When my love sweares that she is made of truth,
I do beleeve her though I know she lyes,
That she might thinke me some untuterd youth,
Unlearned in the worlds false subtilties.
Thus vainely thinking that she thinkes me young,   5
Although she knowes my dayes are past the best,
Simply I credit her false speaking tongue,
On both sides thus is simple truth supprest:
But wherefore sayes she not she is unjust?
And wherefore say not I that I am old?   10
O loves best habit is in seeming trust,
And age in love, loves not to have yeares told.
   Therefore I lye with her, and she with me,
   And in our faults by lyes we flattered be.

144

Two loves I have of comfort and dispaire,
Which like two spirits do sugiest me still,
The better angell is a man right faire:
The worser spirit a woman collour'd il.
To win me soone to hell my femall evill,   5
Tempteth my better angel from my side,
And would corrupt my saint to be a divel:
Wooing his purity with her fowle pride.
And whether that my angel be turn'd finde,
Suspect I may, yet not directly tell,   10
But being both from me both to each friend,
I gesse one angel in an others hel.
   Yet this shal I nere know but live in doubt,
   Till my bad angel fire my good one out.

EXPLANATORY NOTES

19
3   *yawes* jaws
7   *sweets* fine, lovely things
10 *antique* antic, fantastic; ancient

20

1	*natures . . . painted* coloured by Nature herself; coloured naturally
2	*Haste* hast
5	*rowling* rolling, roving
7	*hew* hue, form, appearance, colouring
10	*a dotinge* became besotted; went mildly mad
11	*addition* honouring you; adding something (a penis)
	defeated deprived
13	*prickt* chose; gave you a penis

29

3	*bootlesse* unavailing, useless
6	*Featur'd* formed, shaped, handsome
	possest endowed
7	*skope* extent of view, outlook; liberties, circumstances
8	*injoy* possess; enjoy
10	*Haplye* by chance; happily
12	*sullen* dark, dull

35

3	*staine* make dim
4	*canker* worm
6	*compare* comparison
7	*salving* softening, palliating as with an ointment
	amisse error, fault, misdeed
9	*sence* mind, reasoning power
14	*sourely* cruelly, hurtfully

36

3	*blots* stains
5	*respect* regard, consideration, care
6	*seperable* causing separation
7	*effect* accomplishment; property
14	*report* repute, reputation

55

2	*out-live* outlast
4	*sluttish* dirty, unchaste, immoral
6	*broiles* tumults, battles
7	*quick* living
13	*that* when

56

6	*winck* close
8	*dulnesse* inactivity; bluntness
9	*Intrim* interim, interlude

66

2   *As* as for example   *desert* worth, merit
3   *trimd* dressed, got up   *jollitie* finery, fancy clothes
6   *strumpeted* prostituted
7   *disgrac'd* robbed of its grace
8   *sway* rule
9   *authoritie* tradition, precedent; the ruling powers
10 *Doctor-like* like a pompous scholar
    controuling directing, overpowering, refuting
11 *miscalde* wrongly called, slandered as
12 *attending* waiting on; listening to

74

1   *fell* fierce, cruel, deadly   *arest* seizure by legal warant; halt, stop
3   *line* of poetry
5   *revewest . . . revew* survey, see again
10 *pray* prey
12 *To* too

94

2   *showe* appear they will do
3   *moving* exciting the feelings of
4   *could* cold
6   *husband* manage, protect
    expence spending, extravagant expenditure
11 *base* foul, vile
12 *basest* lowest, humblest
    out-braves defies; surpasses in fine array

121

5   *adulterat* adulterous; corrupt, impure
6   *sportive* amorous, wanton
9   *I . . . am* cp. Exodus 3:14 'And God said unto Moses, I AM THAT I
    AM'   *levell* guess; aim
10 *abuses* offences   *reckon up* count
11 *straight* honest, not bent   *bevel* slanting, crooked
12 *rancke* corrupt, lustful, foul-smelling, luxuriating
14 *raigne* rule; prosper

124

1   *but . . . state* only the offspring of circumstances
2   *unfathered* made fatherless, illegitimate
5   *accident* chance
8   *inviting* attractive, seductive
9   *policy* contrivance, crafty scheming
11 *pollitick* provident, prudent
13 *foles of time* followers of time, time-servers

129

1   *expence* extravagant expenditure, loss   *Spirit* vital energy; semen
    waste squandering; waist
4   *rude* harsh, brutal
5   *Injoyd* enjoyed; used
9   *Made* usually modernized to 'mad'
11 *in proofe* when experienced   *proud* (usually modernized to 'proved',
    cp. no. 129 l. 20); erect

135

1   *Will* this and the following sonnet in the sequence (136) play on various
    senses of the word 'will'. These include: what is willed, desired; lust,
    desire; the penis; the vagina; and the poet's own name
2   *too boote* in addition, into the bargain
3   *vexe* irritate
5   *large* big, generous, lavish, unrestrained
8   *acceptance* reception, admittance
13 *no . . . no* none; the word of denial, 'no'

138

2   *lyes* tells untruths; fornicates
9   *unjust* unfaithful; dishonest
11 *habit* clothes; way of behaving   *seeming* apparent; handsome; appear-
    ing to
12 *told* counted; revealed
14 *flattered* falsely praised; caressed, pampered

144

2   *sugiest* suggest, incite, tempt, lead astray
4   *collour'd il* of dark colouring; unpleasantly painted
9   *finde* usually modernized to 'fiend'
12 *hel* misery; pudenda
14 *fire* drive with fire, smoke; sexually infect

CHRISTOPHER MARLOWE

Faustus's Bargain

—————

The playwright Christopher Marlowe was born in 1564, an exact contemporary of his colleague William Shakespeare. His father was a shoemaker. Marlowe attended the King's School in Canterbury, and later Corpus Christi College, Cambridge. He took his degree in 1584. Poor attendance and rowdy behavior threatened to deprive him of his degree, but the Queen's Council intervened on his behalf. There is some evidence that Marlowe briefly acted as a government spy while on the Continent. In 1587 Marlowe, who may have flirted with a career in the church, moved to London and became a playwright. Tamburlaine, his first play, was produced in that year. Others followed, including Doctor Faustus (his most famous work), and Marlowe also wrote some highly regarded lyric poetry. Little is known of Marlowe's life outside of his writings. He was arrested for fighting in 1589. In 1593 he was summoned before the council on charges of atheism. Marlowe died violently in 1593 when he recklessly launched a tavern brawl.

Marlowe's plays have been treasured for their beautiful lyricism and his corpus has been admired for its breadth of subject matter. He specialized in tragedies, and many of his plays unfold in historical settings. He certainly influenced the dramatic writing of Shakespeare. Marlowe was widely reported to have been an atheist, but The Tragical History of Doctor Faustus (c. 1588) is his most Christian play. It tells the story of a learned doctor, who exchanges his soul for human knowledge and earthly power. Death and damnation are his eventual rewards. Doctor Faustus should be read in the light of Renaissance cultural ideals, and particularly its humanistic and scientific challenges to scholastic certainties. Faustus's bargain is condemned, and the virtues of Christian otherworldliness and humility upheld, but Marlowe also reveals a subtle sympathy with the doctor's desires and plight.

—————

"Faustus's Bargain," from *Doctor Faustus* in *The Complete Plays*, by Christopher Marlowe, edited by J. B. Steane, copyright © 1969 by J. B. Steane, 66–76.

ACT I
SCENE ONE

FAUSTUS *in his study.*

FAUSTUS: Settle thy studies, Faustus, and begin
   To sound the depth of that thou wilt profess.
   Having commenced, be a divine in show,
   Yet level at the end of every art
   And live and die in Aristotle's works.
   Sweet Analytics, 'tis thou hast ravished me.
   Bene disserere est finis logices.
   Is 'to dispute well logic's chiefest end'?
   Affords this art no greater miracle?
   Then read no more: thou hast attained that end.   10
   A greater subject fitteth Faustus' wit.
   Bid *on cai me on*[1] farewell. And Galen,[2] come.
   Seeing, *ubi desinit philosophus, ibi incipit medicus.*[3]
   Be a physician, Faustus: heap up gold
   And be eternized for some wondrous cure.
   Summum bonum medicinae sanitas:
   'The end of physic is our body's health'.
   Why, Faustus, hast thou not attained that end?
   Is not thy common talk sound aphorisms?[4]
   Are not thy bills hung up as monuments,   20
   Whereby whole cities have escaped the plague,
   And thousand desperate maladies been cured?
   Yet art thou still but Faustus and a man.
   Couldst thou make men to live eternally,
   Or being dead, raise them to life again,
   Then this profession were to be esteemed.
   Physic, farewell. Where is Justinian?[5]
   Si una eademque res legatur duobus,
   Alter rem, alter valorem rei etc.,

---

12 *on cai me on:* being and non-being (Aristotle).

13 *ubi desinit philosophus . . . :* where the natural philosopher ends, there the
   doctor begins (Aristotle).

20 *bills:* prescriptions.

28 *Si una eademque res . . . :* If one and the same thing is bequeathed to two
   people, one of them should have the thing itself, and the other the value of it
   (principle attributed to Justinian).

A petty case of paltry legacies! 30
Exhaereditare filium non potest pater, nisi—
Such is the subject of the institute
And universal body of the law.
This study fits a mercenary drudge,
Who aims at nothing but external trash,
Too servile and illiberal for me.
When all is done Divinity is best.
Jerome's Bible! Faustus, view it well.
Stipendium peccati mors est.[6] Ha! *Stipendium etc.,*
'The reward of sin is death'. That's hard. 40
Si pecasse negamus, fallimur, et nulla est in nobis veritas.[7]
'If we say that we have no sin
We deceive ourselves, and there is no truth in us.'
Why then, belike, we must sin,
And so consequently die.
Ay, we must die, an everlasting death.
What doctrine call you this? *Che sera, sera.*
'What will be, shall be.' Divinity, adieu!
These necromantic books are heavenly,
Lines, circles, scenes, letters and characters: 50
Ay, these are those that Faustus most desires.
Oh, what a world of profit and delight,
Of power, of honour of, omnipotence,
Is promised to the studious artizan!
All things that move between the quiet poles
Shall be at my command. Emperors and kings
Are but obeyed in their several provinces.
Nor can they raise the wind or rend the clouds.
But his dominion that exceeds in this
Stretcheth as far as doth the mind of man: 60
A sound magician is a demi-god.
Here, tire my brains to get a deity.
    Enter WAGNER.
Wagner, commend me to my dearest friends,
The German Valdes and Cornelius.
Request them earnestly to visit me.
WAGNER: I will, sir.
    Exit.

---

31 *Exhaereditare filium . . . :* The father may not disinherit the son (Justinian).

FAUSTUS: Their conference will be a greater help to me
　　Than all my labours, plod I ne'er so fast.
　　　Enter the GOOD *and* EVIL ANGELS.
GOOD ANGEL: Oh Faustus, lay that damned book aside,
　　And gaze not on it lest it tempt thy soul　　　　　　　70
　　And heap God's heavy wrath upon thy head.
　　Read, read the scriptures: that is blasphemy.
EVIL ANGEL: Go forward, Faustus, in that famous art
　　Wherein all nature's treasure is contained.
　　Be thou on earth as Jove is in the sky,
　　Lord and commander of these elements.
　　　Exeunt ANGELS.
FAUSTUS: How am I glutted with conceit of this!
　　Shall I make spirits fetch me what I please,
　　Resolve me of all ambiguities,
　　Perform what desperate enterprise I will?　　　　　80
　　I'll have them fly to India for gold,
　　Ransack the ocean for orient pearl,
　　And search all corners of the new-found world
　　For pleasant fruits and princely delicates.
　　I'll have them read me strange philosophy,
　　And tell the secrets of all foreign kings.
　　I'll have them wall all Germany with brass,
　　And make swift Rhine circle fair Wittenberg.
　　I'll have them fill the public schools with silk,[8]
　　Wherewith the students shall be bravely clad.　　　90
　　I'll levy soldiers with the coin they bring,
　　And chase the Prince of Parma from our land,
　　And reign sole king of all the provinces.
　　Yea, stranger engines for the brunt of war
　　Than was the fiery keel[9] at Antwerp's bridge
　　I'll make my servile spirits to invent.
　　Come, German Valdes and Cornelius,
　　And make me blest with your sage conference.
　　　Enter VALDES *and* CORNELIUS.
　　Valdes, sweet Valdes and Cornelius!
　　Know that your words have won me at the last　　　100
　　To practise magic and concealed arts.

89 *public schools:* lecture rooms of the university faculties.

427

Yet not your words[10] only but mine own fantasy
That will receive no object for my head,
But ruminates on necromantic skill.
Philosophy is odious and obscure.
Both law and physic are for petty wits.
Divinity is basest of the three,[11]
Unpleasant, harsh, contemptible and vile.
'Tis magic, magic that hath ravished me.
Then, gentle friends, aid me in this attempt,   110
And I, that have with subtle syllogisms
Gravelled the pastors of the German Church
And made the flowering pride of Wittenberg
Swarm to my problems as the infernal spirits
On sweet Musaeus[12] when he came to hell,
Will be as cunning as Agrippa[13] was,
Whose shadow made all Europe honour him.

VALDES: Faustus, these books, thy wit and our experience
Shall make all nations to canonize us,
As Indian moors obey their Spanish lords.   120
So shall the spirits of every element
Be always serviceable to us three.
Like lions shall they guard us when we please;
Like Almain rutters with their horsemen's staves;
Or Lapland giants trotting by our sides.
Sometimes like women or unwedded maids,
Shadowing more beauty in their airy brows
Than has the white breasts of the queen of love.
From Venice shall they drag huge argosies,
And from America the golden fleece   130
That yearly stuffs old Philip's treasury
If learned Faustus will be resolute.

FAUSTUS: Valdes, as resolute am I in this
As thou to live, therefore object it not.

CORNELIUS: The miracles that magic will perform
Will make thee vow to study nothing else.
He that is grounded in Astrology,

---

103 *that will receive . . . :* that will let me think of no other subject.
112 *Gravelled:* baffled, defeated.
124 *Almain rutters:* German cavalry-men.

Enriched with tongues, well seen in minerals,
Hath all the principles magic doth require.
Then doubt not, Faustus, but to be renowned,   140
And more frequented for this mystery
Than heretofore the Delphian oracle.
The spirits tell me they can dry the sea,
And fetch the treasure of all foreign wracks.
Yea, all the wealth that our forefathers hid
Within the massy entrails of the earth.
Then tell me, Faustus, what shall we three want?
FAUSTUS: Nothing, Cornelius! Oh, this cheers my soul.
Come, show me some demonstrations magical,
That I may conjure in some bushy grove,   150
And have these joys in full possession.
VALDES: Then haste thee to some solitary grove
And bear wise Bacon's and Albanus'[14] works,
The Hebrew Psalter and New Testament;
And whatsoever else is requisite
We will inform thee e're our conference cease.
CORNELIUS: Valdes, first let him know the words of art,
And then, all other ceremonies learned,
Faustus may try his cunning by himself.
VALDES: First I'll instruct thee in the rudiments,   160
And then wilt thou be perfecter than I.
FAUSTUS: Then come and dine with me, and after meat
We'll canvass every quiddity thereof,
For ere I sleep, I'll try what I can do.
This night I'll conjure, though I die therefore.
        Exeunt.

SCENE TWO

        Enter two SCHOLARS.
FIRST SCHOLAR: I wonder what's become of Faustus, that was
    wont to make our schools ring with *sic probo.*
        Enter WAGNER.
SECOND SCHOLAR: That shall we presently know. Here comes
    his boy.
FIRST SCHOLAR: How now, sirrah, where's thy master?

---

163 *canvass every quiddity:* investigate in detail and depth.
2 *sic probo:* 'Thus I prove': triumphant conclusion of scholar's demonstration.

WAGNER: God in heaven knows.

SECOND SCHOLAR: Why, dost not thou know then?

WAGNER: Yes, I know, but that follows not.

FIRST SCHOLAR: Go to, sirrah. Leave your jesting and tell us   10
    where he is.

WAGNER: That follows not by force of argument, which you,
    being licentiates, should stand upon. Therefore, acknowledge
    your error and be attentive.

SECOND SCHOLAR: Then you will not tell us?

WAGNER: You are deceived, for I will tell you. Yet if you were not
    dunces, you would never ask me such a question. For is he not
    Corpus naturale? And is not that *mobile?* Then wherefore
    should you ask me such a question? But that I am by nature
    phlegmatic, slow to wrath and prone to lechery (to love, I   20
    would say), it were not for you to come within forty foot of
    the place of execution, although I do not doubt but to see you
    both hanged the next sessions. Thus, having triumphed over
    you, I will set my countenance like a precision, and begin to
    speak thus: 'Truly, my dear brethren, my master is within at
    dinner with Valdes and Cornelius, as this wine, if it could
    speak, would inform your worships. And so the Lord bless
    you, preserve you and keep you, my dear brethren.'   30
    Exit.

FIRST SCHOLAR: Oh Faustus, then I fear that which I have long
    suspected:
    That thou art fallen into that damned art
    For which they two are infamous through the world.

SECOND SCHOLAR: Were he a stranger, not allied to me,
    The danger of his soul would make me mourn.
    But come, let us go, and inform the Rector.
    It may be his grave counsel may reclaim him.

FIRST SCHOLAR: I fear me nothing will reclaim him now.

SECOND SCHOLAR: Yet let us see what we can do.
    Exeunt.

SCENE THREE

Thunder. Enter LUCIFER *and* FOUR DEVILS.
FAUSTUS *to them with this speech.*

---

25 *precision:* Puritan.

FAUSTUS: Now that the gloomy shadow of the night,
   Longing to view Orion's drizzling look,
   Leaps from th'Antarctick world unto the sky,
   And dims the Welkin with her pitchy breath,
   Faustus, begin thine incantations
   And try if devils will obey thy hest,
   Seeing thou hast prayed and sacrificed to them.
   Within this circle is Jehova's name
   Forward and backward anagrammatised:
   The abbreviated names of holy saints,   10
   Figures of every adjunct to the heavens,
   And characters of signs and evening stars,
   By which the spirits are enforced to rise.
   Then fear not, Faustus, to be resolute
   And try the utmost magic can perform.
     Thunder.
   Sint mihi dei acherontis propitii, valeat numen triplex Jehovae,
   ignei areii, aquatani spiritus salvete: orientis princeps Belzebub,
   inferni ardentis monarcha et demigorgon, propitiamus vos, ut
   appareat, et surgat Mephostophilis (Dragon)[15] *quod tumeraris:*
   per Jehovam, gehennam, et consecratam aquam quam nunc   20
   spargo; signumque crucis quod nunc facio; et per vota nostra
   ipse nunc surgat nobis dicatus Mephostophilis.
     Enter a DEVIL.
   I charge thee to return and change thy shape.
   Thou art too ugly to attend on me.
   Go, and return an old Franciscan friar:
   That holy shape becomes a devil best.
     Exit DEVIL.
   I see there's virtue in my heavenly words.
   Who would not be proficient in this art?
   How pliant is this Mephostophilis!
   Full of obedience and humility,

16 *Sint mihi . . . :* May the gods of the underworld (Acheron) be kind to me; may
the triple deity of Jehovah be gone; to the spirits of life, air and water, greetings. Prince of the east, Beelzebub, monarch of the fires below and Demo-
gorgon, we appeal to you so that Mephostophilis may appear and rise. Why
do you delay (*Quod tu moraris*)? By Jehovah, Hell and the hallowed water
which I now sprinkle, and the sign of the cross, which I now make, and by
our vows, let Mephostophilis himself now arise to serve us.

Such is the force of magic and my spells. 30
Now, Faustus, thou art conjuror laureate:[16]
Thou canst command great Mephostophilis.
Quin redis Mephostophilis fratris imagine.
   Enter MEPHOSTOPHILIS.
MEPHOSTOPHILIS: Now, Faustus, what wouldst thou have me do?
FAUSTUS: I charge thee wait upon me whilst I live,
  To do whatever Faustus shall command,
  Be it to make the moon drop from her sphere,
  Or the ocean to overwhelm the world.
MEPHOSTOPHILIS: I am a servant to great Lucifer, 40
  And may not follow thee without his leave.
  No more than he commands must we perform.
FAUSTUS: Did not he charge thee to appear to me?
MEPHOSTOPHILIS: No, I came now hither of mine own accord.
FAUSTUS: Did not my conjuring speeches raise thee? Speak.
MEPHOSTOPHILIS: That was the cause, but yet *per accidens;*
  For when we hear one rack the name of God,
  Abjure the scriptures and his saviour Christ,
  We fly in hope to get his glorious soul.
  Nor will we come unless he use such means 50
  Whereby he is in danger to be damned.
  Therefore the shortest cut for conjuring
  Is stoutly to abjure all godliness
  And pray devoutly to the prince of hell.
FAUSTUS: So Faustus hath already done, and holds this principle:
  There is no chief but only Belzebub,
  To whom Faustus doth dedicate himself.
  This word 'damnation' terrifies not me,
  For I confound hell in elysium.
  My ghost be with the old philosophers.[17] 60
  But leaving these vain trifles of men's souls,
  Tell me, what is that Lucifer, thy lord?
MEPHOSTOPHILIS: Arch-regent and commander of all spirits.
FAUSTUS: Was not that Lucifer an angel once?
MEPHOSTOPHILIS: Yes, Faustus, and most dearly loved of God.
FAUSTUS: How comes it then that he is prince of devils?
MEPHOSTOPHILIS: Oh, by aspiring pride and insolence,

---

34 *Quin redis . . . :* Why do you not return, Mephostophilis, in the appearance of
   a friar? (cf. l. 25 above).

For which God threw him from the face of heaven.
FAUSTUS: And what are you that live with Lucifer?
MEPHOSTOPHILIS: Unhappy spirits that fell with Lucifer,   70
    Conspired against our God with Lucifer,
    And are for ever damned with Lucifer.
FAUSTUS: Where are you damned?
MEPHOSTOPHILIS: In hell.
FAUSTUS: How comes it then that thou art out of hell?
MEPHOSTOPHILIS: Why, this is hell, nor am I out of it.
    Think'st thou that I that saw the face of God
    And tasted the eternal joys of heaven,
    Am not tormented with ten thousand hells
    In being deprived of everlasting bliss?   80
    Oh, Faustus, leave these frivolous demands,
    Which strike a terror to my fainting soul.
FAUSTUS: What, is great Mephostophilis so passionate
    For being deprived of the joys of heaven?
    Learn thou of Faustus manly fortitude,
    And scorn those joys thou never shalt possess.
    Go, bear these tidings to great Lucifer,
    Seeing Faustus hath incurred eternal death
    By desperate thoughts against Jove's deity.
    Say he surrenders up to him his soul,   90
    So he will spare him four and twenty years,
    Letting him live in all voluptuousness,
    Having thee ever to attend on me,
    To give me whatsoever I shall ask,
    To tell me whatsoever I demand,
    To slay mine enemies and to aid my friends
    And always be obedient to my will.
    Go, and return to mighty Lucifer,
    And meet me in my study at midnight,
    And then resolve me of thy master's mind.   100
MEPHOSTOPHILIS: I will, Faustus.
    Exit.
FAUSTUS: Had I as many souls as there be stars,
    I'd give them all for Mephostophilis.
    By him I'll be great emperor of the world,
    And make a bridge through the air
    To pass the ocean. With a band of men
    I'll join the hills that bind the Affrick shore,

And make that country continent to Spain,
And both contributory to my crown.
The Emperor shall not live but by my leave,   110
Nor any potentate of Germany.
Now that I have obtained what I desired,
I'll live in speculation of this art
Till Mephostophilis return again.
    Exit.

EXPLANATORY NOTES

1. *on cai me on:* Oncaymaeon in 1604 text. Printed as Oeconomy in subsequent editions till Bullen's (1885).
2. *Galen:* (130–200 A.D.), most famous of ancient physicians.
3. *Seeing, Ubi desinit . . . :* line omitted in B.
4. *Is not thy common talk . . . :* line omitted in B.
5. *Justinian:* Justinian I (c. 482–565), codifier of Roman law.
6. *Stipendium peccati . . . :* Romans, VI, 23.
7. *Si peccasse negamus . . . :* 1. John, I, 8.
8. *with silk:* Bullen's emendation: all quartos have 'skill'.
9. *the fiery keel:* a fire-ship used to destroy the Duke of Parma's bridge across the Scheldt in 1585.
10. *Yet not your words . . . skill:* lines omitted in B.
11. *Divinity is basest . . . vile:* lines omitted in B.
12. *Musaeus:* legendary Greek poet, perhaps here confused with Orpheus, to whom the spirits thronged in Hades (Virgil, *Georgics,* IV, 453–527).
13. *Agrippa:* Cornelius Agrippa, famous early 16th century German magician. The 'shadows' are the shades or spirits he invoked.
14. *Bacon's and Albanus' works:* Roger Bacon, 13th century philosopher, reputedly practising black magic. Albanus, perhaps Pietro d'Abano (?1250–1316), a supposed sorcerer, burnt by the Inquisition in effigy after his death.
15. *Dragon:* formerly taken as part of the invocation, now seen as an inserted stage-direction. The Admiral's men, who performed the play, had 'j dragon in fostes' (included in a list of props drawn up probably by Henslowe in 1598). Leo Kirschbaum (*Revue of English Studies,* 18, 1942) suggests that this was a warning to stage hands to prepare for the dragon's appearance at the end of the invocation.
16. *Now, Faustus, thou art . . . :* line omitted in B.
17. *My ghost be . . . :* those who disbelieved in the doctrine of punishment after death.

The Tragedy of Hamlet, Prince of Denmark

DRAMATIS PERSONAE

CLAUDIUS, *King of Denmark*

HAMLET, *son of the late King Hamlet, and nephew to the present King*

POLONIUS, *Lord Chamberlain*

HORATIO, *friend to Hamlet*

LAERTES, *son to Polonius*

VOLTEMAND
CORNELUIS
ROSENCRANTZ
GUILDENSTERN } *courtiers*
OSRIC
GENTLEMAN

MARCELLUS
BARNARDO } *officers*

FRANCISCO, *a soldier*

REYNALDO, *servant to Polonius*

FORTINBRAS, *Prince of Norway*

NORWEGIAN CAPTAIN

DOCTOR OF DIVINITY

PLAYERS

Two CLOWNS, *grave-diggers*

ENGLISH AMBASSADORS

GERTRUDE, *Queen of Denmark, and mother to Hamlet*

OPHELIA, *daughter to Polonius*

GHOST *of Hamlet's Father*

LORDS, LADIES, OFFICERS, SOLDIERS, SAILORS, MESSENGERS, *and* ATTENDANTS

SCENE: Denmark

[ACT III, SCENE I]

Enter KING, QUEEN, POLONIUS, OPHELIA, ROSENCRANTZ,
GUILDENSTERN, LORDS.

King.   An' can you by no drift of conference
     Get from him why he puts on this confusion,
     Grating so harshly all his days of quiet
     With turbulent and dangerous lunacy?

Ros.   He does confess he feels himself distracted,
     But from what cause 'a will by no means speak.   6

Guil.   Nor do we find him forward to be sounded,
     But with a crafty madness keeps aloof
     When we would bring him on to some confession
     Of his true state.

Queen.   Did he receive you well?   10

Ros.   Most like a gentleman.

Guil.   But with much forcing of his disposition.

Ros.   Niggard of question, but of our demands
     Most free in his reply.

Queen.   Did you assay him
     To any pastime?   15

Ros.   Madam, it so fell out that certain players
     We o'erraught on the way; of these we told him,
     And there did seem in him a kind of joy
     To hear of it. They are here about the court,
     And as I think, they have already order   20
     This night to play before him.

Pol.   'Tis most true,
     And he beseech'd me to entreat your Majesties
     To hear and see the matter.

King.   With all my heart, and it doth much content me
     To hear him so inclin'd.   25

III.i. Location: The castle

1. **An':** and. **drift of conference:** leading on of conversation.   7. **forward:** readily willing.
sounded: plumbed, probed.   8. **crafty madness:** i.e. mad craftiness, the shrewdness that
mad people sometimes exhibit.   12. **disposition:** inclination.   13. **question:** conversation. **demands:** questions.   14. **assay:** attempt to win.   17. **o'erraught:** passed (literally,
overreached).

Good gentlemen, give him a further edge,
And drive his purpose into these delights.

Ros. We shall, my lord.

Exeunt Rosencrantz and Guildenstern.

King. Sweet Gertrude, leave us two,
For we have closely sent for Hamlet hither,
That he, as 'twere by accident, may here   30
Affront Ophelia. Her father and myself,
We'll so bestow ourselves that, seeing unseen,
We may of their encounter frankly judge,
And gather by him, as he is behav'd,
If't be th' affliction of his love or no   35
That thus he suffers for.

Queen. I shall obey you.
And for your part, Ophelia, I do wish
That your good beauties be the happy cause
Of Hamlet's wildness. So shall I hope your virtues
Will bring him to his wonted way again,   40
To both your honors.

Oph. Madam, I wish it may.   *[Exit Queen.]*

Pol. Ophelia, walk you here. — Gracious, so please you,
We will bestow ourselves. *[To Ophelia.]* Read on this book,
That show of such an exercise may color
Your [loneliness]. We are oft to blame in this—   45
'Tis too much prov'd—that with devotion's visage
And pious action we do sugar o'er
The devil himself.

King. *[Aside.]* O, 'tis too true!
How smart a lash that speech doth give my conscience!
The harlot's cheek, beautied with plast'ring art,   50
Is not more ugly to the thing that helps it
Than is my deed to my most painted word.
O heavy burthen!

Pol. I hear him coming. Withdraw, my lord.
[Exeunt King and Polonius.]

Enter HAMLET.

26. **edge:** stimulus.   27. **into:** on to.   29. **closely:** privately.   31. **Affront:** meet.
33. **frankly:** freely.   44. **exercise:** i.e. religious exercise (as the next sentence makes clear).
44–45. **color Your loneliness:** make your solitude seem natural.   46. **too much prov'd:**
too often proved true.   47. **action:** demeanor.   51. **to . . . it:** in comparison with the
paint that makes it look beautiful.

437

Ham. To be, or not to be, that is the question: 55
Whether 'tis nobler in the mind to suffer
The slings and arrows of outrageous fortune,
Or to take arms against a sea of troubles,
And by opposing, end them. To die, to sleep—
No more, and by a sleep to say we end   60
The heart-ache and the thousand natural shocks
That flesh is heir to; 'tis a consummation
Devoutly to be wish'd. To die, to sleep—
To sleep, perchance to dream—ay, there's the rub,
For in that sleep of death what dreams may come,   65
When we have shuffled off this mortal coil,
Must give us pause; there's the respect
That makes calamity of so long life:
For who would bear the whips and scorns of time,
Th' oppressor's wrong, the proud man's contumely,   70
The pangs of despis'd love, the law's delay,
The insolence of office, and the spurns
That patient merit of th' unworthy takes,
When he himself might his quietus make
With a bare bodkin; who would fardels bear,   75
To grunt and sweat under a weary life,
But that the dread of something after death,
The undiscover'd country, from whose bourn
No traveller returns, puzzles the will,
And makes us rather bear those we have,   80
Than fly to others that we know not of?
Thus conscience does make cowards [of us all],
And thus the native hue of resolution
Is sicklied o'er with the pale cast of thought,
And enterprises of great pitch and moment   85

---

56. **suffer:** submit to, endure patiently.   62. **consummation:** completion, end.   64. **rub:** obstacle (a term from the game of bowls).   66. **shuffled off:** freed ourselves from. **this mortal coil:** the turmoil of this mortal life.   67. **respect:** consideration.   68. **of . . . life:** so long-lived.   69. **time:** the world.   74. **his quietus make:** write paid to his account. 75. **bare bodkin:** mere dagger. **fardels:** burdens.   78. **undiscover'd:** not disclosed to knowledge; about which men have no information. **bourn:** boundary, i.e. region.   79. **puzzles:** paralyzes.   82. **conscience:** reflection (but with some of the modern sense, too). 83. **native hue:** natural (ruddy) complexion.   84. **pale cast:** pallor. **thought:** i.e. melancholy thought, brooding.   85. **pitch:** loftiness (a term from falconry, signifying the highest point of a hawk's flight).

> With this regard their currents turn awry,
> And lose the name of action. —Soft you now,
> The fair Ophelia. Nymph, in thy orisons
> Be all my sins rememb'red.

Oph.   Good my lord,
> How does your honor for this many a day?   90

Ham.   I humbly thank you, well, [well, well].

Oph.   My lord, I have remembrances of yours
> That I have longed long to redeliver.
> I pray you now receive them.

Ham.   No, not I,
> I never gave you aught.   95

Oph.   My honor'd lord, you know right well you did,
> And with them words of so sweet breath compos'd
> As made these things more rich. Their perfume lost,
> Take these again, for to the noble mind
> Rich gifts wax poor when givers prove unkind.   100
> There, my lord.

Ham.   Ha, ha! are you honest?

Oph.   My lord?

Ham.   Are you fair?

Oph.   What means your lordship?   105

Ham.   That if you be honest and fair, [your honesty] should admit no
discourse to your beauty.

Oph.   Could beauty, my lord, have better commerce than with
honesty?   109

Ham.   Ay, truly, for the power of beauty will sooner transform honesty from what it is to a bawd than the force of honesty can translate beauty into his likeness. This was sometime a paradox, but
now the time gives it proof. I did love you once.   114

Oph.   Indeed, my lord, you made me believe so.

Ham.   You should not have believ'd me, for virtue cannot so [inocu-
late] our old stock but we shall relish of it. I lov'd you not.

Oph.   I was the more deceiv'd.   119

Ham.   Get thee [to] a nunn'ry, why wouldst thou be a breeder of sinners? I am myself indifferent honest, but yet I could accuse me of
such things that it were better my mother had not borne me: I am

---

88. **orisons:** prayers.   102. **honest:** chaste.   113. **sometime:** formerly. **paradox:** tenet
contrary to accepted belief.   116–18. **virtue . . . it:** virtue, engrafted on our old stock (of
viciousness), cannot so change the nature of the plant that no trace of the original will
remain.   121. **indifferent honest:** tolerably virtuous.

very proud, revengeful, ambitious, with more offenses at my beck
than I have thoughts to put them in, imagination to   125
give them shape, or time to act them in. What should such fellows
as I do crawling between earth and heaven? We are arrant knaves,
believe none of us. Go thy ways to a nunn'ry. Where's your father?

Oph. At home, my lord.   130

Ham. Let the doors be shut upon him, that he may play the fool no
where but in 's own house. Farewell.

Oph. O, help him, you sweet heavens!

Ham. If thou dost marry, I'll give thee this plague for thy dowry: be
thou as chaste as ice, as pure as   135
snow, thou shalt not escape calumny. Get thee to a nunn'ry,
farewell. Or if thou wilt needs marry, marry a fool, for wise men
know well enough what monsters you make of them. To a nunn'ry,
go, and quickly too. Farewell.   140

Oph. Heavenly powers, restore him!

Ham. I have heard of your paintings, well enough. God hath given
you one face, and you make yourselves another. You jig and amble,
and you [lisp,] you nickname God's creatures and make your wantonness   145
[your] ignorance. Go to, I'll no more on't, it hath made me mad. I
say we will have no moe marriage. Those that are married already
(all but one) shall live, the rest shall keep as they are. To a nunn'ry,
go.   149

                                                                  Exit.

Oph.   O, what a noble mind is here o'erthrown!
          The courtier's, soldier's, scholar's, eye, tongue, sword,
          Th' expectation and rose of the fair state,
          The glass of fashion and the mould of form,
          Th' observ'd of all observers, quite, quite down!
          And I, of ladies most deject and wretched,   155
          That suck'd the honey of his [music] vows,
          Now see [that] noble and most sovereign reason
          Like sweet bells jangled out of time, and harsh;
          That unmatch'd form and stature of blown youth

---

138. **monsters.** Alluding to the notion that the husbands of unfaithful wives grew horns.
139. **you:** you women.   144–45. **You . . . creatures:** i.e. you walk and talk affectedly.
144–46. **make . . . ignorance:** excuse your affectation as ignorance.   147. **moe:** more.
152. **expectation:** hope. **rose:** ornament. **fair:** Probably proleptic: "(the kingdom) made fair
by his presence."   153. **glass:** mirror. **mould of form:** pattern of (courtly) behavior.
154. **observ'd . . . observers:** Shakespeare uses *observe* to mean not only "behold, mark
attentively" but also "pay honor to."   159. **blown:** in full bloom.

Blasted with ecstasy. O, woe is me   160
T' have seen what I have seen, see what I see!

                          [Ophelia withdraws.]
                    Enter KING and POLONIUS.

King.   Love? his affections do not that way tend,
        Nor what he spake, though it lack'd form a little,
        Was not like madness. There's something in his soul
        O'er which his melancholy sits on brood,   165
        And I do doubt the hatch and the disclose
        Will be some danger; which for to prevent,
        I have in quick determination
        Thus set it down: he shall with speed to England
        For the demand of our neglected tribute.   170
        Haply the seas, and countries different,
        With variable objects, shall expel
        This something-settled matter in his heart,
        Whereon his brains still beating puts him thus
        From fashion of himself. What think you on't?   175
Pol.   It shall do well; but yet do I believe
        The origin and commencement of his grief
        Sprung from neglected love. *[Ophelia comes forward.]*
                          How now, Ophelia?
        You need not tell us what Lord Hamlet said,
        We heard it all. My lord, do as you please,   180
        But if you hold it fit, after the play
        Let his queen-mother all alone entreat him
        To show his grief. Let her be round with him,
        And I'll be plac'd (so please you) in the ear
        Of all their conference. If she find him not,   185
        To England send him, or confine him where
        Your wisdom best shall think.
King.   It shall be so.
        Madness in great ones must not [unwatch'd] go.

                                             Exeunt.

---

160. **Blasted:** withered. **ecstasy:** madness.   162. **affections:** inclinations, feelings.   166.
doubt: fear. **disclose:** Synonymous with *hatch*.   178. **neglected:** unrequited.   183. **his**
grief: what is troubling him. **round:** blunt, outspoken.   185. **find him:** learn the truth
about him.

[SCENE II]

Enter HAMLET and three of the PLAYERS.

Ham.   Speak the speech, I pray you, as I pronounc'd it to you, trippingly
on the tongue, but if you mouth it, as many of our players do, I
had as live the town-crier spoke my lines. Nor do not saw the air
too much with your hand, thus, but use all gently, for in the very   5
torrent, tempest, and, as I may say, whirlwind of your passion, you
must acquire and beget a temperance that may give it smoothness.
O, it offends me to the soul to hear a robustious periwig-pated fellow
tear a passion to totters, to very rags, to spleet the ears of the   10
groundlings, who for the most part are capable of nothing but in-
explicable dumb shows and noise. I would have such a fellow
whipt for o'erdoing Termagant, it out-Herods Herod, pray you
avoid it.

[1.] Play.   I warrant your honor.   15

Ham.   Be not too tame neither, but let your own discretion be your
tutor. Suit the action to the word, the word to the action, with this
special observance, that you o'erstep not the modesty of nature:
for any thing so o'erdone is from the purpose of playing,   20
whose end, both at the first and now, was and is, to hold as 'twere
the mirror up to nature: to show virtue her feature, scorn her own
image, and the very age and body of the time his form and pressure.
Now this overdone, or come tardy off, though it makes the un-   25
skillful laugh, cannot but make the judicious grieve; the censure of
which one must in your allowance o'er-weigh a whole theatre of
others. O, there be players that I have seen play—and heard others
[praise], and that highly—not to speak it profanely, that,   30
neither having th' accent of Christians nor the gait of Christian,
pagan, nor man, have so strutted and bellow'd that I have thought
some of Nature's journeymen had made men, and not made them
well, they imitated humanity so abominably.   35

III.ii. Location: The castle.

2. **mouth:** pronounce with exaggerated distinctness or declamatory effect.   3. **live:** lief,
willingly.   10. **totters:** tatters. **spleet:** split.   11. **groundlings:** those who paid the lowest admission price and stood on the ground in the "yard" or pit of the theatre. **capable of:**
able to take in.   13. **Termagant:** a supposed god of the Saracens, whose role in medieval
drama, like that of Herod (line 14), was noisy and violent.   19. **modesty:** moderation.
20. **from:** contrary to.   23. **scorn:** i.e. that which is worthy of scorn.   24. **pressure:**
impression (as of a seal), exact image.   25. **tardy:** inadequately.   27. **censure:** judgment.
which one: (even) one of whom. **allowance:** estimation.   30. **profanely:** irreverently.
33–35. **some ... abominably:** i.e. they were so unlike men that it seemed Nature had not
made them herself, but had delegated the task to mediocre assistants.

[1.] Play. I hope we have reform'd that indifferently with us, [sir].

Ham. O, reform it altogether. And let those that play your clowns
speak no more than is set down for them, for there be of them that
will themselves   40
laugh to set on some quantity of barren spectators to laugh too,
though in the mean time some necessary question of the play be
then to be consider'd. That's villainous, and shows a most pitiful
ambition in the fool that uses it. Go make you ready.   45
[Exeunt Players.]

Enter POLONIUS, GUILDENSTERN, and ROSENCRANTZ.
How now, my lord? Will the King hear this piece of work?

Pol. And the Queen too, and that presently.

Ham. Bid the players make haste.   *[Exit Polonius.]*
Will you two help to hasten them?   50

Ros. Ay, my lord.   *Exeunt they two.*

Ham. What ho, Horatio!
Enter HORATIO.

Hor. Here, sweet lord, at your service.

Ham. Horatio, thou art e'en as just a man
As e'er my conversation cop'd withal.   55

Hor. O my dear lord —

Ham.   Nay, do not think I flatter,
For what advancement may I hope from thee
That no revenue hast but thy good spirits
To feed and clothe thee? Why should the poor be flatter'd?
No, let the candied tongue lick absurd pomp,   60
And crook the pregnant hinges of the knee
Where thrift may follow fawning. Dost thou hear?
Since my dear soul was mistress of her choice
And could of men distinguish her election,
Sh' hath seal'd thee for herself, for thou hast been   65
As one in suff'ring all that suffers nothing,
A man that Fortune's buffets and rewards
Hast ta'en with equal thanks; and blest are those

36–37. **indifferently:** pretty well.   40. **of them:** some of them.   45. **fool:** (1) stupid person; (2) actor playing a fool's role. **uses it.**   46–47. **piece of work:** masterpiece (said jocularly).   48. **presently:** at once.   54. **thou … man:** i.e. you come as close to being what a man should be (*just* = exact, precise).   55. **my … withal:** my association with people has brought me into contact with.   60. **candied:** sugared, i.e. flattering. **absurd:** tasteless (Latin sense).   61. **pregnant:** moving readily.   62. **thrift:** thriving, profit.

Whose blood and judgment are so well co-meddled,
That they are not a pipe for Fortune's finger   70
To sound what stop she please. Give me that man
That is not passion's slave, and I will wear him
In my heart's core, ay, in my heart of heart,
As I do thee. Something too much of this.
There is a play to-night before the King,   75
One scene of it comes near the circumstance
Which I have told thee of my father's death.
I prithee, when thou seest that act afoot,
Even with the very comment of thy soul
Observe my uncle. If his occulted guilt   80
Do not itself unkennel in one speech,
It is a damned ghost that we have seen,
And my imaginations are as foul
As Vulcan's stithy. Give him heedful note,
For I mine eyes will rivet to his face,   85
And after we will both our judgments join
In censure of his seeming.

Hor.   Well, my lord.
If 'a steal aught the whilst this play is playing,
And scape [detecting], I will pay the theft.   89

*[Sound a flourish. Danish march.] Enter Trumpets and Kettle-
drums, KING, QUEEN, POLONIUS, OPHELIA,
[ROSENCRANTZ, GUILDENSTERN, and other LORDS
attendant, with his GUARD carrying torches].*

Ham.   They are coming to the play. I must be idle; Get you a place.
King.   How fares our cousin Hamlet?
Ham.   Excellent, i' faith, of the chameleon's dish: I eat the air, promise-
         cramm'd—you cannot feed capons so.   95
King.   I have nothing with this answer, Hamlet, these words are not
         mine.

---

69. **blood:** passions. **co-meddled:** mixed, blended.   73. **my heart of heart:** the heart of
my heart.   79. **very ... soul:** your most intense critical observation.   80. **occulted:** hidden.   81. **unkennel:** bring into the open.   82. **damned ghost:** evil spirit, devil.
84. **stithy:** forge.   87. **censure ... seeming:** reaching a verdict on his behavior.   90. **be
idle:** act foolish, pretend to be crazy.   92. **fares:** Hamlet takes up this word in another
sense.   93. **chameleon's dish:** Chameleons were thought to feed on air. Hamlet says that
he subsists on an equally nourishing diet, the promise of succession. There is probably a
pun on *air/heir*.   96. **have nothing with:** do not understand.

Ham. No, nor mine now. *[To Polonius.]* My lord, you play'd once i'
th' university, you say?

Pol. That did I, my lord, and was accounted a good actor. 101

Ham. What did you enact?

Pol. I did enact Julius Caesar. I was kill'd i' th' Capitol; Brutus kill'd
me.

Ham. It was a brute part of him to kill so capital a calf there. Be the
players ready? 106

Ros. Ay, my lord, they stay upon your patience.

Queen. Come hither, my dear Hamlet, sit by me.

Ham. No, good mother, here's metal more attractive. *[Lying down at
Ophelia's feet.]*

Pol. *[To the King.]* O ho, do you mark that? 111

Ham. Lady, shall I lie in your lap?

Oph. No, my lord.

Ham. I mean, my head upon your lap?

Oph. Ay, my lord. 115

Ham. Do you think I meant country matters?

Oph. I think nothing, my lord.

Ham. That's a fair thought to lie between maids' legs.

Oph. What is, my lord? 120

Ham. Nothing.

Oph. You are merry, my lord.

Ham. Who, I?

Oph. Ay, my lord. 124

Ham. O God, your only jig-maker. What should a man do but be
merry, for look you how cheerfully my mother looks, and my
father died within 's two hours.

Oph. Nay, 'tis twice two months, my lord.

Ham. So long? Nay then let the dev'l wear black, for I'll have a suit of
sables. O heavens, die two months ago, and not forgotten yet? 130
Then there's hope a great man's memory may outlive his life half a
year, but, by'r lady, 'a must build churches then, or else shall 'a suffer not thinking on, with the hobby-horse, whose epitaph is, "For
O, for O, the hobby-horse is forgot."

---

97. **mine:** i.e. an answer to my question. 105. **part:** action. 116. **country matters:**
indecency. 125. **only:** very best. **jig-maker:** one who composed or played in the farcical
song-and-dance entertainments that followed plays. 127. **'s:** this. 129–30. **let . . .
sables:** i.e. to the devil with my garments; after so long a time I am ready for the old man's
garb of sables (fine fur). 134. **no thinking on:** not being thought of, i.e. being forgotten.

The trumpets sounds. Dumb show follows.

Enter a King and a Queen [very lovingly], the Queen embracing him and he her. [She kneels and makes show of protestation unto him.] He takes her up and declines his head upon her neck. He lies him down upon a bank of flowers. She, seeing him asleep, leaves him. Anon come in another man, takes off his crown, kisses it, pours poison in the sleeper's ears, and leaves him. The Queen returns, finds the King dead, makes passionate action. The pois'ner with some three or four [mutes] come in again, seem to condole with her. The dead body is carried away. The pois'ner woos the Queen with gifts; she seems harsh [and unwilling] awhile, but in the end accepts love.   *[Exeunt.]*

Oph.	What means this, my lord?	136
Ham.	Marry, this' [miching] mallecho, it means mischief.	
Oph.	Belike this show imports the argument of the play.	140

Enter PROLOGUE.

Ham.	We shall know by this fellow. The players cannot keep [counsel], they'll tell all.	
Oph.	Will 'a tell us what this show meant?	
Ham.	Ay, or any show that you will show him. Be not you asham'd to show, he'll not shame to tell you what it means.	146
Oph.	You are naught, you are naught. I'll mark the play.	
Pro.	For us, and for our tragedy,	
	Here stooping to your clemency,	150
	We beg your hearing patiently.	*[Exit.]*
Ham.	Is this a prologue, or the posy of a ring?	
Oph.	'Tis brief, my lord.	
Ham.	As woman's love.	

Enter [two Players,] KING and QUEEN.

[P.] King.	Full thirty times hath Phoebus' cart gone round	155
	Neptune's salt wash and Tellus' orbed ground,	
	And thirty dozen moons with borrowed sheen	
	About the world have times twelve thirties been,	
	Since love our hearts and Hymen did our hands	

135. **For . . . forgot:** line from a popular ballad lamenting puritanical suppression of such country sports as the May-games, in which the hobby-horse, a character costumed to resemble a horse, traditionally appeared.   137. **this' miching mallecho:** this is sneaking mischief.   139. **argument:** subject, plot.   142. **counsel:** secrets.   145. **Be not you:** if you are not.   147. **naught:** wicked.   152. **posy . . . ring:** verse motto inscribed in a ring (necessarily short).   155. **Phoebus' cart:** the sun-god's chariot.   156. **Tellus:** goddess of the earth.   159. **Hymen:** god of marriage.

    Unite comutual in most sacred bands.   160

[P.] Queen.   So many journeys may the sun and moon

    Make us again count o'er ere love be done!

    But woe is me, you are so sick of late,

    So far from cheer and from [your] former state,

    That I distrust you. Yet though I distrust,   165

    Discomfort you, my lord, it nothing must,

    [For] women's fear and love hold quantity,

    In neither aught, or in extremity.

    Now what my [love] is, proof hath made you know,

    And as my love is siz'd, my fear is so.   170

    Where love is great, the littlest doubts are fear;

    Where little fears grow great, great love grows there.

[P.] King.   Faith, I must leave thee, love, and shortly too;

    My operant powers their functions leave to do,

    And thou shalt live in this fair world behind,   175

    Honor'd, belov'd, and haply one as kind

    For husband shalt thou—

[P.] Queen.   O, confound the rest!

    Such love must needs be treason in my breast.

    In second husband let me be accurs'd!

    None wed the second but who kill'd the first.   180

Ham. [Aside.]   That's wormwood!

[P. Queen.]   The instances that second marriage move

    Are base respects of thrift, but none of love.

    A second time I kill my husband dead,

    When second husband kisses me in bed.   185

[P.] King.   I do believe you think what now you speak,

    But what we do determine, oft we break.

    Purpose is but the slave to memory,

    Of violent birth, but poor validity,

    Which now, the fruit unripe, sticks on the tree,   190

    But fall unshaken when they mellow be.

---

160. **bands:** bonds.   165. **distrust:** fear for.   167. **hold quantity:** are related in direct proportion.   169. **proof:** experience.   174. **operant:** active, vital. **leave to do:** cease to perform.   177. **confound the rest:** may destruction befall what you are about to speak of—a second marriage on my part.   182. **instances:** motives. **move:** give rise to. 183. **respects of thrift:** considerations of advantage.   189. **validity:** strength, power to last.

Most necessary 'tis that we forget
To pay ourselves what to ourselves is debt,
What to ourselves in passion we propose,
The passion ending, doth the purpose lose.   195
The violence of either grief or joy
Their own enactures with themselves destroy.
Where joy most revels, grief doth most lament;
Grief [joys], joy grieves, on slender accident.
This world is not for aye, nor 'tis not strange   200
That even our loves should with our fortunes change:
For 'tis a question left us yet to prove,
Whether love lead fortune, or else fortune love.
The great man down, you mark his favorite flies,
The poor advanc'd makes friends of enemies.   205
And hitherto doth love on fortune tend,
For who not needs shall never lack a friend,
And who in want a hollow friend doth try,
Directly seasons him his enemy.
But orderly to end where I begun,   210
Our wills and fates do so contrary run
That our devices still are overthrown,
Our thoughts are ours, their ends none of our own:
So think thou wilt no second husband wed,
But die thy thoughts when thy first lord is dead.   215

[P.] Queen.   Nor earth to me give food, nor heaven light,
Sport and repose lock from me day and night,
To desperation turn my trust and hope,
[An] anchor's cheer in prison be my scope!
Each opposite that blanks the face of joy   220
Meet what I would have well and it destroy!
Both here and hence pursue me lasting strife,
If once I be a widow, ever I be a wife!

Ham.   If she should break it now!

[P.] King. 'Tis deeply sworn. Sweet, leave me here a while,   225

192–93. **Most ... debt:** i.e. such resolutions are debts we owe to ourselves, and it would be foolish to pay such debts.   194. **passion:** violent emotion.   196–97. **The violence ... destroy:** i.e. both violent grief and violent joy fail of their intended acts because they destroy themselves by their very violence.   199. **slender accident:** slight occasion. 209. **seasons:** ripens, converts into.   212. **devices:** devisings, intentions. **still:** always. 219. **anchor's cheer:** hermit's fare. **my scope:** the extent of my comforts.   220. **blanks:** blanches, makes pale (a symptom of grief).

My spirits grow dull, and fain I would beguile
The tedious day with sleep.   *[Sleeps.]*
[P.] Queen.   Sleep rock thy brain,
And never come mischance between us twain!   *Exit.*
Ham.   Madam, how like you this play?
Queen.   The lady doth protest too much, methinks.
Ham.   O but she'll keep her word.   231
King.   Have you heard the argument? is there no offense in't?
Ham.   No, no, they do but jest, poison in jest—no offense i' th'
world.   235
King.   What do you call the play?
Ham.   "The Mouse-trap." Marry, how? tropically: this play is the
image of a murther done in Vienna; Gonzago is the duke's name,
his wife, Baptista. You shall see anon. 'Tis a knavish piece   240
of work, but what of that? Your Majesty, and we that have free
souls, it touches us not. Let the gall'd jade winch, our withers are
unwrung.

Enter LUCIANUS.

This is one Lucianus, nephew to the king.
Oph.   You are as good as a chorus, my lord.   245
Ham.   I could interpret between you and your love, if I could see the
puppets dallying.
Oph.   You are keen, my lord, you are keen.
Ham.   It would cost you a groaning to take off mine edge.   250
Oph.   Still better, and worse.
Ham.   So you mistake your husbands. Begin, murtherer, leave thy
damnable faces and begin. Come, the croaking raven doth bellow
for revenge.
Luc.   Thoughts black, hands apt, drugs fit, and time agreeing, 255

---

233. **offense:** offensive matter (but Hamlet quibbles on the sense "crime"). 234. **jest:** i.e. pretend. 237–38. **tropically:** figuratively (with play on *tropically*—which is the reading of Q1—and probably with allusion to the children's saying *marry trap*, meaning "now you're caught"). 238. **image:** representation. 242. **free souls:** clear consciences. **gall'd jade:** chafed horse. 243. **winch:** wince. **withers:** ridge between a horse's shoulders. **unwrung:** not rubbed sore. 245. **chorus:** i.e. one who explains the forthcoming action. 246–47. **I . . . dallying:** I could speak the dialogue between you and your lover like a puppet-master (with an indecent jest). 248. **keen:** bitter, sharp. 251. **better, and worse:** i.e. more pointed and less decent. 252. **So:** i.e. "for better, for worse," in the words of the marriage service. **mistake:** i.e. mis-take, take wrongfully. Their vows, Hamlet suggests, prove false. 253. **faces:** facial expressions. 254. **the croaking . . . revenge.** Misquoted from an old play, *The True Tragedy of Richard III.*

[Confederate] season, else no creature seeing,
Thou mixture rank, of midnight weeds collected,
With Hecat's ban thrice blasted, thrice [infected],
Thy natural magic and dire property
On wholesome life usurps immediately.   260
                    [Pours the poison in his ears.]

Ham.   A poisons him i' th' garden for his estate. His name's Gonzago, the story is extant, and written in very choice Italian. You
shall see anon how the murtherer gets the love of Gonzago's wife.

Oph.   The King rises.   265
[Ham.   What, frighted with false fire?]
Queen. How fares my lord?
Pol.   Give o'er the play.
King.   Give me some light. Away!
Pol.   Lights, lights, lights!   270
                    Exeunt all but Hamlet and Horatio.

Ham.   "Why, let the strooken deer go weep,
        The hart ungalled play,
        For some must watch while some
        must sleep,
        Thus runs the world away."   274
        Would not this, sir, and a forest of feathers—if the rest of my for-
        tunes turn Turk with me—with [two] Provincial roses on my raz'd
        shoes, get me a fellowship in a cry of players?

Hor.   Half a share.
Ham.   A whole one, I.   280
        "For thou dost know, O Damon dear,
        This realm dismantled was
        Of Jove himself, and now reigns here
        A very, very"—pajock.
Hor.   You might have rhym'd.   285
Ham.   O good Horatio, I'll take the ghost's word for a thousand
        pound. Didst perceive?

---

256. **Confederate season:** the time being my ally.   258. **Hecat's ban:** the curse of Hecate,
goddess of witchcraft.   266. **false fire:** i.e. a blank cartridge.   271. **strooken:** struck, i.e.
wounded.   272. **ungalled:** unwounded.   273. **watch:** stay awake.   275. **feathers:** the
plumes worn by tragic actors.   276. **turn Turk:** i.e. go to the bad.   276–77. **Provincial
roses:** rosettes designed to look like a variety of French rose.   277. **raz'd:** with decorating
slashing. **fellowship:** partnership.   278. **cry:** company.   282. **dismantled:** divested,
deprived.   284. **pajock:** peacock (substituting for the rhyme-word *ass*). The natural history of the time attributed many vicious qualities to the Peacock.

Hor.	Very well, my lord.	
Ham.	Upon the talk of the pois'ning?	
Hor.	I did very well note him.	290
Ham.	Ah, ha! Come, some music! Come, the recorders!	

    For if the King like not the comedy,
    Why then belike he likes it not, perdy.
    Come, some music!   295

Enter ROSENCRANTZ and GUILDENSTERN.

Guil.	Good my lord, voutsafe me a word with you.	
Ham.	Sir, a whole history.	
Guil.	The King, sir—	
Ham.	Ay, Sir, what of him?	300
Guil.	Is in his retirement marvellous distemp'red.	
Ham.	With drink, sir?	
Guil.	No, my lord, with choler.	
Ham.	Your wisdom should show itself more richer to signify this to the doctor, for for me to put him to his purgation would perhaps plunge him into more choler.	307
Guil.	Good my lord, put your discourse into some frame, and [start] not so wildly from my affair.	
Ham.	I am tame, sir. Pronounce.	310
Guil.	The Queen, your mother, in most great affliction of spirit, hath sent me to you.	
Ham.	You are welcome.	
Guil.	Nay, good my lord, this courtesy is not of the right breed. If it shall please you to make me a 315 wholesome answer, I will do your mother's commandement; if not, your pardon and my return shall be the end of [my] business.	
Ham.	Sir, I cannot.	
Ros.	What, my lord?	320
Ham.	Make you a wholesome answer—my wit's diseas'd. But, sir, such answer as I can make, you shall command, or rather, as you say, my mother. Therefore no more, but to the matter: my mother, you say—	325

---

294. **perdy:** assuredly (French *pardieu*, "by God").   303. **choler:** anger (but Hamlet willfully takes up the word in the sense "biliousness").   305–6. **put ... purgation:** i.e. prescribe for what's wrong with him.   309. **frame:** logical structure.   316. **wholesome:** sensible, rational.   317. **Pardon:** permission for departure.

Ros.   Then thus she says: your behavior hath strook her into amazement and admiration.

Ham.   O wonderful son, that can so stonish a mother! But is there no
sequel at the heels of this mother's admiration? Impart.   330

Ros.   She desires to speak with you in her closet ere you go to bed.

Ham.   We shall obey, were she ten times our mother. Have you any
further trade with us?

Ros.   My lord, you once did love me.   335

Ham.   And do still, by these pickers and stealers.

Ros.   Good my lord, what is your cause of distemper? You do
surely bar the door upon your own liberty if you deny your griefs
to your friend.

Ham.   Sir, I lack advancement.   340

Ros.   How can that be, when you have the voice of the King himself
for your succession in Denmark?

Ham.   Ay, Sir, but "While the grass grows"—the proverb is something musty.   344

Enter the PLAYERS with recorders.

O, the recorders! Let me see one.—To withdraw with you—why
do you go about to recover the wind of me, as if you would drive
me into a toil?

Guil.   O my lord, if my duty be too bold, my love is too unman-
nerly.   349

Ham.   I do not well understand that. Will you play upon this pipe?

Guil.   My lord, I cannot.

Ham.   I pray you.

Guil.   Believe me, I cannot.

Ham.   I do beseech you.   355

Guil.   I know no touch of it, my lord.

Ham.   It is as easy as lying. Govern these ventages with your fingers
and [thumbs], give it breath with your mouth, and it will discourse
most eloquent music. Look you, these are the stops.   360

Guil.   But these cannot I command to any utt'rance of harmony. I
have not the skill.

---

327. **amazement and admiration:** bewilderment and wonder.   328. **stonish:** astound.
331. **closet:** private room.   336. **pickers and stealers:** hands; which, as the Catechism
says, we must keep "from picking and stealing."   344. **proverb:** i.e. "While the grass
grows, the steed starves." **something musty:** somewhat stale.   346. **recover the wind:**
get to windward.   347. **toil:** snare.   357. **ventages:** stops.

Ham.   Why, look you now, how unworthy a thing you make of me!
You would play upon me, you would seem to know my stops, you
would pluck out the   365
heart of my mystery, you would sound me from my lowest note to
[the top of] my compass; and there is much music, excellent voice,
in this little organ, yet cannot you make it speak. 'Sblood, do you
think I am easier to be play'd on than a pipe? Call me what   370
instrument you will, though you fret me, [yet] you cannot play
upon me.

Enter POLONIUS.

          God bless you, Sir.
Pol.   My lord, the Queen would speak with you, and presently.   375
Ham.   Do you see yonder cloud that's almost in shape of a camel?
Pol.   By th' mass and 'tis, like a camel indeed.
Ham.   Methinks it is like a weasel.
Pol.   It is back'd like a weasel.   380
Ham.   Or like a whale.
Pol.   Very like a whale.
Ham.   Then I will come to my mother by and by. *[Aside.]* They fool
me to the top of my bent.—I will come by and by.   385
[Pol.] I will say so.   *[Exit.]*
Ham.   "By and by" is easily said. Leave me, friends.
                                        [Exeunt all but Hamlet.]

'Tis now the very witching time of night,
When churchyards yawn and hell itself [breathes] out
Contagion to this world. Now could I drink hot blood,
And do such [bitter business as the] day   391
Would quake to look on. Soft, now to my mother.
O heart, lose not thy nature! let not ever
The soul of Nero enter this firm bosom,
Let me be cruel, not unnatural;   395
I will speak [daggers] to her, but use none.
My tongue and soul in this be hypocrites—
How in my words somever she be shent,
To give them seals never my soul consent!   *[Exit.]*

---

368. **organ:** instrument.   371. **fret:** (1) finger (an instrument); (2) vex.   375. **presently:**
at once.   384. **They . . . bent:** they make me play the fool to the limit of my ability.
385. **by and by:** at once.   388. **witching:** i.e. when the powers of evil are at large.
393. **nature:** natural affection, filial feeling.   394. **Nero.** Murderer of his mother.
398. **shent:** rebuked.   399. **give them seals:** confirm them by deeds.

BEN JONSON

Volpone

DRAMATIS PERSONAE[1]

VOLPONE, *a magnifico.*
MOSCA, *his parasite.*
VOLTORE, *an advocate.*
CORBACCIO, *an old gentleman.*
CORVINO, *a merchant.*
BONARIO, *son to Corbaccio.*
SIR POLITIC WOULD-BE, *a knight.*
PEREGRINE, *a gentleman traveler.*
NANO, *a dwarf.*
CASTRONE, *an eunuch.*
ANDROGYNO, *an hermaphrodite.*

GREGE *(or Mob)*

COMMENDATORI, *officers of justice.*
MERCATORI, *three merchants.*
AVOCATORI, *four magistrates.*
NOTARIO, *the register.*

LADY WOULD-BE, SIR POLITIC'S *Wife.*
CELIA, CORVINO'S *Wife.*
SERVITORI, *Servants, two* WAITING-WOMEN, etc.

---

1. Many of the characters' names are in Italian, and their translations are the names of animals—Volpone: fox; Mosca: fly; Voltore: vulture; Corbaccio: raven; Corvino: crow. Bonario means "good-natured"; Nano means "dwarf"; Castrone means "gelding"; and Androgyno means "man-woman," from the Greek.

Excerpt from *Volpone*, by Ben Jonson, reprinted from *The Chief Elizabethan Dramatists, Excluding Shakespeare*, (1911), Riverside Press.

SCENE—VENICE

THE ARGUMENT

V OLPONE, childless, rich, feigns sick, despairs,
O ffers his state to hopes of several heirs,
L ies languishing: his parasite receives
P resents of all, assures, deludes; then weaves
O ther cross plots, which ope themselves, are told.
N ew tricks for safety are sought; they thrive: when, bold,
E ach tempts th' other again, and all are sold.

PROLOGUE

Now, luck yet send us, and a little wit
    Will serve to make our play hit;
According to the palates of the season,
    Here is rhyme, not empty of reason.
This we were bid to credit from our poet,
    Whose true scope, if you would know it,
In all his poems still hath been this measure,
    To mix profit with your pleasure;
And not as some, whose throats their envy failing,
    Cry hoarsely, "All he writes is railing":
And when his plays come forth, think they can flout them,
    With saying, he was a year about them.
To this there needs no lie, but this his creature,
    Which was two months since no feature:
And though he dares give them five lives to mend it,
    'T is known, five weeks fully penn'd it,
From his own hand, without a coadjutor,
    Novice, journeyman, or tutor.
Yet thus much I can give you as a token
    Of his play's worth, no eggs are broken,
Nor quaking custards with fierce teeth affrighted,
    Wherewith your rout are so delighted;
Nor hales he in a gull,[1] old ends reciting,
    To stop gaps in his loose writing;
With such a deal of monstrous and forc'd action,
    As might make Bethlem[2] a faction:

---

1. *gull*] an imposition, a trick.

2. *Bethlem*] or Bedlam, popular name for the Hospital of St. Mary of Bethlehem, the London insane asylum.

Nor made he his play for jests stol'n from each table,
   But makes jests to fit his fable;
And so presents quick comedy refin'd,
   As best critics have design'd;
The laws of time, place, persons he observeth,
   From no needful rule he swerveth.
All gall and copperas[3] from his ink he draineth,
   Only a little salt remaineth,
Wherewith he'll rub your cheeks, till, red with laughter,
   They shall look fresh a week after.

ACT I

SCENE I. — A ROOM IN VOLPONE'S HOUSE

Enter VOLPONE, MOSCA.

VOLP.   Good morning to the day; and next, my gold!
    Open the shrine, that I may see my saint.

[MOSCA *withdraws the curtain, and discovers piles of gold, plate, jewels, etc.*]

    Hail the world's soul, and mine! More glad than is
    The teeming earth to see the long'd-for sun
    Peep through the horns of the celestial Ram,
    Am I, to view thy splendour dark'ning his;
    That lying here, amongst my other hoards,
    Show'st like a flame by night, or like the day
    Struck out of chaos, when all darkness fled
    Unto the centre.[4] O thou son of Sol,
    But brighter than thy father, let me kiss,
    With adoration, thee, and every relic
    Of sacred treasure in this blessed room.
    Well did wise poets, by thy glorious name,
    Title that age which they would have the best;
    Thou being the best of things, and far transcending
    All style of joy, in children, parents, friends,
    Or any other waking dream on earth:

---

3. *coperas*] green vitriol, used in making ink.

4. *centre*] center of the earth.

Thy looks when they to Venus did ascribe,
They should have given her twenty thousand Cupids;
Such are thy beauties and our loves! Dear saint,
Riches, the dumb god, that giv'st all men tongues,
That canst do nought, and yet mak'st men do all things;
The price of souls; even hell, with thee to boot,
Is made worth heaven. Thou art virtue, fame,
Honour, and all things else. Who can get thee,
He shall be noble, valiant, honest, wise—

MOS.   And what he will, sir. Riches are in fortune
A greater good than wisdom is in nature.

VOLP.   True, my beloved Mosca. Yet I glory
More in the cunning purchase of my wealth,
Than in the glad possession, since I gain
No common way; I use no trade, no venture;
I wound no earth with ploughshares, I fat no beasts
To feed the shambles; have no mills for iron,
Oil, corn, or men, to grind them into powder;
I blow no subtle glass, expose no ships
To threat'nings of the furrow-faced sea;
I turn no monies in the public bank,
No usure private.

MOS.   No, sir, nor devour
Soft prodigals. You shall ha' some will swallow
A melting heir as glibly as your Dutch
Will pills of butter, and ne'er purge for it;
Tear forth the fathers of poor families
Out of their beds, and coffin them alive
In some kind clasping prison, where their bones
May be forthcoming, when the flesh is rotten:
But your sweet nature doth abhor these courses;
You loathe the widow's or the orphan's tears
Should wash your pavements, or their piteous cries
Ring in your roofs, and beat the air for vengeance.

VOLP.   Right, Mosca; I do loathe it.

MOS.   And, besides, sir,
You are not like the thresher that doth stand
With a huge flail, watching a heap of corn,
And, hungry, dares not taste the smallest grain,
But feeds on mallows, and such bitter herbs;
Nor like the merchant, who hath fill'd his vaults

With Romagnia, rich and Candian[5] wines,
Yet drinks the lees of Lombard's vinegar:
You will not lie in straw, whilst moths and worms
Feed on your sumptuous hangings and soft beds;
You know the use of riches, and dare give now
From that bright heap, to me, your poor observer,
Or to your dwarf, or your hermaphrodite,
Your eunuch, or what other household trifle
Your pleasure allows maintenance—

VOL.   Hold thee, Mosca,
Take of my hand; thou strik'st on truth in all,
And they are envious term thee parasite.
Call forth my dwarf, my eunuch, and my fool,
And let 'em make me sport.   *[Exit MOS.]*
                    What should I do,
But cocker[6] up my genius, and live free
To all delights my fortune calls me to?
I have no wife, no parent, child, ally,
To give my substance to; but whom I make
Must be my heir; and this makes men observe[7] me:
This draws new clients daily to my house,
Women and men of every sex and age,
That bring me presents, send me plate, coin, jewels,
With hope that when I die (which they expect
Each greedy minute) it shall then return
Tenfold upon them; whilst some, covetous
Above the rest, seek to engross me whole,
And counter-work the one unto the other,
Contend in gifts, as they would seem in love:
All which I suffer, playing with their hopes,
And am content to coin 'em into profit,
And look upon their kindness, and take more,

---

5. *Romagnia . . . Candian*] Romagna is a district in Northern Italy on the Adriatic Sea. Candia is the Isle of Crete.

6. *cocker*] to pamper.

7. *observe*] pay obsequious attention to.

And look on that; still bearing them in hand,[8]
Letting the cherry knock against their lips,
And draw it by their mouths, and back again. —
How now!

SCENE II. — THE SAME

*To him re-enter MOSCA, with NANO, ANDROGYNO, and
CASTRONE.*

NAN.   "Now, room for fresh gamesters, who do will you to know
They do bring you neither play nor university show;
And therefore do intreat you that whatsoever they rehearse
May not fare a whit the worse, for the false pace of the verse.
If you wonder at this, you will wonder more ere we pass,
For know, here[9] is inclos'd the soul of Pythagoras,
That juggler divine, as hereafter shall follow;
Which soul, fast and loose, sir, came first from Apollo,
And was breath'd into Aethalides, Mercurius his son,
Where it had the gift to remember all that ever was done.
From thence it fled forth, and made quick transmigration
To goldy-lock'd Euphorbus, who was kill'd in good fashion
At the siege of old Troy, by the cuckold of Sparta.
Hermotimus was next (I find it in my charta).
To whom it did pass, where no sooner it was missing,
But with one Pyrrhus of Delos it learn'd to go a-fishing;
And thence did it enter the sophist of Greece.
From Pythagore, she went into a beautiful piece,
Hight Aspasia, the meretrix; and the next toss of her
Was again of a whore, she became a philosopher,
Crates the cynick, as itself doth relate it:
Since kings, knights, and beggars, knaves, lords, and fools gat it,
Besides ox and ass, camel, mule, goat, and brock,[10]
In all which it hath spoke, as in the cobbler's cock.[11]
But I come not here to discourse of that matter,

---

8. *bearing . . . hand*] deceiving them by false hopes

9. *here*] in Androgyno.

10. *brock*] badger.

11. *cock*] This interlude is based on Lucian's dialogue between a cobbler and a cock.

Or his one, two, or three, or his great oath, BY QUATER![12]
His musics, his trigon,[13] his golden thigh,
Or his telling how elements shift; but I
Would ask, how of late thou hast suffer'd translation,
And shifted thy coat in these days of reformation.

AND.   Like one of the reform'd, a fool, as you see,
      Counting all old doctrine heresy.

NAN.   But not on thine own forbid meats hast thou ventur'd?

AND.   On fish, when first a Carthusian I enter'd.

NAN.   Why, then thy dogmatical silence hath left thee?

AND.   Of that an obstreperous lawyer bereft me.

NAN.   O wonderful change, when sir lawyer forsook thee!
      For Pythagore's sake, what body then took thee?

AND.   A good dull mule.

NAN.   And how! by that means
      Thou wert brought to allow of the eating of beans?

AND.   Yes.

NAN.   But from the mule into whom didst thou pass?

AND.   Into a very strange beast, by some writers call'd an ass;
      By others a precise,[14] pure, illuminate brother
      Of those devour flesh, and sometimes one another;
      And will drop you forth a libel, or a sanctifi'd lie,
      Betwixt every spoonful of a nativity-pie.[15]

NAN.   Now quit thee, for heaven, of that profane nation.
      And gently report thy next transmigration.

AND.   To the same that I am.

NAN.   A creature of delight,
      And, what is more than a fool, an hermaphrodite!
      Now, prithee, sweet soul, in all thy variation,
      Which body wouldst thou choose to keep up thy station?

AND.   Troth, this I am in: even here would I tarry.

NAN.   'Cause here the delight of each sex thou canst vary?

AND.   Alas, those pleasures be stale and forsaken;
      No, 't is your fool wherewith I am so taken,

---

12. *Quater*] quatre, the four in dice.

13. *trigon*] a triangular lyre.

14. *precise*] puritanical.

15. *nativity-pie*] Christmas-pie.

The only one creature that I can call blessed;
For all other forms I have prov'd most distressed.

NAN.   Spoke true, as thou wert in Pythagoras still,
This learned opinion we celebrate will,
Fellow eunuch, as behoves us, with all our wit and art,
To dignify that whereof ourselves are so great and special a part."

VOLP.   Now, very, very pretty! Mosca, this
Was thy invention?

MOS.   If it please my patron,
Not else.

VOLP.   It doth, good Mosca.

MOS.   Then it was, sir.

[NANO and CASTRONE sing.]

SONG.

"Fools, they are the only nation
Worth men's envy or admiration;
Free from care or sorrow-taking,
Selves and others merry making:
All they speak or do is sterling.
Your fool he is your great man's darling,
And your ladies' sport and pleasure,
Tongue and bauble are his treasure.
E'en his face begetteth laughter,
And he speaks truth free from slaughter;[16]
He's the grace of every feast,
And sometimes the chiefest guest;
Hath his trencher[17] and his stool,
When wit waits upon the fool.
     O, who would not be
     He, he, he?"

One knocks without.

VOLP.   Who's that? Away! Look, Mosca.
Fool, begone!

[Exeunt NANO, CAST. and ANDRO.]

MOS.   'T is Signior Voltore, the advocate;
I know him by his knock.

VOLP.   Fetch me my gown,
My furs, and night-caps; say my couch is changing

---

16. *free from slaughter*] with impunity.

17. *trencher*] plate.

461

And let him entertain himself a while
Without i' th' gallery. *[Exit MOSCA.]* Now, now my clients
Begin their visitation! Vulture, kite,
Raven, and gorcrow,[18] all my birds of prey,
That think me turning carcase, now they come:
I am not for 'em yet.

[Re-enter MOSCA, with the gown, etc.]

How now! the news?
MOS.   A piece of plate, sir.
VOLP.   Of what bigness?
MOS.   Huge,
Massy, and antique, with your name inscrib'd,
And arms engraven.
VOLP.   Good! and not a fox
Stretcht on the earth, with fine delusive sleights,
Mocking a gaping crow? ha, Mosca!
MOS.   Sharp, sir.
VOLP.   Give me my furs.

                              [Puts on his sick dress.]
                    Why dost thou laugh so, man?
MOS.   I cannot choose, sir, when I apprehend
What thoughts he has without now, as he walks:
That this might be the last gift he should give,
That this would fetch you; if you died to-day,
And gave him all, what he should be to-morrow;
What large return would come of all his ventures;
How he should worshipp'd be, and reverenc'd;
Ride with his furs, and foot cloths; waited on
By herds of fools and clients; have clear way
Made for his mule, as letter'd as himself;
Be call'd the great and learned advocate:
And then concludes, there's nought impossible.
VOLP.   Yes, to be learned, Mosca.
MOS.   O, no: rich
Implies it. Hood an ass with reverend purple,
So you can hide his two ambitious[19] ears,
And he shall pass for a cathedral doctor.

---

18. *gorcrow*] carrion crow.

19. *ambitious*] also a reference to the word's etymological sense of "moving round."

VOLP.   My caps, my caps, good Mosca. Fetch him in.
MOS.   Stay, sir; your ointment for your eyes.
VOLP.   That's true;
      Dispatch, dispatch: I long to have possession
      Of my new present.
MOS.   That, and thousands more,
      I hope to see you lord of.
VOLP.   Thanks, kind Mosca.
MOS.   And that, when I am lost in blended dust,
      And hundreds such as I am, in succession—
VOLP.   Nay, that were too much, Mosca.
MOS.   You shall live
      Still to delude these harpies.
VOLP.   Loving Mosca!
      'T is well: my pillow now, and let him enter.
                                    [Exit MOSCA.]

    Now, my feign'd cough, my phthisic,[20] and my gout,
      My apoplexy, palsy, and catarrhs,
      Help, with your forced functions, this my posture,
      Wherein, this three year, I have milk'd their hopes.
      He comes; I hear him—Uh! [*coughing*] uh! uh! uh! O—

---

20. *phthisic*] phthisis, a progressively wasting or consumptive condition.